The Cinematic Mirror for Psychology and Life Coaching

Mary Banks Gregerson
Editor

The Cinematic Mirror for Psychology and Life Coaching

Published in association with
Division 46 of the American
Psychological Association –
Media Psychology

 Springer

Editor
Mary Banks Gregerson
1116 South Esplanade
Leavenworth, KS 66048-3522
USA
oltowne@aol.com

ISBN 978-1-4419-1113-1 (hardcover)   e-ISBN 978-1-4419-1114-8
ISBN 978-1-4419-8156-1 (softcover)
DOI 10.1007/978-1-4419-1114-8
Springer New York Dordrecht Heidelberg London

Library of Congress Control Number: 2009938165

Springer is part of Springer Science+Business Media (www.springer.com)

Foreword

Is there one among us who does not cherish the memories of our favorite movies from childhood? These motion pictures may have been captivating, awe inspiring, romantic, informative, scary, or even may have transported us to another reality – the world of science fiction, of wonderland, of Camelot, of swashbuckling unlawful behavior, or of Over the Rainbow. Movies sometimes provoked our curiosity, titillated, exhilarated, precipitated dreams of grandeur and accomplishments, bewildered, or offered us escape from a tawdry, less interesting, less spectacular reality.

In this intriguing volume, talented, ebullient editor Mary Banks Gregerson brings together a collection of creative authors who are experts in various genre and usages of film. These contributing authors use films instructively and constructively in their adult professional lives in a significant number of ways – including but not limited to providing ideas and options for individuals they are treating, mentoring, coaching, or teaching; offering images of others who might be facing similar problems or situations and affording the chance for those they are working with to observe and grapple with how others problem-solve, cope, and perhaps triumph; offering opportunities to hear different perceptions that are more positive and lead to greater self-actualization; recommending films that are motivational and inspiring and ever so much more. It becomes evident that films can be utilized throughout the life cycle with patients and consultees from a variety of socioeconomic, cultural, racial, religious, ethnic, and educational backgrounds and those from the full panoply of biopsychosocial types of families and communities.

Those teaching courses in film making approach films through yet another lens – that of what makes a film interesting and admirable visually – and also through sound effects as well as through the plot and story line. The script writer, producer, director, costumer, set designer, actors, etc., all work together to convey certain ideas or messages; to provoke thoughts or influence attitudes; or to instill views on different aspects of the world. The viewer may go to be entertained, enlightened, informed, distracted, or simply to enjoy or be transformed.

Media psychologists and life coaches want to know how to use films most efficaciously in their work. Films can be rich adjuncts to therapy and provide excellent stimulus for in-session discussions. This compelling volume offers some suggestions and commentaries with luminosity, humor, and wisdom – even alchemy and magic. Perhaps you have your own accrued wisdom to add to the stunning mix.

Media psychologists' interest in the informational, motivational, and inspirational value of films and their potential to create distortions as well as to broaden world views also leads them to engage in other significant roles. Some serve as consultants to producers and directors of films on development of characters so that the characters are realistic as well as vital and interesting, or on their portrayal of psychologists and other therapists so that these depictions are more accurate and scripted to fall within ethical professional guidelines. Other psychologists help those coordinating film festivals to select high-quality, meaningful films that are congruent with the purpose of the festival and/or serve as discussants on the films; it is imperative that they be astute in the analysis of human behavior and of relationships.

Division #46 (Media Psychology) of the American Psychology Association is proud to add this zesty treatise as the third volume to its book series on *Psychology and the Media*.

Without further ado, we now lift the curtain on Movie Magic and the indomitable search for living "happily ever after" in positive psychology land. Enjoy the cinematic journey on which you are about to embark.

Florence W. Kaslow, Ph.D., ABPP
Board Certified in Clinical, Couple and
family, and Forensic Psychology
e-mail: drfkaslow@bellsouth.net

Contents

Story Board: The "Filmist" Fall of the Cinematic Fourth Wall 1
Mary Banks Gregerson

Act One: Introduction 17
Frank S. Pittman III

When Will Hollywood Get the Family Right? 29
Jack Cashill

The Dawning of Desire Skewed Through a Media Lens and the
Loss of American Adolescence: M I 4 U? 51
Mary Banks Gregerson

Lives Through Film: *49 UP* and the *UP* Series as a Longitudinal
Study of Personality and Social Change 77
Kevin Lanning, Samantha A. Montgomery, Justin Bright,
Lenore Broming, Misty Hudelson, Rachel E. Pauletti,
Garreth Rosenzweig, and Rachel Starkings

Cinematherapy: Using Movie Metaphors to Explore Real
Relationships in Counseling and Coaching 89
Judy Kuriansky, Amy Vallarelli, Jamie DelBuono,
and Jeremy Ortman

International Cinema: An Abundant Mental Health Resource
of Films for Education, Communication, and Transformation 123
Ryan M. Niemiec

Trauma and the Media: How Movies can Create and Relieve Trauma . 155
Ani Kalayjian and Lisa Finnegan Abdolian

The Myth of Mental Illness in the Movies and Its Impact
on Forensic Psychology 171
L.E.A. Walker, M. Robinson, R.L. Duros, J. Henle, J. Caverly,
S. Mignone, E.R. Zimmerman, and B. Apple

**Looking at Disability Through a Different Lens: Reinterpreting
Disability Images in Line with Positive Psychology**   193
Rochelle Balter

**Cinema as Alchemy for Healing and Transformation: Using
the Power of Films in Psychotherapy and Coaching**   201
Birgit Wolz

Deconstructing: Perspectives on Perspective-Making   227
M. Gene Ondrusek

The Final Curtain: Movies as Models   247
Danny Wedding

Film Reference List – Compiled by Mary Banks Gregerson   251

Subject Index   277

Editor's Note: All film citations in every chapter can be found in the *Film Reference List* found in this volume on pages 251–275.

Contributors

Lisa Finnegan Abdolian, M.S., Nice, France

B. Apple, Psy.D., J.D., Nova Southeastern University Center for Psychological Studies, Ft. Lauderdale, FL 22214, USA

Rochelle Balter, Ph.D., J.D., Department of Psychology, John Jay College of Criminal Justice, New York, NY, 10019, USA

Justin Bright, B.A., Wilkes Honors College, Florida Atlantic University, Boca Raton, FL, USA

Lenore Broming, B.A., Wilkes Honors College, Florida Atlantic University, Boca Raton, FL, USA

Jack Cashill, Ph.D., Ingram's Magazine, Kansas City, MO 64141-1356, USA

J. Caverly, B.A., Nova Southeastern University Center for Psychological Studies, Ft. Lauderdale, FL, 33314, USA

Jamie DelBuono, M.A., Teachers College, Columbia University, New York, NY 20017-6096, USA

R.L. Duros, Psy.D., J.D., Nova Southeastern University Center for Psychological Studies, Ft. Lauderdale, FL 33314, USA

Mary Banks Gregerson, Ph.D., Health, Environment, and Professional Psychology, Leavenworth, KS 66048-3522, USA

J. Henle, Psy.D., Nova Southeastern University Center for Psychological Studies, Ft. Lauderdale, FL 33314, USA

Misty Hudelson, B.A., Wilkes Honors College, Florida Atlantic University, Boca Raton, FL, 33458, USA

Ani Kalayjian, Ed.D., DDL, RN BCETS, DSc(Hom), Fordham University, New York, NY 10023, USA

Florence W. Kaslow, Ph.D., ABPP, Palm Beach Gardens, FL 33418, USA

Judy Kuriansky, Ph.D., Teachers College, Columbia University, New York, NY 20017-6096, USA

Kevin Lanning, Ph.D., Wilkes Honors College, Florida Atlantic University, Jupiter, FL 33458, USA

S. Mignone, Psy.D., Nova Southeastern University Center for Psychological Studies, Ft. Lauderdale, FL 33314, USA

Samantha A. Montgomery, B.A., Wilkes Honors College, Florida Atlantic University, Boca Raton, FL, 33458, USA

Ryan M. Niemiec, Psy.D., VIA Institute on Character and Hummingbird Coaching Services, Cincinnati, OH, 45202, USA

M. Gene Ondrusek, Ph.D., San Diego, CA 92123

Jeremy Ortman, M.A., Teachers College, Columbia University, New York, NY 20017-6096, USA

Rachel E. Pauletti, B.A., Wilkes Honors College, Florida Atlantic University, Boca Raton, FL, 33458, USA

Frank S. Pittman III, M.D., Northside Hospital Doctos Centre, Atlanta, GA 30342, USA

M. Robinson, Psy.D., Nova Southeastern University Center for Psychological Studies, Ft. Lauderdale, FL 33314, USA

Garreth Rosenzweig, B.A., Wilkes Honors College, Florida Atlantic University, Boca Raton, FL, 33458, USA

Rachel Starkings, B.A., Wilkes Honors College, Florida Atlantic University, Boca Raton, FL, 33458, USA

Amy Vallarelli, B.A., Teachers College, Columbia University, New York, NY 20017-6096, USA

L.E.A. Walker, Ed.D., Nova Southeastern University Center for Psychological Studies, Ft. Lauderdale, FL 33314, USA

Danny Wedding, Ph.D., Missouri Institute of Mental Health, St. Louis, MO 63139, USA

Birgit Wolz, PhD., Oakland, CA 04611

E.R. Zimmerman, Psy.D., Nova Southeastern University Center for Psychological Sutdies, Ft. Lauderdale, FL 33314, USA

Story Board: The "Filmist" Fall of the Cinematic Fourth Wall

Mary Banks Gregerson

Abstract An invisible cinematic fourth wall separates the audience and the performances. A new approach to film appreciation that capitalizes upon the dissolution of this celluloid fourth wall is the "filmist" approach. For filmists, the stimulus (movie) fades into the background, and their responses (appreciation) take center stage. Films stir life, like modern day fairy tales, to provide templates for living. Using special guidelines, filmists relax, focus, and, later, discuss their reactions with others to magnify the value they receive from film viewing. Movies, like magic, cinematically "color in" for clients'/students' imagined happy futures – filling in the fairy-tale ending typically left to fantasy with the phrase " . . . happily ever after . . . . " Postmodern critics of positive psychology command adding the pessimistic realism of " . . . or not . . . " to the traditional romanticized fantasy ending. The many chapters in this edited volume illustrate particular themes to assist therapy, coaching, or teaching that is amplified with the filmist approach to breach the cinematic fourth wall for "happily ever after . . . or not." Cinematic artistic expression infiltrates clients' and students' lives, melding fantasy with reality. The range of what is possible expands with both the integration of celluloid realities into actual living and also the mirrored reflection of real living in cinematic performances and portrayals. Cinema mirrors reality, and reality contours cinema.

The "Filmist" Fall of the Cinematic Fourth Wall

Reciprocal Relations

An invisible cinematic fourth wall separates audience and performances. This "wall" mirrors reality. The mirror is not one way whereby the audience only sees

M.B. Gregerson (✉)
Health, Environment, and Professional Psychology, Leavenworth, KS 66048-3522, USA
e-mail: oltowne@aol.com

Dedicated to my husband Christopher Gregerson for his instrumental interest and support during the years this book evolved, and to my friends, family, and pets Takahata (Tips) and Suburo (Andy) for their loyalty, companionship, and inspiration.

through the looking glass while the cinematic action unfolds, innocent of the viewers' influence. A two-way communication occurs – films influence viewers and viewers influence films. Reflection from the cinematic mirror indelibly refracts upon both the viewer and the players.

This new approach to film appreciation is the "filmist" approach. The dramaturgical convention of a cinematic "wall" falls away when therapy/coaching/education uses film to touch the lives of clients/students. Viewers and films enter into a reciprocal relationship. A filmist influences the cinema as well as being touched ever more intently when thus viewing.

Using special guidelines outlined within this introduction, filmists relax, focus, and afterward discuss with others their reactions to magnify the value of film viewing. Purposefully, like electric charges arcing through the air from the screen onto the viewers, filmist connections create bridges of meaning, influence, and energy between the fantasy portrayed and the reality the audience is living. Films stir life and mirror living. And, the charge rebounds from the audience back to the screen for a bidirectional electric transmission.

The Reach of Films

Recognition for the import of films comes from many sources. For example, in 2008, *Time* magazine seriously considered Zhang Yimou, a renowned Chinese filmmaker, a finalist for *Time* Person of the Year. Since he in 1984 became the ringmaster of the show, Zhang, a cinematographer, who also began acting in 1986, has made so many films and received so many awards that the Chinese have nicknamed him the "Award Winning Expert." In the summer of 2008, he codirected alongside Zhang Jigang the Opening and the Closing Ceremonies at the Summer Olympics in Beijing. That these cultural contributions warrant such singular recognition as *Time's* consideration for Person of the Year indicates the elevation of film to a heroic level and film viewing to a potent, moving cultural experience.

Filmists, and Others

Movie Magic

There is one main difference in being a filmist from a typical film viewer. For filmists, the stimulus (movie) fades into the background, and the response (appreciation) takes center stage. The viewer is writ large while the film becomes the means to the end. Actually, it is like entertainment, which has as its primary focus the audience's reactions to the stimulus being performed. In cinematherapy, though, healing and not simple pleasure is the goal writ large. For life coaches, actualization experienced by clients is writ large. For teachers, what is writ large is the relevance of the cinematic topic to students' lives.

This edited volume colors in what is "writ large" for clients and students.

Movies, like magic, can "color in" clients' imagined happy futures – filling in the fairy-tale ending left to fantasy with the phrase " . . . and they lived happily ever after . . . . " balanced in postmodern times with the added message of " . . . or not . . . " Both clinicians and life coaches may access the value of movie images and research on their effects which, like beacons, may guide clients in getting well and optimizing that wellness. Reciprocal relations add value.

Chapters in this edited volume *Films and Psychology* select movies for a particular theme, whether pleasant or not. This selection improves films as cogent, creative, and concrete assets valuable as therapy, coaching, and teaching adjuncts. Other chapters speak to the conceptual and policy basis for the psychological use of films and television.

As a prelude, Dr. Florence Kaslow's prologue soliloquizes about being a filmist. With stage plays, the word prologue means "preface to a play, from the Greek *pro-logos*, part of a Greek play preceding the entry of the chorus" (Merriam-Webster, 2008). Just so for films, too. So, Dr. Kaslow chimes in her Foreword before the various voices of the chapter authors even begin speaking. Then each chapter voices what happens after the fairy-tale ending " . . . happily ever after . . . " is uttered, or the leavening agent of " . . . or not . . . " is added to this sobriquet.

In classic therapy, that moment when "happily ever after" is voiced typically signifies that time of success with life when therapy closes. Movies are like modern day classic fairy tales that are like therapy, coaching, or teaching. Both have the protagonists – in films, the hero and heroine; in therapy and coaching, the client(s); and in teaching, the student(s) – on the precipice of a new life or understanding. This precipice is reached through struggles and triumphs over dragons and other dangers like in-laws, finances, and sex for therapists; goals, barriers, and values for coaches; and concepts, principles, and facts for students. With the birth of a new beginning in life, both fairy tales and therapy/coaching/education leave to the imagination what occurs beyond that sunset.

Happily Ever After, or Not

Filmist potential has been available for quite some time. Classic film fairy tales, like *The Heiress* (1949) and modern movie morality tales like *The Painted Veil* (2006) reveal character crises resolved positively. Life after the close of the film, though, remains an enigma for the viewer's imagination. For clients, too, after their character and life crises resolve, what happens as they walk out of therapy/coaching room toward the sunset on a distant horizon? Film images and stories can show what to do, and what not to do, to create a "happily ever after" to avoid " . . . or not . . . ", and show what happens after the cinematic curtain falls.

Current sober understanding of life reveals that sometimes what happens may not be pleasant. Thus, the " . . . or not . . . " provides the needed balance to " . . . an epistemological position that contributes to 'reality problems' for positive psychologists" (Held, 2004, p. 11). As positive psychology critic Held (2004) points out, the initial, almost "pop" psychology message within positive psychology tyrannically eschews realistic assessment of possible unpleasantness. Viewers become Pollyannas, removing further from reality rather than delving deeper into personal realities. Balance is needed to restore and expand reality rather than to cultivate and create fantasy.

A "second wave" of positive psychology replaces rigidly optimistic positive psychology with a more balanced integrative message of realism, so that current positive psychology gives proper due to the virtues of the negativity also (Held, 2004). The recent compendium on positive psychology, *A Psychology of Human Strengths*, by editors Aspinwall and Staudinger (2003a) fielded chapters by the editors, Carstensen and Charles (2003), Cantor (2003), Carver and Scheier (2003), Ryff and Singer (2003), and Larsen, Hemenover, Norris, and Cacioppo (2003). Works like these which delve into unpleasantness as well as positivity right the imbalance of unmitigated pleasantness by many adherents to positive psychology. Pessimism is given its rightful due in the field. So, the entire range of possible happenings after the cinematic curtain falls can be fully expected and explored.

In entertainment, whether cinematic or stage, this curtain closes to create the fourth wall. Yet when the cinematic fourth wall fails to connect fantasy and reality in therapy/coaching/education, the curtain never closes. The reverberations of the staged scenes vibrate into the life of an audience member to create connection, spill over, and paint an enlivening, moving "ever after" larger than the still portrait moment when crisis becomes health.

In modern times, life coaching joins therapy for mental wellness after mental health is restored. This enterprise brushes aside the romanticized ending of "happily ever after." Life coaching walks alongside the protagonists at the horizon's edge where the sunset becomes a new day. For those of us thirsting for more of the story, the actualization enterprise of life coaching slakes that dryness. The cinematic fourth wall crumbles, and the curtain stays down while life gushes onward mixing with cinematic reality.

Freeing of energy previously occupied by distress and dysfunction brings renewed vigor, vitality, and truth. Vigor refers to the style of movement, the spring in the client's step, and the pace of motion. Vitality means the inner sense of engagement with life. Truth spellbinds reality rather than fantasy as actuality becomes more daring, more satisfying, and more direct. Life becomes so absorbing that retreat to an inner reality pales in comparison in intent, attraction, and result. Life is the "more."

This edited guide is for mental health/wellness professionals who want more, who want visions that "more" may mean not just the absence of distress and dysfunction. These clients/students want to know what this phrase means and want to live their lives "happily ever after." Clinicians, coaches, and educators serve these clients/students.

Now, though, positive psychology extends the mandate to include the time beyond "happily ever after." An emphasis on the positive, its development, its maintenance, and its growth can easily be conveyed in the stories certain films show.

As these chapters indicate, extant movie guides center on the "sturm und drang" of therapy, getting to the sunset, and omit the upbeat and vibrant world of life coaching beyond the sunset. The sole exception is the new book that analyzes film from a positive psychology perspective (Niemiec & Wedding, 2008).

This recent book by Niemiec and Wedding (2008) focuses on positive psychology and film, and, yet, also magnifies pleasantness with a strengths approach. Now is the time to apply positive psychology to therapy and life coaching, and for positive psychology to emphasize pleasant experiences and overcome unpleasantness for optimal living. For our edited volume, Niemiec has contributed a balanced chapter on international cinema and positive psychology and Wedding has written a postlude. Positive psychology points clinicians into directions after healing, steers life coaches in the basic motivational goals of their enterprises, and orients educators to the entire field. Clinicians, coaches, and educators can access movie depictions of life lessons to optimize the foundations of health whether gained through therapy, or not.

Therapy is not a necessary precursor to life coaching. A client can start from health and simply want assistance to actualize "more" in life. Although life coaching is a marvelous sequel to therapy, life coaching exists independently, too. Education in positive psychology encompasses both these enterprises. This volume will not address the professional controversies and parsimonious dovetailing that exist between therapy and coaching, rather, it will provide a common ground for those conducting therapy and for those conducting life coaching as well as educators teaching both by applying psychology to film.

Beyond "Happily Ever After"

Much of the "beyond happily ever after" realm is ineffable. Fairy tales rarely show the living after the story's positive resolution – with the modern exception of the animated movie series *Shrek* (2001), *Shrek 2* (2004), and *Shrek 3* (2007). The popularity of this animated series may indicate that the audience now wants to see what happens beyond "happily ever after."

Fong (1997) delved into Bettleheim's fascination with the enchantment of fairy tales. He noted, " . . . the happy endings of fairy tales serve as a substitute of the wishes and dreams of readers. In other words, they satisfy readers' spiritual wants" (p. 1). Bettleheim (1976) believed that fairy tales allowed readers, young and old alike, to emotionally grow through the gentler mode of symbolism rather than the harshness of realities.

For our edited volume, movies selected that are relevant for a target theme like father–son relationships can dispel this ineffability. For example, mother–daughter relationships find expression in *Postcards from the Edge* (Nichols, 1990), *Mommie Dearest* (Perry, 1961), *Steel Magnolias* (Ross, 1989), while *I Never Sang for My Father* (Cates, 1970), *Liar, Liar* (Shadyac, 1997), and *Kramer vs. Kramer* (Benton,

1979) show perfect examples of various father–son film relationships. Clients and students can examine what should happen and what should not.

This ineffability made describable through movie images can seem like magic. That is, it seems like magic until science identifies effects and their mechanisms as well as other parameters like population and gender influences. Science anchors such magic in reality.

Science Forms the Field

This edited volume weds science with media film analysis to provide a consummate evidence-based guide for clinicians, coaches, and any learned reader. Now is the time for science to chime in with media analysis. Media scientists need to dispel myths, parse antecedents and consequences, and identify mechanisms to develop the necessary scientific evidence base. In this volume, Walker and her colleagues write about myths of mental illness perpetuated by films. What research evidence exists is presented, with future directions of inquiry clearly articulated. No "happily ever after" vagueness is allowed in the world of science. Mental health scientists want to know how it happens, why it happens, what will make it not happen, and when it will stop naturally.

This edited volume is the first step to transform an essentially clinical and conceptual approach into an evidence-based intervention strategy. When this evidentiary base amasses, the strength of science will anchor all of the other current guides steeped in clinical experience and analytical judgment. With science in the field of film and psychology, a first step need be taken.

First, hypotheses need to be formulated. For this stage, we look to those experienced in the field, and those already making clinical judgments. Their perspectives may provide the first direction for science to move. So, this edited volume turns to clinical experts in various aspects of psychology and film, including those already mentioned, that is, Niemiec and Wedding, as well as Walker and her colleagues. Gregerson turns to scenes of adolescence depicted in movies to comment on the collapse of this rite of passage in American culture. Kuriansky and her colleagues write about the psychology of relationships as shown in film, and American studies specialist Cashill deconstructs modern Californian culture as it reflects/molds visions of the family in films. Balter articulates how those with disabilities are portrayed. Kalayjian and Finnegan Abdolian focus on portrayals of trauma in films. Lanning and his colleagues report on the series of documentaries that follow a group of people over the course of their lives. Wolz provides a conceptual framework with a wealth of clinical and coaching applications. Finally, Ondrusek comments on the interface between television enterprises like reality series and films while critiquing the contributions of authors. These experts have the exciting mandate to spearhead the formation of the scientific field investigating movie adjuncts relevant to clinical treatment programs and life coaching enterprises.

Cinematherapy: State of the Art

Currently, many clinicians instinctively reach for the stimuli of popular films and movies to bolster therapy initiatives. In such film fantasies, clients can experientially "learn" possibilities for behavior, emotions, or thoughts. Such movies "magically" guide clinicians and life coaches to transform clients' visionary aims into concrete realities.

To reiterate an earlier metaphor, these film images can "color in" the fairy tale "happily ever after" fade out found at the end of many fairy tales, so that clients view "real" possibilities. For instance, films like:

- *Guess Who's Coming to Dinner* (Kramer, 1967; Caucasian and African-American), *Lone Star* (Sayles, 1996; Caucasian and Hispanic), and *Dances with Wolves* (Costner, Huneck, & Pfeiffer, 1990; Caucasian and Native American) can explore biracial liaisons.
- Other theme examples are blended families shown in *Step Mom* (Columbus, 1998, another woman replacing birth mother), *The Family Stone* (Bezucha, 2005, dying mother irreplaceable while brood adds spouses and children), *Cheaper By the Dozen* (Levy, 2003) and *Cheaper By the Dozen 2* (Shankman, 2005; the courtship and remarriage of two widowed adults, each with a brood of six), *On Golden Pond* (Rydell, 1961; young divorcée with young child remarries single spouse), and *The Courtship of Eddie's Father* (Cooper, H., Senensky, R., Bixby, B., Komack, Falk, Nelson, Weis, & Sweeney, 1963; young son of a widower matchmakes for his father).
- Still another series of movies addresses identity formation for youths as seen in *Chariots of Fire* (Hudson,1981; the clash of religious and sports values defines young men), *Sky High* (Mitchell, 2005, young man belatedly discovers superpowers inherited from superhero parents), *To Kill a Mockingbird* (Mulligan, 1962, children catapult into young adulthood through social shunning and dangers that their father experiences when living his egalitarian values), *Clueless* (Heckerling, 1995, young girl learns her values independent of and defined by her social set), *Babe* (Noonan, 1995) and *Babe: Pig in the City* (Miller & Paris, 1998, animated, young pig surprisingly excels when assuming the social role of sheepdog), *Good Will Hunting* (van Sant, 1997, professors discover mathematics genius school custodian and socialize him via psychotherapy), and *Say Anything* (Crowe, 1989, young man with modest goals courts and wins young woman with lofty career and personal ambitions).

As noted earlier, "happily ever after" is the actual beginning of the motivational trek to maximize positive functioning. Without any reference point for their desired outcomes, clients may flounder rather than experience efficient, directed progress. Movies can provide such an orienting reference point. Movies and films like *Chariots of Fire* (Hudson, 1981), *My Big Fat Greek Wedding* (Zwick, 2002), and *The Pursuit of Happyness* (Muccino, 2006) can show clients a positive future after triumphing over adversity.

A growing legion of books on psychology and movies indicates the time is here for such books as *The Cinematic Mirror for Psychology and Life Coaching*.

A coterie of books (see the bibliography section of "Other Films and Psychology Books") already appeals to the clinician's healing mission. Furthermore, a respectable smorgasbord of self-help books centers on film and movies.

Each of these books truncates the visionary goals at healing negativity, that is, bringing the dysfunctional and wounded to the minimum thought to be healthy. None show how health transforms into wellness. So, a guide useful for both clinicians and coaches would add positive visions of wellness beyond simple health as well as update what is apropos for healing and transformation that is readying to morph into wellness.

A small group of wellness and movie books for the general public have just started appearing (see "Movies and Wellness for the General Audience" section). These books motivate, stimulate, and inspire with a learned, but nontechnical, nonscientific psychology presentation. Thus, the professional clinician and learned life coach may find these presentations less than satisfying.

Other Film Guides for the Clinician

Over the last decade, the number of film guide books appropriate for clinicians has burgeoned (see the bibliography section "Other Films and Psychology Books"). This reverse annotated chronology notes the authors, date of publication, title, edition number, and the publishers.

Both clinician and life coach should be able to access positive psychology in movie images to move clients' optimizing toward wellness. Now they cannot. To reiterate, none of these film therapy books and those noted subsequently aim at either positive psychology, until Niemiec and Wedding's 2008 volume, or at the wellness impulse of life coaching.

None embrace science either. And, when science is omitted, then lore, intuition, and experience provide a less technically based and a more opinionated guide. This currently opinion-based field of literature calls for the evidence-based popular psychology oriented guide, *The Cinematic Mirror for Psychology and Life Coaching*.

A general public interested in self-help and movies has emerged (see the citations in the reference list section "Other Films and Psychology Books"). *The Cinematic Mirror for Psychology and Life Coaching*. Each entry in this series of books seems approximately equally and respectably popular. The Amazon search engine indicates that many buyers have purchased more than one book in this series.

In the past 5 years a smaller number of books aimed at wellness in relation to film topics have just started to appear (see the reference section "Other Films and Psychology Books"). Popular books such as these capitalize on the large part of life that movies occupy for many people. To wit, US films provide the majority of home entertainment products (MPAA, 2008). In 2006 and 2007, a steady 603 new films were released in more than 150 countries worldwide, and provide the majority of home entertainment.

Books about movies for a purpose other than entertainment beneficially and blissfully co-opt the films' pleasure motive. As the field of film and psychology moves into a stage of scientific inquiry, the systematization of these various non-intended aspects may magnify their value. To repeat an earlier injunction: "We want to know how it [movie magic] happens, why it happens, what will make it not happen, and when it will stop naturally." The use of popular movies to heal and to optimize positively extends their value.

To summarize, none of these wellness books systematizes wellness nor provides a scientific evidence base. A positive psychology model emerging from within this current edited book and the Niemiec and Wedding 2008 volume could give scientifically studied concepts as guideposts. An evidence base would examine the experientially proven words both clinicians and life coaches now offer clients on film images relevant to specific life challenges. Finally, the ability and opportunity to talk about what is seen in the film extends its value.

Who the Readers Are

Life coaches have professional organizations like IDEA, a health and fitness professional association. IDEA has over 19,000 members worldwide. Organizations and associations like CanFitPro (Canadian Fitness Professionals) and training institutions like Bakara Center for Creative Change provide Certified Life Coach Trainings. Such sources access books on life coaching.

In addition, those who also purchased the popular cinematherapy books, some of which are in their second printing, will find this edited volume of interest. For instance, the American Psychological Association (APA) has over 150,000 members with sometimes as many as 20,000 attending the annual conference; APA hosts a huge onsite bookstore there. Many years, films of psychological import are shown through the auspices of the APA Film Committee, and an award is given annually to an outstanding film through the auspices of the APA Division 46 Media Psychology committee called The Media Watch. This edited volume could serve as an excellent source book.

Within APA, Division 46 Media Psychology specifically has an interest in movies and their utilization in promoting health. At the 2006 APA Annual Meeting in New Orleans, LA, the APA Division 46 symposium on "Media, Myth, and Mental Illness" received a deluge of e-mailed and phoned requests for cosponsorship. The Walker and colleagues' chapter in this volume elaborates upon this popular presentation. The entire volume itself is a part of the APA Division 46 Media Psychology Book Series: *Psychology and the Media* with the Editor-in-Chief Florence W. Kaslow, Ph.D., ABPP. Books in this APA published series include:

Kirschner, S., & Kirschner, D. (Eds.). (1972). *Perspectives on psychology and the media.*
Schwartz, L. L. (1999). *Psychology and the media: A second look.*

So, few books until now applied positive psychology for both clinicians and life coaches in terms of films and psychology. The systematic reviews based around specific topics demonstrate the strategic approach when using film in consultation sessions, whether clinical or coaching. Whatever scientific information is gleaned, still, all this data rests upon the process in which clients engage, whether in therapy or life coaching.

The process of viewing films has an august history in film appreciation. A more than 80-year-old pedagogical approach called "cinema education" has been used for a range of teaching – from a skill like bowling to neuroscience medical education (Alexander, Pavlov, & Lenahan, 2007; Low, 1925; Meyers, 2006). The cognitive behavioral approach presented in this introduction could add value for every single viewing for educational purposes.

This introduction "Story Board: The Fall of the Cinematic Fourth Wall" concludes with a suggested approach of über-appreciation. Because learned lay persons and not professionals are the target audience, this presentation of the approach will foster the cultivation of films, as Niemiec and Wedding (2008) have termed the process.

Belief in the power of movies and television to transform has captured the popular imagination. In last year's *Transformers* (Bay, 2007), heroic alien robots, called Autobots, learned to communicate with fleshlings, as earthen humans were called, by watching classic films and television. Ten years before, in the docu-fantasy *Elvis Meets Nixon* (Arkush, 1997), an ingenuously adrift Elvis says he never thought beyond the ending of his many movies when he kissed the girl and they lived happily ever after; he is at a loss in terms of his life direction now that he has won career accolades, kissed his girl (wife Priscilla Presley), and they have walked off into the sunset. A conscious turn toward movies as guides for living, as lights illuminating into the darkness of the future, could enrich not only the passage but also the destination.

Years ago at the 2006 American Psychological Association in New Orleans, I presented the first talk on becoming a "filmist." This approach applies mindfulness (Lanager, 1990) to film viewing. In short, mindful filmists consider a multiplicity of meanings, based upon predetermined choices. Being a filmist means getting the most out of your movie experience.

A filmist watches movies like an artist paints pictures. The movie experience becomes the canvas inside the viewers. Such creativity cultivates meaning, appreciation, and value.

On Being a Filmist

Ever walk out of a film and want the experience to continue? How about simply walking out before the film ended? Has a second screening made a first film viewing richer? Then, you have the makings of a filmist.

Movies. How can we get more for our money with movies on the big or little screen? How? – Watch actively, yet effortlessly. Be a filmist.

A filmist "devours" movies, digesting them in conversation with friends and family after viewing while alertly relaxed, like a hunter awaiting a prey. So a filmist does not just "go" to a film, but rather, a filmist "does" a film. This "doing" involves choice before going, alert yet passive attention while viewing, and then discussion afterward.

Dramaturgy: The Art of Storytelling

The discussion after the film is the *pièce de resistance* for the filmist. A discussion guide under development called *The Filmist* forms the basis for a Friends Film Social Club for filmists. Based upon screen-writing principles called dramaturgy, this 12-month guide overall provides consummate movie viewing. Yet each month stands alone in its value and purpose. Both the year and monthly topics provide a foundation for discussion, for socializing among filmists. These 12 months of Elements for filmists in a social club are as follows:

Character
    The Signature
    Internal Conflict
    Fatal Flaw
Plot
    The Goal
    The Barrier
    The Struggle
Scene
    Sight
    Sound
    Special Effects
Relationship
    Romance
    Family
    Friend/Nemesis

Each element has an explanation, illustrations, and applications so that a range of readers might access this socializing feature. The cohesion of the Filmist Social Club is the process of *SEE*ing (see below), while the satisfaction and the outcome are at once individual and interpersonal. A group of filmists mix individual experiences through the funnel of a single elemental focus to stimulate a foundation for discussion and discovery together.

And the Moral of this Tale is: *SEE*ing Brings Home a Film's Meaning

Prepare first. Three basic steps help the viewer *SEE* instead of just watching films.

√ Start with a blank screen.
√ Establish what will be important – that is, the focus of attention.
√ Express to others your response to the particular dramaturgy, or technique of dramatization/comedy of interest.

Again, although the parsimony of this approach appears simple, its application is not easy. We are entrained to experience films as entertainment – to absorb ourselves in plots, in relationships, in aesthetic judgments. Filmists rise above these mundane entertainment involvements. Filmists brush aside these common experiences in order to heighten satisfaction, cultivate comprehension, and maximize value.

Set a Blank Screen: A Tabula Rasa

Clear your mind of all other thoughts, concerns, musing, and preoccupation. I find helpful envisioning in my mind's eye a blank, white movie screen like those used for viewing home movies or school films. Then my imagination controls what plays on the screen, how fast, whether moving forward or back, or even stopped as in a portrait. In essence, I become my own movie director.

This "blanking" is not easy. An activity typically used for entertainment changes to an activity for educational enhancement. Instead of being drawn along plot lines and character relationships, the filmist abstracts from the viewing details specifically predetermined as the most important. This transformation takes effort, dedication, and practice. The rewards are great.

A trick to setting a blank screen is a mindfulness technique (Lanager, 1990) combined with diaphragmatic deep breathing (Borysenko, 2008). Mindfulness actively processes experiences and considers multiple possible paths, multiple possible outcomes, and multiple possible meanings. Diaphragmatic breathing relaxes the body so that the active mindfulness progresses unimpeded. This combination of relaxing the body and mind, then focusing the mind for creative "audiencing" magnifies bottom-line enjoyment and top-shelf satisfaction.

Establish What Is Important

Ironically for filmists, the focus of one's attention occurs based upon preconceptions. This predetermined focus, either by the filmist her/himself or by the filmist social viewing group, culls from the movie what aspects to include in one's subsequent movie responses. If you are on a personal odyssey, then decide your destination yourself. If, though, viewing as a member of a group, say a friendship social film viewing club (Gregerson, 2006), then establish collectively what is important, that is, what the group's destination will be. Like a sieve or a magnetic net which catches pertinent images, information, relationships, plots, and characteristics, this focus establishes beforehand what is important.

Express to Others: "'To Be or Not To Be' That Is the Question" (Shakespeare, circa 1600).

This step is crucial to complete the filmist experience. Talk to others. Express your experience, discuss whether:

> To be, or not to be: that is the question:
> Whether 'tis nobler in the mind to suffer
> The slings and arrows of outrageous fortune,
> Or to take arms against a sea of troubles,
> And by opposing end them?
> (William Shakespeare,
> Hamlet, circa 1600).

Take your response on the inside and bring it out. Talk and listen. The talking and the listening deepen the experience.

When you know how to appreciate, what to appreciate, and how to make it personally relevant, you will be a filmist. You will SEE differently. Your destination will be different than the usual audience member floating along the entertainment train. You will have a special basis for communicating to others. After this easy yet challenging skill starts, its development deepens each time the skill is used.

Two steps precede and one step follows the movie experience.

But what of the movie viewing experience itself? Finally, after the "S" and "E" of, respectively, setting a blank screen and establishing what's important, relax, and let go while you watch, readying yourself for the subsequent "E" to express yourself. Afterward, talk to your friends, communicate your experiences, and discuss your impressions to intensify the original value of the movie viewing.

More for Your Investment

Think of being a filmist as wise investing. Choose wisely which movie and where in that movie, to invest your attention; then sit back, watch it, and experience enjoyment magnify when communicating with others. This filmist experience is your ticket to value, your passport to meaning, and your certificate for appreciation.

The enjoyment is in easy viewing – enriched by the deciding, enlivened by the discovery, enhanced by the sharing.

When you talk with others before and after the film different experiences occur.

Before the film, you create a "frame" or context which will draw out certain aspects of the film to the forefront. These particular aspects will play over in your mind, your emotions, and your body, all of which are at rest because you set the blank screen.

What sticks will comprise the discussion after viewing. And, what sticks is that unique combination of who you particularly are with your one-of-a-kind experiences and of the pre-viewing context that you as a member of your group chose.

The pre-chat is like knotting a skein to catch fish. The caught fish are the images, the thoughts, the experiences culled from the actual viewing which is the preparation. The absorption comes from discussing with other through expression, like eating the fish at a shared banquet. The post-chat mixes your fishes with your friends' fishes to make quite a feast!

Ah, the secret is in the calming, deciding, expressing.

A filmist is like a movie viewing Sherlock Holmes, a subtle, poised, confident detective that astounds the casual viewer by directed focus that "outs" nuances hidden to others, and, then, harvests meaning.

Being a filmist gives a new meaning to the injunction "Go forth, and multiply." Multiply the value of your movie tickets. Multiply the meaning of the viewing experience. Multiply the things you have in common with others. Even if you differ in the meaning extracted, you will find common ground in the process. You all will be flimists.

References

Alexander, M., Pavlov, A., & Lenahan, P. (2007). Lights, camera, action. Using film to teach ACGME competencies. Literature and arts in medical education issues. *Family medicine, 39*(1), 20–23.

Aspinwall, L. G., & Staudinger, U. M. (2003a). *A psychology of human strengths: Fundamental questions and future directions for positive psychology.* Washington, DC: American Psychological Association.

Aspinwall, L. G., & Staudinger, U. M. (2003b). A psychology of human strengths: Some central issues of an emerging field. In L. G. Aspinwall & U. M. Staudinger (Eds.), *A psychology of human strengths: Fundamental questions and future directions for a positive psychology* (pp. 9–22). Washington, DC: American Psychological Association.

Bettleheim, B. (1976). *The uses of enchantment.* New York: Knopf.

Borysenko, J. (2008) Meditation and staying centered. In: *Stress reduction.* Joan Boysenko's Homepage. Available via Internet Explorer. http://www.joanborysenko.com/cms.cfm?fuseaction=articles.viewThisArticle&articleID=191&pageID=420. Cited September 7, 2008.

Cantor, N. (2003). Constructive cognition, personal goals, and the social embedding of personality. In L. G. Aspinwall & U. M. Staudinger (Eds.), *A psychology of human strengths* (pp. 49–60). Washington, DC: American Psychological Association.

Carstensen, L. L., & Charles, S. T. (2003). Human aging: Why is even good news taken as bad? In L. G. Aspinwall & U. M. Staudinger (Eds.), *A psychology of human strengths* (pp. 75–86). Washington, DC: American Psychological Association.

Carver, C. S., & Scheier, M. F. (2003). Three human strengths. In L. G. Aspinwall & U. M. Staudinger (Eds.), *A psychology of human strengths* (pp. 87–102). Washington, DC: American Psychological Association.

Fong, K. (1997). The effect of classic fairy tales on readers and society. http://www.cs.siu. edu/~kfong/research/fairytales.html. Cited August 21, 2008.

Gregerson (Jasnoski), M. B. (2006). On becoming a filmist with your friends. *The amplifier,* Fall/Winter, *3*, 17–18 (abstract) Available via the American Psychological Association Division 46 Media Psychology newsletter website homepage. http://www.apa.org/divisions/div46/AmpFall-Win06_final.pdf. Cited September 7, 2008.

Held, B. S. (2004). The negative side of positive psychology. *Journal of humanistic psychology, 44*(1), 9–46.

Langer, E. (1990). *Mindfulness.* Cambridge, MA: De Capo Press.

Larsen, J. T., Hemenover, S. H., Norris, C. J., & Cacioppo, J. T. (2003). Turning adversity to advantage: On the virtues of the coactivation of positive and negative emotions. In L. G. Aspinwall & U. M. Staudinger (Eds.), *A psychology of human strengths* (pp. 211–225). Washington, DC: American Psychological Association.

Low, B. (1925). The cinema in education. Some psychological considerations. *Contemporary reviews, 128*, 628–635.

Meyers, L. (2006). Lights, camera, action: Movies, music and other media can enliven your classroom. *GradPSYCH, 4*(2). Available at American Psychological Association Online. http://gradpsych.apags.org/mar06/cover-action.html. Cited August 28, 2008.

Merriam-Webster Online dictionary. (2008). Accessed at http://www.merriam-webster.com/dictionary/prologs on August 28, 2008.

Motion Picture Association of America (MPAA). (2008). *Research and statistics.* Accessed at http://www.mpaa.org/researchStatistics.asp on August 10, 2008.

Niemiec, R., & Wedding, D. (2008). *Positive psychology at the movies: Using films to cultivate.* Gottingen, Germany: Hogrefe & Huber.

Ryff, C. D., & Singer, B. (2003). Ironies of the human condition. Well-being and health on the way to mortality. In L. G. Aspinwall & U. M. Staudinger (Eds.), *A psychology of human strengths* (pp. 271–287). Washington, DC: American Psychological Association.

Other Film and Psychology Books

Movies and Psychotherapy for Professionals

Cambridge Studies in Film. (2003). *The 'I' of the camera: Essays in film criticism, history, and aesthetics.* Cambridge, UK: Cambridge University Press.

Gabbard, G. O., & Gabbard, K. (1999). *Psychiatry and the cinema* (2nd ed.). Arlington, VA: American Psychiatric Publishing.

Hertlein, K. M. (Ed.), & Viers, D. (2005). *The couple and family therapists' notebook: Homework, handouts, and activities for use in marital and family therapy* (Haworth Practical Practice in Mental Health). Philadelphia, PA: Haworth Press.

Hesley, J. W., & Hesley, J. G. (2001). *Rent two films and let's talk in the morning: Using popular movies in psychotherapy* (2nd ed.). San Francisco, CA: John Wiley & Sons, Inc.

Kaplan, A. (1989). *Psychoanalysis and cinema* (Afi Film Readers Series). New York: Routledge.

Lee, J. Y. (2006). *A group therapy manual using cinematherapy to improve adjustment in adolescents after parental divorce.* ProQuest/UMI.

Peake, T. H. (2004). *Cinema and life development: Healing lives and training therapists.* Westport, CT: Praeger Publishers.

Reich, J. (2004). *Beyond the Latin lover: Marcello Mastroianni, Masculinity, and Italian cinema.* Bloomington, IN: Indiana University Press.

Robinson, D. J. (2003). *Reel psychiatry: Movie portrayals of psychiatric conditions.* Port Huron, MI: Rapid Psychler Press.

Smith, J. H. (1987). *Images in our souls: Cavell, psychoanalysis, and cinema* (psychiatry and the humanities). Baltimore, MD: The Johns Hopkins University Press.

Solomon, G. (1995). *The motion picture prescription: Watch this movie and call me in the morning: 200 movies to help you heal life's problems.* Fairfield, CT: Aslan Publishing.

Solomon, G. (2001). *Reel therapy: How movies inspire you to overcome life's problems.* Fairfield, CT: Aslan Publishing Corp.

Wahl, O. F. (1997). *Media madness: Public images of mental illness.* Chapel Hill, NC: Rutgers University Press.

Wedding, D. & Boyd, M. A. (1998). *Movies and mental illness.* Columbus, OH: McGraw Hill College.

Wedding, D., Boyd, M. A., & Niemiec, R. (2005). *Movies and mental illness: Using films to understand psychotherapy* (2nd Rev ed.). Gottisgen, Germany: Hogrefe & Huber Publishing.

Self-Help and Movies

Bergund, J., & West, B. (2004). *Gay cinematherapy: The queer guy's guide to finding your rainbow one movie at a time.* Bel Air, CA: Delta.

Bunch, C. K. (2006). *The Wizard of Oz. The symbolic quest to find your inner heroes, face your worst enemy, and attain wholeness. This timeless movie is cinematherapy for the soul.* Bloomington, IN: iUniverse, Inc.

Peske, N., & West, B. (2003). *Cinematherapy for lovers: The girl's guide to finding true love one movie at a time.* Cayon, CA: Delta.

Peske, N., & West, B. (2004). *Cinematherapy for the soul: The girl's guide to finding inspiration one movie at a time.* Bel Air, CA: Delta.

Peske, N. & West, B. (2004). *Cinematherapy goes to the Oscars.* Bel Air: Delta.

Solomon, G. (2005). *Cinemaparenting: Using movies to teach life's most important lessons.* Fairfield, CT: Aslan Publishing Corporation.

West, B., & Bergund, J. (2005). *TVtherapy: The television guide to life.* New York: Delta.

West, B., & Peske, N. (1999). *Cinematherapy: The girl's guide to movies for every mood.* Cayon, CA: Delta.

West, B., & Peske, N. (2002). *Advanced cinematherapy: The girl's guide to finding happiness one movie at a time.* Cayon, CA: Delta.

Wolz, B. (2004). *E-motion picture magic: A movie lover's guide to healing and transformation.* Cayon, CA: Glenbridge Publishing Ltd.

Zimmerman, J. N. (2003). *People like ourselves: Portrayals of mental illness in the movies (Studies in Film Genres, Pt.).* Lanham, MD: Scarecrow Press.

Wellness and Movies for the General Audience

Anker, R. M. (2005). *Catching light: Looking for god in the movies.* Grand Rapids, MI: Wm B. Eerdman's Publishing Company.

Clemens, J., & Wolff, M. (2000). *Movies to manage by.* Columbus, OH: McGraw Hill.

Hendricks, G., & Simon, S. (2005). *Spiritual cinema.* Carlsbad, CA: Hay House.

Simon, S. (2002). *The force is with you: Mystical movie messages that inspire our lives.* Charlottesville, VA: Hampton Roads Publishing Company.

Teague, R. (2000). *Reel spirit: A guide to movies that inspire, explore and empower.* Wellington, AU: Unity Books.

Act One: Introduction

Frank S. Pittman III

Abstract It has been said that we go to the movies to fall in love. We know that is true and we fall in love regularly with an enormous screen there in the dark. But we also go to the movies to get wisdom about how life works, to predict the future, to learn how to see what is over the next hill, and what is down the next road. For a lifetime, I have looked to the movies for lessons in reality. But none of these sources of the immortal myths and legends by which we structure our lives could compare in reality or in mythic moment with what was taking place as the pictures and stories and faces – never forget the faces – were transferred from the big screen to the even bigger screen in my head.

We have to look quite a way back to find films about families who are earnestly trying to get along, rather than trying to decide whether it will make them happy to remain in the family with their loved ones. Even if no one else does so, at least the therapists must believe that people have the power to make relationships work, to pull together in times of crisis, and to actually live together without driving one another crazy. The primary skill of therapists is optimism, the belief that we humans can change and do whatever needs to be done for our life and for the lives of our loved ones.

It has been said that we go to the movies in order to fall in love. We know that is true and we fall in love regularly with an enormous screen full of Cyd Charisse, Laurence Olivier, Susan Sarandon, Sophia Loren, Meryl Streep, Morgan Freeman, or Gene Kelly, there in the dark. But we also go to the movies to get wisdom about how life works, to predict the future, to learn how to see what is over the next hill, what is down the next road. For a lifetime, I have looked to the movies for lessons in reality.

F.S. Pittman III (✉)
Northside Hospital Doctors Centre, Atlanta, GA 30342, USA
e-mail: fsp3md@aol.com

M.B. Gregerson (ed.), *The Cinematic Mirror for Psychology and Life Coaching*,
DOI 10.1007/978-1-4419-1114-8_2, © Springer Science+Business Media, LLC 2010

My Life at the Movies

I grew up in a series of small Southern Gothic towns with an alcoholic mother, a father off at war, two adoring grandmothers, one the editor of the daily newspaper, the other the undertaker and church organist. What's more, we had a cemetery full of kinfolk, each with a story or two. When I was not listening to family stories at my grandmothers' knees, I went down the street to the movies. My first job was delivering fliers for the local picture show. To me, the movies were far more real than the life my family was living in their decaying antebellum mansions with little or no inside plumbing. It was an ideal stage setting for earthy romantic fantasy.

My mother's cousin Charles, with whom she had been raised, had run the pentathlon in the 1920 Olympics, had won a Rhodes Scholarship and the Metropolitan Opera Auditions, and had gone to Hollywood hoping to play Ashley in *Gone with the Wind*. He didn't get the role but he did get on with the telephone company for a while. Mother would send him $50 every Xmas and he would send her a letter about the famous elbows he had rubbed. Hollywood became part of our neighborhood.

I was 2 when *Snow White* (Disney, 1937) came out and the wicked stepmother scared the BeJeesus out of me; I was 4 when I nestled in my Mammy's lap in the balcony to see *Gone with the Wind* (Fleming, 1939), which I still insist is real, more real than either Kansas or Oz in 1939. I learned compassion from the Joads trying to get from their dust bowl in Oklahoma to the gardens of California. I learned morals and character from *Hopalong Cassidy* (Bretherton, 1935), whose real last name (Boyd) was that of my most loving grandmother. All the war movies fighting it out in my mind starred my missing father; all the love stories starred my once beautiful mother.

I wrote movie reviews in college at Washington and Lee, another mythical atmosphere, and even took courses (from a mentor I shared with Tom Wolfe) on how to watch movies. For 4 years, I did not miss a single flick that came to either theater in the little college town or the theaters at any of the surrounding towns.

In medical school, I was busy and became an amateur movie goer. In time I became a doctor and a husband to another dedicated moviegoer. We could go to the movies again.

I went into psychiatry, of course, perhaps to learn what a normal life was like. I ignored the bloodless diagnoses in the Diagnostic and Statistical Manual. Instead, I read Freud, whose case histories were something between novels and mysteries. (Freud and Sherlock Holmes had more in common than cocaine.) I came to see that I could be more helpful to people when we had together turned their life or situation into a story, as the causes and effects in their lives roll around and enwrap one another. We explored the forces that impacted or determined the things people did, how they came to do them, where they picked up the misinformation about the human condition that would make their self-defeating behavior make sense within the context of their family, their town, and perhaps even within the context of the movies they had seen or the novels they had read.

Interestingly, much of the misinformation people carry through life was picked up from self-help books written by well-meaning people who just hadn't lived enough life yet to understand how complex it can be, and how simple.

As psychiatry did in those days, our primary goal was to convince people that whatever their parents had told them or modeled for them was well intentioned, even if stark raving mad. Only if people know what other people feel in life can they be compassionate or optimistic or effective in negotiating the interactions of their lives on the same planet with other human beings. One thing that was inescapably clear was that those people, usually men, who read the sports pages but have rarely if ever read fiction, have bypassed the crucial experience of knowing what life feels like to people outside themselves. They may go to movies in which people on screen don't talk much to one another, while the audience is kept awake by glass shattering and things exploding.

This was of course long before television got to our neck of the woods. When it did come in, I was grown and gone. (My parents then kept several TV's blaring around the clock, stopping all the conversation that made life with them feel like someone was alive there.) We could watch the little TV screen and see competitive seductions, contests about who would get the girl (or the guy). Around the clock we watched bad guys chase good guys, and good guys chase bad guys, and we might ponder who would live and who would die. Most of the plots were familiar from the polygamous and bloodthirsty Old Testament. Between burning bushes and man-eating whales, brothers killed brothers and fathers killed sons, and kings killed the husbands of the women they lusted after. Sick people got well and bad people got caught and everyone good lived happily ever after.

My hobby is writing movie reviews. For 25 years, my reviews have appeared in the *Psychotherapy Networker* (formerly *The Family Therapy Networker*) with reviews of – or at least comments about – 450 movies. In these reviews I try to underline what the moviemakers are trying to say and trying to do. I want to identify what the movie is showing us, what effect it is having upon us, and what it tells us about the human condition, about the relationships of human beings in their natural state. I may be making some use of the hours I've spent in the dark thinking about what sort of creatures we are and what we are doing to one another when we act out the scripts we have been given, directly or inadvertently, in our families.

In therapy, patients and I talk about the messages from the movies. When I teach, I show or explain or even act out scenes from movies that demonstrate the interaction or the emotions people go through in life.

Marriage: The Mysteriously Fragile Institution

We talk a lot about marriage, the institution that confuses us most. Marriage in recent decades has somehow become the most fragile of our human institutions. It is not holding and therefore children are growing up with single parents, if any at all, and are failing to grow into adults. It is a disaster for all of us. Children who grow up without fathers do not understand what grown men are about; they cannot become one and they cannot choose one. They may actually think that women who run from marriage are showing great maturity and courage. Yet they somehow have confidence that, once they get rid of this imperfect husband, they can go to the "perfect husband store" and pick up a shiny new one.

Boys growing up without fathers may become male impersonators, exaggerating the display of masculinity it takes to look like a man. Boys who grow up fatherless are many times more likely to end up imprisoned for violent crimes, jumping from marriage to marriage and running out on kids, terrified of an equal relationship with a female partner.

Marriage is not likely to work if you don't understand it and instead expect a totally different sort of arrangement, like a high romance or a suicide pact.

The most important things we need to know about marriage are, first, that "Marriage is not marriage unless both partners are working to make it equal, total, and permanent" and, second, that "Marriage is not supposed to make you happy: it is supposed to make you married and thus bring coherence into your life."

We are supposed to learn such things about marriage from our parents, grandparents and siblings, but our families, even if they manage to stay together and don't kill one another, protect us from unpleasant reality and hide things from us. Unfortunately we learn about marriage from romantic fantasies, from pornography, or from Cialis 4-hour erection ads. (I don't know which is worse in raising people's expectations too high.) Perhaps the worst source of information about marriage would be romance novels. Interestingly, the best place to learn about men, women, and marriage might be women's magazines.

Television is not a reliable source of insight about what it takes to make a marriage work. The day time talk shows tend to be impatient with imperfect men or indecisive women and they want to get it over with fast, "Leave the jerk! You deserve better. Put the children up for adoption, they'll be fine. Think of what will make you happy, right this minute. All women are in danger of being romantically disappointed or verbally abused, so you should surely run away from your home and your loved ones."

Television also tends to dumb marriage down for us, so we must go to the movies to get a close-up, bigger than life, picture of the horrors and splendors of the blessed and cursed state of marriage. There are certain movies that radiate such wisdom, everyone needs to know and understand them. There are many of them, but here are a few I often present to therapists and patients.

Romance and Suicide

Wuthering Heights (Wyler, 1939) was made from the broodingly romantic novel of 1847 by Emily Bronte. This film makes romance seem dangerous, deadly, and doomed – somewhat of a suicide equivalent. It dramatizes and debunks the notion that marriage has something to do with high romance and soul mates. Narcissistically romantic Cathy (Merle Oberon) is about to marry the rich guy next door (David Niven) but she is in love with the gypsy foundling Heathcliff (Laurence Olivier), with whom she's been raised and now who is the family stable boy. Oberon demands that Heathcliff "Make the world stop right here. Make the world stand still.

Make the moors never change. Make you and I never change." Heathcliff says "The moors and I will never change. Don't you, Cathy." Her response is "No matter what I ever say or do, Heathcliff, this is me standing here on this hill with you forever." In other words, "do not let the future happen, since our love would not survive all that reality. We cannot marry therefore our choices are to suicide or to live in misery." Sure enough, she goes ahead and marries David Niven that afternoon, makes him miserable until she dies and comes back to haunt everyone. Hollywood, forced to offer happy endings to its prospective audience, lets each movie end with true love being requited, so the audience feels a moment of happiness until they stop to think about it.

Woody Allen used to believe in romantic love, yet he let both Jonathan Rhys Meyers playing Chris Wilton in *Match Point* (Allen, 2005) and Martin Landau playing Judah Rosenthal in *Crimes and Misdemeanors* (Allen, 1989) escape punishment for murdering their mistresses. In a recent Woody Allen film, *Vicky Cristina Barcelona* (Allen, 2008), the still more or less married Spanish artist and wild man Juan Antonio played by Javier Bardem invites two American tourists, adventurous Cristina done by Scarlett Johansson and the circumspect Vicky done by Rebecca Hall to share his weekend and his bed. They are soon joined by his homicidal ex wife Marcia Elena played by Penelope Cruz, as Bardem regularly changes partners or just adds to the rotation and explains his actions by assuring us he feels like doing it. The landlady Judy Nash played by Patricia Clarkson wants to join the *rondele*, or at least some *rondele*, but restrains herself and instead encourages everyone else to get on the merry-go-round. Allen's sympathies are clearly with those who make decisions on bases other than the passion of the moment. He, who once was cynical about marriage, now seems to have soured on romance.

Romance is about the measure of true love, i.e., the eagerness to die for it, like *Romeo and Juliet* (Cukor, Castellani, Zeferelli, & Luhrmann, 1936/54/68/96). One of the more outrageously romantic films of my youth was *Duel in the Sun* (Vidor, 1946) in which a good brother Jesse McCaules (Joseph Cotton) and a bad brother Lewton "Lewt" McCaules (Gregory Peck) vie for their dangerous half breed cousin Pearl Chavez (Jennifer Jones). When she chooses Cotton, Peck shoots him, so Jones shoots Peck, and Peck, after crawling for bloody miles across the desert, shoots her, and they bleed and die together among the cacti – for love.

The Hill of Beans

As I watch love stories unfold so inevitably, I keep hearing in my head Bogart as Rick's final words to the love of his life, Ingrid Bergman as Ilsa, at the airport in *Casablanca* (Curtiz, 1942). She is planning to leave her husband, Paul Henreid as Victor Lazslo, the freedom fighter who is the last hope for Western Civilization. Bogey switches the plane tickets and sends Bergman off to help her husband save the world. He tells her, "Ilsa, I'm no good at being noble, but it doesn't take much to see that the problems of three little people don't amount to a hill of beans in this crazy world. Someday you'll understand that, not now. – But we'll always have Paris."

It is usual for Hollywood to assure us that true love is the secret of happiness, and refreshing when it suggests that there are other considerations, particularly children whose emotional stability is threatened by threats to the parental marriage. In *Bridges of Madison County* (Eastwood, 1995), Robert Kincaid (Clint Eastwood), a National Geographic photographer in a dirty truck comes to Iowa and seduces a farm wife Francesca Johnson (Meryl Streep). They bathe together and peel carrots at the sink and plan to run off together, leaving behind a perfectly serviceable husband and children. Streep explains to Eastwood why she can't go (she would know she had treated her loved ones unfairly and she would end up hating the marriage-breaking interloper who blew her honorable little life apart). And, of course, she would always have Paris. She understands that exciting memories are fun, and nice things to have tucked away somewhere.

In the fascinating and talky Patrick Farber play about love and sex, *Closer* (Nichols, 2003/I), Julia Roberts as Anna explains to Natalie Portman as Alice why she took up with Portman's mate, Jude Law as Dan. "I fell in love with him, Alice." Portman replies: "That's the most stupid expression in the world. 'I fell in love' – as if you had no choice. There's a moment, there's always a moment; 'I can do this, I can give in to this or I can resist it.' I don't know when your moment was, but I bet there was one. – You didn't fall in love, you gave in to temptation."

Falling in love, especially when the fallers already have mates, brings great pain to all of the participants and even the bystanders. It is not the reparation of a misspent life. Matching everyone up at the end, as in Shakespeare's comedies and Hollywood movies of the 60s and 70s and adolescent films for the dating singles, seems puerile, like the solutions offered on daytime TV.

Marriage of Comfort

The movie that most totally buried the primacy of romance was *Marty* (Mann, 1955) a deliberately drab film in which Ernest Borgnine as Marty Piletti, a fat ugly butcher, pestered by his mother to get married, meets a girl he describes as a dog when all his friends decree that she is not the girl of their dreams. He is standing her up as he spends the evening with his usual buddies. After listening to their banal chatter, Marty announces: "What are you doing tonight? I don't know, what are you doing tonight? Miserable and lonely, miserable and lonely and stupid. What am I, crazy or something? What am I doing with you guys? I've got something good here. You don't like her, my mother don't like her, she's a dog and I'm a fat ugly man but I had a good time last night and I'll have a good time tonight and if I have enough good times I'll get down on my knees and beg that girl to marry me. And if we make a party on New Year's I'll have a date for that party. You don't like her? That's too bad." He enters the phone booth and says to one of his friends: "When are you getting married, Angie? You ought to be ashamed of yourself. You're 33 years old and your kid brothers are married already."

This man is not expecting to be blown off his feet by physical and emotional perfection. He wants a life, and a family and adulthood. He wants a buddy, a partner, not too much to ask – unless you are a romantic who wants life to be magical. He is seeking comfort, companionship and, if he's lucky, someone who is willing to live with him, like him, and share his life. The world does not have to stand still for him, as it does for Cathy and Heathcliff.

Perhaps the wisest pronouncement from the movies is Bea Vecchio's (Beatrice Arthur) words to her son Joseph Hindy as Richie, who at the time of his brother's wedding in *Lovers and Other Strangers* (Howard, 1970) announces that he is divorcing Diane Keaton as Joan Vecchio, because he is not happy. She intones in her booming baritone, "Don't look for happiness, Richie. It will only make you miserable."

At the point of marriage, what is expected of you? In *She's Having A Baby*, (Hughes, 1988) Kevin Bacon as the earnest Jefferson is at the altar to marry the delicately beautiful Elizabeth McGovern as Kristy Biggs. The preacher asks: "Wilt thou, Jefferson, have this woman to be they wedded wife? Wilt thou comfort and keep her in sickness and in health? Wilt thou provide her with credit cards and a 4 bedroom 2 and a half bath house with central air and professional decorating, a Mercedes Benz, and 2 weeks in the Bahamas every spring? Wilt thou try to remember the little things that mean so much, like flowers on her anniversary, a kind word when she's had a rough day, an occasional "you look pretty today?" Wilt thou be understanding when she's tired, headachy or upset about something. Wilt thou try not to be such a pig when thou shave and shower. Wilt thou listen patiently to long stories about kids, clothes, and decorator checkbook covers?"

Jefferson: "I will."

Sometimes, the expectations are up front, and sometimes you gradually realize what you are expected to do, feel, say, and take care of. In *Raisin in the Sun* (Petrie, 1961), Sidney Poitier as Walter Lee Younger, despite his aspirations, is a chauffer, living with his wife and son on the charity of his mother. His wife, Ruby Dee as Ruth Younger, is not compassionate over how humiliating this all is for him. And even if he is desperately ashamed of his failures, he can't see what he could do about it, and they bicker and blame each other rather than pulling together. Poitier crawls out of bed when pulled by Dee, and he counters her impatience with: "You look good this morning, Baby." She glares and he declares: "The first thing a man needs to learn is never to make love to a woman in the morning. You all are some evil creatures early in the morning."

Families Surviving

In *Grapes of Wrath* (Ford, 1940), the Joad family, uprooted from their dust farm in Oklahoma, head west for the promised land in California. In the family truck, Jane Darwell as Ma Joad dampens the family optimism for work, picking cotton.

Ma Joad. "For a while there it looked as if we were beat, good and beat, like we didn't have nobody in the whole wide world but enemies, like nobody was friendly no more. Made me feel kinda bad and scared too, like we was lost and nobody cared."

Pa Joad (Russell Simpson): "You're the one that keeps us going, Ma. I ain't no good no more and I know it. It seems like I spend all my time these days thinking about how it used to be, thinking of home. I ain't never going to see it no more."

Ma Joad: "Pa, a woman can change better than a man. A man lives sorta, well in jerks, a baby's born or somebody dies and that's a jerk. He gets a farm or loses it and that's a jerk. With a woman its all in one flow like a stream, little eddies, and waterfalls, but the river, it goes right on. A woman looks at it that way."

Pa Joad: "Well, maybe, but we sure taken a beating".

Ma Joad, laughing: "That's what makes us tough."

If men see life as a series of contests one wins or loses, life will be jerky, but if one views life as a process which unfolds and reveals much the same experiences for everyone, as the human condition is what it is, then there is nothing to fear. None of us will get out of life alive anyway but we can get tough enough with crisis after crisis so we aren't afraid of the next crisis that inevitably comes our way. That fearlessness in the face of change and adaptation makes women naturally embrace therapy and men shrink from it.

It was not just Ma Joad who survived without prevailing. Even *Rocky* (Avidsen, 1976) did not win his boxing match, but he hung in there honorably and felt like a man.

The Discovery of Adolescence

Hollywood brought a fair amount of wisdom into our lives, in addition to all the mind numbing pap. It may be that the problem began in 1955 when in *Rebel without a Cause* (Ray, 1955) James Dean as Jim Stark appeared, discovered (or maybe invented) adolescence, muttered self pityingly and incoherently, and then self destructed in his new Porsche. This was just a decade after WWII, and *The Greatest Generation* (András, 1985) that went to war and saved the world. We knew then what a man was supposed to be, i.e. a warrior ready to die for humanity. But Dean, and his successors like Marlon Brando, Montgomery Clift, and Paul Newman offered a quite different model, one of self-absorption and alienation. They were followed by a generation of men who gave little of themselves. Women were expected to find these narcissistic postadolescents so attractive, they tolerated anything from them and provided everything.

In the mid-1950s children disappeared from the family picture on the screen. Shirley Temple, Judy Garland, Mickey Rooney, Margaret O'Brien grew up and retired. The only children we saw on screen were either ersatz adults (like Jody Foster as Iris Steensma in *Taxi Driver* (Scorsese, 1976), Tatum O'Neal as Addie Loggins in *Paper Moon* (Bogdanovich, 1973), Alfred Lutter as Tommy in *Alice Doesn't Live Here Anymore* (Scorsese, 1974), Anna Paquin as Flora McGrath in *The Piano* (Campion, 1993) or, a generation later, Ross Malinger as Jonah Baldwin in

Sleepless In Seattle (Ephron, 1993); children who serve as therapists, matchmakers, and advisors to single parents, constantly reassuring the fragile grownups that their hyper-mature offspring don't really need parents, so the parents need not grow up.

No matter how resilient the children were, the grownups were quite delicate and must be kept from feeling guilty about the disruption of the family. Those children who were in any way needy were depicted as monsters, as in *Omen* in 1976 (Donner) and *Exorcist* in 1973 (Friedkin) and *Rosemary's Baby* in 1968 (Polanski), sent from the devil to make us grownups feel guilty for not dedicating ourselves as totally to raising children as we should. It was a wholesale societal denial of the needs and vulnerabilities of children.

The Rediscovery of Childhood

Thirty years later, in the mid-1980s, a series of movies (mostly foreign language) such as *The Last Emperor* (Bertolucci, 1987), *Hope and Glory* (Boorman, 1987), *Au Revoir Les Enfants* (Malle, 1987), *My Life as a Dog* (Hallström, 1985), *and Fanny and Alexander* (Bergman, 1982) rediscovered children. Unfortunately the emphasis in the rediscovery that children were indeed children was on preventing sexual, or sometimes physical, abuse. The solution to this, since so many of the abusers were male, was to run fathers even further out of family life. Actually, fathers rarely molest their children: it was stepfathers, or more likely the mother's live-in boy friends, who did most of the molesting, torture, or murder of children. But fathers became increasingly afraid of touching their children and a generation of children grew up without being hugged. And, a dysfunctional family, in some circles, was one which still had a man in it.

On TV, there were many fathers – Hugh Beaumont as Ward Cleaver, Bill Cosby as Chet Kincaid, Dan Castellanata as the voice of Homer Simpson, Robert Young as Jim Anderson, and Andy Griffith as Sheriff Andy Taylor in, respectively, *Leave it to Beaver* (Tokar, Butler, Abbott, Beaumont, Bellamy, Reynolds, Haas, Leader, Barton, & de Cordova, 1957–1963), *The Bill Cosby Show* (Ruskin, Sandrich, Serensky, Hart, Cosby, & James, 1969–1971), *The Simpsons* (Kirkland, Moore, Reardon, Anderson, Archer, Anderson, Silverman, Nastuk, Kruse, Moore, Polcino, Lynch, Dietter, Michels, Kramer, Baeza, Polcino, Sheetz, Persi, Scott III, Affleck, Marcantel, MacMullan, Ervin, Kamerman, Clements, Gray, Bird, Butterworth, Sosa, Faughnan, & Oliver, 1989 to present), *Father Knows Best* (Russell & Tewksbury,1954–1960), *My Three Sons* (Whorf, Bellamy, Tewksbury, Kern, de Cordova, Considine, Reynolds, & Sheldon, 1960–1972), and *The Andy Griffith Show* (Sweeney, Philips, Rafkin, Ruskin, Weis, Crenna, Hayden, Morris, Bellamy, Baldwin, Reynolds, Flicker, Leonard, Irving, Nelson, Ruben, & Dobkin, 1960–1968) – but they were increasingly presented as incompetent and optional. This was contrary to the usual pattern on the big screen in which fathers and father figures are heroic and wise, but find themselves without a partner. Jimmy Stewart as Charlie Anderson in *Shenandoah* (McLaglen, 1965), Spencer Tracy in *Boy's Town*

(Taurog, 1938; as Father Flanagan), or *Captains Courageous* (Fleming, 1937; as Manuel Fidello), Gregory Peck as Atticus Finch in *To Kill A Mockingbird* (Mulligan, 1962), and John Wayne as foster father Thomas Dunson to Montgomery Clift as Matt Garth in *Red River* (Hawks, 1948) were among the classics. Nowadays, Tom Hanks and Denzel Washington play the father often, while Morgan Freeman plays everyman's father figure or the voice of the father. But the father figure is rarely married, rarely actually in the same home with the rest of the family.

In a recent and a unique great movie, *Brokeback Mountain* (Lee, 2005), sheepherder Jack Twist, played by Jake Gyllenhaal, falls in love with cowboy Ennis Del Mar, played by the late Heath Ledger, meets him several times a year for sex, love, and fishing. But Gyllenhaal wants Ledger to leave his children (he's already left his wife) and set up house with him. Always rebuffed, he insists "I don't know how to quit you." Ledger can't seem to get across that he can't do that to his children. Whatever else he is or isn't, he's a father and that must come first. This has no meaning for the more romantic Gyllenhaal who has no children and gets little from his own father.

The Importance of Fathers

So far, the movies have not done a very good job of pulling the myths of the family together and make us see the importance of fathers in family life and the importance of marriage in the lives of children. Adolescent boys are still showing their vulnerability and entitlement. Rich, skinny, teenage girls seem to have gone to jail and/or rehab a time or two too often, and they have outstayed their welcome. Wives are off somewhere with their new jobs and men are learning to change diapers and wash dishes, but the marriage has not come together well enough to form a sanctuary for people of different generations to live together contentedly ever after.

Harrison Ford as the eponymous title character in the latest *Indiana Jones: Kingdom of the Crystal Skull* (Spielberg, 2008) manages to finally find himself a wife (Karen Allen as Marion Ravenwood) and a son (Shia LeBeuf as Mutt Williams). Maybe in time, Christian Bale's Bruce Wayne as *Batman Begins* (Nolan, 2005) will get a wife and children, or James Bond will do so. *Rocky* (Avidsen, 1976) did.

But in order to study family relations in our millennium, we have to look to the courtship rituals and careful preoccupation with economics, class, and character in the six very similar novels of Jane Austen, all of which have been filmed repeatedly and inspire readers and viewers to see what life was like back in a more practical and civilized, and a less sexually charged time.

The latest examination of a family on film is the remake of *Brideshead Revisited* (Jarrold, 2008), from Evelyn Waugh's novel about the impact of their mother's rigid, antisexual Catholicism on the relationships of the other members of the family. The new film, with Emma Thompson as the mother Lady Marchmain, cannot compare with the 11-hour BBC series (1981),, which takes the time and pace in which to let us live in the family estate and come to fall in love with the family's son, daughter, child, and the house itself. We can even come to see the horrors of a religion or philosophy that makes one hate and fear life itself.

Searching for Models of Family Life

We have to look quite a way back to find films about families who are earnestly trying to get along, rather than trying to decide whether it will make them happy to remain in the family with their loved ones. How did family become such a scary place to live, always on the verge of blowing apart, much like standing on an earthquake fault? Did we do this to the world? Even if no one else does so, at least therapists must believe that people have the power to make relationships work, to pull together in times of crisis, and to actually live together without driving one another crazy. Therapists who are afraid that family members may hurt one another, and interfere with one another's happiness, can blow apart every family they see and do enormous damage that lasts for generations.

Again, the primary skill of therapists is optimism, the belief that we humans can change and do whatever needs to be done for our life and the lives of our loved ones. As therapists, we must above all believe in the human capacity for change.

When Will Hollywood Get the Family Right?

Jack Cashill

> *I was still looking for a panacea, for some kind of relief from all of that life, from all that damage.*
>
> Tatum O'Neal, *A Paper Life* (2004)

Abstract Films themselves not only provide a useful reflection of the society creating them but also contribute to a reshaping of that very society. Unfortunately, an examination of family portrayals in contemporary films reflects a microcosmic California film community largely deformed by deracination and divorce. That deformation leads, in turn, to films that may encourage in the audience a sense of anomie and estrangement. Such deformation and dysphoria, in karma-like fashion, echoes reminiscently the fractured African American "family" legacy from slavery practices. This Hollywood reflection and spread of personal anomie and estrangement as well as relationship fluidity and family instability reaches global proportions with the vigorous export of Hollywood fare, and, thus, Hollywood values. Hollywood may accidentally champion the attraction toward cohesion among cultures worldwide, but at what cost if the content of the cohesion capriciously escapes scrutiny and lacks sculpting toward healthy function? This does not have to be so. Hollywood has a responsibility not only for successful exportation, but also for what is being sent abroad and at home. Like it or not. Films have the power to reveal a positive psychology, pro-social construction of "healthy family," which includes—and encourages—stability, faith, community, growth, personal responsibility, and rich extended relationships. The problem is not that Hollywood no longer wishes to make such films. The problem may be that Hollywood may no longer know how.

J. Cashill (✉)
Ingram's Magazine, Kansas City, MO 64141-1356, USA
e-mail: jackcashill@yahoo.com

M.B. Gregerson (ed.), *The Cinematic Mirror for Psychology and Life Coaching*,
DOI 10.1007/978-1-4419-1114-8_3, © Springer Science+Business Media, LLC 2010

29

The Media-Holding Environment Replaces the Family

Social scientists have voiced concern for pro-social media influences on children, teens, and families for more than a decade (Allen, 1994). For example, research has documented increased cultural influence on children from television, VCRs, and Anglo education which replaces the Apachean Grandmother for transmission of culture (Bahr & Bahr, 1995). This growing reliance on electronic media rather than human connections results in teens self-socializing. They exercise more control through choice of media consumed than they can in choosing family and other human social influences (Arnett, 1995). In essence, they indulge their preferences rather than have a concerned environment nurturing them. Children are making choices for which they may not be prepared.

Media is replacing the extended family, upending human interaction that disciplines the individual to fit with the group. This replacement impact appears most potent in terms of thoughts and ideas, but not in terms of behavior, which is most influenced by human interaction and modeling (Boulay, Storey, & Sood, 2002). Reliance on media "parenting" may unmoor our children's actions. Individuals drift in learning any behavioral discipline from others that promotes translating thoughts, ideas, and attitudes into actions.

Adults receive no better messages from media modeling. Fracture occurs between generations, between peers, and between thought and action (Gregerson, M. B., 2008, Personal communication). This media cultivation of individualism, rather than connectedness, undermines the strength and stability of the collective (Dion & Dion, 1988; Triandis, 1994). As social and economic barriers to divorce crumbled, marital unions became more short-lived (Guiness, 1993). Such an individualistic-holding environment influences elders and young alike by blending the virtual and physical worlds (Gamble, 2007). We need to examine this new polymorphous holding container, and those that both fill and drink from that container.

Hollywood Rules and Reflects

One major purveyor of mass media is California. More than one-fourth of California's people live in Los Angeles County. For better or worse, what these people think matters. Their social influence seeps through their main product, entertainment. With entertainment the number one American export (MPAA, 2008), this influence reaches global proportions.

For very nearly a century Los Angeleans have had more influence on world culture than any comparable group of people since imperial Rome. This influence began with the movies, then bled into television, then into music, then music videos, and now, even into video games. Since 1958 (Lerner) the social control aspects of media influence have concerned psychologists. Today, media and media moguls have palpable power.

Local Californians sense their power. One screenwriter in informal conversation referred to himself casually as a "Roman citizen" in just the sense meant above, namely someone who shapes the world, satisfies his own whims, and leaves the potholes to the plebeians. "Back where you come from [Kansas] you have the freedom to do this," he confided, holding his hands about half a foot apart. "Here [California]," he said stretching his hands about three feet apart, "we have the freedom to do this." (Uhl, S., 2006, Personal communication)

As much as we might like to deny it, Hollywood still has a grip on us. Hollywood is not what it once was (Cashill, 2008). It has gone wrong in a thousand different ways, one of which is entirely relevant to the focus of this chapter, that is, the Hollywood take on family. Or, rather, the Hollywood deconstruction of the American family.

The American movie image of "family" has disintegrated into emotional satisfaction rather than cognitive commitment (Arriga, 2001; Arriaga & Agnew, 2001). This focus on the ephemeral rather than the stable—that is, passion rather than thoughts translated into actions—promulgates relationship instability and fluidity. The indulgence in the bestial and the individual replaces the allegiance to ideals and to the effects on others. Cultures more individualistic rather than communal cultures have higher divorce rates (Dion & Dion, 1988; Triandis, 1994). The shift from a group to an individual ethic reflects ethnic roots that affirm and replace with serial monogamy the traditional golden standard of one lifetime nuclear family (Barash & Lipton, 2001; Mead, 1930, 1970; Smith & Smith, 1974).

This deracination, family disintegration, and individualism surprisingly echoes the slavery ethnic heritage of African-Americans (Black & Jackson, 2005; Hines & Boyd-Franklin, 2005). The slave heritage is one of violently and malevolently disrupted family and kinship bonds (Akbar, 1985; Nobles, 2004) to serve the needs of overlords (Bennett, 2003; van Sertima, 1976). The recent proliferation of ethnically based films at once romanticizes and criticizes this deracinated, fractured family history (The Belknap Collection for the Performing Arts, 2008). Instead of eschewing such fluid family "structures," perhaps mainstream culture has drifted unwittingly into mimicking them (Gregerson, M. B., 2008, Personal communication).

Has fascinated preoccupation with diversity ironically propelled homogenization of the historical fractured African American "family" connections into mainstream culture (Gregerson, M. B., 2008, "Personal communication")? Homogenization reflects a trend toward cultural cohesion rather than highlighting lines of diversity (Bhawuk, 2008; Fu, 2006), and media plays a great part in creating such singular worldwide iconic images (Gammack, 2002). Watchers of the African-American cinema scene have noted a modern lack of addressing racial, and thus, diversity themes (Sheridan, 2006). A singular image of relatedness and connected concerns may be appearing, and it is not a pretty image.

What becomes institutionalized nationwide, and ultimately worldwide, needs careful consideration. With the export of Hollywood fare, both mainstream and ethnic, the responsibility becomes a global one (Gregerson, M. B., 2008, Personal communication). The past *does not* have to define the future, even unwittingly.

Families, both models and critiques of families, exist in film land. Over 20 years ago, Levy (1991) identified six major cycles of family films:

1. Decline of family in the late 1960s;
2. Substitution of alternative for nuclear family in the late 1960s and early 1970s;
3. White suburban families in mid- to late 1970s;
4. Tormented and troubled families in the late 1970s and early 1980s;
5. Youth-oriented films in mid-1980s; and
6. Return to traditional family values and structure in the late 1980s.

What of the last two decades? Early in the 1990s Zillmann, Bryant, and Huston (1994) issued the challenge to use the media pro-socially, rather, for good.

The African American prototype, especially father–son as will be discussed in more detail later, appears an important bond for this culture.

Films, though, do not have as positive a history as the small screen. Hollywood films, of course, have the power to reveal a positive psychology construction of healthy family, which includes—and encourages—stability, faith, community, growth, personal responsibility, and rich extended relationships. The problem is not that Hollywood no longer wishes to make such films. The problem may be that Hollywood no longer knows how.

Rebels Without Causes—or Fathers

In a mercenary way, at least, family matters a great deal in Hollywood, perhaps more than ever. There is no other rational explanation for the career of television impresario Aaron Spelling's daughter Tori, even if she didn't show up at her father's funeral.

Nepotism rules in this Southern California film community more so than in any other competitive endeavor. How many winners of the US Open or the Nobel Prize in Literature or the Tchaikovsky Competition have spawned a winning heir or even one who made the final cut? None. None. None. By contrast, Ryan O'Neal's 10-year-old daughter Tatum took home an Oscar on her very first try, and she is just one of scores, nay hundreds, of the Hollywood offspring to prosper thusly. The Douglas clan's legacy extends three generations from Kirk to Michael to Cameron. Drew Barrymore descends fourth generation from the great legendary theatrical family, the Barrymores.

The problem, however, goes much deeper than the triumph of the half-talented and the homely. Hollywood has become a closed loop of bad vibes and worse information, especially on the issue of family. "I didn't want to be this crazy mother," Tatum O'Neal says of her own mom, "which I sort of ended up later on being" *(Dateline NBC*, 2004).

Many in this film industry simply have never seen a happy, functioning family— let alone a community of such families. They who provide reference points have none themselves. "We are a little bit out of touch in Hollywood every once in a while," boasted Rosemary Clooney's handsome nephew, George Clooney, at the 2006 Oscars. "I think it's probably a good thing" (Clooney, 2006). No, George, it is not. Ignorance never is, not when you have the power to teach the world.

To test these assumptions about Hollywood and the family, the names of the 20 prominent children of the entertainment industry had their family status traced through the International Movie Data Base (IMDB; see Table 1). There is minimal science about this archival survey. If the reader thinks some personality should be on this list and is not, it is an unwitting omission.

In every one of the "divorced" cases cited, the parents did so when their children were still minors. Many children watched their parents divorce more than once. Curiously, those that have become bigger names than their parents—Jeff Bridges (Lloyd Bridges), Charlie Sheen (Martin Sheen), Sean Penn (actress Eileen Ryan and director Leo Penn), and Gwyneth Paltrow (actress Blythe Danner and the late director Bruce Paltrow)—are the ones that grew up in two-parent homes. Divorce is not the key to emotional depth, nor to star appeal.

Plus, as the cases of Sheen and Penn make clear, a two-parent household is no guarantee of sanity in a universe where family disorder has reached critical mass. "The family grows best in a garden with its kind," California historian Josiah Royce observed correctly more than a century ago (Royce, 2002). "Where family life does not involve healthy friendship with other families, it is apt to be injured by unhealthy if well-meaning friendships with wanderers." Look at even the paragons of normalcy like Reese Witherspoon that have succumbed to the Hollywood disease

Table 1 Twenty most prominent children of the entertainment industry and their family status

Children	Family status
Drew Barrymore	Parents divorced
Jeff Bridges	Parents together
Jamie Lee Curtis	Parents divorced
Laura Dern	Parents divorced
Michael Douglas	Parents divorced
Robert Downey, Jr	Parents divorced
Carrie Fisher	Parents divorced
Bridget Fonda	Parents divorced
Jane Fonda	Parents divorced
Melanie Griffith	Parents divorced
Kate Hudson	Parents divorced
Timothy Hutton	Parents divorced
Angelina Jolie	Parents divorced
Jennifer Jason Leigh	Parents divorced
Gwyneth Paltrow	Parents together
Sean Penn	Father previously married
Campbell Scott	Parents divorced
Charlie Sheen	Parents together
Keifer Sutherland	Parents divorced
Patrick Wayne	Parents divorced

of divorce. She recently lamented that, despite the stability from her own non-Hollywood family, "...my parents are still married, and my grandparents stayed married, but it's [her divorce from her ex-husband Ryan Phillipe] a situation my own children will have to deal with, so it was of interest to me" (Sullivan, 2008).

Their insight into the reasons for their dilemma from divorce seems limited. Yet despite their limited perspective, these wanderers and friends are the very same people who have been tasked to show the rest of the world how American family life and culture work. This makes no sense.

To be fair to our myopic media pals, they do at least sense that something is the matter. They are just not sure what it is. The fractionating culture seems to undermine even the stalwart like Reese, and in previous generations, Robert Redford. This anxiety reveals itself in those few serious cinematic attempts to explain contemporary family life in California, beginning with the archetypal California movie, 1955's *Rebel without a Cause* (Ray), a movie whose cluelessness is built into the very title.

"Man existing alone seems an episode of little consequence," a scary old astronomer at LA's Griffith Observatory tells the gnarly young rebels at the film's beginning. It is left to them to find whatever consequence can be had (Ray, 1955). In this still innocent era—*Rebel* (Ray, 1955) premiered the same year as Disneyland—Writer/director Nicholas Ray felt free to pose the idea of family as an alternative to that aloneness. The idea is one thing, however. The reality was another, and in mid-1950s California, at least for the *Rebel*'s (Ray, 1955) three main characters, family just wasn't happening. All were estranged from their folks. The parents of Sal Mineo's poor rich kid, Plato, skipped town and left him with the maid. By the time of Bret Easton Ellis' documentary-style novel of early 1980s LA, *Less Than Zero* (Kanievska, 1987), everyone seemed to be skipping town and leaving the kid with the maid, but in 1955 that still seemed pretty shocking.

Desperately adrift, Plato tries to find safe harbor with James Dean's stuttering Jim and Natalie Wood's equally unsteady Judy. "If only you could have been my dad," Plato tells Jim before being gunned down by the overeager LA cops. "He tried to make us his family," sighs Jim afterwards. In real life, there would not be much family for any of the three actors.

When 16-year-old Natalie Wood first read the script for Rebel she heard a voice buzzing in her head saying, "You are Judy." (Finstad, 2001, p. 139). In many ways, hers was the perfectly synthetic California life. Born Natalia Nikolaevna Zakhraenko to Russian parents in San Francisco, young Natalia had metamorphosed into the all-American girl-next-door Natalie Wood by the age of 5. After just one small film role, Natalie's overly ambitious, once-divorced mother uprooted her, her half-sister, and her alcoholic father—"a shadow figure in his own household" (Finstad, 2001, p. 144)—to Los Angeles in the hope that Natalie would become a star. That she did, experiencing just about every culture shock California had to offer along the way. These included an affair with the 43-year-old Ray when she was still a 16-year-old "jailbait," a brutal rape at the same age by a major Hollywood star 20 years her senior, and a marriage to movie star Robert Wagner undone, according to Wood at least, when she caught him in bed with another man (Finstad, 2001).

Wood would go on to divorce Wagner and remarry him. She shouldn't have. On Thanksgiving weekend 1981, the 43-year-old actress, Wagner, and their friend actor Christopher Walken sailed to Catalina Island, a surprisingly untouched and un-peopled slice of California 26 miles across the sea from Long Beach. After a disturbed, deeply alcoholic evening, the hydrophobic Wood apparently tried to escape their yacht and ended up drowning, her cries for help either unheard by Wagner or, more likely, unheeded. That Wagner walked away from this tragedy legally unscathed is a testament to the enduring clout of Hollywood.

As it happens, Wood outlived her *Rebel without a Cause* (Ray, 1955) co-stars. James Dean met his untimely end on what is now Route 46 near Cholame when a Cal Poly student with the unfortunate name of Donald Turnupseed crossed blindly into Dean's lane and ran head on into his Porsche 500 Spyder. "My fun days are over," Dean reportedly said to the EMTs who carted him off (City-Data.com, 2008). His pre-release death helped make *Rebel without a Cause* (Ray, 1955) a huge hit. In 1976, the 37-year-old Sal Mineo was in rehearsal for his role as a gay burglar in the LA production of the play, *P.S. Your Cat Is Dead!* (Guttenberg, 2002), when a not-so-gay burglar stabbed him fatally in a West Hollywood alley. Nick Adams, another *Rebel without a Cause* (Ray, 1955) co-star, died of a drug overdose in his Beverly Hills home in 1968 at the age of 36. Volumes have been written about the alleged gayness or bi-sexuality of all three of these actors, some of which may even be true.

At the time of *Rebel without a Cause*'s release in 1955 (Ray), Hollywood still saw the family as worth saving, worth reconstructing. On television especially, the nuclear family dominated that decade and into the next, as evidenced by chirpy classics like *Leave It to Beaver* (Tokar, Butler, Abbott, Beaumont, Bellamy, Reynolds, Haas, Leader, Barton, & de Cordova, 1957–1963), *Father Knows Best* (Russell, Tewksbury, Rodney, & Briskin,1954–1960), and *The Adventures of Ozzie and Harriet* (Nelson & Nelson, 1952–1966), each with a stable father figure and a loving mother.

In those shows without two parents, typically it was the mom who went missing—chastely to her grave, of course—and it was the dad who soldiered on even as he mothered his children. *Andy Griffith* (Sweeney, Philips, Rafkin, Ruskin, Weis, Crenna, Hayden, Morris, Bellamy, Baldwin, Reynolds, Flicker, Leonard, Irving, Nelson, Ruben, & Dobkin, 1960–1968), *My Three Sons* (Whorf, Bellamy, Tewksbury, Kern, de Cordova, Considine, Reynolds, & Sheldon, 1960–1972), and *The Courtship of Eddie's Father* (Cooper, Senensky, Bixby, Komack, Falk, Nelson, Weis, & Sweeney, 1969–1972) all mined this theme as did westerns like *The Rifleman* (Lewis, Laven, Nadel, Nelson, Medford, Donner, Allen, Dobkin, Hiller, Hopper, Peckinpah, Landres, Taylor, Post, Claxton, Johnson, Neilson, Slavell, Moder, Rich, & Wendkos, 1958–1963) and *Bonanza* (Claxton, Allen, Benson, McDougall, Witney, Nyby, Landon, Florea, Penn, Daugherty, Oswald, Richardson, Altman, Wjard, Garnett, Golden, Springsteen, Daves, Pevney, Black, Neilson, Rich, Vogel, Kane, Landres, Haas, C. F., Lubin, A., Moder, D., Friend, R. L., Daniels, M., Leacock, P., Yarbrough, Carr, Faralla, Nadel, McEveety, Totten, Mayer, Webster, Colasnto, & Kjellin, 1959–1973). The movies meanwhile served up the apotheosis of widower pop-hood in Atticus Finch, the hero of 1962's *To Kill a Mockingbird* (Mulligan).

The Fatherless, and Faithless, Microcosm Called Southern California

Yet even in these families, at least the ones set in contemporary California, no one had cousins or aunts or even grandmothers. No one went to christenings or first communions or even to church. No one prayed on Fifties TV, not Beaver, not Bud, not David, nor Ricky. If they still saluted the flag, they had lost touch with the rituals of extended family and faith. They were as deracinated as the young families in the modern overnight communities of Southern California.

No one exploited the vulnerability of the unmoored more dramatically than California serial murderer and cult leader Charles Manson. "All your roots are cut," he would tell his young cult charges. "You are freed from your families and all their old hang-ups. You are cut loose into the now." (Atkins, 1978, p. 83)

To cushion these lost souls from the shock of "the now," Manson created his idea of a family with himself at the head. "Charlie had instantly seemed more a father to me," says Susan Atkins, "than my own father." (Atkins, 1978, p. 76) On the night of August 8, 1969, Manson directed four of his children—Atkins, Linda Kasabian, Patricia Krenwinkel, and Tex Watson—to kill the inhabitants of a certain house in Beverly Hills.

Manson was a freak, but Atkins, Kernwinkel, Kasabian, Van Houten, and the twenty or so other young women under Manson's sway were not. To see them now is to see one's own sisters and wives and mothers: attractive, middle aged, middle class women, well spoken and well spoken of, even if at least four of them are still in prison. Under slightly different circumstances, they might all have prospered.

As it happens during the same year that Manson was preparing his flock for Helter Skelter, state assemblyman Jim Hayes of Long Beach was going through a nasty divorce. To make life easier for people like himself he introduced a bill, which would result in the nation's most progressive no-fault divorce law. Not that Californians needed much help getting divorced. Josiah Royce had argued that California divorces were "far too numerous and easy," and that was in the 1850s. (Royce, 2002, p. 318)

On September 4, 1969, just 4 weeks after the Tate–LaBianca murders, Governor Ronald Reagan signed into the California Family Law Act of 1969, an endorsement that he would later regret. "He wanted to do something to make the divorce process less acrimonious, less contentious, and less expensive," son Michael Reagan writes of his once-divorced dad in his book *Twice Adopted* (Reagan, 2004, p. 42). He also made divorce a whole lot more available.

Marin County divorce authority Dr. Judith Wallerstein calls the bill "an upheaval akin to a cataclysmic earthquake." "People were jubilant," adds Wallerstein (2000, p. xxviii). They rejoiced in the same shortsighted way the people in England did when Chamberlain brought back "peace in our time." Only in California, they celebrated by getting divorced.

In 1970, the first full year of the no-fault law, the state registered a record 112,942 divorces, a 38% increase from just the year before (Christian Party, 2008). To put that number in perspective consider that in 1960, there had been only 105,352 *marriages* in California. Population growth—27% for the decade—accounts for some of the discrepancy, but the marriage/divorce ratio, no matter what the qualifiers, signaled a massive disruption in family life.

In 1970, California's divorce rate was 60% higher than the nation as a whole and continued to trend upwards throughout the decade. By 1980, California had registered a new record 138,361 divorces. In other words, some 276,000 Californians got divorced in 1980 alone. That was more than twice as many as in 1966, and in 1966, the California divorce rate was already 50% higher than the national norm. In fact, the divorce rate increased four times faster than the population did in the years 1966–1980.

Only Oklahoma had no-fault divorce before California, and no one paid attention to Oklahoma (Parejko, 2008). People did pay attention to California. A national lawyers group, the self-designated Uniform Law Commission, quickly composed a model no-fault law based on California's, and by 1985, just about every state in the union had adopted it in one form or another with predictable results. By 1980, the nation's divorce rate was higher than California's was in 1969.

In 1980, embarrassed by the divorce plague in their midst, California lawmakers implemented a quick fix of world class caliber: they would no longer keep or publish statistics! Imagine the anxiety lawmakers could have spared their constituents if they had tackled AIDS with the same ingenuity.

These divorce reforms went unchallenged, argues Wallerstein (2000, p. xiii), in her breakthrough book *The Unexpected Legacy of Divorce*, because of "an almost conspiratorial silence" about its unhappy effect on kids. Wallerstein began rethinking her own relatively tolerant take on divorce after a chance encounter with a child she had counseled long ago. Twenty-five years after her parents' divorce, the young woman was still struggling with its consequences. This meeting inspired Wallerstein to undertake a long-range, close-up study of the kids with whom she had worked 25 years earlier, the deepest such study ever undertaken. The results, as Wallerstein admits, "hit a raw nerve" in America. Many in positions of influence simply did not want to know what she had learned.

Among her discoveries is that most children never really recover. "Divorce is a life-transforming experience," Wallerstein writes (2000, p. xxxiii). "After divorce, childhood is different. Adulthood—with the decision to marry or not and have children or not—is different." (Wallerstein, 2000, p. 300) She refrains from judging that difference good or bad, but her subjects don't. Not one of the roughly 100 interviewees wanted their own children to go through what they had.

In general, adolescence begins early and lasts late for these kids (Wallerstein, 2000). The girls are more likely to seek out sex, the boys seek out drugs and alcohol. They marry later if at all, get divorced more, trust less, and have fewer children. Although the fewer children finding does not echo the African-American progeny proliferation associated with the slavery legacy, the wariness and instability in their own marital unions do reflect the slavery heritage.

Divorce and the Media

When not ignoring divorce completely, the media have done their best to trivialize it, just as slave owners did. In July 1999, the PBS children's show *Sesame Street* offered a perky little vignette on the subject (as reported in Wallerstein, 2000, p. xxvii; DiNapoli, Simon, Squires, Clash, Diego, May, Martin, Gordon, Guadarrama, Mazzarino, J., Feldman, S., Zylstra, N., Dilworth, J., Stone, J., Henson, J., Broder, Saks, Balsmeyer, DeSeve, Lathan, & Schwarz, 1969). In it, Kermit the Frog, here an inquiring reporter, asks a cute little bird where she lives. As she tells Kermit merrily, she lives part of the time in one tree where she frolics in her mother's nest and the rest of her time in a separate tree where she frolics with her dad. "They both love me," she chirps.

Had James Ellroy written this scene—*Sesame Street Confidential?*—the tone might have been a little different. He remembers his own nest-hopping as a "bifurcated life divvied up between two people locked in an intractable mutual hatred" (Ellroy, 1996, p. 106).

Ellroy's hard stare is too much for Hollywood as well. "Oh, my dear Katie," counsels Aunt Euphegenia Doubtfire on her kiddie TV show (Columbus, 1993). "You know, some parents get along much better when they don't live together. They don't fight all the time and they can become better people. Much better mommies and daddies for you."

Such is the sappy and largely false advice Robin Williams' drag character, Mrs. Doubtfire, offers at the end of the movie comedy of same name. What sets the movie apart, though, is not that it takes a wrongheaded stand on divorce—"You'll have a family in your heart forever"—but that it takes any stand at all. *Mrs. Doubtfire* (Columbus, 1993) is one of the handful of halfway serious cinematic looks at the effects of divorce on children, even if its message is no deeper, or different really, than *Sesame Street*'s (DiNapoli, Simon, squires, Clash, Diego, May, Martin, Gordon, Guadarrama, Mazzarino, J., Feldman, S., Zylstra, N., Dilworth, J., Stone, J., Henson, J., Broder, Saks, Balsmeyer, DeSeve, Lathan, & Schwarz, 1969 to present).

One shared trait Wallerstein finds among her subjects is a relentless "fear of loss, fear of change, and fear that disaster will strike, especially when things are going well." (Wallerstein, 2000, p.301) This may help explain "Helter Skelter." Susan Atkins and the others interpreted this innocuous phrase from a Beatles' song to mean that "things were going out of control in the world, and the end was coming" (Atkins, 1978, p. 108). Another trait is that even as adults, children of divorce nurse a "continuing anger at parents," more often at the dads, whom the kids regard as "selfish and faithless."

In film, especially in serious films about California, the feud between the emotionally fragile child and a faithless father has become something of an angry staple. Directors Robert Altman in *Short Cuts* (1993), Irwin Winkler in *Life As A House*

(2001), Erik Skjolbjaerg in *Prozac Nation* (2001), and Paul Thomas Anderson in *Magnolia* (1999) serve up some of the least attractive screen dads since Director Stanley Kubrick's Jack "Here's Johnny" Torrance in *The Shining* (1980).

In the equally angry 1993 Joel Schumacher film, *Falling Down*, the Michael Douglas character, William Foster, wanders across the baroque badlands of Los Angeles on a deranged odyssey to reclaim his estranged wife and daughter. "I'm coming home," he tells them repeatedly and pathetically.

For Michael Douglas, this film has an element of the personal. His father, Kirk Douglas, quit the nest when Michael was six. Michael saw his dad and his new half-brothers only on holidays. In turn, Michael left his wife Diandra and son Cameron. According to the IMDB, Diandra "was sick of [Michael's] womanizing, absenteeism, and not being 'a proper father to Cameron' " In *Falling Down* (Schumacher, 1993), Douglas's character is shown to be no more proper a father than Douglas himself, his memory of a happy home proving pure illusory. As with Plato, the police shoot Foster down, too, a standard *deus ex machina* in Hollywood.

By century's end, the film community had so lost touch with the workings of a normal, happy family that it began to treat such a family as myth, a hoax even, and in no movie more insidiously than 1998's seemingly benign *Pleasantville* (Ross). Gary Ross, an occasional speechwriter for Michael Dukakis and Bill Clinton, wrote and directed this sly little bit of cinematic subversion. The LA-born son of a blacklisted screenwriter—or, so he alleges, commie roots being boast worthy in Hollywood—Ross has an agenda. Unlike the other *auteurs*, his is political, not personal. He does not try to illuminate the family but to undermine it.

The movie opens in a contemporary California high school with an apocalyptic bent. In one class, a counselor tells the students that the job market is collapsing. In another, a health teacher cautions them that HIV is running wild. In a third, a science teacher warns them that the globe is on high broil. "Okay. Who can tell me what famine is?" he asks.

If anything, life at home is scarier still. "No—you have custody the first weekend of every month and this is the first weekend," the mom shouts on the phone. Her two high-school-age children meanwhile suffer visibly through this messy divorce and their mother's ensuing affair with a man 9 years her junior. Jennifer is a mindless slut; her brother, David, a feckless nerd who seeks refuge from his chaotic life in an old *Leave It To Beaver*-like sitcom (Tokar, Butler, Abbott, Beaumont, Bellamy, Reynolds, Haas, Leader, Barton, & de Cordova, 1957–1963) called *Pleasantville* (Ross, 1998).

Through some mildly entertaining gimmickry, David and Jennifer find themselves teleported into a living, breathing, black and white Pleasantville. Here, they emerge as Bud and Mary Sue Parker, model children of the equally perfect George and Betty Parker. A serious student of the show, David has the inside skinny not only on the quirks of the characters, but also on the culture of the town. He attempts to instruct his wayward sister in both.

Jennifer will have none of it. From minute one, she can sense Pleasantville's psychic shackles and proceeds to pare them off as quickly as she can. Sex, Jennifer understands, cuts through everything. When she liberates the town's virginal jocks from their restraints, they mutate from black and white to color. They, in turn, spread the charms of sex to their friends. These newly deflowered lads and lasses blossom in full color as well. So do the flowers around them in this anti-Eden. Soon enough, Jennifer enlists David in her polychromatic rebellion—I would say "rainbow," but Hollywood had yet to discover gay sex—and the revolution is on.

The quietly restless Betty Parker discovers her own color by—blush—masturbating in the bathtub. She becomes fully radiant when she betrays the dull but decent George and beds down with the aptly named "Mr. Johnson," the soda shop manager. Mr. Johnson taps his inner palette not just through adulterous sex but through truly awful abstract art.

The forces of change soon shake, rattle, and roll the once complacent burg. The kids at the soda shop switch from sweet 1950s pop to raunchy R & B. David introduces his new friends to literature—as if!. They now read presumably subversive classics like *Catcher in the Rye* (Salinger, 1951) and *Huckleberry Finn* (Twain, 1884).

In writing about Gold Rush San Francisco, Royce had described "the true sin of the community" as a general sense of "irreligious liberty" (Royce, 2002, p. 313) As Royce saw it, San Franciscans "considered every man's vices, however offensive and aggressive they might be (short of crime), as a private concern between his own soul and Satan." As Ross sees it a century or so later, that same "irreligious liberty" is the salvation of the community.

This plot line might have been amusing enough were our heroes merely rebelling against *Pleasantville* (Ross, 1998), the show. But by blurring the line between the fictional Pleasantville and the real Mid-America, Director Ross grinds his edgy Blue provocations right up in the face of the Red.

It is only a matter of time before the town fathers, black and white to the man, fascist to the core, attempt to suppress "the coloreds" and reinstate their own "values," a word that drips acid when spoken. This frantic little effort climaxes in a court trial whose set smugly, if preposterously, mimics that of *To Kill a Mockingbird* (Lee, 1960; Mulligan, 1962). But it's too late. The 1960s are spreading through Pleasantville like the Blob, and folks are too buzzed to get the fire extinguishers from the high school to freeze it in its tracks.

Ross targeted the young and hit home. "The film addresses the limits of conservatism, the hypocracy (sic) of hiding your head, the fascism of fear," writes one typical reviewer on *Ain't It Cool News* (Harry's Reviews, 1998). "It brings up the other C word, not communism, but Change. The most violent act we have."

Before they contract AIDS, catch fire freebasing, or start up Pleasantville's own Trench Coat Mafia, David and Jennifer are miraculously teleported back to the present. To his tiny credit, Ross acknowledges the chaos of the world these kids inhabit. Nothing has changed in their absence. The mom, distraught over a botched weekend with her cub scout of a beau, tearfully tells David, "It's not supposed to be like this."

Before his Pleasantville experience, David would have agreed. But like the epic hero-trippers of yore, David has returned home a savvier if more cynical dude. He has learned that morals are a scam, marriage a fraud, innocence an illusion, and "family values" a euphemism for bigotry. The wise man, he knows now, avoids moral judgment at all costs or at least pretends to do so.

If the adults of California insist on blinding themselves to the obvious, the children are all eyes. It would take a 13-year-old, Nikki Reed, to write the screenplay for the truest and scariest cinematic portrait of a family in meltdown, 2003's *Thirteen* (Hardwicke).

In the way of background, Reed's California parents divorced when she was two. As Judith Wallerstein (2000, p. 299) might have predicted, Reed's problems exploded when she hit adolescence. Her father's girlfriend, production designer Catherine Hardwicke, suggested that Reed keep a diary to cope. She wrote a screenplay instead. Impressed, Hardwicke helped her shape it and went on to direct the film, her directorial debut.

Shot in semi-documentary style, and set at and around the very real Portola Middle School in the San Fernando Valley, *Thirteen* (Hardwicke, 2003) ingenuously captures the mayhem that the culture of divorce has wrought on California life. The film's protagonist, the shrewdly named Tracy Freeland, begins her 7th grade career at Portola as a studious innocent. From day one, she finds herself awed and intimidated by the school "hot" girls already well along in their self-liberation. Envious of their status on campus, Tracy begins to mimic them.

Following the lead of one Evie Zamora—a rare Biblical allusion these days—Tracy proceeds to dispense with one cultural restraint after another: Modesty first, then temperance, then chastity. Living in the sexually overcharged LA environment, the girls and their friends spread the spirit of "irreligious liberty" throughout the junior high. They steal clothes, drink, do drugs, tramp around, self-mutilate, and sample gay sex, all the things that David and Jennifer might have gotten to do if *Pleasantville* (Ross, 1998) had had a sequel.

Left by her parents with a drugged and indifferent relative, the shackle-free Evie leads the way. Tracy has all the restraint that a divorced and distracted mom can impose. Those distractions include a full time business, a house, two children, an unhelpful ex, and a sometimes live-in boy friend struggling with his own coke habit. In a reversion of roles much like the one seen in *Pleasantville* (Ross, 1998) and not at all uncommon in divorced families, Tracy asks her mom, "Why are you doing this to yourself?" The mom, who looks, as Evie points out, *"like the hot big sister,"* has no good answer. The yuppie dad has no answers at all. When called in to help by the older brother, he chafes, "Can someone please tell me what is the problem—in a nutshell?"

Only in a world where life and love are so routinely commodified could a problem possibly come in a "nutshell." This one, however, is not so easily cracked. As much as the dad would like to help, he cannot let his little bird frolic in his nest even for a weekend. "I am trying to kick ass at this new job," he tells Tracy. "I am trying to get you and your mom more money."

The movie, painfully realistic and believable, has no answers either. It offers hope at film's end that the mother's desperate love for her daughter will save her from a dissolute culture, but it offers no guarantee for Tracy and not a prayer for Evie—nicely played by Nikki Reed herself. In the wrong time and place, Evie becomes Susan Atkins. In general, the critics liked the film, but not one that I read talks about the role of divorce in Tracy's fevered embrace of the vulgar. A typical review cites as the "themes" of the movie, "insecurity, confusion, wanting to be liked and accepted" (Anonymous, 2008). Yeah, OK, Mack, but why?

What the movie shows smartly and un-self-consciously is how broken homes undermine the common culture and how that culture, in turn, undermines the home. In this regard, it is the exact opposite of the absurd *Pleasantville* (Ross, 1998), which the same critics liked even more.

One telling feature of the film is that Tracy and Evie hook up almost exclusively with minority boys, mostly black. They do so for no particular reason other than that the black kids in their orbit have even fewer checks and balances in their lives than they do.

The un-bloodied 13-year-olds in Tracy's circle have turned an un-sweet 16 when they show up on the mean streets of Inglewood in the LA-based *Grand Canyon* (Kasdan, 1991). Mack, the film's lawyer protagonist played by Kevin Kline, encounters the lads one night after a Lakers' game when they drive by his stalled Lexus and come back to harass him. "You know, this is a nice car, mister," says one of them in a scene that sends chills down the collective California yuppie spine, if yuppies do indeed have spines. "I could use me a car with a phone in it."

Were the makers of *Thirteen* (Hardwicke, 2003) and *Grand Canyon* (Kasdan, 1991) merely dabbling in stereotype, California would be a happier place. But unfortunately, they are not. These lost boys represent the rolling, pulsating edge of what in the year of *Grand Canyon*'s release, 1991, was California's most volatile cultural plate. A year later their real-life models would spark the single greatest shock to the state since the Manson murders of 1969. They sent even their sympathizers scrambling for ornamental iron and the locks to secure it.

Yet, a half block in any direction from the epicenter of the 1992 Rodney King riots, the intersection of Florence and Normandie, one finds rows of pleasant bungalows with generally trim lawns. In San Francisco Hunter's Point, the vegetation is lush and the views of the East Bay are extraordinary. This isn't Bed-Sty or Harlem or Chicago's South Side. This is 21st century California, sunny, open, free of restraint, at least semi-prosperous, and potentially mobile in every which way.

So Why the Mayhem?

Hollywood, when it bothers to try, cannot muster even a dumb rationale. "This ain't the way it's supposed to be," laments Danny Glover's everyman character, Simon, the black tow-truck driver as he negotiates Mack's way out of the carjacking in *Grand Canyon* (Kasdan, 1991). "Everything is supposed to be different than the way it is." Unfortunately, neither Simon nor the writer/director, Lawrence Kasdan, has any more sense of how anything in post-shackle California is supposed to be than the mom in *Pleasantville* (Ross, 1998).

Neither do the other characters in *Grand Canyon* (Kasdan, 1991). "What's going on in the world?" asks Mack in despair. "The world doesn't make any sense to me anymore," agrees Mack's wife, Claire. And while the characters sit at the literal edge of the Grand Canyon trying to conjure some sense up, carloads of wayward young boys continue to roam the streets of Los Angeles locked and loaded for Armageddon.

The young black directors who have tried to answer the question—why the mayhem?—have done so with considerably more insight, most notably John Singleton in his 1991 feature, *Boyz n The Hood*. Perhaps because these African Americans have come to terms with their own slavery heritage, they can illuminate the current struggle for the individual, the couple, and the family. Just 23 years old at the time of the film's release, Singleton tells a South Central coming of age story, not unlike his own. As the film's protagonist, Tre Styles, approaches adolescence, his divorced mother ships him to his father's house knowing full well the pressure the streets can bring to bear on a fatherless boy.

"You may think I'm being hard on you right now, but I'm not," the father explains to Tre. "I'm trying to teach you how to be responsible. Your friends across the street, they don't have anybody to show them. You gonna see how they end up, too."

These friends, a pair of half-brothers living with their strung out single mom, fulfill the father's prophecies. The one is murdered, and his brother turns murderer in revenge. In an impressive act of will, Tre opts out of the revenge party. As the movie makes clear, the moral reinforcement from his father has given him the strength to do so.

At film's end, the surviving brother tells Tre about watching TV the day after his brother's murder and scanning the news in vain for some mention. "I started thinking, man," he continues. "Either they don't know, don't show, or don't care about what's going on in the 'hood'." For a variety of reasons, the "they" care less even today. "They" may be preoccupied with their own slavery-like heritage, with no understanding of its roots, or where to point a finger of rebuke; nor grasp of the forces of cultural homogenization gone awry by promulgating fractionation rather than the other way with health the contagion; nor defense against the lure of romanticizing the noble savage often associated with ethnicity.

In 1993, twin brothers Albert and Allen Hughes co-wrote and directed the film *Menace II Society* (1993). They were just 21 at the time. Although rougher edged than *Boyz* (Singleton, 1991), *Menace II Society* (Hughes & Hughes, 1993) imposes something of a Biblical allegory on the mindless chaos of contemporary California.

In the way of prologue, we see the young protagonist, Caine Lawton, growing up in a Watts household awash in drugs and violence. In one scene he and his junky mom watch his dope-dealing dad needlessly shoot a man. The dad is himself shot and killed when Caine is ten, and Caine is dispatched to his grandparents' home in the projects.

In their portrayal of the grandparents, the Hughes brothers signal their recognition of a stronger and more orderly African American past. Critical to that order is the grandparents' traditional Christianity. As best they can, they infuse Caine with love enough to keep him whole and values enough to keep him focused at least until high school graduation, a rare distinction among the young men in his lost world. "The Lord's Grace is with you, boy," says his Grandpapa. Such focus on pre-American roots and American faith seems the salvation reconciliation these young black directors believe possible, if improbable.

The Lord has his work cut out for him in contemporary LA. Once out on the streets, Caine proves as resistant to grace and as keen on violence as his namesake. "We supposed to be brothers!" pleads one black victim of Caine's swelling greed, but Caine is clearly not this or any other brother's keeper. He robs this one, beats another, and kills another still. All of his victims are black just as all the victims and victimizers in *Boyz* (Singleton, 1991) are black as well. Unable to help, and unwilling to condone, his grandparents are finally moved to cast Caine out.

As Caine suspects, the violence he has unleashed comes back to haunt him and ultimately to kill him. "I had done too much to turn back, and I had done too much to go on," he regrets as he lay dying. "And now it's too late."

A less artful film from this same period, Steve Anderson's *South Central* (1992), focuses even more intently on the role of the father. Based on Donald Baker's book, *Crips, South Central* (1997) tells the story of O. G.—original gangster—Bobby Johnson. After 10 years in prison, Johnson returns to the streets of South Central LA a wiser man. He has one mission in mind—to save his young son from the gangbanging life that he himself had led.

In the movie's climactic scene, Bobby faces off against the new gang leader, who has all but stolen his son's heart and mind. "Ray-Ray," implores Bobby, "that boy you're holding is my son. My son. I told a man in prison that I would save my son's life, even if it took my life." When Ray-Ray resists, Bobby hits home with a plea so universal in its appeal that Ray-Ray relents, "All I want is to give him something that you or I never had—a father."

Unlike their white counterparts, these young black writers and directors know that life is supposed to be about something. The white film makers, whether establishment or independent, seem to still be in the process of nadir seeking before their eyes can turn upward in hope of something better. The young blacks know that the key to that something is the love of a woman and the transmission of values from father to son. And although there is some peripheral rhetoric in all three movies about white this and that, they know too that the essential problem is theirs to solve.

Black television showed positive images include the ground-breaking *The Bill Cosby Show* (Ruskin, Sandrich, Senensky, Hart, Cosby, & James, 1969–1971), *Fresh Prince of Bel-Air* (Jensen, Melman, Falcon, Rogers, Vinson, Virgil, Cripe, Allen, Kraus, & Walian, 1990–1996), *The Red Foxx Show* (Lathan, Barnette, Martin, & Singletary, 1986), *In Living Color* (Miller, McCoy, Wayans, & Wickline, 1990–1994), and *The Jeffersons* (Shea, Lally, Scott, Singletary, & Smith, 1975–1985). The sad real-life killing of Bill Cosby's own adult son Ennis in 1997 poignantly underlined the continued disruption of relationships, even in the most positive of model and model families reflected in semi-autobiographical portrayals. During this time of personal tragedy, such a series, *Cosby* (Scardino, Whitesell, & Ryder, 1996–2000) actually portrayed a son's successful destiny to become an educator as had been planned for Bill's own murdered son.

A number of African American stars shot from these series, notably Will Smith, who recently starred with his son Jaden in a film *The Pursuit of Happiness*

(Muccino, 2006). In this poignant true life story, Chris Gardner (portrayed by Will Smith) and his son Christopher (played by Jaden) cling to each other through divorce and destitution, eventually winning the day with their relationship intact. As a matter of fact, the argument could be made that this father–son relationship was the basis for bouncing back from the nadir of modern homeless shelters, penniless pockets, and a harsh unseeing surrounding world.

Unfortunately, just as Gardner's world was blind to his plight, the larger Hollywood community offered families, no matter what color, little help or guidance in weathering life's vicissitudes. Earlier films of families like *Peter Pan* (Hogan, 2003), *Captains Courageous* (Fleming, 1931), *The Sound of Music* (Wise, 1965), *To Kill a Mockingbird* (Mulligan, 1962), *The Wizard of Oz* (Fleming, 1939), *Ordinary People* (Redford, 1980), *Kramer vs. Kramer* (Benton, 1979), *The Parent Trap* (Swift/Meyers, 1961/1998), and *The First Wives Club* (Wilson, 1996) showed divorce, dysfunction, or imbalance with an absent or non-functional member. Exceptions to this rule were the holiday classics *A Christmas Story* (Clark, 1983) and *It's a Wonderful Life* (Capra, 1946).

Next came a transitional period with blended families or alternative families the rule in *Yours, Mine, and Ours* (Gosnell, 2005), *Stepmom* (Columbus, 1995), *Running with Scissors* (Murphy, 2006), *The Royal Tennenbaums* (Anderson, 2001), *Duets* (Paltrow, 2000), *Riding in Cars with Boys* (Marshall, 2001), *Home Fries* (Parisot, 1998), *The Family Stone* (Bezucha, 2005), *Harry Potter* series (Columbus, 2001; 2002; Cuarón, 2004; Newell, 2005; Yates, 2007). Alongside were intact families that functioned less than perfectly and abandoned children—the *Home Alone* series (Columbus, 1990, 1992; Gosnell, 1997), alienated children—*American Beauty* (Mendes, 1999), lied to children and provided role models of infidelity, disloyalty, or risqué behavior—*Rumor Has It* (Reiner, 2005), *Dan in Real Life* (Hedges, 2007), and *Failure to Launch* (Dey, 2006), or asked children to support seemingly odd behavior—*Bruce Almighty* (Shadyac, 2003). Perhaps only distress, dysfunction, and instability make good entertainment?

This community context seems steps behind the young blacks who were taking giant steps, and had great strides yet to take before no longer blaming an unnamed force, before no longer flailing about with guttural angst, and before realizing it is their lives to live, or to lose. The lost souls who inhabit Hollywood and export its products have no help to give and no moral authority with which to give it.

Can Hollywood make a film of a healthy family, compelling not in oddity but in typicality—an "every family?" Life itself truly does offer crucial challenges to those steady in their character, relationships, and families. Why must we concoct, and perhaps, thus, create imaginal portrayals that foreshadow what occurs later in the real lives corrupted now by these implanted ideas? Why not take the harder challenge of cultivating security, sanity, and salubrity. Otherwise, it's pure sloth and expediency that robs the American public and the audience worldwide of true value for the dollar or yen well spent.

Perhaps the industrial organizational psychology aspects of the entertainment profession itself fosters this fractionation (Gregerson, M. B., 2008, Personal communication). Denizens of Hollywood move from project to project, from locale to locale, from production staff to production staff, from co-stars to co-stars. In the entertainment industry, a continuing ensemble like that seen in the *Ocean*'s series, the *Indiana Jones* quartet and the *Star Wars* series typically is found mainly on successful television series like *Seinfeld,* the *Law and Order* trilogy, or the *Crime Scene Investigation* quartet (*Ocean*'s: Soderbergh, 2001, 2004, 2007; *Indiana Jones:* Spielberg, 1981, 1984, 1989, 2008; *Star Wars:* Filoni, 2008; Kershner, 1980, Lucas, 1977, 1999, 2002, 2005, Marquand, 1983; *Seinfeld:* Ackerman, Cherones, Steinberg, & Trainer, 1990–1998; *F-r-i-e-n-d-s:* Halvorson, Bright, Lembeck, Burrows, Mancuso, Bonerz, Schwimmer, Weiss, Benson, Jensen, Hughes, de Vally Piazza, Epps, Fryman, Myerson, Schlamme, Zuckerman, Christiansen, 1994–2004; *Law and Order* trilogy [*Prime:* Makris, Alexander, Dobbs, Sherin, Platt, Penn, Scardino, Mitchell, Misiano, Quinn, Forney, Gould, de Segonzac, Swackhamer, Sackhelm, Pressman, Gerber, Muzio, Frawley, Misiano, Gillum, Wertimer, Watkins, Whitesell, Robman, Florek, Mertes, Correll, Arner, Hayman, Shilton, Ellis, Shill, Martin, Chapples, Hunter, & McKay, 1990 to present; *Special Victims Unit:* Platt, Makris, Leto, Campanella, de Segonzac, Forney, Shill, Zakrzewski, Kotcheff, Dobbs, Taylor, Fields, Wallace, Kaplan, Lipstadt, Glatter, Rosenthal, Wertimer, Quinn, Beesley, Pattison, & Woods, 1999 to present; *Criminal Intent:* Prinzi, de Segonzac, Shill, Makris, Martin, Zakrzewski, Chapple, Barba, Swartout, DiCillo, Muzio, Platt, Scardino, Norton, Wallace, Smith, Girotti, Coles, Fields, Campanella, Chopra, Torres, McKay, Treviño, & Bray, 2001 to present]; *Crime Scene* quartet [*CSI:* Fink, Lewis, Cannon, Hunt, Smight, Grossman, Clark, Eagles, O'Hara, Antonio, Wright, Correll, Markle, Sarafian, Slovis, Tanenbaum, Beesley, Bailey, Tarantino, Coolidge, Leitch, & Barclay, 2000 to present; *CSI: Miami:* Chappelle, Lautanen, Gaviola, Hill, Sarafian, Egilsson, Clark, Beesley, Lamar, Grossman, Glassner, Yaitanes, Correll, Keller, Barba, Meyer, & Cannon, 2002 to present; *CSI: New York:* Bailey, Moore, Scott, von Ancken, Barba, Hemingway, Sarafian, Glassner, Clark, DePaul, Zakrzewski, Lautanen, Adamns, Hunt, Grossman, Estevez, Thomas, & Jackson, 2004 to present; *Naval Crime Scene Investigation:* Smith, Wright, O'Hara, Whitmore Jr., Bucksey, Levi, Woolnough, Wharmby, Ellis, Libman, Mitchell, Webb, Cragg & Brown, 2003 to present]). Yet the embarrassingly long list of directors and producers associated with each of these television shows belies behind-the-scenes fluidity in production group memberships even though the on-air relationships remained the same. What is it about this culture that fosters disposability rather than endurability?

This professional fluidity may undermine secure attachment patterns in basic relatedness which may reverberate into familial relatedness capability as well (Bowlby, 1979; 1988; Gregerson, M. B., 2008, Personal communication). Attachment refers to a "lasting psychological connectedness between human beings" (Bowlby, 1969, p. 194). The four characteristics of Bowlby's attachment theory raise questions whether this industry CAN foster a healthy relationship-holding environment (van Wagner, 2008) with the following characteristics:

1. *Proximity Maintenance*—Does the nomadic nature of moving project to project heighten the intense connectedness with those proximal rather than with a distal

family group? As folk rocker Steven Stills (1970) eloquently put it, "Love the one you're with."

2. *Secure Base*—Within this gypsy culture, who and what serves as anchor for relationship/personal stability and solidness?

3. *Safe Haven*—Is there any place of refuge and sanctuary, especially when threatened or stressed?

4. *Separation Distress*—Does the typical experience in relationship turnover at work inure industry talent and staff to separation vicissitudes?

The current Hollywood collective wisdom, such as it is, is on display in the final scene of *Pleasantville* (Ross, 1998). When David's distraught mom laments, "It's not supposed to be like this," the wise young man reaches out to his weeping mom and reassures her with a bit of Hollywood sophistry so tellingly empty it could have been this article's title—"It's not supposed to be anything."

References

Allen, E. E. (1994). Strategies for the 1990s: Using the media for good. In D. Zillmann, J. Bryant, & A. C. Huston (Eds.), *Media, children, and the family: Social scientific, psychodynamic, and clinical perspectives. LEA's communication series* (pp. 85–95). Hillsdale, NJ: Lawrence Erlbaum Associates, Inc.

Akbar, N. (1985). Nile Valley origins of the science of the mind. In I. Van Sertima (Ed.), *Nile valley civilizations*. New York: Journal of African Civilization.

Anonymous. (2008). Accessed at www.epinions.com/mvie_mu-11249997/display_~full_specs on June 4.

Almaas, A. H. (2000). Facets of unity. Boston, MA: Shambala Publications.

Arnett, J. J. (1995). Adolescents' use of media for self-socialization. *Journal of youth and adolescence, 24*, 519–533.

Arriga, X. B. (2001). The ups and downs of dating: Fluctuation in satisfaction in newly formed romantic relationship. *Journal of personality and social psychology, 80*, 754–765.

Arriga, X. B., & Agnew, C. R. (2001). Being committed: Affective, cognitive, and conative components of relationship commitment. *Journal of personality and social psychology bulletin, 27*, 1190–1203.

Atkins, S. (1978). *Child of Satan, child of God* (p. 83). New York: Bantam Books.

Bahr, K. S., & Bahr, H. M. (1995). Autonomy, community, and the mediation of value: Comments on Apachean grandmothering, cultural change, and the media. In. C. K. Jacobson (Ed.). *American families: Issues in race and ethnicity. Garland library of sociology, Vol. 30; Garland reference library of social science, Vol. 1015* (pp. 229–260). New York: Garland Publishing.

Barash, D. E., & Lipton, J. E. (2001). *The myth of monogamy: Fidelity and infidelity in animals and people*. Gordonsville, VA: W.H. Freeman.

Bennett, L., Jr. (2003). *Before the mayflower: A history of Black America*. Chicago, IL: Johnson.

Bhawuk, D. P. S. (2008). Globalization and indigenous cultures: Homogenization or differentiation? *International journal of intercultural relations, 32*(4), 305–317.

Black, L. & Jackson, V. (2005). Families of African origin: An overview. In M. McGoldrick, J. Giordano, & N. Garcia-Preto, *Ethnicity and family therapy* (pp. 77–86). New York: The Guildford Press.

Boulay, M., Storey, J. D., & Sood, S. (2002). Indirect exposure to a family planning mass media campaign in Nepal. *Journal of health communications, 7*(5), 379–399.

Bowlby, J. (1969/1982). *Attachment and loss, Vol. 1: Attachment.* New York: Basic Books.

Bowlby, J. (1979). *The making and breaking of affectional bonds.* London: Tavistock.

Bowlby, J. (1988). *A secure base.* New York: Basic Books.

Cashill, J. (2008). *What's the matter with California? Cultural rumbles from the golden state and why the rest of us should be shaking.* New York: Threshold.

Christian Party. (2008). Accessed at http://www.christianparty.net/divorcecalifornia.htm. Cited June 4, 2008.

City-Data.com. (2008). Accessed at http://www.city-data.com/forum/religion-philosophy/203044-famous-last-words.html, June 24.

Clooney, G. (2006). Oscar award ceremony broadcast, March 6.

Dateline NBC. (2004, October 15). Interview.

Dion, K. L., & Dion, K. K. (1988). Romantic love: Individual and cultural perspectives. In R. J. Sternberg & M. L. Barners (Eds.), *The psychology of love.* New Haven, CT: Yale University Press.

Ellroy, J. (1996). *My dark places* (pp. 24–25, 105, 169). New York: Vintage Books.

Finstad, S. (2001). *Natasha: The biography of Natalie Wood* (pp. 139, 144). New York: Harmony Books.

Fu, W. W. (2006). Concentration and homogenization of international movie sources: examining foreign film import profiles. *Journal of communication, 56*(4), 813–835.

Gammack, J. (2002, April). Mindscapes and Internet-mediated communication. *Journal of computer-mediated communication, 7*(3).Accessed via Internet Explorer on November 16, 2008, http://www.centrelink.org/ANTH498/GAMMACK.pdf

Gamble, J. (2007, August) Holding environment as home: Maintaining a seamless blend across the virtual/physical divide, *M/C Journal, 10*(4). Retrieved November.15, 2008, from http://journal.media-culture.org.au/0708/11-gamble.php

Guiness, O. (1993). *The American hour: A time of reckoning and the once and future role of faith.* New York: Free Press.

Harry's Reviews. (1998, October 2). *Ain't it cool news.*

Hines, P. M. & Boyd-Franklin, N. (2005). African American families. In M. McGoldrick, J. Giordano, & N. Garcia-Preto (Eds.), *Ethnicity and family therapy* (pp. 87–100). New York: The Guildford Press.

Lee, H. (1960). *To kill a mockingbird.* Philadelphia, PA: J.B. Lippincott & Co.

Lerner, D. (1958). *The passing of traditional society.* Glencoe, IL: Free Press.

Levy, E. (1991). The American dream of family in film: From decline to a comeback. *Journal of Comparative Family Studies, 22*(2), 187–204.

Mead, M. (1930). *Growing up in New Guinea: A comparative study of primitive education.* New York: Harper Perennial Modern Classics, 2001.

Mead, M. (1970). *Culture and commitment.* London, UK: Bodley Head.

MPAA (Motion Picture Association of America). (2008). Home page. Accessed at http://www.mpaa.org/researchStatistics.asp, November 14.

Nobles, W. (2004). African philosophy: Foundations for black psychology. In R. Joes (Ed.), *Black psychology* (4th ed.). New York: Harper & Row.

O'Neal, T. (2004). *A paper life.* New York: HarperEntertainment.

Parejko, J. (2008). *Stolen Vows: The illusion of no-fault divorce and the rise of the American divorce industry.* Accessed via Google. http://www.stolenvows.com/chapter3.htm. Cited June 4, 2008.

Reagan, M. (2004). *Twice adopted* (p. 42). Nashville. TN: Broadman & Holman.

Royce, J. (2002). *California: A study of American character* (p. 319). Berkeley, CA: Heyday Books.

Salinger, J. D. (1951). *Catcher in the rye.* Boston, MA: Little, Brown & Co.

Sheridan, E. (2006). Conservative implication of the irrelevance of racism in contemporary African American cinema. *Journal of black studies, 37*(2), 177–192.

Smith, J. R., & Smith, L. G. (1974). *Beyond monogamy: Recent studies of sexual alternatives in marriage.* Baltimore, MD: Johns Hopkins University Press.

Sullivan, R. (2008, November 4). Reese Witherspoon's innocence abroad. *Vogue*. Accessed at http://www.style.com/vogue/feature/2008_Nov_Reese_Witherspoon/, November 13.

The Belknap Collection for the Performing Arts. (2008). *Cinema: African American cinema*. Accessed via Internet Explorer, November 13, 2008. http://www.uflib.ufl.edu/SPEC/belknap/cinema/cinemaaa.htm

Triandis, H. C. (1994). *Culture and social behavior*. New York: McGraw-Hill. http://lucy.ukc.ac.uk/Anthsoc/multi-choice.html

Twain, M. (1884). *Huckleberry Finn*. New York: Charles L. Webster and Company.

van Sertima, I. (1976). *They came before Columbus. The African presence in ancient America*. New York: Random House.

van Wagner, K. (2008). Attachment styles. *About.com: Psychology*. Accessed via Internet Explorer. December 15, 2008. http://psychology.about.com/od/loveandattraction/ss/attachmentstyle.htm

Wallerstein, J. (2000). *The unexpected legacy of divorce: The 25 year landmark study* (pp. xiii, xxvii, xxviii, xxxiii, 299, 301). New York: Hyperion .

Zillmann, D., Bryant, J., & Huston, A. C. (Eds). (1994). *Media, children, and the family: Social scientific, psychodynamic, and clinical perspectives. LEA's communication series*. Hillsdale, NJ: Lawrence Erlbaum Associates, Inc.

The Dawning of Desire Skewed Through a Media Lens and the Loss of American Adolescence: M I 4 U?

Mary Banks Gregerson

Abstract Desire dawns both publicly and privately for adolescents in our media-rich American culture. Adolescent youths come of age simultaneously physically, cognitively, and socially. Research finds about one-third of a teen's day consuming media (Roberts, 2000). Mass media, like films and movies, can both reflect and influence a healthy adolescent awakening for our young. Or, not.

Adults' best interests worldwide perhaps are served with media portrayals of adolescence depicting sexuality and vitality, a positive psychology concept, rather than those too prolific portrayals of sexualization. Thus, teens and elders are separate and shared stakeholders in this rite of passage, and may have complementary dawnings of desire, of intent. Teens desire to mold their identity for a firm foundation for future peer relatedness apart and separate from the family-centered relatedness of childhood. Elders may desire the satisfaction of generativity, that is, passing along their wisdom to the young, and then, of being appreciated.

Introduction

Desire dawns both publicly and privately for adolescents in our media-rich American culture. Youth simultaneously come of age physically, cognitively, and socially. During adolescence, research finds approximately one-third of a teen's day devoted to media consumption (Roberts, 2000). Thus, distal influences beyond the immediate face-to-face social nexus and family and community controls have a large impact on teens transitioning between the world of childhood and the universe of adulthood. Mass media, like films and movies, can both reflect and influence a healthy sexual awakening for our young. Or, not.

M.B. Gregerson (✉)
Health, Environment, and Professional Psychology, Leavenworth, KS 66048-3522, USA
e-mail: oltowne@aol.com

M.B. Gregerson (ed.), *The Cinematic Mirror for Psychology and Life Coaching*,
DOI 10.1007/978-1-4419-1114-8_4, © Springer Science+Business Media, LLC 2010

There is a choice. Elders design and cultivate the "holding environment" for the young (Winnicott, 1975). *"Holding environment* is a psychical and physical space within which the infant is protected without knowing he is protected . . . .[that] Allows the young to become more autonomous" (Gamble, 2007).

An apt metaphor for the relationship between the holding environment and the teen is:

> The seedling needs a particular holding environment in order to develop into a tree: the right soil, enough water, the right nutrients, the right amounts of light and shade. If it doesn't have the proper holding environment, it won't grow steadily and healthily and it might not grow at all. A good holding environment, then, is the environment that is needed for the human soul to grow and develop into what she can become. It needs to provide a sense of safety and security, the sense that you are, and can count on, being taken care of.
>
> (Almaas, 2000, p. 38)

Elders create the holding environment, and know its nurturance quotient by the health or illness it breeds in the young.

The media often characterize teens as victims of their desires. Classic films like *The Heiress* (Wyler, 1949) and *Now, Voyager* (Rapper, 1942) indicate the enduring struggles between carnal desires, identity formation, social obligations, and personal wishes. Such classic films firmly plant the passage of adolescence as a timeless challenge for the young. Yes, adolescence is a time of new hormonal heights. Teen years are also a time of identity formation, social awakening outside the family, and finding a place in society. Recent films like *Clueless* (Heckerling, 1995) and *Atonement* (Wright, 2007) echo other classic films like *Rebel without a Cause* (Ray, 1955) and *Splendor in the Grass* (Kazan, 1961) in their exploration of the many challenges faced by adolescents.

How their expanding social environment influences them can crucially stimulate or undermine health development in children through adolescence into adulthood. Elders have major input into qualities of the social holding environment.

Vitalization

There is no term or phrase to describe healthy adolescence in American culture, as if it does not exist, or hasn't the importance to be identified. The closest positive psychology concept is "vitality" (Peterson & Seligman, 2004), meaning the power to live or grow (Random House, 2006). A companion concept is "flexibility," meaning the capability of withstanding stress without injury. Yet vitality better describes the immense energy and robustness inherent in healthy teen living.

Vitality is one of the "key five strengths that are most highly correlated with happiness and well-being (the other four strengths are curiosity, an interest in the world, hope and optimism, gratitude, and the capacity to love and be loved)"; (Dean, 2008). Assessment of vitality has occurred in research with nursing home residents (Ryan & Frederick, 1997). So research in this area has developed from qualitative to quantitative, empirically grounding the validity of the concept.

For instance, not until Hernstein (1970) quantitatively systematized Thorndike's (1898) operant conditioning model, did its logical tautology resolve. Then scientific thought could unabashedly embrace this model. Similar research on vitality and youth could further our understanding not only of vitality but also of adolescence and what is the most nurturing holding environment.

One opposite of vitalization for teens might be termed "sexualization." Sexualization inappropriately saps wholesome vitality by making teenagers uni-dimensional, sensationalized objects bandied about by the whim of their puberty/social experiences. Too easily media fictionalize these harmful über-sexualized images into single dimensioned teens rather than depicting a balanced picture of teen living, vitalized with self-control and self-care while enlivened with exploration in the context of relatedness to others. Contrast the classic *Animal House* (Landis, 1978) and *The Breakfast Club* (Hughes, 1985) with modern fare of *Napoleon Dynamite* (Hess, 2004) and *Save the Last Dance* (Carter, 2001) to see how similar adolescent themes remain.

Vitalization of youth imbues crucial meaning, harmony, and direction into living infused with vibrant life energies and attitude. Society roles, institutions, and norms can foster vitality (Peterson & Seligman, 2004). Excellent examples of vitalization are the *Last Picture Show* (Bogdanovich, 1971), *American Graffiti* (Lucas, 1973), *Grease* (Kleiser, 1978), *Back to the Future* (Zemeckis, 1985), *Election* (Payne & Parra, 1999), and *Mean Girls* (Waters, 2004). The broad role of the media, in particular, in adolescent lives has received recent attention in terms of vitalization, or lack thereof, of teens (American Psychological Association Task Force on the Sexualization of Girls, 2007). Only recently has the role of media in creating the holding environment come under scrutiny (Gamble, 2008).

Physiologically, structurally, socially, and psychologically teens have a qualitatively different experience than children. So, their holding environment changes, and needs to change. Healthy development into adulthood rests a great deal on sexual well-being for teenagers (Satcher, 2001). Appropriately, socially for teens, peers gain importance as friends and romances straddle the private and public worlds and family involvement recedes. In their private world, children's pubescent bodies have "minds of their own."

Hormonal changes literally send blood rushing to new places as sexual response matures. View how Emmeline (portrayed by Brooke Shields) and Richard (played by Christopher Atkins) in the primitive setting of *Blue Lagoon* (Kleiser, 1980) discover their body changes without elders to guide them. Teens blossom with adult characteristics like body hair. Experiences like onset of their sex drive phenomenologically and literally rock the adolescents' worlds. Life is different.

Both public and private worlds exert control without asking permission from the child or, rather, dawning adult. Yet we expect the child traversing adolescence increasingly to make decisions affecting their bodies, their lives, their friends, their loves, their souls (Rubin, 2002; Steele, 1999). The dawning of such social responsibility is not always enticing. Note how *Buffy the Vampire Slayer* (Kuzui, 1999) resists the responsibilities thrust upon her. This awakening cognitive sophistication does not protect teens from untoward outside influences. The holding environment is crucial.

The media can help, or the media can hinder. What is considered culturally appropriate and inappropriate is tele-communicated (Iyengar, 1991). *Rushmore* (Anderson, 1998) eloquently shows these growing pains as a precocious young man vies with a teacher for the affections of a young woman. Unfortunately, few intervening transformative societal images or models ease the sexual and social transition from child to adult. Distorting sexualization images permeate our cultural milieu (APA, 2007). This is more of a harming environment than a holding environment.

Sexualization

In teens' public world, media like movies and television thrust more and more "teeny" adult images onto children already challenged with body transitions. *Bratz: The Movie* (McNamara, 2007) is based upon dolls which little girls dress seductively like sexed up Barbie dolls (it should be noted that when Barbie premiered as the first teenage fashion model doll in 1959 eyebrows raised at her blossomed bosom and tiny waist). Researchers have termed "sexualization" an inappropriate, unhealthy sensationalization (American Psychological Association [APA], 2007). In American culture sexualization is a documented detriment linked to impaired cognitive performance, body dissatisfaction, eating disorders, low self-esteem, depressive affect, and physical health problems in both older and younger women (APA, 2007). This detriment is a pervasive and persistent problem.

Where are you Hilary Duff (Miley Cyrus)? In 2008 the America cultural pop scene veritably lost Hilary Duff, a shining, if "black hole"-like (Delehanty, 2000–2008), example of clean teen development under the spotlight's glare. The term "train wreck teens" refers to many of her hapless contemporaries. Hilary shines because she embraces teenage abstinence, clean living, stable relationships, and well-mannered public interactions. But, where is she? Why has her powerful presence disappeared like a "black hole"? And why has the previous darling Miley Cyrus been zapped from the title of this section with a "strike out?"

The astronomical term "black hole" refers to a powerful dark section of the universe. Its power exists not in twinkling brilliance, like other stars, but in its absence of light. Being un-seeable, its power magnifies. We know black holes exist although their image is non-existent.

So, it goes with Hilary. Her Disney Lizzie McGuire brand is popular, positive, and vitalizing. Yet she drops from our radar screens in between television show (Holland, de Jarnatt, Rosman, Williams, Montgomery, Roberts, Israel, & Carradine, 2001–2004) and movies (Fall, 2003). A brief recent appearance in the media concerned a relationship breakup and then, later, a new one starting.

And, the strike out of Miley Cyrus? She is the 2007 teen sensation and daughter of Billy Ray Cyrus, a country star since 1993. Her Disney teen pop sensation television show as persona Hannah Montana (Christiansen, Kendall, Correll, Margolin, Flynn, Savage, Chemel, & Cendrowski, 2006–present) embraces family values, education, stable friendships, and healthy navigation of teenage dating experiences.

Then her wildly popular pop music tour (2007–2008) exceeded all expectations. Miley's father assured the public that he would protect his daughter from the "train wreck" fate of other high profile Hollywood teens like Britney Spears, Lindsay Lohan, and Nicole Richie (Wilz, 2007).

Under the guise of concern and oversight (pun intended), the celebrity media typically serves a steady diet of the drug, sex, and feuds among the celebrity young. Britney, Lindsay, and Nicole moved from teen to young woman while in the public eye. Our hearts broke as did theirs, and they reeled. In the ever spawning number of celebrity magazines, these latter three reeled from club to club; from bed to bed, from hospital to jail, from marriage to divorce, and from parenting to losing custody of children to reveal their trials, their tempers, their addictions, and their instability by literally and figuratively exposing themselves. They grabbed headlines. Paparazzi followed their every move; one paparazzo, in what he termed only a marriage of convenience, even "moved in" to date and "marry" in Mexico one of the vulnerable pop stars. Any young woman reading might wonder how she herself should act after reading about these modern day "Perils of Pauline" starlets. In the past the crashing and burning celebrity ingenues were older than teens (like Marilyn Monroe, Dorothy Dandridge, and Judy Garland) even though they may have portrayed teens, but nevertheless they were "train wreck girls," those that sacrifice themselves at the altar of fame (Wiltz, 2007). Certainly if the ruler of success is fame, if not fortune, then the number of people who know your name wins, and since bad behavior receives more press than the good behavior, being bad wins.

How lovely to be able to say that all these three have, of late, turned corners for the better. Britney is stable enough to have her children on a more regular basis, perform on a television series, and have a new single "Womanizer" zip to Number 1 on the pop charts. Nicole has two children and fiancé (perhaps by the time this reaches print he will be husband) as well as a philanthropic children's foundation. Lindsay seems settling into a stabilizing, happiness engendering relationship with an older woman, and is returning to work. Perhaps the flame-out fiasco era for high profile young women is passing?

Regrettably, the media holding environment pushed Miley Cyrus into the titillating "tsk, tsk" culture, despite her father's vows to save her from "train wrecking." What makes our voyeurism snap up the tawdry, the tempestuous, and the deceitful? In June 2008 for what would become the most popular *Vanity Fair* issue of the year; famed photographer Annie Liebowitz photographed tousled haired Miley clad only in bed sheets for just a feature, but not cover, story! Close upon the heels of this reputation-tarnishing but profile-elevating "success" followed a number of negatively charged public events for Miley including Internet photos of her in suggestive or rude poses. For the *Vanity Fair* fiasco, the public blamed Miley's parents Billy Ray *and* Tish Cyrus as well as photographer Annie Liebowitz, all of whom protested these "art" photos had been misinterpreted. What these adults deemed apropos, a large portion of American culture found lacking. For the future, Gabriella Cilmi, Lea Marie, Laree Belen, Forest Lipton, and Selena Gomez are all teen sensations in the making, and nipping at Miley Cyrus' heels. Miley's "summer of shame" has now ended, although she was recently questioned as to how she would respond if her star had set by the time she is 20. How would she as a person feel if her professional life were over by 20?

Imagine thinking that being a star is so central that an "ending" of life would occur when the spotlight moved away! Jung (Jung, Campbell, & Hull, 1976) called this a pathological identification with the persona. When the core of self fuses with the part of the self projected out to others, that is, the persona, then too much dependence on others occurs, and "strangulation" by others can occur. Jung advised healthy development of the persona as a *part* of oneself, with others aspects like solitary reflection, too, developed. "I" continues breathing and living whether or not "you" acknowledge, love, hate, or ignore me. This independent sense of self is still impacted by others, just not wrecked or destroyed by others.

Redemption is possible. At the end of summer 2008, Miley joined the vocal young pop stars Selena Gomez and Nick Jonas in wearing chastity, or purity, rings. Public proclamations of their private vows eschew active sexuality until after marriage. *E News!* featured this "trend" somewhat quizzically and yet affirmatively. Recall Jessica Simpson's loudly proclaimed chastity under marriage to Nick Lachey; and her subsequent return as a divorcée to the pack mentality of freewheeling sexual mores.

And, of boys? Nick Jonas aside, sadly, train wrecking almost seems a rite of passage expected of a young man. A recent DUI accident for young Shia LeBeouf, the heir apparent for the Indiana Jones franchise, does not bode well. Young LeBeouf, on the other hand, supplies winter housing for his recovered drug addict father. Neither does bode well the maiming and subsequent jail time caused by the drunken driving of young Nick Bollea, son of larger-than-life personality Hulk Hogan.

Other young men like Chace Crawford, Justin Timberlake, and Benji Madden, to name a few, usually grab headlines without skirting the edge of decency. Besides the major flurry of Justin's role in Janet Jackson's wardrobe malfunction at the 2006 Super Bowl half time show, only a minor flurry occurred when Chace Crawford broke up a high profile romance with country music star Carrie Underwood, and then spent quantities of time with his co-star Ed Westwick. Chace's representative felt obliged to categorically deny rumors of Chace's gay sexual preference (*US* magazine, 2008a). A previous dust storm of Chace's objects of desire became fodder for the popular press earlier this year when, curiously, an affair was alleged with N'SYNC's JC Chavez, who felt compelled to defend publically his own heterosexuality (*US* magazine, 2008b). An online gabfest called *Gawker* asserts:

> Our theory: "is he [Chace] or isn't he" gay speculation is one of the cornerstones of success for a show like *Gossip Girl*, which will never openly court the gays, but always make winking nods in their direction. This is all just the CW manipulating their product and continually tweaking their floppy haired sex robot's hardwiring.
>
> (Gawker, 2008)

Other Gawker headlines relevant to this speculation were "Is Chace Crawford Being Gay-Framed on Craig's List?" and "How to Un-Gay Chace Crawford". This perhaps concocted flurry around this young actor is technically not relevant to the age of adolescence since Mr. Crawford is 23. An earlier reference to Shia LeBoeuf, age 22, is also technically not teen territory. Yet, popular wisdom totes the late blooming nature of males relative to females. Let us pray that "train wreckage" is not one such delayed development phenomenon for males. That the media might conceivably reach beyond the bounds of truth to fabricate press and attention underlines the power of the press, that is, any type of press.

The relatively fewer lines of analysis and consideration in this chapter for the males as "train wrecks" is not sexism on the author's part. Yet a curious double standard might still exist. Perhaps the males' behavior appears less sensational either because their boundaries are less strict, or they behave themselves more. Another consideration is that the pressures upon the young female star are greater or of a different caliber than those on the young males. Certainly, acting out of American females whets the American appetite for the vulgar. Recall that Miley Cyrus' provocative photos jettisoned the best selling issue of a popular women's magazine.

As an exemplary female, though, one young star, Hayden Panettierre (TV's *Heroes)* grabs headlines for devotion to environmentally sound movements. Still, her relationship with a much older co-star Milo Ventimiglia raised eyebrows in some reportage. Why would we seek to find a seamy side, or somehow nod our heads and sigh in resignation that even exemplars raise suspicion about psychosocial/sexual judgment?

Positive Spins Make Romance Veil Reality

Why Do We Watch Infamy?

Some might say social comparison (Festinger, 1954) makes us appreciate our relatively quiet lives. Sure, Miley may have millions from her music tour, but she can't go out on a date without the whole world knowing.

Some might say that prurient tastes for sensationalism or "yellow" journalism fuel public appetite for the unsavory, the sordid, and the sad (Winchester, 1995). We privately and smugly appreciate that Miley's parents exploit her for making family fortune now that Billy Ray's country music star seems to have set, that is, until his new Reality TV show proves him an audience draw once again.

Others might insist that defensive pessimism (Norem, 2002) draws us to tales of woe, worry, and tragedy to prepare us positively to counter such forces in our own lives. If only Miley's father Billy Ray and mother Tish, to say nothing of photographer Annie Liebowitz, had pessimistically assessed the possible publicity fall out of the *Vanity Fair* photos, they might have chosen differently and more wisely to protect this daughter as her parents adamantly and steadfastly had avowed to protect, but have not.

Others think along Calvinistic lines. We want to punish those who do wrong (Kushner, 1983). We exalted Miley and now we smite her for not living up to our exalted image. It's her fault that we found her so perfect and now are disappointed with her fall from grace.

And, lastly, others point to the famous Irish playwright Brendan Behan's quote, "All publicity is good publicity—except an obituary notice." How many of you, dear readers, do not know who Hilary Duff is but do recognize the name Miley Cyrus? Then, the truth of this possibility becomes evident.

There is one American teen star in 2007 at age 16, though, for whom worldwide notoriety appeared and the innocence of adolescence truly vanished. In December 2007, a celebrity news magazine announced then 16-year-old Jamie Lynn Spears was pregnant (*OK! Magazine*, 2007). Before that moment, Jamie Lynn had appeared as the young version of her famous older sister Britney's role in the ill-fated movie *CrossRoads* (Davis, 2002) and a few other public performances, and headlined her own successful television show Nickelodeon's *Zoey 101* (Hoefer, Weissman, Grossman, Kendall, Holland, Christiansen, & Savage, 2005–2008). This year, 17-year–old Jamie Lynn has given birth. The same celebrity news magazine published an upbeat announcement of conception and what some critics called a glamorized accounting of birthing and parenting an infant (Lu, 2008). This courageous young woman and her young fiancé have shouldered the responsibilities for their actions without complaint and without sensationalism nor encouraging others to follow suit. Isn't young Jamie Lynn showing "vitality" when facing this unplanned very adult child rearing while still at the edge of childhood herself?

Experts on teenage medicine caution about such highly publicized positive spins on teenage pregnancy:

> The media doesn't show the downside to teenagers getting pregnant," says Warren Seigel, a pediatrician who founded the Adolescent Medicine Program at Coney Island Hospital. "All they're seeing is the upside . . . . This concept of having a baby might feel good emotionally when you look at the magazines, but its not reality.
>
>   (Kliff, 2008)

In his magazine's defense, Editor Rob Shuter averred that "Babies are the new 'it' factor in the celebrity market." (Kliff, 2008), and answered thusly the question Kliff (2008) posed:

> **How big was the story of Jamie Lynn's pregnancy for [*Newsweek*]?**
> The attention and press, it might be one of the biggest stories that [magazine]'s has ever had in America if not the world. It was an international story. It was on the cover of the London newspapers, the German newspapers, the French newspapers. It was just an extraordinary moment. I think we knew it was a very big story but it took us a little bit by surprise just how big this story became. The nightly news was talking about it.

Without moralizing, the psychosocial question remains whether or not the story of a social model like Jamie Lynn reflects or influences culture. Did other young girls become pregnant before (Jamie Lynn reflecting) or after (Jamie Lynn influencing)?

Perhaps an answer to this question begins with viewing another media event. Additionally, last year the movie *Juno* (Reitman, 2007) relayed the story of a pregnant high school student played by Academy Award nominated Ellen Page. This teen carried her baby to term while attending high school before giving the child to an adoptive parent. Young Juno returned to her life *sans* baby but still with the same boyfriend, parents, and friends. Her pregnancy may have seemed with few repercussions except for a hazy hiatus away for the birth, and the growing awkwardness of wearing teen grunge clothing while pregnant.

Concurrent with Jamie Lynn's *vivant tableau* and Juno's fictional portrayal, mainstream American media noted in 2006 an overall surge in teen pregnancies (Kingsbury, 2008). As a microcosm, in a New England high school, students' quizzically asked school health officials for pregnancy tests in the early Fall, and many showed great disappointment in negative results. This trend occurred well before Jamie Lynn's pregnancy announcement in December. At that same high school a young 2008 graduate and mother (named Ireland) of a toddler tries to dispel the romantic notions other students express when calling her "lucky" to have a baby:

> They're so excited to finally have someone to love them unconditionally," Ireland says. "I try to explain it's hard to feel loved when an infant is screaming to be fed at 3 a.m.

Perhaps those conceiving in early winter 2007 were less leaders in this teen pregnancy upsurge in New England in 2007 than a reflection of our culture's new romantic appeal of pregnancy and parenthood.

This trend also seems echoed world wide of late. The previous year (2006), the first U.S. upsurge in teen pregnancy occurred in 15 years. This fact seemed, again, reflective of rather than influenced by the teen pregnancy of *Whale Rider*'s (Caro, 2002) star 16-year-old Keisha Castle-Hughes from New Zealand (People magazine, 2006). Around the world young teens are having sex, becoming pregnant, and keeping their children, or not. The high profile teens seem at the middle of the bell curve rather than outliers leading this psychosexual phenomenon.

Jamie Lynn truly typifies the loss of adolescence lamented in this chapter. Instead of moments for self-reflection during which her blossoming identity can develop, this young mother has moments of self-reflection on whether or not she is a good mother. During her baby's infancy this role imposes its presence 24/7. Jamie Lynn as a person may be slighted by premature closure from the demands of mothering. The social role of mother should follow identity formation rather than be a tool of identity formation.

At which step in this process can we influence more age appropriate life tasks for these young? Certainly the responsibility evidenced in child rearing might indicate a consciousness in conception—or, not—but at least in parenting responsibilities. We need to know more about antecedents as well as consequences for these teens whose dawning of desire sped directly into the high noon of parenting without lingering in the morning of child-free young adulthood. The ultimate goals for social scientists perhaps might best be described as to elevate all societal members into a higher quality of life.

Does spotlight on young role models who probably reflect rather than mold behavioral patterns absolve the media from their influence? Social engineering to contour media influence might counter what seems now like media reflections of societal trends. More systematic archival analyses of teen intimacy habits and births, as well as parenting patterns could speak more definitely to what here are simple surmises based upon a smattering of observations. Perhaps a strong dose of defensive pessimism, rather than rosy-eyed optimism, might counter this trend toward precocious adulthood for some possibly unwary and unsuspecting young teenagers. When cultural media messages squarely convey the vicissitudes of parenting, and the very real possibilities of unprotected sex as well as the socio-emotional challenges of young passion, our young will have true choice.

As it stands, does misguided positive spinning foist a fairy tale-like fantasy upon young people's imagination or innocence regarding sex, birth, and parenting? Perhaps a dialectical synthesis is occurring. First, the admonitions against the evils of sex (thesis), then the idealization of young love and parenthood (antithesis), and, finally, the synthesis of the joys and stresses of such unusual psychosocial precocity. Such media social engineering might present worldwide a more accurate message to the young about the ups and downs of teenage sex, the challenges and sacrifices of young pregnancy and parenthood as well as the alternative of the joys and benefits of unfettered participation in mainstream adolescent activities before meeting the chores of young adulthood without the added pressures of parenting. I find it somewhat shocking to pose as the "alternative" child-free adolescence. Yet this perspective problem of foreground and background is endemic to the media–culture relationship in terms of adolescents.

Media vs. Culture

Mass media informs people about what is important and how to think about events and people in those events (Kosicki, 1993), or does the underlying culture inform media transmission? Media psychologists already investigate bi-directionality of causality (e.g., Elliott, 2003) to answer the question: Do media form culture, or culture form media?

Cultivation theory (Gerbner, Gross, Morgan, & Signorelli, 1994) proposes that a populace gradually adopts the image of reality that media presents. Consistent exposure over time leads the audience to adopt the presented world view. For example, extremely frequent viewers of television perceive their social reality parallels closely the televised reality (Buerkel-Rothfuss, Gorenberg, Atkin, & Neuendorf, 1982).

Our society is on the verge of losing adolescence. A 6% increase in teenage pregnancies during American adolescence is a prolonged time of transition from child to adult (Kingsbury, 2008). Recall that independence increases in decision making for teens (Rubine, 2002; Steele, 2002). Teens, especially girls, develop identities by imitating media representations (Hutson & Wright, 1998).

As we see, the mass media of films and movies reflect, for the most part, a preternatural skewed image of matured, not maturing, teen years. This distortion departs from a healthy, enabling image to guide and benefit teens gradually becoming adults. Our youth seem to go directly from diapers to dating.

Advertisers (CBC Marketplace, 2005) term "age compression" the purposefully mismatching images of social precocity with biological age. Ironically, age compression also finds elders encouraged to dress and act younger than their age. No matter what age, Americans are encouraged to be what they are not, and to purchase products to assist this "plasticizing."

Such commercial symbolism like ads, cartoons, and movies construct perceptions of reality (Guffman, 1959; Macrae, Milne, & Bodenhauser, 1994; Sherman & Frost, 2000). In particular, media depiction of "male" and "female" fundamentally form gender identity (Gordon & Chavez, 1990). A similar mechanism may be a primary source for images of sexuality, which guides the youths' genesis of desire. Research needs to address this proposition formed through archival analysis of film depictions of young love: Do images of sexuality parallel the perceptual mechanisms research has found with gender identity? This question, and many others, emerge when examining media and psychology, especially in relation to depictions of adolescent sexuality.

What responsibility do media leaders have through conscionable choice of images presented to guide rather than exploit our children? A recent grassroots protest thwarted the doll merchandising of the burlesque girl group called the Pussycat Dolls. What will make "grasstops," that is, the higher echelon media take proactive rather than reactive action? To answer these questions, guide adult action, and illuminate future decision making and directions for scientific research, we first need to know where we are now. The picture is not pretty.

Media Images as Ideals and Stereotypes

We stereotype. This is not *all* bad. A stereotype simplifies life for us (Schneider, 2003), decreasing decision making time by condensing all nuances of differences into larger categories. The "cognitive miser" theory (Macrae, Milne, & Bodenhauser, 1994; Sherman & Frost, 2000) proposes that humans rely upon images from commercial symbolism to form stereotypes. These stereotypes then streamline decision making to conserve cognitive resources.

One such stereotype concerns sexuality. Spence and Bruckner (2000) found that children connect between stereotypes and preferences for types of social activities and relationship choices. Classically, Freud (reprint edition 1997) worked against cultural stereotypes of sexuality as taboo.

Since his time our culture has been trying to prove him wrong, *or* follow his sage advice, depending upon your preconceived bias for or against Freud. This very preconceived bias is exactly what a stereotype is—a pre-judgment. In our more sexual permissive times, perhaps restraint and decorum have become the taboos. As classic psychological theories note, the time when sexuality first blooms, that is, adolescence, deserves special attention. As modern media analysts note, mass communication sends messages to and from our young.

Adolescence, in particular, commands a prominent place in the development of both sexuality and stereotypy capacity (Mortimer, Larson, Brown, et al., 2003). Our modern expressive society literally teems with expressions of sexuality in contrast to Freud's sexually repressive Victorian society. Stereotypy capacity concerns the abstract ability to understand the world in more general abstract rather than concrete terms. Both cognitive development of stereotypy and sexuality occur circa onset of the teen years, which have other important tasks, too, as noted by other psychology theorists.

Adolescence

At the crucial time of adolescence our young have two psychosexual tasks, according to psychologist Erik Erikson (1968): Identity Formation and Fostering Intimacy. From birth, Erikson saw us as sexual beings, with particular life tasks at each life stage. He conceptualized eight psychosexual life stages over the development of our lifetime. Adolescence concerns relatedness to oneself and to others. Identity concerns "Who I am." Intimacy concerns "How I relate to others." Teens dually develop their sense of self and of self in relation to others. Recall that teen identity is thought to be indelibly influenced by media sources (Hutson & Wright, 1998). Girls specifically report identity as a major concern during teen years (Brown, 1991).

Furthermore, post-Freudian theorists highlighted adolescence as an important psychosocial time. Elaborating upon Erikson, for instance, Hill (1983) identified five tasks for adolescents:

(1) Identity—discovering and understanding the self as an individual;
(2) Intimacy—forming close relationships with others;
(3) Autonomy—establishing a healthy sense of independence;
(4) Sexuality—coming to terms with puberty and expressing sexual feelings; and
(5) Achievement—becoming a successful and competent member of society.

These theorists form one voice to note that societal values influence adolescent sexuality. At this time, teens search curiously. They sift through people as well as media images to guide their choices and formation of their sense of self, sexuality, and relatedness to others. Media are an important source of guidance, whether intended or not (Hutson & Wright, 1998).

As biomedical and social scientists we, in particular, search and investigate sex and sex stereotypes. Adolescence, in particular, has captured more and more of the scientific imagination and curiosity. Psychologists consider how societal values both reflect and impinge upon adolescents' dawning of desire, that is, the onset of puberty.

Sexualization vs. Vitality, That Is, Healthy Sexuality

Recently the American Psychological Association (2007) has published a *Report of the APA Task Force on the Sexualization of Girls*. In particular, this Task Force noted the difference between healthy sexuality and sexualization, the latter which occurs when (APA, 2007, p. 2):

- a person's value comes only from his or her sexual appeal or behavior, to the exclusion of other characteristics;
- a person is held to a standard that equates physical attractiveness (narrowly defined) with being sexy;
- a person is sexually objectified—that is, made into a thing for others' sexual use, rather than seen as a person with the capacity for independent action and decision making; and/or
- sexuality is inappropriately imposed upon a person.

Healthy sexuality (vitality) and sexualization differ fundamentally. Scientific investigation of this distinction comes from socialization, socio-cultural, cognitive psychoanalytic, objectification approaches (APA, 2007). Self-objectification may occur rather than a healthy self-integrity, self-esteem, and self-worth (Fredrickson & Roberts, 1997; McKinley & Hyde, 1996). Healthy sexuality emanates from and creates intimacy, attachment, sharing, and respect (Satcher, 2001; Sexuality Information and Education Council of the United States [SIECUS]). Sexualization may undermine successful navigation of the other tasks of adolescents, as mentioned previously. An excellent societal monitor of the relatively predominance of sexualization and healthy sexuality is media images.

As media psychologists we have particular interest in how technology influences healthy sexuality and sexualization stereotypes. In 2005 Escobar-Chaves and her colleagues reported that the 2,522 media and sexuality scientific studies between 1983 and 2003 had less than 1% focused on adolescents, a crucial time in psycho-sexual development. This relative neglect indicates that adolescents have been lost in our societal scientific search on the dawning of desire.

This large gap in the scientific literature does NOT reflect popular culture, which now focuses upon this new economic force. In the current zeitgeist expressions of sexuality onset are often mediated by technology, that is, media. Do media really influence the adolescent's experience of sexuality?

The Media, Sexuality, and Adolescence

As children mature, an increasing dependence on media has been noted (Rubin, 2002; Steele, 1999). Research has documented that adolescents spent more time watching TV than being in school or with parents (Chapin, 2000). Entertainment ranked third behind school and sleeping in terms of how teens say they spend their time (D. Roberts, Foehr, & Rideout, 2005). In a Kaiser Family Foundation study (Hoff, Green, and Davis, 2003), tweens (those between 8 and 14 years) reported using the Internet 4 days per week and 2 hours online each log on. Both children and parents reported the media as a major source for information on sex (Malamuth & Impett, 2000).

Movie images themselves provide answers to this question. Almost a decade ago in the 1999 movie *Superstar* (McCulloch), Molly Shannon, a former television *Saturday Night Live* player, played teenaged Mary Katherine Gallagher (Wilson, McCarthy-Miller, Miller, Schaffer, King, Weis, Signorelli, Wachtenheim, Williams, Marianetti, Schiller, Sedelmaier, Brooks, McKay, Shannon, Steinmacher, Taccone, McGrath, Lipson, Zander, Judge, White, Hader, Samberg, Idle, Wegman, Ichaso, Dear, Kelly, Guest, Corbett, McCulloch, Gianas, Warburton, Wetterhahn, Alt, Lovelace, Brooks, Lennert, Miles, Smigel, DeSeve, Kerven, & Slesin, 1975 to present). This after-school video store clerk and schoolgirl's only wish in life is for a kiss, "not just any kiss, mind you—a big-time, hold-your-breath-'till-you're-gonna-faint, Hollywood-style kiss." This movie is a perfect example of youth believing celluloid reality and letting movies guide their behavior—life imitates art. Mary Katherine's rapt absorption and cognitive schema formed by celluloid occurs because she lives with her grandmother—Mary Katherine had no personal experience with female–male relatedness, except through popular culture images.

A decade earlier another movie, 1987's *Dirty Dancing* (Ardolino), depicted what guidance, or lack thereof, a healthy, if staid, doctor's family provided for 17-year-old "Baby," the youngest daughter. Baby wanders away from the protection of adult supervision by leaving the sedate nighttime family entertainment furnished by a Catskills resort. She wanders into territory forbidden for guests—the staff quarters area. Baby is drawn by a raucous dance cacophony and bright lights, like the proverbial moth to a flame. Opening the door where the lights and sounds are drawing her, she awkwardly and shyly watches the "hot" dancing of other couples. Yet the "hottest couple" is not even a couple; they are simply two childhood friends who grew up dancing and evolved their style as they entered teendom. In the movie, Baby fast-forwards her transition from child to adult by being dumped directly into a seething, undulating sticky situation when she replaces the female in this platonic yet sexy dancing duo. Baby bursts into sexual awareness complete with relational complexity and identity searching. As a communication to audience teens, this media image of adolescence provides hazy relational boundaries, identity confusion, and age compression (CBC Marketplace, 2005). Furthermore, Baby's basically sound father–daughter relationship broke down around the sexual situations evoking the father's sexual stereotypes. The Message is: Girls require supervision; a woman does not.

Music Speaks

As Britney Spears' 2003 song tells it: "I'm not a girl, not yet a woman," reflecting the finding that in 1999 teen-oriented radio had 22% sexual content (Donnerstein, 2002). Girls require supervision. A woman does not. Later we shall see how this sexualization in songs and films pervades many other aspects of culture, but now, a further comment on music is warranted to underline the seriousness of this cultural static.

Music videos in general are guilty of sexualization (Gow, 1996; R. C Vincent, 1989). Content analysis research has found 44–81% of music videos have sexual content (Gow, 1990; Greeson & Williams, 1986; Pardun & McKee, 1995; Sherman & Dominick, 1986). Sommers-Flanagan and her colleagues (1993) concluded about sexualization in country music videos that "...the concept of a whole person is clearly absent from the video's message" (p. 752).

Teens consume more sexual content more frequently in music than in TV, movies, or magazines (Pardun, L'Engle, & Brown, 2005). Later, as more detailed examination of these other parts of teen media diet supports, the concern about messages and models that films give to teens. These "tweens," those 8 to 14 are in a nether land of both needing and eschewing adults.

Films and Boys

And, what of boys and movies? How are societal values reflected in the film images supplied of the male coming of age? Images of male sexual awakenings prove equally concerning. Yet no complementary APA Task Force has been formed yet to address the sexualization of boys. Evidently dual concerns and standards exist for boys and girls. Around sexual issues, girls seem to get more attention, both good and bad.

In the 1983 movie *Risky Business* (Brickman) a young Tom Cruise plays 19-year-old Joel Goodson, Cruise's breakout role. When his parents leave for a week, his troublemaking friends call an escort service for Joel. Let us bypass Tom's famous "air" rock-and-roll dance in his "tighty whitie" briefs and shirt—even though this scene was what years ago first attracted his now wife Katie Holmes. In the movie, when Joel is in bed alone post-call girl, his ambivalence toward his "bad boy" behavior tortures him. The young man, without developing a relationship, experiences sex "way over his head." Sexualization occurs. Ironically, this bad boy behavior receives cultural rewards like entrance into an ivy league college. What a message given to young men!

Another example of a young man's sexual initiation outside of healthy sexuality, that is, vitality, and a normal one-on-one relationship comes from the 2000 movie *Almost Famous* (Crowe). Rather than attend high school classes, young William Miller convinces Rolling Stone magazine to hire him to write about a rock group. William bonds with the band's groupies called the Band-Aids, who relieve their boredom in middle America by deflowering young William. In a role reversal, young William and not the young women later feel used and confused. Not even Rolling Stone magazine had prepared William for the disorientation and distress he feels after his group deflowering. He, though, ultimately is rewarded with a cover story.

For boys, sexualization have may different value than for girls. Sexualization for boys seems on the road to societal job success while for girls it may be the end of the road. For girls, success is relational, so any mechanism like sexualization that undermines healthy relationships, undermines their whole *raison d'etre*.

Young girls, also, are not immune to skirting the bounds of propriety in media portrayals of their sexuality, but do they reap "rewards?" In the 1999 straight-to-video *Passport to Paris* (Metter), American 'tween sweethearts Mary Kate and Ashley Olsen escape their grandfather's supervision in Paris and find "trouble" with two French boys. On a secluded bridge, the Paris boys invite Ashley and Mary Kate to a dance the next evening and start to kiss them when the Paris police "bust" them. Mary Kate and Ashley receive their reward—an invitation and then attendance at the dance. A social invitation for girls and not the career success for boys emanates from the sexualization.

Both boys and girls triumph over temporary setbacks attached to their initiation into youthful sexualization to ultimately receive cultural rewards. Healthy sexuality sanctioned by adults, producing pleasant experiences with little endangerment, escapes both boys and girls. Yet in *Dirty Dancing* (Ardolino, 1977) and *Passport to Paris* (Metter, 1999) for girls, but not in both *Risky Business* (Brickman, 1983) and *Almost Famous* (Crowe, 2000) for boys, the law and outside authorities regulated or attempted to regulate sex by strict enforcement. The common, even if subtle, shared message is of teens sexual expression being "trouble" and not amenable to self-regulation—especially, for girls.

For these four media images of adolescent dawning of desire, families transition from a protective cover to a stranglehold to be eluded. Besides foisting adult attitudes, behaviors, expectations, and acceptability upon the young with sexualization, adults also appear as foils and foilers for teens. Few depictions show healthy parent–child relatedness around healthy sexuality, although some do exist as we shall see in the last section of this chapter.

In the two examples of films depicting American boys' arrested or diverted healthy sexual expressions, no emotional turmoil results toward self although unpleasantness is aimed at adults. When William Miller and Joel Goodson each consummate their sexual initiations outside of a healthy intimate relationship, confusion and conflict with their paramours result. And even for the girls too, their parents weren't there to protect them, and they eluded other authorities.

Media Images of Adolescent Sexuality in Other Cultures

Sexuality in other cultures can vary greatly (Greene, 2000; Hurtado, 2003). Research has documented that historically stereotypes predominated by sexuality and physicality stigmatize girls of color and immigrant girls (Hill Collins, 2004). In Mexico, at the turn of the century, parental control over children's sexuality was absolute, as seen in the 1993 movie *Like Water for Chocolate* (Arau). Young Pedro has fallen madly in love with neighboring Mama Elena's youngest daughter, Tita, fulfilling her nanny's curse—when Tita was born, the unhinged nanny said that the first man to look at the infant as a young girl would fall head over heels in love.

The single Mama Elena, though, has other plans for youngest daughter Tita, whom Mexican family tradition dictates care for the mother. Mama Elena thwarts Tita and Pedro's union by diverting him to Tita's eldest sister. The middle sister, at first kidnapped as a child by the locale bandoleros, now actively joins them as the leader's consort. Years later after Mama Elena and the eldest sisters' deaths, when Tita and Pedro finally do consummate their relationship, further tragedy ensues. No where in this movie is healthy sexuality shown.

Such family control is still seen in media depictions emanating from other cultures like India, colloquially termed Bollywood. In *Monsoon Wedding* (Nair, 2001), an adult Cousin Ria's recall of her adolescent sexual abuse by an uncle results in the family shunning the uncle. The family shuns the uncle and flutters protectively around Ria. Also, the young bride of this arranged marriage is having an illicit affair, so healthy sexuality in the young does not appear in *Monsoon Wedding*.

We see that ethnic cultures tend to bring the group to bear on sexual coming of age. Desire dawns for the ethnic teen amid adult chaos, repression, and interference. In these media images both ethnic and American cultures seem conflict-ridden over what is healthy sexual awakening.

Merchandise Reflects Film Images

In advertising parlance, age compression means "pushing adult products and teen attitudes on younger and younger kids" (CBC Marketplace, 2005). 'Tweens now provide incredible consumer clout—an estimated $1.7 billion! Sexuality more appropriate for those older is being used to attract, to mesmerize, and to close the sale with younger and younger children.

A classic example of age compression emanates from the 1950s when controversy surrounded the introduction of the Barbie doll with curves to replace the ubiquitous baby dolls. Currently, new sexuality replaced the now deemed non-realistic hourglass figured Barbie, who has even lost her Ken these days in an unfortunate updating.

Now, a bevy of new products present ever more brazen depictions of gender attributes and of sexual behaviors. For example, Bratz dolls and Internet sources like Much Music and Tony Hawk's Underground fast-forward teen sexuality (Donnerstein, 2002). In the Web site Tony Hawk's Underground, a skateboarding video game oddly has background scenarios of strip teases slipping by. Whether indirectly, as in this Web site, or more directly expressed, sexualization attracts an audience.

If commercial images contour adolescents' images and stereotypes of sexuality, new technologies, that is, personal blogs, e-zines, and room art give access. An assessment technique called "room tours" has teens walk around their bedrooms while describing the wall decorations, artifacts, electronics, and other personalized aspects (Steele & Brown, 1995). Today's adolescents oftentimes highly sexualize what environmental psychologists call the "environmental load" of their rooms.

Certainly such new methods speak to the need to scientifically scrutinize the effects of adolescent/sexuality/media phenomena like age compression.

Print Media Reflects Film Images

Magazines were often the preferred media for sexual information for both boys and girls (Treise & Gotthoffer, 2002). Sexualization is prevalent in magazines (Krassas, Blauwkamp, & Wesselink, 2001, 2003; Plous & Neptune, 1997). Content analysis of the popular culture magazine *Rolling Stone* identified social stereotypes that undermined healthy gender and ethnic stereotypes (Gerbher, Gross, Morgan, & Signorelli, 1986; Wilson, 1990). What specifically do these magazines purvey?

Since the 1990s lad magazines like *Maxim, Stuff,* and *FHM* (*For Him Magazine*) have become commonly accepted as "salacious but not pornographic" with "bawdy" humor (Carr, 2003). Originally a number of retail stores banned their sale. Content analysis of these three lad magazines, that is, *Maxim, Stuff,* and *FHM* (*For Him Magazine*) revealed these nine themes:

- Improving One's Sex Life
- What Women Like
- Sexual Satisfaction
- Unorthodox Sexual Behaviors or Positions
- Unorthodox Sexual Locations
- Drugs and Alcohol
- Relationship States
- How positive and negative the main relationship is
- How explicit are the accompanying photos, and what is their interpersonal nature

For girls, one study even reported that those reading women's lifestyle magazines like *Cosmopolitan* and *Elle* also endorsed sexual stereotypes (Kim & Ward, 2004). Content analyses of *Seventeen* and *YM* magazines revealed conflicted sex messages (Durham, 1998; Garner, Sterk, & Adams, 1998):

- Encouragement to be sexy
- Emphasis on importance of romantic relationships
- Instruction on how to please young men
- Simultaneous emphasis on patience and control

Television Reflects Film Images

Televised media exposes teens to "sexual scripting of behaviors" not available elsewhere (Gagnon & Simon, 1987). Sexual remarks are pervasive on television (Ward, 2007). Recall that cultivation theory (Gerbner et al., 1997) underlines the important influence of media upon perceptions of reality, especially for very frequent media users (Chapin, 2000). The wedding of marketing and television, that is commercials in particular, sexualize images (Lin, 1997).

Nielsen Media Research (1998) found that children/teens watched television for an average of 3 hours per day, with a combined media consumption of 6 hours 32 minutes per day. So the media influence on teens in palpable, but is it palatable? What do teens view?

- Sexual content accounted for approximately 1/3 of prime time shows popular with teens (Greenberg, Richards, & Henderson, 1980; Ward, 1995).
- In one study (Ward, 1995) almost 60% sexual dialogue and innuendo comprised the most highly sexed show.
- Female sexuality was less frequent content than male sexuality.
- The top three sexual themes were

  - relationship oriented with competition,
  - female physicality valued as selection criteria for males, and
  - a sense of masculinity derived from sex.

- From 1980 to 1985, references or scenes of sexuality increased 103%, resulting in around 2,000 sexual references (Greenberg et al., 1993a), with a nominal number about preventing pregnancy or sexually transmitted diseases.
- In a normal day of a young 'tween, researchers observed over 280 instances of sexual content from a media source (CBC Marketplace, 2005).
- Prime-time TV features premarital and extramarital sex far more frequently than sex between spouses, with the comparison skyrocketing to 24:1 in soap operas (Lowry & Towles, 1989) compared to 32:1 in R-rated movies (Greenberg et al., 1993).
- Action–adventure series feature premarital sex and prostitution most often (Greenberg et al., 1993).

How does this affect teens? Controversy exists in answering this question. On the one hand, researchers and adults say "a lot." A 1991 longitudinal study documented prospectively that early adolescents who watch sexy TV reported earlier initiation of sexual intercourse in middle and late adolescence (Petersen, Moore, & Furstenberg, 1991).

On the other hand, teens say "not much," at least personally. They have a double standard for themselves and for their friends (Kaiser Family Foundation, 2002). Although the media affect their friends, those studied tenaciously asserted they themselves were above media influence and that they resented the media being blamed for their behavior (Fay & Yanoff, 2000).

Scientifically, the importance of media for teens may be an experimental confound. When the demand characteristics of the forced-choice research method mentioning media were absent, teens rarely spontaneously mentioned the media (Werner-Wilson, Fitzharris, & Morrissey, 2004). Recently teens most often cited peers or friends as the source of sex information (Andre, Dietsch, & Cheng, 1991;

Andre, Frevert, & Schuchmann, 1989; Ballard & Morris, 1998; Kaiser Family Foundation et al., 2003), although in other research over a number of years and diverse samples, teens noted reading as the most important source of information on sex (Andre et al., 1991; Andre et al., 1989; Bradner, Ku, & Lindberg, 2000; Spanier, 1977). These findings do not vary across gender and experience level.

Who Is Responsible?

This selected movie analysis echoes, in part, the 2007 report from the American Psychological Association Task Force on the Sexualization of Girls (see http://www.apa.org/pi/wpo/sexualization.html). Both the current chapter and the APA Task Force agree to challenge parents, educators, news staff, entertainers, and other interested adults to become responsible shamanistic shepherds of the onset of relationship sexuality. Shamans are native healers whose own successfully traversed healing experiences, like trials by fire, have made them apt guides for others.

Who is responsible—the teens, their peers, their parents, their teachers, the media? Legally, until teens reach majority, however a particular state defines majority, parents and adults are responsible. Yet Shari Graydon (2004), who wrote a book about beauty stereotypes and marketing, succinctly observes, "Parents do have a responsibility, no question about it. But kids spend more time with media than they do with their parents."

Movies, in particular, find their largest audience in teens (Steenburger, 1995). Thirteen percent of children have reported daily movie going while 35% reported video or DVD viewing (Roberts et al., 2005).

Yet responsibility shifting can occur, as one teen's mother put it, "I am glad I don't have to do [talking about sex] because she gets that at school" (CBC Marketplace, 2005). In 2001 Donnerstein and Smith showed that parents who view television with their teens and openly communicate may inoculate teen and 'tweens (those 8–14) from the potentially adverse effects of the media bombardment of sexuality.

We the elders are all responsible. Parents, teachers, media, and leaders. We make the holding environment by what we tolerate and what we do not. Discernment is a necessary first step for disciple. So, perhaps the first step will be for adults to convince teens of potential pitfalls and to teach discernment when viewing media images of sexuality.

And, closely following that step is the next—teens commanding respect so that adults stop exercising the ostrich solution. Ignoring the dawning of desire does not make it go away. Believing that truthful warning may start the navigation of these shoals with minimal anguish and angst.

So, the "dawning of desire" may be also the heightening of motivation, or intent, for adults to contour a health-engendering holding environment. To attend, recognize, and facilitate the social, sexual, and personal challenges adolescents face. Psychology can help, especially media psychology. Media magnifies the holding environment, and it creates the holding environment as well. This double strength responsibility puts media squarely in a role of responsibility for our youth. This role cannot be escaped. It can be shaped. Now, is the time to do so.

Positive Psychology and Today's Dawning of Desire

The picture may be changing both in terms of societal reflection and influence about onset of teen puberty. In newer movies, both girls and boys have received recent makeovers so that teens evidence more autonomy and judgment, but not after the inevitable pitfalls of naïveté and inexperience. This interim stage of societal modeling for the dawning of desire demonstrates that change is possible and can be popular.

For girls, two recent movies, 1995's *Clueless* (Heckerling) and 2003's *The Lizzie McGuire Movie* (Fall) reflect a transformation in societal views on teen girls. In *Clueless* (Heckerling, 1995), young Cher Horowitz (played by Alicia Silverstone), named for a rock diva and who is preternaturally wise in the romantic ways of the world, missteps as her friends' matchmaker, and in her own pursuit of love—until her father deftly and subtly intervenes. Instead of hovering and banning, her father Mel Horowitz (acted by Dan Hedaya) contrives for Cher to choose as her paramour Mel's adopted son from a previous marriage. Although Cher chooses, without her knowledge her choice is contrived by her father. Almost a decade later in *The Lizzie McGuire Movie* (Fall, 2003), Lizzie (played by Hilary Duff) is cast upon her own auspices as she goes to Europe *sans* parents. Her adult chaperones simply watch as she endures mishaps and finally charts her own course. Lizzie's peers, and not her parents, help her triumph over the romantic evil to which she unwittingly succumbs.

For boys, in the 2005 movies *Sky High* (Mitchell, 2005) and *Harry Potter and the Goblet of Fire* (Newell, 2005) male puberty has special plot import. In *Sky High* (Mitchell, 2005), young Will Stronghold (portrayed by Michael Angarnao) enters high school for the super-power gifted and is, at first, bedazzled by a villainess disguised as an honor student leader. She dupes the guileless Will, who violates direct orders from his father resulting in a weapon of mass destruction being stolen. Ultimately, though, Will saves his parents and his school when he uncovers the truth and by himself solves the dilemma. Harry Potter (acted by Daniel Radcliffe), on the other hand, always a bumble buss, fumbles his way through first infatuation with Cho Chang (portrayed by Katie Leung), a young Hogwarts School of Magic wizardess-in-the-making. At one point it seems, although untrue, as if Harry has murdered Cedric, a rival for Cho's affections. Whenever Harry sees Cho, he blushes, stutters, or his stomach "feels funny." He does manage to invite her to the Hogwart's Yule Ball, although Cedric (played by Robert Pattison) has beaten him to the punch. So, in *Sky High* (Mitchell, 2005) the young hero triumphs over evil within and outside himself while in *Harry Potter and the Goblet of Fire* (Newell, 2005) the young anti-hero continues his streak of bad-luck strewn conquest that triumphs in spite of his foibles. Will makes his fate while fate elevates Harry.

All of these newer visions of adolescence restrain expressions to affection, with sexuality an absent element. More classic films like the 1962 *Lolita* (Kubrick) which was remade in 1997 (Lyne) and 1971's (Mulligan) *Summer of '42* feature the deflowering of a young one by a feckless or reckless elder. Such child exploitation seems out of favor at the moment, thankfully.

Yet adults have recessed into the background rather than seemingly collaborated as guides and mentors with the young grappling with the onset of puberty. Even in the positive psychology examples furnished above, no collaboration existed between adult and teenager. Either the adult was absent because of locale or imprisonment. Dramatically this *parents absentia* made the youngster rely upon her/his own resources to save the day. Interestingly, in each case, the budding romantic yearnings of the teen were implicated in a plot twist potentially calamitous if a *deus ex machina* did not miraculously save the teen from her/himself. The crucial moment was the teen seeing the destruction and potential disaster caused by the romantic duping, and stepping back.

Conclusion

So, the phrase "dawning of desire" may refer both to the teens and their elders. For teens, desire may dawn with the onset of puberty and new social roles moving from family of origin to peers in order one day to establish their own families. For elders, an altruistic desire, or intent, called positive generativity (Erikson, 1968) may dawn. Then elder influence nurtures the development of healthy sexuality in teens rather than either avoiding the issue or selfishly exploiting teens for economic gains and as sexual objects in sexualization. Sexuality is healthy; sexualization is not. Teens are not just pocket books nor stimuli currency. Teens are humans, deserving respect, understanding, and relaxed oversight.

Teens deserve elders' respect, attention, and guidance. One day the roles will reverse, and teens will be the caretakers of the elders. Then cultural karma will "pay back" the treatment afforded the teens by elders. Truly how we treat our teens today may be how they treat us tomorrow.

Mary Banks Gregerson, PhD, Leavenworth, KS, is 2009–2012 Treasurer for the American Psychological Association (APA) Division 46 Media Psychology and the 2008–2011 Council Representative for the APA Division 10 Society for the Psychological Study of Aesthetics, Creativity, and the Arts.

References

Almaas, A. H. (2000). Holding environment. *Facets of unity: The ennegram of holy ideas*. Boston, MA: Shambala Publications.

American Psychological Association Task Force on the Sexualization of Girls. (2007). *Report of the APA task force on the sexualization of girls*. Washington, DC: American Psychological Association. Accessed on July 27, 2008, from www.apa.org/pi/wpo/sexualization.html

Andre, T., Dietsch, C., & Cheng, Y. (1991). Sources of sex education as a function of sex, coital activity, and type of information. *Contemporary educational psychology, 16*, 215–240.

Andre, T., Frevert, R. L., & Schuchmann, D. (1989). From whom have college students learned what about sex? *Youth and society, 20*, 241–268.

Ballard, S. M., & Morris, M. L. (1998). Sources of sexuality information for university students. *Journal of sex education and therapy, 23*, 278–287.

Bandura, A. (1977). *Social learning theory.* New Jersey: Prentice Hall.

Bradner, C. H., Ku, L., & Lindberg, L. D. (2000). Older, but not wiser: How men get information about AIDS and sexually transmitted diseases after high school. *Perspectives on sexual and reproductive health, 32*, 33–38.

Buerkel-Rothfuss, N. L., Greenberg, B. S., Atkin, C. K., & Neuendorf, K. (1982). Learning about the family from television. *Journal of communication, 32*(3), 191–201.

Carr, D. (2003, October 20). Maxim's 'hidden' cover spoofs breathless headlines. *New York times*, p. C1

CBC Marketplace. (2005, January 9). Your finance: Marketing to kids. *Broadcast.*

Chapin, J. (2000a). Adolescent sex and mass media a developmental approach. Adolescence, Winter. Accessed on August 28, 2008 at http://www.findarticles.com/p/articles/mi_m2248/is_140_35/ai_70777841

Chapin, J. (2000b). Third-person perception and optimistic bias among urban minority at-risk youth. *Communication research, 27*(1), 51–81.

Dean, B. (2008). Vitality. *Getting to know creativity newsletter. Series introduction,* 2(12). Accessed on August 28, 2008. http://www.coachingtowardhappiness.com/AHC/vol2num26.htm

Donnerstein, H. (2002). The Internet. In V. C. Strasburger & B. J. Wilson (Eds.), *Children, adolescents, and the media* (pp. 301–321). Thousand Oaks, CA: Sage.

Donnerstein, E., & Smith, S. (2001). Sex in the media: Theory, influences, and solutions. In D. Singer & J. Singer (Eds.), *Handbook of children and the media* (pp. 289–307). Thousand Oaks, CA: Sage Publications.

Durham, M. G. (1998). Dilemmas of desire: Representations of adolescent sexuality in two teen magazines. *Youth and Society, 29*, 369–389.

Elliott, M. R. (2003). Causality and how to model it. *BT technology journal, 21*(2), 120–125.

Erikson, E. (1968). *Identity, youth and crisis.* New York: Norton.

Escobar-Chavez, S. L., Tortolero, S. R, Markham, C. M., Low, B. J., Eitel, P., & Thickstun, P. (2005). Impact of the media on adolescent sexual attitudes and behaviors. *Pediatrics, 116*(1), 303–326.

Festinger, L. (1954). A theory of social comparison processes. *Human relations, 7*(2), 117–140.

Fay, J., & Yanoff, J. M. (2000). What are teens telling us about sexual health? Results of the Second Annual Youth Conference of the Pennsylvania Coalition to Prevent Teen Pregnancy. *Journal of sex education and therapy, 25*(2/3), 169–177.

Fredrickson, B. L., & Roberts, T. A. (1997). Objectification theory: Toward understanding women's lived experience and mental health risks. *Journal of women quarterly, 21*, 173–206.

Gagnon, J., & Simon, W. (1987). The sexual scripting of oral genital contacts. *Archives of sexual behavior, 16*, 1–25.

Gamble, J. M. (2007, August). Holding environment as home: Maintaining a seamless blend across the virtual/physical divide. *M/C journal: A journal of media and culture 10*(4), http://journal.media-culture.org.au/0708/11-gamble.php Accessed August 25, 2008. Posted August 26, 2008.

Garner, A., Sterk, H. M., & Adams, S. (1998). Narrative analysis of sexual etiquette in teenage magazines. *Journal of communication, 48*, 59–78.

Gawker. (2008). *Is this man gay? Watch gossip girls Mondays at 8pm on The CW to (not) find out!* Accessed on August 9, 2008. http://gawker.com/364202/is-this-man-gay-watch-gossip-girl-mondays-at-8-on-the-cw-to-not-find-out.

Gerbner, G., Gross, L., Morgan, M., & Signorielli, N. (1994). Growing up with television: The cultivation perspective. In J. Bryant & D. Zillman (Eds.), *Media effects: Advances in theory, and research (*pp. 17–41). Hillsdale, NJ: Lawrence Erlbaum Assoc.

Gow, J. (1990). The relationship between violent and sexual images and the popularity of music videos. *Popular Music and Society, 14*, 1–9.

Gow, J. (1996). Reconsidering gender roles on MTV Depictions in the most popular music videos of the early 1990s. *Communication reports, 9*, 151–161.

Graydon, S. (2004). *In your face: The culture of beauty and you.* Toronto, ON, Canada: Annick Press.

Greenberg, B., Richards, M., & Henderson, L. (1980). Trends in sex-role portrayals on television. In B. Greenberg (Ed.), *Life on television: content analyses of U.S. drama* (pp. 65–88). Norwood, NJ: Ablex.

Greenberg, B. S., Stanley, C., Siemicki, M., Heeter, C., Soderman, A., & Linsangan, R. (1993a). Sex content on soaps and primetime television series most viewed by adolescents. In B. S. Greenberg, J. D. Brown, N. L. Buerkel-Rothfus, (Eds.), *Media, sex, and the adolescent.* (pp. 29–44). Cresskill, NJ: Hampton Press.

Greenberg, B. S., Siemicki, M., Dorfman, S., Heeter, C., Lin, C., Stanley, C., et al. (1993b). Sex content in R-rated films viewed by adolescents. In B. S. Greenberg, J. D. Brown & N. L. Buerkel-Rothfuss (Eds.), *Media, sex and the adolescent* (pp. 45–58). Cresskill, NJ: Hampton Press, Inc.

Greene, B. (2000). African American lesbian and bisexual women. *Journal of social issues, 56*, 239–250.

Greeson, L. E., & Williams, R. A. (1986). Social implications of music videos for youth: An analysis of the content and effects of MTV. *Youth & society, 18*, 177–189.

Hernstein, R. J. (1970). On the law of effect. *Journal of experimental analysis of behavior, 13*, 243–266.

Hill, J. (1983). Early adolescence: A research agenda. *Journal of Early Adolescence, 3*, 1–21.

Hill Collins, P. (2004). *Black sexual politics: African-Americans, gender, and the new racism.* New York: Routledge.

Hurtado, A. (2003). Negotiating the color line. In A. Hurado (Ed.), *Voicing Chicana feminism: Young women speak out on sexuality and identity* (pp. 176–197). New York: New York University Press.

Hutson, A. C., & Wright, J. C. (1998). Mass media and children's development. In W. Damon, I. E. Sigel, & A. Renninger (Eds). *Handbook of child psychology, 5th ed., vol. 4 Child psychology in practice*, pp. 999–1058. Hoboken, NJ, US: John Wiley & Sons Inc.

Iyengar, S. (1991). *Is anyone responsible? How television frames political issues.* Chicago: University of Chicago Press.

Jung, C. G. (Author), Campbell, J. (Ed.), & Hull, R. F. C. (Trans.). (1976). *The portable Jung.* New York: Penguin (Non-classics).

Kaiser Family Foundation. (2002, May). *Survey on teen, sex, and TV.* Accessed May 23, 2002, from http://www.kff.org/entmedia/3229-index.cfm

Kaiser Family Foundation, Hoff, T., Green, L., & Davis, J. (2003). *National survey of adolescents and young adults: Sexual health knowledge, attitudes, and experiences.* Menlo Park, CA: Henry J. Kaiser Family Foundation.

Kim, J. L., & Ward, L. M. (2004). Pleasure reading: Associations between young women's sexual attitudes and their reading of contemporary women's magazines. *Psychology of woman quarterly, 28*, 48–58.

Kliff, S. (2008). Baby 101. *Newsweek WEB exclusive.* http://www.newsweek.com/id/145837. Accessed July 27, 2008.

Kingsbury, K. (2008, June 18). Pregnancy Boom at Glouster High. *Time Magazine.* http://www.time.com/time/world/article/0,8599,1815845,00.html. Accessed July 27, 2008.

Kosicki, G. (1993). Problems and opportunities in Agenda-setting research. *Journal of communication, 43*(2): 100–127.

Krassas, N. R., Blauwkamp, J. M., & Wesselink, P. (2001). Boxing Helena and corseting Eunice: Sexual rhetoric in Cosmopolitan and Playboy magazines. *Sex roles, 44*, 751–771.

Krassas, N. R., Blauwkamp, J. M., & Wesselink, P. (2003). "Master your Johnson:" Sexual rhetoric in *Maxim* and *Stuff* magazines. *Sexuality & culture, 7*, 98–119.

Kushner, H. S. (1983). *When bad things happen to good people.* New York: Avon.

Lin, S. S. J., & Tsai, C. C. (2002). Sensation seeking and Internet dependence of Taiwanese high school adolescents. *Computers in human behavior, 18*, 411–426.

Lowry, D., & Towles, D. (1989). Soap opera portrayals of sex, contraception, and sexually transmitted diseases. *Journal of communication, 39*(2), 76–83.

Lu, A. (2008). *Jamie Lynn Spears' new motherhood role seems glamorized in new magazine interview.* AHN Media Corporation. http://www.allheadlinenews.com/articles/7011557419. Accessed July 27, 2008.

Malamuth, N., & Impett, E. (2001). Research on sex in the media: What do we know about effects on children and adolescents? In D. Singer & J. Singer (Eds.), *Handbook of children and the media* (pp. 289–307). Thousand Oaks, CA: Sage Publications.

McKinley, N. M., & Hyde, J. S. (1996). The objectified body consciousness scale. *Psychology of women quarterly, 20*, 181–215.

Neilson Media Research. (1998). *1998 Report on television.* New York: Author.

Norem, J. K. (2002). *The positive power of negative thinking: Using defensive pessimism to harness anxiety and perform at your peak.* New York: Basic Books.

OK! Magazine. (2007, December 18). *World exclusive: Jamie Lynn Spears–"I'm pregnant!".* http://www.okmagazine.com/news/view/3425. Accessed July 27, 2008.

Pardun, C. J., & McKee, K. B. (1995). Strange bedfellows: Symbols of religion and sexuality on MTV. *Youth & society, 26*, 438–449.

Pardun, C. J., L'Engle, K. L., & Brown, J. D. (2005). Linking exposure to outcomes: Early adolescents' consumption of sexual content in six media. *Mass communication & society, 8*(2), 75–91.

People magazine. (2006, October 6). *Whale rider's keisha castle-hughes expecting.* http://www.people.com/people/article/0,26334,1543222,00.html. Accessed July 27, 2008.

Petersen, J., Moore, K., & Furstenberg, F. (1991). Television viewing and early initiation of sexual intercourse: Is there a link? *Journal of homosexuality, 21*(1/2), 92–118.

Peterson, C., & Seligman, M. E. P. (Eds.). (2004). *Character strengths and virtues: A handbook and classification.* New York: Oxford University Press.

Plous, S., & Neptune, D. (1997). Racial and gender biases in magazine advertising: A content analytic study. *Psychology of women quarterly, 21*, 62–644.

Random house unabridged dictionary. (2006). New York, NY: Random House.

Roberts, D. (2000). Media and youth: Access, exposure, and privatization. *Journal of adolescent health, 27*(2), 8–14.

Roberts, D., Foehr, U., & Rideout, V. (2005, March). *Generation M: Media in the lives of 8–18 year olds.* Menlo Park, CA: Kaiser Family Foundation.

Rubin, A. M. (2002). The uses-and-gratifications perspective of media effects. In J. Bryant & D. Zillmann (Eds.), *Media effects: Advances in theory and research* (2nd ed., pp. 525–548). Mahwah, NJ: Erlbaum.

Ryan, R. M., & Frederick, C. (1997). On energy, personality, and health: Subjective vitality as a dynamic reflection of well-being. *Journal of personality, 65*, 529–565.

Satcher, D. (2001). *The surgeon general's call to action to promote sexual health and responsible sexual behavior.* Washington, DC: U.S. Department of Health and Human Services, Office of the Surgeon General. Retrieved from www.surgeongeneral.gov/library/sexualhealth/call.pdf

Sherman, B. L., & Dominick, J. R. (1986). Videos and sex in music videos: TV and rock 'n'roll. *Journal of communication, 36*, 79–93.

Sommers-Flanagan, R., Sommers-Flanagan, J., & Davis, B. (1993). What's happening on music television? A gender role content analysis. *Sex roles, 28*, 745–753.

Spanier, G. B. (1977). Sources of sex information and premarital sexual behavior. *Journal of sex research, 13*, 73–88.

Spence, J., & Buckner, C. (2000). Instrumental and expressive traits, trait stereotypes, and sexist attitudes: What do they signify? *Psychology of women quarterly, 24,* 44–63.

Steele, J. R. (1999). Teenage sexuality and media practice: Factoring in the influences of family, friends and school. *The journal of sex research, 36,* 331–341.

Steele, J. R. (2002). Teens and movies: Something to do, plenty to learn. In J. D. Brown, J. R. Steele, & K. Walsh-Childers (Eds.), *Sexual teens, sexual media: Investigating media's influence on adolescent sexuality. LEA's communication series,* pp.227–252. Mahwah, NJ, US: Lawrence Erlbaum Associates Publishers.

Steele, J., & Brown, J. (1995). Adolescent room culture: Studying media in the context of everyday life. *Journal of youth and adolescence, 24*(5), 551–576.

Thorndike, E. L. (1898). Animal intelligence: An experimental study of the associative processes in animals. *Psychological review Monograph supplement, 8,* 1–109.

Treise, D., & Gotthoffer, A. (2002). Stuff you couldn't ask your parents: Teens talking about using magazines for sex information. In J. D. Brown, J. R. Steele, & K. Walsh-Childers (Eds.), *Sexual teens, sexual media: Investigating media's influence on adolescent sexuality* (pp. 173–189). Mahwah, NJ: Erlbaum.

US magazine. (2008a, July 27). *Chace Crawford and Ed Westwick Gay Rumors "Absolutely Untrue."* Accessed July 27, 2008.

US magazine. (2008b, March 26). *JC Chasez: I'm "not dating" Chace Crawford,* Accessed July 27, 2008.

Vincent, R. C. (1989). Clio's consciousness raised? Portrayal of women in rock videos, reexamined. *Journalism quarterly, 66,* 155–160.

Ward, M. (1995). Talking about sex: Common themes about sexuality in the prime-time television programs children and adolescents view most. *Journal of youth and adolescence, 24,* 595–615.

Wilz, T. (2007, January 6). Divas of disaster: People just can't look away from the train wreck girls. *Washington post,* C01.

Winchester, M. D. (1995). Hully gee, It's a WAR! The yellow kid and the coining of yellow journalism, *Inks: Cartoon and comic art studies, 2*(3), 22–37.

Winnicott, D. W. (1975). The concept of a healthy individual. In C. Winicott, R. Shepherd, & M. Davis, *D.W. Winnicott: Home is where we start from: Essays by a psychoanalyst.* New York: Penguin.

Lives Through Film: *49 UP* and the *UP* Series as a Longitudinal Study of Personality and Social Change

Kevin Lanning, Samantha A. Montgomery, Justin Bright, Lenore Broming, Misty Hudelson, Rachel E. Pauletti, Garreth Rosenzweig, and Rachel Starkings

Abstract In this chapter we examine the *UP* series of documentary films, a longitudinal examination of the lives of 14 British individuals. The first film, *7 UP!*, depicted participants at age 7 and was produced in 1963. The most recent, *49 UP*, was produced in 2005. We consider the value and the limitations of the series as a study of personality development and describe the trajectories of the lives of three participants in some detail.

In 1963, Granada Television produced *7 UP!* (Almond, 1964), a documentary portrait of a group of 7-year-old English schoolchildren. The program was an episode of Granada's then-innovative *World in Action* series; it was intended both as a study of the effects of social class and as a preview of what was to come of England in the year 2000. In that first film, ten boys and four girls participated, a gender bias reflective of the difference in expectations and opportunities for men and women of the time and place.

At this writing, all but a few of the participants in that first film have returned to participate at 7-year intervals. Following *7 UP!* (Almond, 1964), came *7 Plus Seven* (Apted, 1970), *21 UP* (Apted, 1977), *28 UP* (Apted, 1984), *35 UP* (Apted, 1991), *42 UP* (Apted, 1998), and in 2005, *49 UP* (Apted, 2007).[1] When viewed as a series, the films document not only the charms of childhood, but also the crises of adolescence, emerging adulthood, and middle age. At this writing, most of the participants have become parents and some are grandparents. Each has been seen coping with loss: Most have suffered the death of one or both parents, some have seen marriages falter, a few have left the country of their birth, and some struggle with problems of health and mobility. We have seen them achieve and struggle in the world of work, deriving both satisfaction and frustration from their career paths as they now begin contemplation of retirement.

K. Lanning (✉)
WB 218, Wilkes Honors College, Florida Atlantic University, Jupiter, FL 33458, USA
e-mail: lanning@fau.edu

[1] The films are available on DVD as a boxed set from http://firstrunfeatures.com/UPseries.html.

M.B. Gregerson (ed.), *The Cinematic Mirror for Psychology and Life Coaching*,
DOI 10.1007/978-1-4419-1114-8_5, © Springer Science+Business Media, LLC 2010

Taken together, the *UP* series is a remarkable achievement, one that film critic Roger Ebert has called "an inspired, even noble use of the film medium" (Ebert, 1998).

Yet while the aesthetic and dramatic value of the *UP* series seems clear, its value for counseling psychologists and others in the helping professions may not be self-evident. What can a series of films – any films – tell us about personality strengths and optimal development? And what, if anything, can we learn from this particular series of brief film portraits of different participants at different ages, each facing different problems, and each responding to different cues by the filmmakers?

In the present essay, we consider the significance of the film series for counseling and clinical psychologists. We address both potential therapeutic applications of the films and reflect upon its contribution to our understanding of personality and social development. Finally, we consider a positive psychology standpoint, exploring some of the ways in which watching the film series may itself be an avenue toward psychological growth.

The UP Series and Psychology

For the psychologist, the films of the *UP* series can be considered to provide a large and unusual longitudinal data set that highlights the complexities and patterns within a number of individual lives. Within each film, each scene can be understood in terms of a particular participant at a particular time and in a particular place. Reflecting the complexity of both the everyday interpretation of behavior and more formal longitudinal studies of development, the broad parameters of place, age, and time are typically confounded or linked. When, for example, we observe that Lynn and Jackie are both married by *21 UP* while Andrew, Bruce, and John are attending university, we cannot know of the extent to which these outcomes are a product of the different backgrounds of the participants, the expectations of the culture in which they lived, or the time this particular episode was filmed.

Each installment of the series can be seen as a time capsule. Taken together, the series illuminates both cultural consistency and change. Changes in style, in clothing, mannerisms, and hairstyles, are quickly seen, while deeper cultural changes emerge more slowly. Nonetheless, we recognize evolving attitudes toward single parenthood and working mothers, the impact of increasing globalization and new technologies, and, beneath it all, the still pervasive effects of social class. These cultural effects remind us of the importance of time, place, and setting in understanding our own lives and the lives of others.

Quantifying Impressions Using the California Q-Set

In our own viewings of the *UP* series, we have used Block's (1971) *Lives through Time* study as a template for structuring the data and articulating our perceptions of the participants. In that earlier study, Block analyzed several large and heterogeneous archival studies of personality development, rating each participant on each occasion using the items of the California Child and Adult Q-sets (CCQ and CAQ, respectively). These measures rely upon an ipsative methodology, in which ratings are assigned in the framework of individual lives rather than in comparison with other persons.

For our purposes, the items of the CCQ and CAQ function as a robust, standard, and largely comprehensive language for examining personality (Block, 1961, 2008; Lanning, 1994). We can use Q-sets to assess stability and change, for example, by comparing the ratings of a particular *UP* series participant at ages 21 and 49. Similarly, we can use Q-sets to compare women and men, the upper class and the working class, or those with and without children. In studies of personality development, Q-sets have been used to quantify the extent to which a person fits into a particular type. Q-sets can also be used to examine the correspondence with a preexisting personality "ideal" or prototype, such as the *Optimally Adjusted* person, who is characterized by dependability, insight, ethical behavior, and a capacity for close relationships.

For the present purposes, it is instructive to consider the Q-set items judged to be most characteristic of the participants in the *UP* series. Eight undergraduate college students each rated two target participants at each age, using the CCQ for the 7- and 14-year olds and the CAQ for the remaining ages. In Table 1, the most characteristic items are listed for each age; because of space limitations, only three items are shown, necessarily providing only a glimpse into the participants and how they are seen. The content of these items appears to be multiply determined, reflecting not only the developing personalities of the participants, but also the time and culture in which the films were made and the increasingly strong attachment felt by the raters toward the targets. At ages 7 and 14, our raters were impressed by the children's deference, at 21, by their intelligence, and from ages 28 through 42 their responsibility. Beginning at age 35, the participants are seen as compassionate. Finally, at age 49, raters are struck by the ethical codes of the participants. Although this portrait is necessarily skeletal, it suggests increasing depth and desirability, something which is also seen in the correspondence between the profile for each age and the *Optimally Adjusted* prototype: Although participants are seen positively at every age, this is particularly true for the adults beginning at age 35.

Our quantitative analyses of the *UP* series, based on systematic ratings using Q-sets and other measures, have been illuminating. Despite a limited sample size, the data are coherent in a number of respects. For example, the participants typically show greater resemblance on adjacent (7-year) occasions than over broader (14, 21, etc.) periods. A particularly striking finding is that participants from the same social class appear more similar over time, suggesting that the role of social class becomes greater rather than smaller over the life course (Lanning et al., 2006). These findings notwithstanding, a purely quantitative approach cannot do justice to the series, cannot provide a comprehensive portrait of the participants, and can only provide a starting point for the counselor, life coach, or clinician.

Table 1 Q-set items most characteristic of *UP* Series participants at ages 7–49

Age	Item text
Age 7	Is open and straightforward
	Is obedient and compliant
	Is an interesting, arresting child
Age 14	Is obedient and compliant
	Behaves in a feminine/masculine style and manner
	Is open and straightforward
Age 21	Is verbally fluent; can express ideas well in words
	Appears to have a high degree of intellectual capacity
	Is calm, relaxed in manner
Age 28	Is dependable and responsible
	Is calm, relaxed in manner
	Has insight into and understands own needs, motives, behavior; knows self well
Age 35	Has warmth; has the capacity for close relationships; compassionate
	Is dependable and responsible
	Appears straightforward, candid, frank in dealing with others
Age 42	Is dependable and responsible
	Has a clear-cut internally consistent personality
	Has warmth; has the capacity for close relationships; compassionate
Age 49	Has warmth; has the capacity for close relationships; compassionate
	Interested in members of the opposite sex
	Behaves ethically; has a personal value system and is faithful to it

Note: Entries are the highest scored Q-set items in 16 separate sets of ratings. For ages 7 and 14, items are drawn from the California Child Q-Set (CCQ); for the remaining years, items are from the California Adult Q-set (CAQ).

Three Lives in Progress

The group of participants initially profiled in 7 *UP!* was chosen with the intention of sampling different social classes and, as previously noted, was biased in favor of boys over girls. Beyond this effect, the sampling criteria are unclear. While each participant is in her or his own way compelling and charismatic, space constraints limit us to considering only three in any detail.

Neil

Arguably the most fascinating and challenging of the 14 lives profiled in the series is that of Neil. At age 7, Neil is seen as talkative and full of childlike wonder. He tells us that living in the city is good because its numerous overhangs allow one to be outside in the rain without getting wet, and when asked about "colored people" he giggles about people with purple faces. His career aspirations are a mix of the conventional and the idiosyncratic, as he considers the possibilities not only of becoming an astronaut but also a coach driver. While both jobs describe a theme of adventure or wanderlust that will play an important role in Neil's life, the second of these is in some ways more telling. The aspiration to become a "coach driver" appeals to Neil because he could enjoy taking people to the seaside and "telling them about everything." On the Q-set, he is described as emotionally expressive, vital, and autonomous (see Fig. 1).

Fig. 1 Neil at 14 (printed with permission from First Run Features/www.first run features.com)

Seven years later, Neil is more serious. We see him playing chess and speaking of the importance of competition, of the need to keep working. Although he does not seem as happy, on the Q-set he is nonetheless seen as intelligent, warm, and tending to arouse liking and acceptance in adults.

As previously noted, the *UP* series provides not only profiles of individual lives, but also time capsules of particular occasions and, confounded with this, pictures of particular ages or stages in the life cycle. The challenges of early adulthood are apparent in watching *21 UP*, which is in some ways the saddest of all the films in the series. Here, as in no other film, the modal participant appears to be struggling with both normative and idiosyncratic life crises. No participant embodies this more dramatically than Neil, who at 21 is a drifter seeking to find fulfillment. He lives in an abandoned "squat" and appears unable, unwilling, or uninterested in living the life laid out for him. He claims to feel satisfied, yet his words seem hollow; he speaks with resentment and bitterness when he discusses his parents and his failure to complete university. Though trying to keep up appearances, Neil seems increasingly disconnected from the lives of those who would care about him. On the Q-set, he is seen as introspective, concerned, and ruminative.

The happy Neil that was seen in *7 UP!* is gone in *28 UP* – not only to the viewer, but, more importantly, to Neil himself. It is, in the words of one of the raters watching the series, "heartbreaking." He has withdrawn further. On the Q-set, he is seen as needing his own autonomy, as unpredictable, introspective, as avoiding others, and as anxious. We see his distress manifest at a molecular or behavioral level in his rocking to-and-fro, and at a more molar level in his homelessness and geographic isolation. He tells us that he will never have children, for no matter how perfect a woman the mother might be, the children still would be likely – and here he speaks haltingly – to inherit something from him. The cinematography accentuates his struggles. Neil is small, framed by a panoramic sky above a Scottish Loch. He is alone, unbuffered in his solitude against the vicissitudes of nature. Frankly, we fear for him.

Seven years later we find, in *35 UP*, that Neil is doing more than merely hanging-on. He is living in a council flat, no longer itinerant. He is more engaged with others and is acting in community theater. Though we begin to get a sense of his resilience, we recognize that he is still deeply troubled: When asked if he feels like he is going insane, Neil responds that he "doesn't think it, [he] knows it." He is again seen as introspective and ruminative, and here as moody as well.

The arc of Neil's life continues to swing upwards when we see him in *42 UP.* Here, Neil is involved in local politics as a Liberal Democratic member of the Hackney council. His faith plays an increasingly central role in shaping his everyday life, as does his long-held social interest. (When asked why he got involved in politics, Neil claimed that he was unhappy with the government, so he felt that he should participate). He is still anxious, though it is anxiety that now seems bounded, and perhaps more importantly, is no longer entirely dystonic but subjectively sensible. He says that, of course, he gets nervous when he speaks, but that this is a good thing, presumably because it implies a sensitivity to the audience. He tells us that he has never been busier or in contact with so many people. Here, he is again seen as introspective, but also as intellectually capable, self-aware, arousing of nurturance, and as ethically consistent.

In the most recent episode, we find Neil once again in the countryside. But, unlike 21 years earlier, he now seems in harmony with nature and not overwhelmed. At the end of *49 UP*, Neil reminds is that "life comes once, and it's quite short, so you have to appreciate what's good in it." He seems to have a sense of purpose, perhaps even optimism. On the Q-set, he is still seen as moody and introspective, but also as concerned with deep issues, interesting, and intelligent.

Jackie

Though the early films in the series give relatively little screen time to the female participants, Jackie's charisma and charm are immediately apparent in *7 UP!* In the episode shot in 1963, Jackie is extraverted and open, eager not merely to express her opinions about boys, but also to give voice to her progressive social beliefs. She tells us that if she had money "she would give it to the poor people," and speaks out against racism. On the Child Q-set, she is seen as feminine, warm, cheerful, and sociable.

Seven years later, in *7 Plus Seven*, we find Jackie attending a comprehensive school, giggling about boys, and describing her wish to merely "live comfortably" when she is older. Here, in addition to the themes seen as characteristic at 7, she is also described as responsive to humor, open, and assertive.

Jackie at age 21 is still extraverted, but is now struggling with the normative crises of intimacy and identity. She is married and seen establishing a home in Essex with her husband. Although she has been working in a bank for the last three and a half years, she emphasizes her domestic role and even shows off her planned nursery. She displays her sense of humor in discussing the collapse of the cake on her wedding day, but there is a moment of tension as well. Her ratings here are less favorable, appearing defensive and sensitive to criticism (see Fig. 2).

Fig. 2 Jackie at 21 (printed with permission from First Run Features/www.first run features.com)

At 28, Jackie continues to be married. She does not have children, which she explains as due to her own "selfishness." She appears content with her work in an insurance company, though she does not express ambition to advance further. At this stage in her life, she shows little correspondence with the normative paths described by Helson's *Feminine Social Clock* or *Masculine Occupational Clock* (Helson, Mitchell, & Moane, 1984). As a young adult freed from the issues of adolescence, Jackie is increasingly autonomous and reflective, less concerned with self-presentation than with self-understanding. She is seen on the Q-set as assertive and candid.

The departure from convention, and perhaps toward fulfillment, continues in *35 UP*. We find that Jackie is a single mother, divorced, and having had a son following a brief romance. Motherhood has changed her life, yet is not without its challenges. She is struggling financially and now works at a pub to make ends meet. She mourns the loss of her own mother to cancer while appreciating the support of her father in her life. In response to Apted's questions about the difficulties of the working class, Jackie is now less defensive and more willing to acknowledge the social constraints she has personally faced. While recognizing that the rich have more choices, she is not envious. Rather, she emphasizes the need for people to make the best of what they have. She is resilient in the face of financial and emotional hardship. Raters again describe her as candid, but also as gregarious and protective.

At 42, Jackie is seen at the breakfast table, serving cereal to three young boys, with the two younger children added since the prior episode. We learn that Jackie is no longer romantically involved with Ian, the father of the two younger boys, but that he continues to play an important role in their family. Ian lives not far from Jackie and the boys, all in rural Scotland in a place which is reminiscent, for Jackie, of how the East End of her childhood used to be, that is, child-friendly and safe. She takes pride in her children while hoping to push them harder than she was pushed academically. Although Jackie suffers both financial and physical hardships, she nonetheless rejects pity and remains adamant that she is not depressed about her life choices. She finds a purpose in her children, something a mere 14 years earlier she thought she would never do. The Q-set items here echo those from prior years: She is seen as candid, assertive, and protective.

In *49 UP*, we find that Jackie still lives in Scotland where she continues to raise her three sons with the support of their father. We appreciate both the idiosyncracy and the coherence of Jackie's family. While Ian is not Charlie's biological father, and does not live with Jackie and her sons, Ian acts as – is – the father to all three boys. Meanwhile, Ian's mother, Liz, serves at least three important roles: She is an involved grandparent to the boys, a source of financial support, and a friend and companion for Jackie.

Perhaps because of the security of this safety net provided to Jackie by her family, perhaps too because of Director Apted's own changing notions of his role in the series, Jackie achieves something important in *49 UP*. In an escape from the role of passive subject, she talks to Apted about their relationship with each other, reminding him of an episode that occurred in *21 UP*, in which Apted insensitively had asked Jackie if she felt that she had "missed out" by marrying young. One senses this earlier slight had colored the relationship between the two of them for fully 28 years. Our raters again describe her as candid and assertive, but also appreciate her directness in a way that they did not previously. When Director Apted defers to her and asks what she would like to discuss, Jackie speaks of her goals for the future, including returning to school.

Bruce

In 1963, we meet Bruce as a gentle and jug-eared 7-year old in a boarding school where he studies Latin grammar, exercises unsmilingly, and obeys while suffering the minor brutalities imposed upon him in what appears to be a rigid and authoritarian environment. Religious faith plays an important role for this sensitive boy who, in a comment reflecting the vestiges of colonialism, tells us that he aspires to missionary work, to "teach people who are not civilized to be more or less 'good.' " He seems unhappy and tells us that he wants nothing more than "to see [his] Daddy, who lives six thousand miles from here." On the Q-set, he is seen as involved in what he does, concerned with moral issues, and easily victimized by other children.

At 14, Bruce appears introspective, serious and soft-spoken, traits which seem to make the changes of adolescence even more challenging. He tells us that he no longer feels that he could do missionary work, since he does not consider himself a good public speaker. Despite his doubts, he continues to be socially engaged, telling us that he sides with the Labour party and does not agree with the social and racial policies of the Conservatives. He does not have a girlfriend yet, but tells us that he is "sure it will come." In addition to the moral concerns noted at 7, he is described at 14 as obedient, empathic, and solitary.

Seven years later we find 21-year-old Bruce studying Mathematics. He seems cognitively mature yet socially vulnerable, in some ways even childlike in his countenance. He tells us that he has never fallen in love or even misbehaved and that he would like to become a mapmaker and travel the world. But still there is doubt, for he tells us that his dreams are unlikely to be realized. He is seen as protective, giving, and concerned with deep issues.

In *28 UP* we learn that the boy who wanted to improve the lot of others is now using his Oxford education to teach underprivileged children in London's East End. He is again seen as concerned with deep issues, but also as ethically consistent and aware of his own motives.

In *35 UP* we find that this path has taken him to Bangladesh. Here, his attitude toward the people and the place can no longer be characterized by the patronizing vision of his childhood: He aims not merely to help others to become "civilized," but to attain something more symmetrical or reciprocal. We see him not only teaching schoolchildren but also learning Bangla, and we believe him when he tells us that he has traveled to overcome his fear of the unfamiliar. The viewer senses that his fears extend to and explain his continuing failure to find love. In addition to the Q-set items characteristic of him at 21 and 28, he is seen as "arousing liking in others." Yet Bruce seems lonely and is still looking for a partner.

At age 42 he has found her, or perhaps she – Penny – has found him. Their wedding appears as one of the more dramatic moments of the series, one in which the long-suffering nice guy not only gets the girl, but is presented as truly heroic. As the camera pans across the wedding party we see none other than Neil, whom Bruce befriended and who is on the road to recovery. On the Q-set, Bruce is seen in broadly favorable terms: intelligent, ethical, dependable, warm, and relaxed.

At age 49, Bruce's life has turned inward; his pro-sociality is now narrower in its focus. He has moved out of the East End and is now living in middle-class comfort, teaching the children of the affluent in one of England's oldest independent schools. We sense that he has traded his earlier idealism for a more commonplace and easier dream. He is now dedicated to his children, to his marriage, and, as a reminder that real lives possess a complexity that cannot be reduced to one single theme, to the game of cricket. Yet the Q-set items paint a more complex picture than seen at 42, with raters describing Bruce not only as warm and concerned with deep issues, but also as prone to guilt (see Fig. 3).

Fig. 3 Bruce at 49 (printed with permission from First Run Features/www.first run features.com)

Some Lessons from the Participants

In addition to providing information about personality development over time, the *UP* series also provides us with lessons from the lives of each of the participants. From Jackie, for example, we recognize that each family is unique not merely in its struggles, achievements, and secrets, but also in its very structure. We are reminded, too, of the challenges of understanding a person through the filter of film. From Bruce, we observe the calibration of life plans, the channeling of the pro-social, and perhaps the idea that virtue and altruism cannot, ultimately, be unbounded. Neil's story is evocative in many ways of the struggles seen and successes achieved in the lives of some of Carl Rogers' best known clients; in Neil one observes resilience, hope, and even wisdom.

While compelling, Jackie, Bruce, and Neil are not the only participants in the *UP! Series* to offer lessons to the viewer. Nick and Paul differentially view the impact of emigrating from their natal homeland; each reminds us of the importance of a sense of place. Tony and Lynn describe the profound sadness they felt on the deaths of their parents, while Suzy eventually becomes a grief counselor to help others in the coping process. Nick considers his divorce to be worse than the death of a spouse whereas Simon views his own divorce as an opportunity to start over. Jackie and Bruce both delight in their late arrival to parenthood, whereas Lynn and Tony relish the opportunity to act as young grandparents. Another compelling lesson is offered by Paul, who was first seen in a children's home at age 7 and who will become a shy and introverted adult; one senses that a solid and loving marriage has served as an important buffer against his proneness to depression. He reminds us, as do Bruce and Neil, of the power of relationships in shaping personality.

The lessons that counselors and clients can draw from the *UP* series are as varied as the clients themselves. In watching Nick, one sees the power of serendipity: He attributes his career as an academic and his expatriation, indeed, the opening of his eyes to a whole world beyond the Yorkshire Dales, to the simple fluke of being chosen for the film series. In watching John, we are reminded of the need to accommodate and sacrifice: For him, each new installment of the film is like "a little pill of poison" to be endured for a greater good. Neil's story illustrates resilience and evokes tenderness. There is hope reflected in his rear-view mirror of the car as he drives, autonomously and for the first time on screen at age 49. We are rapt when he shares the experience of watching a butterfly seem to take pleasure in the simple opening and closing of its own wings. He muses, "perhaps that's all there is to life . . . just being happy with what you are. That life goes on all around. That there are millions of creatures who all have to find their parts as well."

As Roger Ebert (1998) has said of the *UP* series, "anyone watching these films goes through a similar process of self-examination. *Why am I me and why not you? Why am I here and why not there?*" In our current work with the films, we are trying to understand what makes them so powerful. In particular, we are examining the hypothesis that watching the films constitutes something of a "life salience" induction antithetical to the mortality salience induction used in studies of terror management. The films remind us that we are directly related to other living things, eliciting feelings of humility. We feel compassion and concern for the welfare of the participants and hope that they can direct us to our own positive outcomes. By watching the participants successfully navigate the challenges of life, the *UP! Series* serves as a reminder of resiliency, a source of strength for those viewers who face similar struggles.

Final Remarks

While the effect of the series on participants is unknowable, the loss of privacy that they have suffered is evident. For most persons there can be nothing easy in the asymmetry of fame, in knowing *that* one is seen but not knowing *how*. And so it is appropriate to consider the almost existential question raised by John: "Do the films have any value?"

As an "objective" archive, surely their value must be called into question. Our understanding of the participants is biased not just by their self-presentation strategies, the intentions of the director, and our own needs, but also by the editor, whose role as a filter cannot be overestimated. In film as in everyday perception, the primary cognitive task lies in deciding what *not* to see (Erdelyi 1974; Ondaatje, 2002). With all of these filters – and with only a few minutes shown of each person on each occasion – it is clearly presumptuous to assume that one has a complete sense of these people's lives.

Yet despite this, we remain struck by the fact that for us the participants have become more than transient film images, statistical prototypes, or moral object lessons. They are recognized as familiar, that is, as members of the human family. Like another study of family in film, Steichen's 1955 photographic exhibit *The Family of Man*, the *UP* series fosters in the viewer not voyeurism but attachment, or, rather, connectedness, that is, the sense that others matter and that we are not alone. And so, for the next 7 years we will think of Bruce, Jackie, Neil, and the rest from time to time. Like lost relatives, we look forward to seeing them with warmth but also with apprehension, wondering how they have changed, and how we have changed as well.

References

Almond, P. (Director) (1964). *7 UP!* London: Granada Television.

Apted, M. (Director) (2007). *The UP series (7 UP! / 7 plus seven / 21 UP / 28 UP / 35 UP / 42 UP / 49 UP)*. New York: First Run Features.

Block, J. (1961). *The Q-sort method in personality assessment and psychiatric research*. Springfield, IL: Charles C. Thomas Publisher.

Block, J. (1971). *Lives through time*. Berkeley, CA: Bancroft Books.

Block, J. (2008). *The Q-sort in character appraisal: encoding subjective impressions of persons quantitatively*. Washington, DC: American Psychological Association.

Ebert, R. (1998). *The UP documentaries*. Retrieved June 3, 2008, from http://rogerebert. suntimes.com/apps/pbcs.dll/article?AID=/19981025/REVIEWS0 8/401010370/1023

Erdelyi, M. H. (1974). A new look at the new look: Perceptual defense and vigilance. *Psychological Review, 81*, 1–25.

Helson, R., Mitchell, V., & Moane, G. (1984). Personality and patterns of adherence and nonadherence to the social clock. *Journal of personality and social psychology, 46*, 1079–1096

Lanning, K. (1994). The dimensionality of observer ratings on the California Adult Q-Set. *Journal of personality and social psychology, 67*, 151–160.

Lanning, K., Bright, J. W., Broming, L. C., Hudelson, M. D., Evans, R. B., Rosenzweig, G. M.,et al. (2006). *Lives through film: 49 UP and the UP series as a longitudinal study of personality and social change*. Paper presented at the 114th annual meeting of the American Psychological Association, New Orleans, August.

Ondaatje, M. (2002). *The conversations: Walter Murch and the art of editing film*. New York: Knopf.

Steichen, E. (1955). *The family of man*. New York: The Museum of Modern Art.

Cinematherapy: Using Movie Metaphors to Explore Real Relationships in Counseling and Coaching

Judy Kuriansky, Amy Vallarelli, Jamie DelBuono, and Jeremy Ortman

Abstract In this chapter, "cinematherapy" is reviewed and evaluated as a tool and technique in therapy, counseling, and coaching to help individuals and couples become aware of and cope with real-life problems. In using this approach, film characters and scenarios present metaphors, or archetypes, which can serve as triggers for reflection and discussion. Specific details about the method of using this technique are presented, as well as case examples of assigning viewing of particular films for specific situations, for example, when facing dating, divorce, or abuse. Special issues are explored, including application of the technique in particular settings and with new client populations. Cautions in using the technique, and the need for systematic research, are also discussed.

Introduction

Individuals and couples face many problems in their relationships which present roadblocks to forming a deep and lasting bond. Often they pick inappropriate partners, perpetuate unhealthy patterns, or cannot communicate about personal or interpersonal issues in order to reach resolutions. Such issues are commonly presented in therapy, counseling, and coaching and are also often depicted in major motion pictures, making the use of commercial films as a tool in therapy potentially helpful and increasingly popular. This chapter describes this practice – commonly referred to as "cinematherapy" – and its theoretical underpinnings. Examples are given of major motion pictures, which can be appropriate for types of relationship issues presented in therapeutic sessions by individual clients and couples, particularly in cases which represent new trends in contemporary society. Case histories and new variations using techniques of cinematherapy are presented, and their value

J. Kuriansky (✉)
Teachers College, Columbia University, New York, NY 20017-6096, USA
e-mail: www.DrJudy.com

M.B. Gregerson (ed.), *The Cinematic Mirror for Psychology and Life Coaching*,
DOI 10.1007/978-1-4419-1114-8_6, © Springer Science+Business Media, LLC 2010

discussed in terms of facilitating healthy relationships (Kuriansky, 2002). The process of cinematherapy offers valuable opportunities for research to validate the techniques and establish their effectiveness.

Background

Motion pictures became a major part of the media culture in the 1920s, and since then have been considered to be a source of not only entertainment but also education for professionals and the public (Toman & Rak, 2000; Orchowski, Spickard, & McNamara, 2006). Movies have been used to educate and supervise counselors (Toman & Rak, 2000) as well as to teach topics like psychiatry and the law (Anderson, 1992) and clinical pharmacology (Koren, 1993). With the synergistic impact of images, music, dialogue, lighting, camera angles, and special effects, films elicit powerful reactions which engage viewers emotionally, physically, and cognitively (Tyson, Foster, & Jones, 2000). Films and film clips have been used in educational settings and classrooms, to demonstrate various issues relevant to course material (Wolz, 2004). Courses also specifically target this topic (King, 2008). For example, in one elective course given by two family medicine physicians on *Movies and Medicine: Using Film to Reflect on The Patient, The Family and Illness*, students watch selected films to discuss and learn how patients and their families are affected by illness (University of Connecticut, 2008).

The use of commercial films as lessons for patients in a therapeutic setting dates back to an early journal submission on the topic (Fritz & Pope, 1979). This approach began drawing increasing interest in the past two decades, with practitioners selecting commercial films for clients to view individually or with others as a means of therapeutic gain (Duncan, Beck, & Granum, 1986; Berg-Cross, Jennings, & Baruch, 1990). The modality has become increasingly popular and is now generally called "cinematherapy" both in the professional literature and in the popular culture (Sharp, Smith, & Cole, 2002; www.cinematherapy.com). The term is used in this chapter, given its ease of understanding and wide use; however, the word has been criticized since cinematherapy is more a tool than a therapeutic modality (Portadin, 2006). As a result, other terms have been offered. For example, since the technique involves a form of mass communication (like art and music), it has been described as a "popular culture intervention" (Dermer & Hutchings, 2000). The process has also been called "video work" (Hesley & Hesley, 2001), "reel therapy" (Solomon, 2001), and more recently an "e-motion picture" path to healing and transformation (Wolz, 2005).

Several journal articles and mass market books have been written about the process of cinematherapy, including a description of the process and lists of films which address particular life issues (Hesley & Hesley, 2001; Ulus, 2003; Wedding, Boyd, & Niemiec, 2005). In using this process, the practitioner carefully selects a film for the client to see which relates to core issues being dealt with in ongoing therapeutic interchanges. The film is then assigned to the client to view as "homework" between sessions and later used as a stimulus for discussion in therapy sessions. Mass market books have also suggested this technique for use not only by the professionals but also by the public, who select their own films for further exploration of an issue (Sturdevant & Gedron, 1998; Solomon, 2001; Teague, 2000; Wolz, 2005; Grace, 2005; Hendricks & Simon, 2005).

Uses of Cinematherapy

In its use of motion pictures produced by Hollywood production companies or independent producers, cinematherapy is distinct from the use of educational films in treatment, as the latter have a more direct message and are produced in an instructional manner. A major reason that major movie pictures are becoming a tool in therapy is their typically universal appeal and versatility in exploring such issues as culture, class, gender, power, and sexual orientation (Dermer & Hutchings 2000). Further, the film viewing can be integrated into any therapy modality and with varied populations, e.g., individuals, couples, and/or families.

It has been noted that there are different levels of intensity in using films for therapeutic change (Mann, 2004). Specifically, "popcorn cinema therapy" involves watching a movie for a needed emotional release; "evocative cinema therapy" involves using films to help people learn about themselves in more profound ways based on how they respond to different characters and scenes; and "cathartic cinema therapy" serves as a precursor or first stage in psychotherapy to open up different levels of emotions and the psyche.

Study Directions

The study of cinema as a tool in psychotherapy has taken several directions, including what movies reveal about cultural myths and collective fantasies; how they depict the practice of psychotherapy; and how they can be used in a clinical setting (Gabbard & Gabbard, 1999; Gabbard, 2001). Some psychologists even give courses about the psychological impact of film (Fischoff, n.d.). In cinematherapy, movies are used to familiarize clients with emotional problems they might have difficulty identifying in themselves but can spot more easily in film characters. By viewing a story similar to their own lives, clients may better be able to learn about and cope with their issues in an objective manner (Rizza, 1997). The film presents an opportunity for change by revealing issues in a nonthreatening way within the safety of distance so that difficult material and alternate ideas and behaviors can be processed indirectly at first, and then more directly processed. In this way, therapists can use movies to externalize problems so that clients can deal with problems from a safe distance (Dermer & Hutchings 2000).

Value of Cinematherapy

Movies further offer a shared language and experience for clients and therapists, which help solidify the therapeutic alliance (Berg-Cross et al., 1990). In addition, cinematherapy gives the client permission to talk about a particular issue, by providing validation that others have been through similar experiences and emotions. Furthermore, watching films provides the client with a powerful means of observational learning with opportunities to choose among different attitudes and behaviors. As such, the movie characters can plant seeds for growth, reframe problems, and model healthy problem-solving behaviors that clients may implement in their own lives (Newton, 1995).

Cinematherapy can be seen as an extension or continuation of the more established technique of bibliotherapy, whereby the client is assigned reading material which reveals characters dealing with similar conflicts and issues, in an effort to help the client better understand and cope with difficulties (Newton, 1995). The approach of bibliotherapy has been noted as applicable to other media, with the use of films offering advantages by providing stimulation on additional sensate levels (visual and auditory), making movies more impactful on people than other art forms (Wedding, Boyd, & Niemiec, 2005). Other advantages include increasing client compliance with a 2-hour movie assignment compared to reading lengthy written material, building on an activity people in popular culture already do frequently, making material accessible to people regardless of educational background or literacy level, and reaching clients difficult to reach emotionally because suspending problems while watching the film bypasses ordinary defensiveness (Dermer & Hutchings, 2000).

The Process and Dynamics of Cinematherapy

The therapeutic technique of cinematherapy uses the experience of processing content and character in films to help clients change negative beliefs, manage destructive emotions, raise insight, develop self-esteem, and rediscover strengths (Dermer & Hutchings, 2000). Through discussing the film, clients can reframe issues and explore alternative solutions to problems, guided by meaningful processing with the therapist (Newton, 1995). It has been pointed out that television viewers can recognize and learn about their personality style from characters with whom they identify (Young, 1987). The practitioner's steps in using films for counseling or coaching have been identified as involving three stages: assessment (of the client and of goals in therapy), implementation (assigning the film), and debriefing (discussing the impact of the film in subsequent sessions) (Caron, 2005).

Watching a film has been described as a dissociative state in which reality is temporarily suspended and viewers perceive events as though they are inside the movie surrounded by the characters in the film (Wedding, Boyd, & Niemiec, 2005). Through identification with characters, individuals project themselves into the action. The film draws the client into the viewing experience and at the same time affords a unique opportunity to retain a perspective outside the experience. As such, the film can help clients better understand their lives, provide catharsis or perspective, and suggest corrective thinking and feeling.

Watching characters in a film becomes a form of vicarious learning for the viewer, as described in social learning theory whereby the viewer models behavior after the characters (Bandura, 1977). In this context, the viewer's process has been described in three steps: projection, identification, and introjection (Ulus, 2003). In the projection phase, the viewer's thoughts, affects, and beliefs are triggered by the events and characters in the film. In the identification phase, the viewer accepts or rejects the characters as relating to oneself, feeling like the character in the film without necessarily conscious awareness. In the introjection phase, the viewer adopts the experiences in the film into his/her own world. Within the therapeutic sessions, the therapist can help the patient work through lessons from each of these stages and resolve issues to help decrease painful emotions (depression or anger) or incorporate positive experiences (self-confidence, self-esteem, empowerment) evoked by these processes.

The plot of the film may not exactly represent the client's life but can serve as a metaphor for an important aspect. Metaphors have been used in psychotherapy for decades to convey meaning to the symbolic, creative parts of the brain while bypassing more analytic and logical parts (Groth-Marnat, 1992). In cases where clients resist messages and interpretations by intellectualizing or denial, metaphors provide a valuable less direct form of communication which speaks to more receptive parts of the personality and allows more open discussion.

Directions for Cinematherapy

Instructions

It is helpful to ask the client to take notes when watching the film, in order to capture their impressions, and be able to recall them for processing in the coaching or therapy session. Recommendations for viewing films include: To stay comfortable and pay attention to the body and breathing, to release tension, and to experience personal reactions without preconceived thoughts or ideas (Wolz, 2005). After the movie is over, self-questioning can address questions like, "Did my breath change when I watched the film?" "What did I like or dislike?" "Which characters did I identify with?" and "What scenes were appealing or upsetting?"

Film Selection

Films can be self-selected by the client or couple or identified by the practitioner. Since films are chosen to provide greater self-understanding, insight, or functioning for the client, the therapist must make a thorough assessment of the client's problems and situation to tailor the choice to the client's situation, problem, needs, and goals, in the same way as with any aspect of counseling or any homework assignment. Other major considerations are diversity issues (the client's background and culture) and the client's interest in films.

To achieve proper selection, the therapist must have previewed the film and be thoroughly familiar with its content. A judgment must be made about whether to assign a film which serves as an example of a severe situation (like drug abuse or domestic violence) or provides positive role models, shows problem-solving, or offers hope and encouragement.

Not all films used in cinematherapy need to be relevant in literal content to the patient's situation, as they may have metaphorical implications (Dermer & Hutchings, 2000). Some films may also have inappropriate content, like profanity, violence, or other content potentially offensive to the client or contradictory to the goals of therapy. These may not exclude the film but would require extensive explanation and processing (Dermer & Hutchings, 2000).

Practitioners using commercial films as therapeutic tools would have to become familiar with a wide variety of films. Background research can be done by reading books on the subject, searching the worldwide web for sites on cinematherapy and on particular films, and asking for recommendations from colleagues interested in films or already using them in their practice (Calisch, 2001). For example, the book *Sex and the Cinema* (Krzywinska, 2006) analyzes the cultural context of sexually themed films, discussing movies like *The Story of O* (Jaekin, 1975), *Emmanuelle* (1974), *Secretary* (Shainberg, 2002), and *Eyes Wide Shut* (Kubrick, 1999) which starred then-married Tom Cruise and Nicole Kidman. *Sex in the Movies* (Frank, 1989) is an in-depth presentation of over 200 films and how they treat sexual themes like infidelity, role reversals, swinging, kinky practices, teen exploitation, and sexual violence. Among the movies analyzed are *Body Double* (de Palma, 1984), *Body Heat* (Kasdin, 1981), *Dressed to Kill* (Nell/dePalma, 1940/1980), *Tootsie* (Pollack, 1982), *Last Tango In Paris* (Bertolucci, 1972), *Behind the Green Door* (Mitchell & Mitchell, 1972), *and La Cage aux Folles (The Bird Cage*; Molinara/Nichols; 1978/1996). Over 1,000 movies are considered in the book *Positive Psychology at the Movies* (Niemiec & Wedding, 2008) with regard to how they address core strengths and virtues (like courage, justice, and humanity) identified by leading psychologists in the emerging field of positive psychology. Counselors and coaches wanting to incorporate cinematherapy into their practice can make good use of the research-based suggested questions for discussion, and the extensive appendixes on the top inspirational films and web resources.

One survey of 37 family therapists' suggestions of movies to use in therapy led to a list of movies useful to therapists who see couples and families (Dermer & Hutchings, 2000). The list presents films that address major issues in therapy, the rational for assigning it, and for whom it is useful. For example, related to the subject of "infidelity," the film *Something to Talk About* (Hallstrom, 1995) is recommended for couples as a useful demonstration of how affairs often emanate out of low marital satisfaction. To address the subject of "conflict resolution and communication," the film *War of the Roses* (de Vito, 1989) is listed as recommended for couples since it demonstrates the end result of dysfunctional processes. The film *Bye, Bye Love* (Weisman, 1995) is recommended for divorced or divorcing parents since it presents three examples of that situation. Films recommended for clients with "intimacy issues in relationships" include *Crimes and Misdemeanors* (Allen, 1989) for its exploration of the complexity of love relationships and efforts in current relationships to repair the past; *Crossing Delancey* (Silver, 1988) for its exploration of the problems of being single and pressured to get married; and *How to Make an American Quilt* (Moorhouse, 1995) for its examples of confronting intimacy fears and committing to adulthood. For couples with marital problems, *Four Seasons* (Alda, 1981) was recommended for its demonstration of marital struggles and *Forget Paris* (Crystal, 1995) was noted for showing how a couple having difficulty making time for each other fail and succeed in their relationship.

Assigning "Homework"

The use of homework assignments has been shown to be a useful technique in therapy (Kazantzis & L'Abate, 2007). Assigning major motion pictures as homework can be well received since watching movies is perceived as a pleasurable activity, and viewing can be done alone or together as a couple or in a group. When working with a couple, the counselor or coach should make it clear whether the couple should discuss their reactions to the film together afterward or write their reactions down for discussion together at a defined time and bring such notes to the session for discussion.

Case Example of Cinematherapy

The following is a case history which provides an example of how a film was used in therapy with a patient.
In Love with Mr. Wrong: *When Harry Met Sally*

Many women come to therapy complaining about persistent attraction to men who treat them poorly. These women usually have a history of choosing men who fit the profile of being emotionally unavailable but meeting the women's "eligibility criteria" for being physically attractive, financially well-off, and socially well-connected (Kuriansky, 2002). At the same time, these women commonly are pursued by, but reject, suitors who treat them well but do not fit their eligibility criteria.

The example of the case of Stephanie. An example of the type of women with the above problems is a 25-year-old female client, Stephanie. Early in her therapy, Stephanie was assigned to view the film, *When Harry Met Sally* (Reiner, 1989). In this film, the young single female character Sally Albright played by Meg Ryan is dating a typical Mr. Wrong – a man who treats her poorly to the point where she is constantly feeling miserable and badly about herself – and develops a close friendship with a good-natured but somewhat neurotic male Harry Burns played

by Billy Crystal. Their relationship deepens as they share extended phone conversations, intimate confessions and tender consolations, and spend holiday time together
– essentially acting like a traditional couple. Yet Sally resists their romance since
Harry hardly fits her "eligibility criteria," in that he is not handsome, suave, or hard
to get. The film addresses common issues in real people's lives as to whether a male
and female can be friends without having sex (Harry insists sex has to happen, Sally
maintains it doesn't) and also whether a woman can accept the "nice guy" who
makes her happy as opposed to the "player" she desires but suffers.

In the post-viewing therapy session, Stephanie admitted that she readily identified with the Meg Ryan character and wished she could similarly accept a "nice
guy." Therapy ensued with steps toward accomplishing this goal (Kuriansky, 1990),
which include demystifying attraction; determining and changing your checklist for
what you are looking for in a partner; evaluating self-deceptions involved in searching for the idealistic "dream lover"; recognizing emotional traps, inner messages,
and lifelong patterns traced to relationships with parents and early dating partners
which lead to compulsively making dysfunctional choices; resisting impulses based
on lust and attraction to money, power, or sex; and building self-esteem to be freer
to make healthier partner choices resulting in being treated well. In following these
steps, the client can be encouraged that good friendship is as an important foundation for a loving romantic partnership. A helpful exercise for these women – and
men since males can suffer a corollary syndrome – is to make a specific list of their
"love criteria" – the qualities they feel they must have in a partner – to reevaluate
those (Kuriansky, 2003).

As Stephanie enjoyed watching movies, she was assigned another film that further explores mate criteria. In *Crossing Delancey* (Silver, 1988), a single woman at
first resists the advances of a suitor, discounting him as ineligible because of his
job as a pickle-maker, but then becoming more open to him because of his caring
character.

Modeling Sexual Responses

Even in contemporary times when women's sexuality is addressed openly and
many books are available about women's sexual pleasure, a considerable number
of women still have trouble having orgasm. This condition is called "anorgasmia,"
referring to the meaning the state "before" a woman has had such a release.

Assigning the film *When Harry Met Sally* (Reiner, 1989) is also helpful in these
cases, when accompanied by instructions to pay particular attention to the famous
"orgasm scene." In that scene, while eating in a deli restaurant with Harry, Sally
mimics the experience of having an orgasm. As other diners look on and listen
in, Meg makes movements and emits loud sounds of ecstasy, to the point where
an older woman looks on with envy and announces, "I'll have what she's having"
(a comment which evokes laughter). A client's discussion of the humor in that scene
is expected and allows for more comfortable exploration of the sensitive issues of
women's orgasmic response.

As the client Stephanie explained in a post-viewing session, "It was hysterical the way she really did that in public, but it was so extreme, I don't think that's real." This response facilitated the therapist's offering corrective thinking about women's orgasm: That such "extreme" reactions displayed in the film can occur in some women; that all women's responses are individual; and that sexual responses can vary for any one woman over time. Most importantly, it was pointed out that while faking an orgasm is not recommended during sex with a partner (because it takes the woman out of the experience of relating to her partner), such faking offers an excellent opportunity to become more comfortable with a full range of sexual responses and is an important step in therapies to teach women to have orgasm (Barbach, 1976; O'Connor, 1986). Mimicking during self-stimulation what the woman thinks is an orgasm further helps the woman get in touch with her expectations and experience the full range of releasing her physical and emotional responses (essentially "faking it until you make it"). Such a practice is substantiated by social learning theory as described above, which emphasizes the importance of observing and modeling behaviors, attitudes, and emotional reactions of others, and maintains that the highest level of observational learning is achieved by organizing and rehearsing the modeled behavior symbolically and then enacting it overtly (Miller & Dollard, 1941; Bandura, 1977, 1994).

As follow-up and further reinforcement of the lessons from the film-viewing homework, clients like Stephanie can be assigned bibliotherapy homework. In Stephanie's case, she was assigned to read the book, *For Yourself: The Fulfillment of Female Sexuality*, which even decades after its release effectively describes women's orgasm and the steps to achieve this response (Barbach, 1976).

Application to Real Relationship Problems

Fear of Commitment

One of the most common problems in relationships today is fear of commitment – the inability to be intimate with one person. The classic commitment-phobic male with "cold feet" recounts in therapy how he dates many eligible women but always breaks up with them without knowing why. Issues to explore which perpetuate this problem include an attachment to mother, anger toward women, and early experiences of having been either suffocated or abandoned. A film which demonstrates such a character with the "Peter Pan syndrome" (inability to grow up and form a mature relationship) is *Failure to Launch* (Dey, 2006) where a 35-year-old commitment-phobic male moves in with his parents to be taken care of while he perpetuates Romeo-like behavior. Commitment-phobes benefit from seeing their actions played out on screen, providing an objective view of their own behavior. Married men can suffer as much as single men and can also benefit from seeing this film, to face underlying fears of commitment and vulnerability that sabotage their emotional connection and sexual performance with their partner.

Cross-gender identification with film characters is also possible. Women who see this film can be guided to view themselves as commitment-phobic similar to the male character. The therapist can point out how women in real life complain about not finding an eligible partner when in reality they are choosing unavailable men to "hide" behind complaining about the man without owning their own resistance. These women suffer from the female corollary to the "madonna prostitute" syndrome in men (where the male splits women into the doting wife and mother figure while directing his erotic interest to another woman) and demonstrate the "daddy-Don Juan" syndrome where the woman disconnects her erotic desire from the man once he becomes her stable partner and father of her children. The film *Runaway Bride* (Marshall, 1999) is a good example of such female Peter Pans, chronicling the antics of Maggie Carpenter, played by Julia Roberts, who leaves her grooms at the altar. The therapist can also point out how life imitates art, as the actress herself (Roberts) broke off with a fiancé right before the wedding and had a short-lived marriage. A happy ending can also be explored, as Roberts has since found commitment with her present husband with whom she has three children.

Sex, Love, Commitment, and Marriage

Perhaps in no one film are there as many examples of issues related to sex, love, commitment, and marriage as in the long-awaited films *Sex and the City* and its sequel (respectively, King, 2008; projected for 2010) based on the long-running popular television series of the same name. These two films will be ideal to recommend for many clients with relationship issues, as they are fun viewing as well as present examples of relationships to discuss with key phrases mentioned in the movie, either as narration or as script, which can be reviewed. Men as well as women can benefit from following the relationship dynamics and patterns experienced by the main male characters as well as by the female characters, and by the sharing of the four female friends, who represent stereotypes of real women. The classic lesson of the film is the value of the female support system evident in the friendship of the four friends, who are always "there" for each other, especially in emotional emergencies.

Many other very relevant issues are presented. In the first film, fear of commitment, as mentioned above, is dramatically portrayed in this film, where not only Mr. Big (played by Chris Noth as the longtime love of the main character of Carrie Bradshaw, played by Sarah Jessica Parker) has cold feet and leaves her at the altar but the female character of Samantha Jones (played by Kim Cattrall) presents an example of female commitment-phobes. Samantha continues to focus on sex (and salivate at fit male bodies) instead of settling down even with the handsome younger lover Smith Jerrod (played by Jason Lewis) who never falters in his desire for her. Her situation highlights important issues often overlooked in counseling with women, where they project their own commitment fears onto the men they complain about. Despite the fact that her younger lover treats her well, Samantha says, "I can't believe that my life revolves around a man" and bemoans that commitment signals an unpleasant state where, "... it's all about the other person..." and where you "... lose yourself...." While the movie character seems to have control of her life, women in real life exhibit codependency in losing themselves when they are in a relationship – a valuable issue to explore in counseling. Samantha ultimately breaks up with her young lover, admitting her problem, that she loves him but loves herself more. Some real-life women, to the chagrin of their male partners, walk out on their union, like Samantha, "in search of themselves." Using the example of Samantha's distress that her lover bought her a gift she admired because she wanted to buy it for herself, can be a trigger to discuss this drive (possibly an over-reaction) for independence, sometimes called counterdependence.

The dilemma of another girlfriend, Charlotte York (played by Kristin Davis), also provides fodder for real-life counseling, in that she acknowledges that she has a "perfect" life – wonderful husband, adorable adopted daughter, and new baby on the way – yet she is afraid to be so happy since "nobody gets it all." Indeed, some real-life couples sabotage their relationship for just this reason; fear that it is too good and therefore bound to be ruined. Yet, in a poignant scene – valuable to point out to a client for positive modeling – Charlotte kisses her husband Harry Goldenblatt (played by Evan Handler) in bed and says, "Thank you for being you."

By the opposite token, Miranda Hobbs (played by Cynthia Nixon) becomes sour on marriage when her husband Steve Brady (played by David Eisenberg) admits having a sexual fling, explaining his frustration that they have not had sex in a long time. Her choice can raise debatable issues in real-life counseling, including Samantha's advice to her friend to forgive her husband's infidelity since "Anyone can slip." Discussing the "violation of trust" which Miranda says "is killing me," can help clients explore their own deep wounds from betrayals in their own life. Despite her husbands' protests that the fling meant nothing, Miranda refuses to take him back and even tells Mr. Big on the eve of his nuptials that "Marriage ruins everything." The impact of sexual infidelity is rich for discussion, comparing reactions based on the nature of the indiscretion (a one-time fling or a long-term affair) and possible options (breaking up or resolving the hurt). Samantha's life also provides food for the proverbial therapeutic couch, as she gains weight at one point in the film, explaining that she "eats so [she] will not cheat." In more positive coping, Miranda and Steve go to therapy and reconcile. Their experience shows how couples can recover from affairs, by exploring feelings and making new agreements (Kuriansky, 2002).

Several stereotypes are revealed in the film, which can be explored in counseling. For example, when two of the girlfriends shop for costumes for one's little daughter, the other observes that the outfits are "all either a witch or a sexy kitten," reflecting two stereotypic female roles: women as a nagging wife or an erotic lover. Another comment made by one of the women – that "Good guys screw you, bad guys screw you, and some don't screw you" – can be trigger talking about the theme of women feeling victimized by men and the possibilities of becoming empowered instead. Another of the film's themes actually breaks gender stereotypes, as Miranda, a female lawyer, is portrayed as the one who avoids emotions, while her husband Steve is approachable and emotional (what can be considered a modern day "emo-man" signaling his capacity to express emotion). In the end, Miranda learns to express her feelings. Miranda's withdrawal from sex, as the reason for Steve's infidelity provides further material for therapeutic discussion about how sexual needs impact infidelity.

Despite problems, love wins out in the film, as Carrie's assistant (played by Jennifer Hudson) reconnects with – and marries – her old flame, and as Mr. Big finally succumbs to exchange vows with Carrie. While the narration says at one point that relationships can't be "all about being happy," love does matter, and happy endings happen – which itself can be reality tested in real-life sessions. Other contemporary relationship issues are planned in the flim's sequel

Sustaining a Long-Term Relationship

Problems like those expressed by Miranda and Steve in *Sex and the City* (King, 2008) are common in real life, whereby couples stop having sex and drift apart. Many films show this dilemma and reflect real-life situations where couples come to therapy complaining of boredom and wanting to spice up their love life. An interesting trend these days to solve these problems is to guide the couple in ancient techniques of tantric connection and tantric sex in order to achieve deeper intimacy through breathing exercises and directing energy (Kuriansky, 2004). Simple practices can be taught where couples set aside special evenings to be together, look deeply into each other's eyes, and breathe deeply, sending love energy into the other person. Tantric sex practices are presented briefly – and humorously – in *American Pie 2* (Rodgers, 2001) but are explored in great detail in the film *Bliss* (Lawrence, 1985), which is a useful assignment for couples, to see how the technique works to encourage a more sacred and joyful union when a couple seeks to revive the flames of passion in their relationship by exploring this path. (Along the way, the female partner in the couple also uncovers sexual abuse in her past, which is another common real-life phenomenon that must be healed in order to stop sabotaging couple's intimacy.)

Affairs

With surveys showing shockingly high numbers of men and women having had an affair during the course of an otherwise committed relationship, many individuals and couples seek counseling for infidelity as either the presenting complaint or a major issue. Topics which need to be explored include reasons for the infidelity, e.g., personal problems like fear of commitment; social circumstances like a drunken evening on an out-of-town work trip; or relationship problems like resentment, or anger, or sexual frustration. A woman's 4-day intensive affair – and rediscovery of her passion – in her husband's absence is poignantly portrayed in *Bridges of Madison County* (Eastwood, 1995). While the therapist must emphasize that assigning this film is not an endorsement of having an affair, the assignment can serve as a trigger to explore the increasing phenomenon of female infidelity. While couples can recover from an affair if they understand their needs, are able to forgive and to make a renewed commitment to each other, some individuals will not stop philandering. The film *Alfie* (Gilbert, 1966/Shyer, 2004) can be a good example for a woman addicted to womanizers to dissuade her from craving such men and a good example for philandering men of the pain of such behavior.

Betrayal from Affairs

Almost everyone has been rejected in relationships at some point in his/her life. Many patients come to therapy after a troublesome breakup resulting in emotional devastation. Past and present pain from these experiences cause people maladjustment in all aspects of their present life and also lead to various extremes of fear of commitment and intimacy (Firestone & Catlett, 1999). A useful film which portrays reactions to rejection and coping mechanisms is *The First Wives Club* (Wilson, 1996). In the film, four female friends have been abandoned by their partners for a younger mate. One of the women is so distraught that she plunges over her balcony, committing suicide. The remaining three friends (Bette Midler who plays Brenda, Goldie Hawn as Elise, and Diane Keaton as Annie whose husband has an affair with their marriage counselor) meet after the funeral, review their unhappy marriages and heartbreaks, and plot their revenge.

They form a club called *The First Wives Club* (Wilson, 1996) and decide to blackmail their husbands and retrieve financial resources they feel are rightfully theirs. Cleverly, they convince their ex-husbands to fund a nonprofit charity in their dead friend's name to help support mistreated women. The movie's plot offers an excellent opportunity for a counselor to address common reactions of rejection with a client, including the narcissistic injury which erodes self-esteem (Rice & Rice, 1986) by referring to reactions of the film characters. For example, Brenda reacts with cynicism and Annie becomes insecure. Common phases of denial, depression, and anger can be discussed, as well as positive coping strategies, like securing support from friends – a strategy which has been proven in real life to be sustaining.

Clients will inevitably react to the memorable line from the film uttered by Ivana Trump (playing herself) who announces at the after-party of the grand opening of the charity, the phrase she is well-known for: "Don't get mad, get everything!" Clients will also likely raise another memorable scene, which has become popular on You Tube, where the three friends sing the popular 1960s Lesley Gore tune, *You Don't Own Me*. The lyrics, "I'm free, and I love to be free, to live my life the way that I want, to say and do what ever I please. No you don't own me!" can offer motivation to a client to assert a similar sense of empowerment.

Specific questions that facilitate this transition from powerlessness to empowerment in a post-viewing debriefing session include "Talk about the characters in the movie" "How did the women feel about being rejected?" "Which character do you most relate to?" "What do you think about how the women reacted to their husbands' unfaithfulness and rejection?" "What are constructive and destructive ways to deal with rejection?" and "How does seeing this film make you feel differently about your coping in your situation?"

Another commercial film addressing rejection is *Under the Tuscan Sun* (Wells, 2003). After the female main character in the film discovers her husband's affair and intentions to take their shared assets, she moves to Italy where she discovers new relationships and renewed self-esteem and joy in life. This adjustment is reassuring to patients in similar situations. Another resourceful movie is *Why Did I Get Married?* (Perry, 2007) where a woman (played by Jill Scott) betrayed by an unfaithful husband (played by Richard T. Jones) finds forgiveness, new self-worth, new love, and renewed strength and faith.

Control and Power Struggles

Great interest centered on the film *Mr. and Mrs. Smith* (Liman, 2005) because its stars Brad Pitt and Angelina Jolie play spouses suffering from the "5-year itch" – boredom and waning passion in their relationship – which is one of the most common complaints of couples who seek counseling. However, the characters in the film are both assassins who end up being assigned to target each other, with resulting tension between the two stimulating excitements. The same excitement was rumored to be the cause of the actors' real-life attraction, resulting in Pitt leaving his wife Jennifer Aniston for his costar Angelina Jolie. Assigning this film to a couple can be a stimulus for discussing how power struggles can be at the source of their relationship problems and can also spark discussion about ways to restore the spark.

Competition between partners – as between the Pitt and Jolie characters – are another common issue in real-life couples. Usually in therapy, the male partner is interested in exploring these fantasies, with accouterments like whips and chains, although increasingly, female partners express the desire to tie up the man or order him around. The film *Secretary* where a young woman (played by Maggie Gyllenhal) just released from a mental hospital has sexual sadomasochistic sex with her lawyer boss (played by James Spader) is a good example of how such sex and power imbalance is addictive until the person develops self-esteem and feels deserving of being loved instead of tortured. The film also raises an interesting question about whether it is possible to have a sadomasochistic relationship that perhaps has therapeutic value where the two people can help each other heal from control and power conflicts (Kelleher, 2002).

Divorce

Despite the increasing numbers of divorces diminishing the social taboo and shame of such breakups, both members of a couple can still suffer severely, especially when children – and custody battles – are involved. With more men fighting for custody of their children, the film *Kramer versus Kramer* (Benton, 1979) is a good suggestion for men to view since it shows a man (played by Dustin Hoffman) left by his wife (played by Meryl Streep) adjusting to caring for himself and wanting to hold on to his child (played by Justin Henry).

The Extreme of Love Addiction: The Case of Fatal Attraction

The Example of the Movie Character of Alex Forrest. Love addiction has been recognized as a real problem, similar to an addiction to drugs, alcohol, food, or shopping, whereby the person is out of control and compulsively engages in the destructive behavior. The problem has been well outlined in the book, *The Marilyn Syndrome: Breaking Your Love Addiction Before It Breaks You* written with a woman, Susan Isrealson, who experienced the problems to such an extreme that she would hand her business card to strangers through her car widow and wake up in a stupor after sex with them (Macavoy & Israelson, 1991). *Fatal Attraction* (Lyne, 1987) is a classic film about this issue and therefore useful to assign to a client suffering from this addiction, to identify the symptoms and potentially tragic outcome. In this film, a single woman named Alex Forrest (played by Glenn Close) has a one night stand with a married man named Dan Gallagher (played by Michael Douglas) and becomes dramatically obsessed with him, pursuing and stalking him, with disastrous consequences. In one memorable scene, the spurned woman becomes so maniacal that she enters his home and boils the pet bunny of his child (played by Ellen Hamilton Latzen) in a pot on the stove. After watching this film, questions to ask a client in order to diagnose a love addiction and to explore behaviors and feelings, include "Do you have to be in love to be happy?" "Do you meet someone and immediately decide s/he is "the one"?" "Do you require that person's approval to appreciate your own experiences?" "Do you feel extreme "highs" or "lows" when deliriously in love?" "Do you panic or feel the world has come to an end if the "love" is not available?" "Do you feel hatred or vengeful towards a loved one who does not return your love?" "Do you feel powerless to stop your feelings towards the love object, despite your advances being clearly unwanted?" and "Do you fantasize that you are desired by the person even when the evidence does not prove that?" The film's denouement can be discussed as a warning for the client to take steps in her or his own life to overcome the addiction. Clients can be given guidelines about the difference between a love addiction and healthy love, i.e., that addictive love is depleting, whereas healthy love is energizing; and, that love addiction comes from codependency and desperation for the partner, whereas healthy love allows both people to be interdependent.

Special Populations

A New Specialized Population

A new population in need of therapy has emerged in today's society: A new generation of combat veterans and their partners – suffering from extreme psychological and emotional devastation constituting posttraumatic stress disorder (PSTD). The shocking high numbers of returning soldiers in emotional distress is becoming more recognized. Reports have uncovered a twice higher rate of suicide for these veterans than for other Americans (CBS Reports, 2007).

A film exploring the pain of a soldier (played by Jude Law) trying to get back home to his wife (played by Nicole Kidman) is *Cold Mountain* (Minghella, 2003). Positive reassurance that love can survive after a partner's tragic injury in combat is touchingly portrayed in the movie, *Coming Home* (Ashby, 1978). In the film, a nurse (played by Jane Fonda) in a veterans' hospital falls in love with a paraplegic (played by Jon Voight) and has her first explosive orgasm during sex with him.

Serious reactions to war are shockingly shown in *The Deer Hunter* (Crimino, 1978) which follows male buddies played by Robert De Niro, Christopher Walken (whose character kills himself playing Russian roulette), and John Savage (playing a soldier who loses his leg) in their painful journey from their Pennsylvania steel worker jobs to a prison camp in Vietnam where they experience extreme horror. Their return is mired in emotional trauma, consistent with what is now commonly recognized as PTSD (Engdahl, Dikel, Eberly, & Blank, 1997). The female partners (played by Meryl Streep, Rutanya Alda, Mandy Kaplan, and Mary Ann Haenel) at home are almost as emotionally scarred as the men; for example, the wife of the paraplegic soldier falls into a catatonic-like state, where she is so emotionally shocked that she can hardly move or speak. The film dramatically demonstrates the importance of counseling now being recognized as counseling for PTSD for returning troops and their partners. For example, the film's character played by Walken is so traumatized by his war experiences that he keeps reliving his trauma (going back to a gambling house to replay the Russian roulette he was forced to play as a prisoner of war) instead of returning home and reacclimating. The character plays by De Niro emerges as the only example of a decent adjustment, in that he strives to never give up his philosophy that "you only get one chance at life." While this film can be painful to watch, it can bring forth painful feelings faced by today's troops and their loved ones. But it can also be useful for others who may suffer from other trauma which can mimic war shock.

Sexual Orientation

In today's society, the issue of sexual orientation and identity is becoming more openly discussed, and an increasing number of patients present such conflicts in therapy. Several movies can be helpful to address these issues, with most showing very dramatic, troubling, and even tragic dilemmas faced by the protagonists. For example, in *Boys Don't Cry* (Peirce, 1999), the main character – a young female (played by Hilary Swank) who attempts to embody her true identity as a male – is brutally tortured and murdered by male peers (played by Rob Campbell and Matt McGrath).

A more uplifting story is told in the film *Transamerica* (Tucker, 2005) – a double entendre about crossing the country and also crossing gender roadmaps. The film presents an education about transgendered persons despite criticism from some professionals about some details. In the film, Bree Osborne (born as a male, Stanley, and played by Felicity Huffman) is hurt when her son Toby (played by Kevin Zegers) finds out she has a penis and calls her a freak. "I am not a freak," she protests;

explaining that she has a genetic disorder, "gender dysphoria." While gender dysphoria is one accurate term for Bree's identification as the gender opposite from
what her genitals and sex characteristics indicated at birth, some experts claim
that the phrase implies pathology and dysfunction and prefer more neutral – and
positive – terms like "mind–body disharmony" and "transsexed persons" (Heath,
2007). Another clarification of terms is necessary, as the operation Bree seeks in the
movie – often referred to as a "sex change operation" – is more accurately called
"genital reconstruction surgery" or "sex reassignment surgery" in professional circles, while an even more positive term is "sex affirmation surgery" (to reflect the
affirmation of the person's decision about who he or she really is). In the film, Bree
is initially denied approval for the operation when her counselor detects unresolved
emotional issues. Indeed, men and women who want sex reassignment traditionally
have to pass what is called the "life test" – living for at least a year as the opposite sex – but they also must be deemed psychologically ready. Some applicants are
considered to be not good candidates based on their motives (to escape pressures of
masculinity or mid-life crises), thrill-seeking and impulsive personality, or depression. But Bree's desire is ultimately deemed legitimate, evidenced in her response
to her doctor's question, "How do you feel about your penis?" (she answers, "It dis-
gusts me") and her feeling of being born into, or "trapped," in the wrong body. The
film portrays realistic challenges, evidenced in family members' negative reactions
(e.g., Bree's mother's ridicule and fear of being blamed for her "son's" condition).
But the film also has a "happy ending" showing that transgendered persons can
be loving parents and that their children can ultimately understand and empathize
with their transsexual parent (e.g., Bree's son finally accepts his "father"). Self-
affirmations also serve as positive examples, as one character in the movie says,
"We are not gender challenged, we are gender gifted." Similarly inspirational, Bree
tells her son, "Native Americans used to call us two-spirit people," a reflection of
cultures' viewing such people with respect and intrigue (e.g., fa'afines in Samoa are
considered an honor in a family).

Gay Relationships

While homosexuality has become more acceptable in society, people still feel conflicted, and watching films with gay characters can be a positive way to help clients
explore their feelings. The 2005 film *Brokeback Mountain* (Lee, 2005) is a good
homework assignment, as it follows the secretive relationship between two cowboys, played by the late Heath Ledger whose character is the more assertive of the
two and by Jake Gyllenhaal as the more resistant young man. *Birdcage,*the 1996 film
directed by Mike Nichols, is another good choice, as Robin Williams is a gay cabaret
owner who with his "'drag queen' partner" (played by Nathan Lane) pretends to be
straight to avoid offending the moralistic parents (played by Gene Hackman and
Dianne Wiest) of the fiancé (portrayed by Calista Flockhart) of his son (played by
Dan Futterman).

   While medicine fortunately has advanced so that more people can live with
HIV/AIDS than previously had a death sentence from the disease (CDC, n.d.), the

threat of the virus is still prevalent. Several films address powerful issues related to this disease; for example, *And the Band Played On* (Guest, 1980) is a motion picture docudrama about the discovery of the AIDS epidemic in America in 1977 and the courageous battles by a doctor confronting the government about the newly discovered deadly virus. The hero in the film (an epidemiologist played by Matthew Modine), who works for the Center for Disease Control, is credited in real life as being the first to become aware of the unexplained retrovirus plaguing mainly gay men in three major cities (San Francisco, Los Angeles, and New York). The character who is infected with the AIDS virus shows viewers the hardships a gay man and his partner endure. Viewers, even those who are not infected, can relate to the pain of the disease and the ensuing social problems, including the contention between the government and the gay community – which persists today. Another film which explores discrimination (of those with positive HIV status) is *Philadelphia* (Demme, 1993). The 1993 drama starring Tom Hanks is based on the real story of a lawyer who sued his firm for unfairly firing him. The film offers inspiration for everyone who faces prejudice.

Issues faced by those infected with HIV are also poignantly presented in *Rent* (Columbus, 2005), a film especially appealing for young people given its young characters. This popular Broadway show made into a movie in 2005 is about young HIV-positive adults (portrayed by Mayumi Ando, Will Chase, Merle Dandridge, Shaun Earl, Eden Espinoza, Renee Elise Goldenberry, Rodney Hicks, Marcus Paul James, Justin Johnston, Adam Kantor, Telly Leung, Caryn Lyn Manuel, Michael McElroy, Jay Wilkinson, Maia Nikenge Wilson, Karmine Alers, Crystal Monee Hall, Trisha Jeffery, Owen Johnston, Todd E. Pettiford, and Kyle Post) who cannot afford their rent, and who help each other, and go to support groups to cope with their tribulations. Viewers can relate to main characters who try to find love while living with the virus and their secrets. For example, Angel, a cross-dresser, stumbles upon a young man who was recently mugged and their relationship blossoms into love. The subjects of homosexuality as well as bisexuality are explored through storylines of a young couple, to which other young adults can relate, when struggling with developmental stages of identity issues.

Positive Examples of Relationships

Most films explore problems since conflict creates compelling drama. But some films can be considered to follow a more positive plot. These can be helpful when assigned to patients as a model of a healthy relationship, consistent with sound psychological theory about modeling behavior and self-efficacy, which maintains that people will emulate behaviors and attitudes to which they are exposed (Miller & Dollard, 1941; Bandura, 1977, 1994).

A positive role model for men is offered in the charming romantic comedy *Kate and Leopold* (Mangold, 2001) where the character played by Hugh Jackman comes from the age of chivalry through a time portal to win the heart of a frustrated New York City single professional female played by Meg Ryan. The story can be used to discuss what is being recognized as the new "emo-man" – a male who is more emotional, expresses feelings, and desires closeness. Similarly, *Something's Gotta Give* (Meyers, 2003) shows how ladies' man and cradle-snatching Harry (played by Jack Nicholson) has a heart attack and comes to terms with his mortality and immaturity, finally, to fall in love, find passion, and commit to a woman his age (played by Diane Keaton).

Notting Hill (Michell, 1999) is another uplifting romance. A beautiful internationally famous American actress (played by Julia Roberts) succumbs to the charm of a starstruck, somewhat goofy British bookstore owner (played by Hugh Grant), who wins her attention by spilling juice on her and inviting her back to his apartment to clean up. In a more serious plot, *The Constant Gardener* (Meirelles, 2005) gives a touching testimony to lasting and devoted love of a man toward a woman when a husband (played by Ralph Fiennes) carries on his murdered wife's (played by Rachel Weisz) legacy, in search of justice for poor Africans being used as guinea pigs by pharmaceutical companies.

Specific Issues

Other specific issues in relationships which present in therapy, counseling, and coaching are addressed below, with suggestions about how professionals can use films in their work with clients.

Race and Class Differences

More women and men are choosing partners from ethnic and racial cultures and backgrounds differing from their own (Alvarez, 2008). This can lead to problems from potential disapproval from friends, family and society, and friction in the relationship over adjusting to each other's attitudes and behaviors. The 1967 film *Guess Who's Coming to Dinner* (Kramer) is encouraging because the young white woman (played by Katharine Houghton) raised to blindly conform to convention, returns home from a vacation with her fiancé (played by Sidney Poitier) who is African-American, forcing the family (father played by Spencer Tracy and mother by Kathryn Hepburn) and others to confront their racial prejudices. Ethnic, cultural, and class differences are also explored in films like the classic 1961 *West Side Story* (Robbins), 1974 *The Great Gatsby* (Clayton), and in the 1997 blockbuster *Titanic* (Cameron). In the latter, star-crossed lovers – rich girl Rose (played by Kate Winslet) and poor boy Jack (played by Leonardo DiCaprio) – demonstrate the extreme of devotion.

Couples need not only be prepared for potential problems arising from cultural clashes but also be encouraged that cooperation and adjustment to each other is possible, with understanding and compromises (Kuriansky, 2004). A typical film showing this possibility is *My Big Fat Greek Wedding* (Zwick, 2002), an autobiographical account of what happens when a young Greek woman (played by Nia

Vardalos) falls in love with a non-Greek man (played by John Corbett) and learns more about her own heritage in the process of trying to convince her family (father played by Michael Constantine and mother by Christinia Eleusiniotis) to accept their union.

Bollywood films – the informal term referring to the film industry in India, merging the word Hollywood with the letter "B" for the Indian city of Bombay – have become more mainstream internationally. Many of these films are musicals with song and dance numbers woven into melodramatic and formulaic plots of romantic relationships, often with love triangles, courtesans, and star-crossed lovers with angry parents. Plots commonly hinge on the tradition of arranged marriage – providing a valuable opportunity to discuss this issue with clients questioning this practice – however, more recent productions are based on more Western practices of dating.

Age Gaps (the December/May Romance)

Real-life relationships where the man is much older than the woman are common, but an increasing trend today is the opposite – romances between older women and much younger men. While these women (popularly called "cougars") are flattered by younger men's attention, they also worry about the appropriateness of having a "boy toy." The real-life example of actress Demi Moore and her 15-year younger husband Ashton Kutcher is a positive role model of such a marriage working out, where the male expresses adoration and support for his much older and wealthier wife. A film that can similarly reassure the woman of the acceptability of this choice is *Crush* (McKay, 2001/I), where a 40-year-old headmistress (played by Andie McDowell) of a country school has contests with her female friends over who is the "Saddest of the Week" until she falls into an affair with a 25–year-old former male pupil (portrayed by Kenny Daghty) and is no longer sad.

Open Marriage

The era of the 1960s sexual revolution led to activities like wife swapping as described in the book *Open Marriage* (O'Neill, 1984) and the film *Bob, Carol, Ted and Alice* (Mazursky, 1969). A more recent trend is "polyamory," where couples may include others in their intimate exchanges, characterized by the desire for "more love for all." The network TV series *Swinging* (Kellett, 2005–2008) has revived interest in these practices – and while polyamory as distinct from swinging does not sanction recreational sex, there is increasing interest in this phenomenon and what happens in such mixes and matches. In the 2006 film, *Kiss Me Again* (Smith, 2006), a young married couple (played by Jeremy London and Katheryn Winnick) searches for excitement in the face of lagging desire for each other (including going to a party with sex toys). In the course of their both falling for the same sexy Spanish female, they explore the boundaries of marriage and their definition of exclusivity, commitment, and love. *Three of Hearts: A Postmodern Family* (Kaplan), a documentary released in 2006, similarly challenges those boundaries, as two young men (Sam Cagnina and Steven Margolin) in love go on a search for a third soul mate – a woman (Samantha Singh) – to share their bed and marriage.

Substance Abuse and Its Impact on Relationships

With millions of men and women suffering from alcoholism, the strain that such an addiction puts on a relationship drives many people to seek help. Addiction specialists know that an addict only changes when he or she wants to or hits bottom but seeing the tragedy of that bottom projected on screen can serve as a wake-up call. The film *Leaving Las Vegas* (Figgis, 1995) traces the descent of a male (portrayed by Nicholas Cage) drinking himself to death after his wife and son leave him, and *Days of Wine and Roses* (Edwards, 1962) shows how a male alcoholic (played by Jack Lemmon) seduces his wife (portrayed by Lee Remick) into similar addiction. The extreme outcome of alcoholism and abuse is painfully evident in the Elizabeth Taylor–Richard Burton portrayals in *Who's Afraid of Virginia Woolf* (Nichols, 1966) which shows the mutual verbal abuse of a drunken couple and the urgency of resolving repressed resentments. As in the personal case of the actress Julia Roberts described above, the real-life example of the relationship between Taylor and Richard Burton can provide added discussion matter for counseling since their tumultuous union was well-publicized.

The problem of female alcoholism is becoming increasingly recognized in society today and is highlighted in the film *When a Man Loves a Woman* where Meg Ryan plays an alcoholic school counselor who neglects her daughters, "hits bottom," and goes to rehab. Yet, on her return home sober and strong, the problem of codependency is highlighted when her controlling husband (portrayed by Andy Garcia), accustomed to her past helplessness, has trouble adjusting to her new sobriety. The couple goes to a marriage counselor to deal with the codependency – providing a positive role model of recovery on a number of levels.

Abuse in Relationships

Statistics show that about 960,000 assaults are reported each year by intimate partners in the United States, and an estimated 400,000 men and women are abusive (Greenfeld et al., 1998). Women and men who have been abused and who are abusive have serious issues and problems in intimate relationships. With such high frequency of abuse in people's background, it is likely that individuals or couples presenting in therapy may have hidden abuse in their background. This devastating experience often plays an important role in disrupting the present relationship, particularly evident in the inability to trust or be intimate (Terr, 1991). Fortunately, support groups are available to help people cope with this trauma (Richmond, 2009).

A useful film to assign in these cases is the movie *The Burning Bed* (Greenwald, 1984). In the film, Farrah Fawcett plays a battered wife, subjected to coercion and control by an abusive husband (played by Paul Le Mat). The film is a realistic portrayal of domestic violence, the pattern of coercive threats and abuse on various levels (emotional, physical, psychological, sexual, and financial), and the tragic progression of the relationship leading to typical patterns of failed attempts to leave the relationship and a potentially drastic outcome (resulting in death in the films. This model developed by Pence & Paymar (1993) has been applied in many professional settings.). Given this film as homework, the client can be directed to observe the typical stages of domestic violence. The beginning of such a relationship often starts passionately – just as the character Francine and her husband Micky have an immediate attraction – representing what has been called the "honeymoon phase" where the relationship shows no apparent problems. A scene which presages problems shows the couple making out on a date, where Micky pressures Francine to have sex which she protests – insisting that she wants to wait to get married – but to which she ultimately succumbs.

The next stage of an abusive relationship is characterized by mounting tension and the abusive partner's progressive aggression, leading to the first event of physical violence, which usually comes as a surprise to the female partner. Typically this event occurs when the man's ego is threatened, as it is in the film when Micky is not working or earning money yet will not allow his wife to work. At a family barbeque, when Francine shows up with a new shirt and manicure, Micky becomes even more threatened and strikes Francine, admitting, "I just can't stand you dressing up for anyone else but me. You look too sexy." The woman's confusion in such situations is evident by Francine's reply, "Before you were married you loved when I dressed up. Why all of the sudden did you change?"

The progression of the batterer's possessiveness and insecurity is evident as Micky persists in making Francine promise she would never leave him and tracks everything she does, even timing her visits to the grocery store. Since many battered women in real life are codependent with their abusive partner and unable to call for help, notify police, or leave the abusive relationship, the film presents a positive role model since Francine, frightened her husband would kill her, ultimately calls the police. Yet, the movie also poignantly and painfully portrays the challenges such women face in secondary abuse from the "system," in the form of loved ones denying the abuse (e.g., Francine's mother rationalizes, "Women have to put up with their man especially if there are children involved.") and police powerlessness to intervene unless they witness the abusive acts (e.g., in the film, cops tell Francine, "We can't arrest him because we didn't actually see that he hit you."). Such frustrations are further evident when a welfare agent tells Francine that there is no way he could provide her with any help unless the head of the house signs a form (which her husband clearly would not do).

While many women in real life refuse to leave or divorce an abusive partner, the movie character does so. Yet, as is also typical in real life, the abusive partner persists in his pursuit; in the film, Micky continually shows up at Francine's house, banging on the door, and screaming typically possessive statements like "It doesn't matter if we are divorced, you are mine." His pleas that he had changed and guilt-inducing assertions about how their children need him as a father break Francine's will, as is also typical in such real-life relationships. Also predictable, the abusive partner is alcoholic and becomes abusive in front of the children. Using the film's example, the counselor can point out to a client how this pattern is addictive to the woman and ultimately exceptionally dangerous for all involved. That danger comes in the form of "marital rape" in the film, which can also happen in real life (Kennedy-Bergen & Barnhill, 2006). The ultimate insult of this act prompts Francine to drastic countermeasures in the most dramatic scene in the film where Francine burns her husband to death in his sleep.

In its portrayal of domestic violence, *The Burning Bed* (Greenwald, 1984) is useful in therapy to help clients notice warning signs of such relationships, the tactics used by abusive men (*Intervene With Violent Men*, 2004), and the cycle of abuse. This cycle is visually displayed in a Power and Control Wheel (Pence & Paymer, 1993) which exhibits tactics abusers use to maintain control over their partner and the impact of physical, sexual, and emotional violence. The wheel can be used as a handout to a client, while discussing the lessons from the film's plot, including that abusive men rarely change even though they protest to the contrary. The therapist can guide the woman into considering alternate options for action which would not result in as drastic an outcomes as shown in the film, and point out how the woman should expect denials of others about the abuse and frustration from the system, and how leaving the relationship for a safe haven (e.g., at a battered women's shelter) is a healthy and empowering choice.

As in the case of Stephanie described above, bibliotherapy is a valuable added tool in such cases where abuse is an issue. Many self-help books have been written on the topic, which can be helpful to clients. A recent book, *Violent Partners*, can also be helpful for counselors, as it challenges traditional notions that most perpetrators are male who should be jailed, to present the dynamics of abuse and new ways of stopping the dynamic of intimate violence (Mills, 2008).

Watching such a film is also useful viewing for some abusive men, who deny their behavior. These men can be directed to relate the husband's actions to their own, to explore how to resolve their own insecurities and past injuries, to restrain their impulses, and to form healthier interactions with their partner. In this way, the male character in a film like *The Burning Bed* (Greenwald, 1984) becomes an important example of some behaviors not to be emulated but a catalyst for discussing alternative behaviors and working through underlying problems.

Battered women are inevitably fearful and discouraged about escaping situations they perceive as a trap. A film which can be reassuring because of the main character's healthy emergence from a severe struggle with past abuse is *Sybil* (portrayed by Sally Field; Petrie, 1976). Clients watching this film can be comforted that they are not experiencing a similarly severe reaction – dissociating into different "personalities" – making it easier for them to confront their own troubled past. The film further offers an opportunity to point out how many women suppress or repress past abuse for decades (Marion, Solomon, & Siegal, 2003). Another film similarly helpful is *Prince of Tides* (Streisand, 1991) since the character of Savannah (played by

Melinda Dillon) represses having been raped, an event which is revealed as a reason for her repeated suicide attempts. Ultimately, the character makes this connection and reconciles her past.

The film is also a healthy affirmation to a client of the helpfulness of exploring past experiences. This is especially useful in contemporary fast-paced times, when psychoanalytic therapy is less popular given the time and financial investments required in contrast to shorter term and focused behavioral and cognitive techniques which offer more promise for quick fixes. The film exhibits how defense mechanisms protect people from experiencing even deeper trauma. The film can be a useful homework assignment not only for survivors of child abuse like Sybil but for survivors of any form of trauma, as inspiration to release anger, face past pain, begin a new life, and fulfill new dreams (Sybil's dream was to become a teacher). Another inspiration is evident in the reaction of Sybil's love interest (played by Brad Loomise) to losing his wife in a car accident. Thinking he could cope with that tragedy, he learns as he says, "You're never ready for what you have to do, you just do it. That's what makes you ready."

The film *Take My Eyes* (Bollain, 2003) shows a productive response to abuse, in the actions of the main female character (played by Laia Marull) who leaves her abusive husband (played by Luis Toscar) after suffering several beatings. She gets a job, becomes successful, makes a new life and friends, and never looks back. Similar to the message in *The Burning Bed* (Greenwald, 1984), the abusive husband in this film becomes possessive and jealous (over other men seeing his wife at her job) and uses the children as a control tactic, making the wife feel guilty that the child "needs a family." Abused women in therapy need to be aware of this tactic (Wagner & Mongon, 1998). The film also highlights a relatively newly recognized abusive dynamic called "emotional abuse" – where the control is on an emotional level. "Emotional abuse" is increasingly common in patients today, where the victim feels mistreated but is unable to identify what is wrong because the criticism and undermining are not easily identifiable or labeled as abusive.

Discussion

General Issues

The advent of new media (DVDs, websites, ipods) has made therapeutic tools like using movies for therapeutic purposes more available to more people. Such technology advances increase the likelihood that cinematherapy will become even more popular and make it even more possible to select and review scenes from films – using a computer or other device during a session.

Clients who enjoy movies can be assigned different films as therapy progresses. To show interest on the therapist's part, DVDs can be displayed on bookshelves in the same way that books reveal a message about the practitioner's interests.

A version of cinematherapy is the "talkback" technique – guided discussions with an audience in a public setting to help them process themes in a film which would relate to their lives (Kuriansky, Walsh, & Laszczak, 2005). For example, in one such discussion after the film *Crush* (McKay, 2001/I), the audience was led in a discussion by a psychologist (the first author) about what constitutes a healthy relationship; whether relationships with vast differences – as with age gaps – can last; and how to handle conflicts over such relationships due to one's own and others' judgments.

Fitting Cinematherapy into the Therapist's Orientation Style

Cinematherapy can be applied in a variety of settings with therapists of varying orientations that have been described by psychologists (Seligman, 2006). Although some practitioners are more inclined or comfortable using motion pictures in therapy, data suggest that practitioners of all different orientations and therapeutic modalities have used them as clinical tools (Lampropoulos, Deane, & Kazantzis, 2004). Cinematherapy can be integrated in gestalt therapy, whereby the gestalt therapist typically asks the patient to assume various identities in order to better understand feelings as well as the perspective of other people in their relationships (Cat, 2007). For example, a client can be asked to imagine that she is the character of Brenda in *First Wives Club* (Wilson, 1996) in order to explore cynicism that can result from being rejected or to imagine assuming the role of the character of Elise who indulges in bad habits (drinking and smoking) in response to being hurt and then to describe alternate coping strategies.

Cinematherapy has been shown to be more consistent with humanistic and behavior approaches than with psychoanalysis (Lampropoulos et al., 2004). From a humanistic perspective, one woman's response in *First Wives Club* (Wilson, 1996) – of plummeting self-esteem – can be explained by her need to belong and be loved and explored from this perspective. Cognitive therapists using this film can identify distorted ways of thinking about being rejected, correct and reframe the experience, and identify positive behaviors in response. However, exploring themes in films is actually consistent with a psychodynamic approach since the technique uses metaphors which are fundamental to psychoanalytic investigations into unconscious connections. For example, the source of Elise's addictive behavior (drinking and smoking) in *First Wives Club* (Wilson, 1996) can be traced to the trauma of having been a success as an Oscar winning actress but now finding herself middle-aged and rarely cast in roles. An even more dramatic example of the value of psychoanalytic explorations is evident in the therapeutic exploration of Sybil's past experience of abuse as a cause of her dissociative state.

The delivery style of the therapist has been pointed out as an important factor in cinematherapy. While it has been suggested that films should be assigned as a strict prescription (Horne & Passmore, 1991), inviting the client to view the film can be equally acceptable (e.g., saying, "It occurs to me that the film [name]is relevant to what you are dealing with. Would you be interested and willing to rent it, and to note what seems relevant to you?").

Formats

Cinematherapy can be used for individuals, couples, or even groups, to address common issues of relationships. A model of group movie therapy has been described, consisting of 8–12 clients seen once a week for 90 minutes for 12 weeks (similar to traditional group therapy) where the group discusses characters, plots, and metaphors they see in the films and as they apply to their real life (Demir, 2007).

Movie One-Liners

While not technically cinematherapy – which involves assigning an entire film for viewing – using notable lines or quotes from films can assist in communicating powerful messages to clients. Movie one-liners are especially useful in cases where the client is a movie buff and might recognize the films, and when the quote is targeted to a valuable conclusion about relationships. Examples of these are the line from *Fried Green Tomatoes* (Avnet, 1991), "I wonder how many people never get the one they want, but end up with the one they're supposed to have" and the line "If you love someone you say it, you say it right then, out loud. Otherwise the moment just passes you by," from *My Best Friend's Wedding* (Hogan, 1997).

References to movie scenes and lines also work when the scene is well-known, as is the case for some Woody Allen films with Allen's typically neurotic expressions of frustration with himself, relationships, and sex. For example, one of the most common sexual complaints of couples – besides the above-mentioned boredom – is incompatible sexual desire, expressed memorably in a scene from the Woody Allen film *Annie Hall* (1997) where the couple gives differing answers to the question about how often they have sex. The female (played by Diane Keaton) says "frequently" and the male (Woody Allen character) complains that it only happens "three times a week." This disagreement can stimulate a discussion between partners in couple counseling about different levels of sexual desire. For example, one couple came to therapy before getting married because she was resisting being abandoned in her sexual expression, which the fiancé missed. Talking about this scene in Allen's film helped her admit to him about her fears of approaching him with the same wanton sexuality as she had expressed as a single woman, as if that would denigrate the sacredness of their union to the level of her previous more casual sexual encounters with other men.

Issues of Transference and Countertransference in Films

In therapy, issues of transference and countertransference inevitably arise which affect the progress of the therapy and therefore must be managed (Gabbard, 2001). Transference refers to patient's projection onto the therapist which recapitulates earlier or other important relationships. Countertransference occurs when the therapist projects aspects of his or her own life onto the patient. These issues are often unaddressed by the patient but when brought out in the open can be helpful to the therapeutic process and clarify the relationship between the therapist and the patient (Imura, 1991). Since these issues may be suppressed or repressed as well as be threatening, assigning a film which exhibits this interpersonal dynamic can be helpful. The film *Sybil* shows a positive relationship between therapist and patient, and a productive long-term therapeutic process, whereby the patient ultimately integrates her dissociative states. *Analyze This* (Ramis, 1999) and *Good Will Hunting* (van Sant, 1997) also show therapist–client relationships, which while not as positive, can highlight how the therapeutic relationship reveals patterns in other relationships. The Media Watch Committee of Division 46 (Media Psychology) of the American Psychological Association gives annual awards to films which accurately portray practitioners behaving in a highly professional manner or that clearly label unprofessional behavior, such as *The Sopranos* (van Patten, Patterson, Coulter, Taylor, Bronchtein, Bender, Buscemi, Attias, & Chase, 1999–2007) and *Law and Order: SVU* (Platt, Makris, Leto, Campanella, de Segonzac, Forney, Shill, Zakrzewski, Kotcheff, Dobbs, Taylor, Fields, Wallace, Kapalan, Lipstadt, Glatter, Rosenthal, Wertimer, Quinn, Beesley, Pattison, & Woods, 1999–present) (Schulz, 2005; http://www.apa.org/divisions/div46/).

Since films should be carefully selected, relevant to the client's issues, and not including inappropriate or misleading content (Sharp et al. 2002), those which portray a therapist in a negative light should be used with caution. This includes popular films which show a therapist violating professional boundaries of the therapist–patient relationship. For example, in the film *Antwone Fisher* (Washington, 2002), Denzel Washington plays a Marine psychiatrist who helps his young soldier client to express feelings and resolve his anger, but in doing so, visits the young man's home – which can give clients a misguided idea about the counselor being open to a dual relationship. In *Anger Management* (Segal, 2003), Jack Nicholson as the eccentric counselor who insists on moving in with his client (played by Adam Sandler), sleeping in the same bed, and serving him breakfast, also oversteps boundaries of traditional therapy.

Caution

Films which present stereotypes can be used to encourage clients to resist rigid roles in their real life. An analysis of 99 movies about therapy, reported at the 2000 APA Division 46 media award ceremony (http://www.fenichel.com/Fischoff.shtml) found that male therapists were presented as ineffective and females often as becoming sexually involved (as in the film, *Prince of Tides* [Streisand, 1991] where Barbra Streisand as the therapist has a sexual affair with her patient Nick Nolte).

Films also present a danger in creating a negative image of mental illness in the viewer's perceptions. For example, a survey of 76 college students showed that after viewing films portraying mental illness (e.g., *One Flew Over the Cuckoo's Nest* [Forman, 1975)] and *Girl, Interrupted* [Mangold, 1999]), almost half of the participants rated people in real life who are suffering from mental illness as a danger to themselves and others (DelBuono, Jusis, Lopez, & Vallarelli, 2008). In addition, almost three-quarters of the students surveyed said that after viewing movies featuring therapists and/or clients (e.g., *Sybil* [Petrie, 1976], *Anger Management* [Segal, 2003], *Silence of the Lambs* [Demme, 1991], *First Wives Club* [Wilson, 1996], *Gothika* [Kassopvitz, 2003], *Antwone Fisher* [Washington, 2002], *Girl Interrupted* [Mangold, 1999], *Good Will Hunting* [van Sant, 1997], *Analyze This* [Ramis, 1999], *Prince of Tides* [Streisand, 1991], *One Flew Over the Cuckoo's Nest* [Forman, 1975]), almost three-quarters of respondents said they would not consult a mental health professional.

Another caution is that certain patients would not be good candidates for cinematherapy. This is particularly true for patients experiencing psychotic episodes who have trouble distinguishing reality from fantasy. It is also not recommended to assign a very sad movie (like the 2003 biographical film *Sylvia* [Jeffs, 2003] about the life of poet Sylvia Plath who descends into deep depression and eventual suicide) to a depressed client unless there was an adequate level of resolution in the plot (Sharp et al., 2002). Warnings have been issued by cinematherapy expert John Hesley who notes that therapists cannot always predict how patients will react to a film, suggesting that watching *Scenes From a Marriage* (Bergman, 1973) could push a couple toward unnecessary divorce (Hesley & Hesley, 2001). This point is supported by the fact that some films have faced legal action for their presentation of violence, as in the case of the movie *Natural Born Killers* (Stone, 1994) where creators were accused of providing examples of murder. The action indicates how films powerfully influence people's behavior.

Need for Evidence Base

To date, proof of the impact and usefulness of movies in therapy from the point of view of patients is only available through anecdotes and case examples. For example, psychoanalyst Foster Cline has been quoted as saying, "You just know if you get a client to watch a particular movie and the person 'gets' what's going on, you'll be able to make some progress" (Mangin, 1999). The late noted political journalist Norman Cousins attested in his book *Anatomy of an Illness as Perceived by the Patient* (2005) that watching humorous (Marx Brothers) films was a crucial part of his recovery from disease – with 10 minutes of belly laughs having a pain-relieving and sleep-inducing effect. Scientific outcome studies of patients assigned cinema homework are not available (Karlinsky, 2003), although an increasing number of books, articles, and even a growing number of websites are available about the technique and its application.

Some studies have been done, however, about practitioners' attitudes toward cinematherapy, with data supporting positive attitudes. For example, in one survey of 401 members of the clinical and counseling division of the American Psychological Association, almost one half of respondents recommended movies to their clients and 68% of these practitioners found films helpful. Only 2% perceived them as harmful (Norcross, 2000). Another survey of 837 practitioners showed that 67%

agreed or strongly agreed that "quality motion pictures that deal with psychological issues can be beneficial or can be used for therapeutic purposes" (Lampropoulos et al., 2004). Of 27 movies featuring practitioners, the highest rated quality movie was *Ordinary People* (Redford, 1980).

A rationale for the effectiveness of using films in counseling settings is based on a theory of learning and creativity that postulates seven intelligences tapped in movie viewing (Wolz, 2003). These intelligences are logical (plot), linguistic (dialogue), visual–spatial (pictures, colors), interpersonal (storytelling), kinesthetic (movement), and intrapsychic (inner guidance). The more of these intelligences accessed in the experience, the more learning is achieved.

The Client's Own Relationship Movie

A technique which represents a variation on cinematherapy is to ask clients to write a movie script about their relationship (Kuriansky, 2003). Clients can consider their life is like a movie script where they are the producer, director, writer determining the plot, and casting director choosing all the actors to enact various dramas that they unconsciously or consciously need or want in their real life. Doing this exercise helps clients feel empowered, that is, that they are in charge of their relationships and life direction. Questions that can be asked in therapy after this assignment include, "Is your movie a comedy or tragedy?"; "Do you like your own role?" "What characters do you consistently cast?" and "What is the outcome of your movie?" To give clients an opportunity to see how they can change, they are also asked to describe what the movie of their ideal relationships would look like, and what the actors would be doing and how they would be interacting.

Further Resources About Cinematherapy

While cinematherapy is a somewhat misleading term since it is not a therapy unto itself but rather a tool to be used in therapy (Portadin, 2006), there is still growing use of the term and several websites devoted to research and training in the technique Extensive information is available at www.cinematherapy.com and www.cinemaalchemy.com, which are hosted by a marriage and family counselor who offers workshops and information for professionals and the public on the topic. Another website, www.cinema-therapy.com, is hosted by a psychologist whose latest innovation of cinematherapy uses films to help parents understand their children.

New variations of the technique of cinematherapy are movie viewing clubs and services offering selections of films which address subjects and storylines with particular inspirational themes or socially conscious messages for individual or group viewing. These films may have been shown in film festivals but were passed over by major Hollywood motion picture production companies and therefore did not get major distribution. Some individuals host movie-viewings of such films in their

homes (D. Heller, 2008, "Personal communication"), while other nonprofit organizations provide DVDs and other corollary services which can be purchased in a
package from an internet site. For example, people can join the Spiritual Cinema
Circle, for recommendations of "movies that matter" that have "heart and soul." An
example is the film *If I Never See You Again* (Villanseñor, 1997) about a group of
older people who play music in nightclubs rather than waste away in a retirement
home, and *Letting Go* about a father who has trouble accepting his son's decision
to put his "blankey" away, evoking issues about the father's own difficulty growing up (www.spiritualcinemacircle.com). Club members receive DVDs with a set
of "reflection questions" to ponder about the spiritual essence of the film and its
application to one's own life. Film festivals, trips, and conferences with well-known
spiritual leaders are also offered.

Therapy training centers and institutions can develop their own film libraries, as
has been done by New York University's Medical School. Their brief yet varied
film and video database lists major Hollywood titles (like *Awakenings* [Marshall,
1990] and *The Doctor* [Haines, 1991]*)* to art-house fare (like *Antonia's Line* [Gorris,
1995] and *Vanya on 42nd Street* [Malle, 1994]. University faculty uses the videos to
acquaint future doctors with situations they or their patients might encounter.

Traditionally in cinematherapy, therapists select the films to assign to patients;
however, patients can be asked to come up with their own ideas. Further, a couple
can be asked to brainstorm ideas in the session about DVDs they can rent. This
process has the added advantage of giving the therapist as well as the couple an
opportunity to observe their cooperation and decision-making process. For example,
one couple in therapy was arguing about whose family they should visit over the
holiday. The male partner wanted them to watch the comedy *National Lampoon's
European Vacation* (Heckerling, 1985) where a family wins a 2-week vacation but
encounters many mishaps along the way, while the female partner insisted on a more
serious drama about a couple's problems. In therapy, they were guided to explore
the underlying reasons for their choice that reveal their divergent styles, in that he
always wanted to make light of their problems, in stark comparison to her more
serious confronting approach.

Conclusions

The use of motion pictures is emerging as a useful and inexpensive supplement to
traditional modalities in therapy for a variety of purposes: To educate, encourage,
and aid individuals and couples in becoming aware of and coping with personal
and interpersonal problems. Therapists, counselors and coaches can use films to
trigger discussion about sensitive issues and to give clients and their partners an
opportunity to confront an issue in a private setting (watching a DVD at home) and
then to process the experience with a professional. Although practitioners report the
value of assigning major motion pictures as homework in working with clients, there
is a paucity of research on the efficacy of this technique. Traditionally, research on
movies and therapy has focused on how psychological treatment and mental health

professionals are portrayed in the movies (Eber & O'Brien, 1982; Schneider, 1987) and attitudes of practitioners toward cinematherapy.

The field of using major motion pictures as a therapeutic tool is in its infancy, and as with any new theory or technique, qualitative and quantitative research needs to be done. A systematic series of empirical investigations should be undertaken to more effectively inform clinical practice. While research and even training is needed to establish the effective use of movies in counseling and psychotherapy as a mainstream therapeutic modality, there is no doubt about the increasing interest and clinical anecdotes showing the usefulness of using commercial motion pictures to enhance treatment and encourage change. New developments pointed out in this chapter include that films, even those made decades earlier, can highlight new or increasing trends in modern relationships, like emotionally available men, older women–younger men unions, and couplings crossing cultural divides. The lives of the actors, besides that of the film characters, can also provide material for therapeutic discussion. New developments in cinematherapy, currently made possible by computer and DVD viewing and internet access, will inevitably evolve as technology advances.

References

Alvarez, A. (2008). *You got some 'splaining to do: Interracial and interethnic relationships, as seen on TV, and heard on the radio, and read on cereal boxes*. Retrieved June 1, 2008, from http://www.racialicious.com/2008/05/08/you-got-some-%E2%80%98splaining-to-do-interracial-and-interethnic-relationships-as-seen-on-tv-and-heard-on-the-radio-and-read-on-cereal-boxes/

Anderson, D. D. (1992). Using feature film as a tool for analysis in a psychology and law course. *Teaching of psychology, 19*, 155–157.

Bandura, A. (1977). *Social learning theory*. New York: General Learning Press.

Bandura, A. (1994). Self-efficacy. In V. S. Ramachaudran (Ed.), *Encyclopedia of human behavior* (Vol. 4, pp. 71–81). New York: Academic Press. (Reprinted in H. Friedman [Ed.], *Encyclopedia of mental health*. San Diego: Academic Press, 1998).

Barbach, L. (1976). *For yourself: The fulfillment of female sexuality* (Rev. 2000). Garden City, NY: Anchor Press.

Berg-Cross, L., Jennings, P., & Baruch, R. (1990). Cinematherapy: Theory and application. *Psychotherapy in Private Practice, 8*, 135–156.

Calisch, A. (2001). From reel to reel: Use of video as a therapeutic tool. *Afterimage: The journal of media arts and cultural criticism, 29*, 22–24.

Caron, J. J. (2005). *DSM at the movies: Use of media in clinical and educational settings.* Retrieved on April 6, 2008 from http://www.counselingoutfitters.com/vistas/vistas05/Vistas05.art38.pdf

Cat, J. (2007). Switching gestalts on Gestalt psychology: On the relation between science and philosophy. *Perspectives on science, 15*(2), 131–177. Retrieved June 1, 2008, from MIT Press Journals database.

CBS News. (2007). *Suicide epidemic among veterans: A CBS news investigation uncovers a suicide rate for veterans twice that of other Americans*. Report posted on November 13, 2007, New York. Retrieved on June 30, 2008, from http://www.thewe.cc/weplanet/news/armed_force/us_soldiers_committing_suicide_vietnam_iraq.html

CDC (n.d.). Retrieved June 4, 2008, from http://www.cdc.gov/hiv/topics/msm/index.htm

Cousins, N. (2005). *Anatomy of an illness as perceived by the patient.* New York: W.W. Norton & Company.

DelBuono, J., Jusis, J., Lopez, A., & Vallarelli, A. (2008, May 10). *The psychological and behavioral impact of cinematic films.* Poster presented at the 16th Annual Pace University Psychology Conference, Pace University, New York.

Demir, E. S. (2007) *Cinema therapy.* Retrieved May 25, 2008 from http://psinema.metu. edu.tr/makale/cinematherapy.pdf

Dermer, S. B., & Hutchings, J. B. (2000) Utilizing movies in family therapy. *The American journal of family therapy. 28,* 163–180.

Duncan, K., Beck, D., & Granum, R. (1986). Ordinary people: Using a popular film in group therapy. *Journal of counseling and development, 65*(1), 50–51.

Eber, M., & O'Brien, J. M. (1982) Psychotherapy in the movies. *Psychotherapy: Theory, research, and practice, 19,* 116–120.

Engdahl, B., Dikel, T. N., Eberly, R., & Blank, A., Jr. (1997). Posttraumatic stress disorder in a community sample of former prisoners of war: A normative response to severe trauma. *American journal of psychiatry, 154,* 1576–1581. Retrieved May 29, 2008, from Trauma Articles database.

Firestone, R. W., & Catlett, J. (1999). *Fear of intimacy.* Washington, DC: American Psychological Association.

Fischoff, S. (n.d.) Retrieved on April 3, 2008, from http://www.apa.org/divisions/div46/images/ fischoff2.pdf

Frank, S. (1989). *Sex in the movies.* Secaucus, NJ Citadel Press.

Fritz, G., & Pope, R. O. (1979). The role of cinema seminar in psychiatric education. *American journal of psychiatry, 136,* 207–210.

Gabbard, K., & Gabbard, G. (1999,). *Psychiatry and the cinema* (2nd ed.). Chicago: University of Chicago Press.

Gabbard, G. O. (2001). Psychotherapy in Hollywood cinema. *Australian Psychiatry, 9,* 365–369.

Grace, M. (2005). *Reel fulfillment: A 12-Step plan to transforming your life through movies.* New York: McGraw-Hill.

Greenfeld, L., Rand, M., Craven, D., Klaus, P., Perkins, C., Ringel,C., et al. (1998). *Violence by intimates: Analysis of data on crimes by current or former spouses, boyfriends, and girlfriends,* U.S. Department of Justice. Retrieved on June 1, 2008, from http://www.ojp.usdoj.gov/bjs/pub/pdf/vi.pdf

Groth-Marnat, G. (1992). Past traditions of therapeutic metaphor. *Psychology, A journal of human behavior, 29,* 41–47.

Heath, R. A. (2007). *Praeger handbook of transsexuality: Changing gender to match mindset.* Westport, CT: Praeger Press.

Hendricks, G., & Simon, S. (2005). *Spiritual cinema: A guide to movies that inspire, heal and empower your life.* Carlsbad, CA: Hay House.

Hesley, J. W., & Hesley, J. G. (2001). *Rent two films and let's talk in the morning: Using popular movies in psychotherapy* (2nd ed.). New York: John Wiley & Sons, Inc.

Horne, W., & Passmore, A. (1991) *Family counseling and therapy* (3rd ed.). Itasca, IL: F. E Peacock Publishers, Inc.

Imura, S. (1991). Transference and countertransference in nursing. *Emphasis nursing, 1,* 77–81.

Karlinsky, H. (2003). Doc Hollywood North: Part II. the clinical application of movies in psychiatry. *Canadian psychiatric association bulletin, 35,* 14–16.

Kazantizis, N. & L'Abate, L. (Eds.) (2007). *Handbook of homework assignments in psychotherapy.* New York, NY: Springer.

Kennedy-Bergen, R., & Barnhill, E. (2006). Marital rape new research and directions. *Applied research forum.* Retrieved May 29, 2008, from National Online Resource Center on Violence against Women database.

Koren, G. (1993). Awakenings: Using a popular movie to teach clinical pharmacology. *Clinical pharmacological therapy, 53,* 3–5.

Kelleher, K. (2002). Can an unconventional tie really bind couples? *Los Angeles times*, Southern California Living section, October 7, pp. E1, 4.

King, T. (2008). Syllabus: PY298 Honors- *Movies and mental disorder*. Retrieved on October 19, 2009, from http://www.bridgew.edu/SYS/Syliabi/PY298hsyIS08.pdf.

Krzywinska, T. (2006). *Sex and the cinema*. London: Wallflower Press.

Kuriansky, J. (1990). *How to love a nice guy*. New York: Doubleday.

Kuriansky, J. (2002). *The complete idiot's guide to a healthy relationship* (2nd ed.). Indianapolis: Alpha Books.

Kuriansky, J. (2003). *The complete idiot's guide to dating* (3rd ed.). Indianapolis: Alpha Books.

Kuriansky, J. (2004). *The complete idiot's guide to tantric Sex* (2nd ed.). New York: Penguin Publishing, Alpha Books.

Kuriansky, J., Walsh, N., & Laszczak, M. (2005, November 25). *Using the "talkback" technique to facilitate discussion after a creative media event and to survey audience members opinions on psychosocial issues*. Poster presented at the 3rd New School Psychology Poster Session. New School for Social Research, New York.

Lampropoulos, G. K, Deane, F. P., & Kazantzis, N. (2004). Psychologists' use of motion pictures in clinical practice. *American psychological association*, *35*, 535–541.

Macavoy, E., & Israelson, S. (1991). *The Marilyn syndrome: Breaking your love addiction before it breaks you*. New York: Donald I. Fine.

Mann, D. (2004). *Cinematherapy movies for mental health: Films that may help change the way we think and feel*. Retrieved on May 3, 2008 from http://www.msnbc.msn.com/id/4264832/

Mangin, D. (1999). Cinema therapy: How some shrinks are using moves to help their clients cope with life and just feel better. *Health and body*. May 27. Retrieved May 25, 2008, from http://www.salon.com/health/feature/1999/05/27/film_therapy/

Marion F. S., & Daniel J. S. (Eds.). (2003). *Healing trauma: Attachment, trauma, the brain, and the mind* (pp. 221–281). New York: Norton.

Miller, N., & Dollard, J. (1941). *Social learning and imitation*. New Haven, NJ: Yale University Press.

Mills, L. G. (2008). *Violent partners: A breakthrough plan for ending the cycle of abuse*. New York: Basic Books.

Newton, A. K. (1995). Silver screens and silver linings: Using theatre to explore feelings and issues. *Gifted Child Today*, *18*(2), 14–19.

Niemiec, R., & Wedding, D. (2008). *Positive psychology at the movies: Using films to build virtues and character strength*. Gottingen, Germany: Hogrefe & Huber.

Norcross, J. C. (2000). Here comes the self-help revolution in mental health. *Psychotherapy*, *37*, 370–377.

O'Connor, D. (1986, reissue). *How to make love to the same person for the rest of your life*. New York: Bantam.

O'Neill, N. (1984). *Open marriage: A new life style for couples*. New York: M. Evans & Company, Inc.

Orchowski, L., Spickard, B., & McNamara, J. (2006) Cinema and the valuing of psychotherapy: implications for clinical practice. *Professional psychology:Research and practice*, *37*(5), 506–514.

Pence, E., & Paymer, M. (1993). *Education groups for men who batter: The Duluth model*. New York, NY: Springer Publishing.

Portadin, M. A. (2006). *The use of popular film in psychotherapy – is there a "cinematherapy"?* Dissertation submitted in partial fulfillment of Ph.D requirements at Massachusetts School of Professional Psychology. Retrieved on May 7, 2008, from http://www.cinematherapy.com/pressclippings/Portadin-dissertation.pdf

Rice, J., & Rice, D. (1986). *Living through divorce – A developmental approach to divorce therapy*. New York: Guilford Press.

Richmond, R. L. (2009). *A guide to psychology and its practice: Trauma support groups*. Retrieved on October 19, 2009, from http://www.guidetopsychology.com/suppport.htm.

Rizza, M. (1997). *A parent's guide to helping children: Using bibliotherapy at home.*The National Research Center on the Gifted and Talented 1997 winter newsletter available at: http://www.ucc.uconn.edu/%26tilde;wwwgt/wintr972.html

Schneider, I. (1987). The theory and practice of movie psychiatry. *American journal of psychiatry, 144,* 996–1002.

Schulz, H. T. (2005, Winter). Good and bad movie therapy with good and bad outcomes. *The amplifier.* Newsletter of Division 46 of the American Psychological Association, p.19.

Seligman, L (2006). *Theories of counseling and psychotherapy.* Upper Saddle River, NJ: Pearson Merrill Prentice Hall

Sharp, C., Smith, J., & Cole, A. K. (2002). Cinematherapy: Metaphorically promoting therapeutic change. *Counseling psychology quarterly, 15,* 269–276.

Solomon, G. (2001). *Reel therapy: How movies inspire you to overcome life's problems.* New York: Lebhar-Friedman Books.

Sturdevant, C. G., & Gedron, M. (Eds.). (1998,). *The laugh & cry movie guide: Using movies to help yourself through life's changes* (2nd ed.). Larkspur, CA: LightSpheres.Publishing.

Teague, R. (2000). *Reel spirit: A guide to movies that inspire, explore and empower.* Unity Village, MO: Unity House.

Terr, L. C. (1991). Childhood trauma: An outline and overview. *American journal of psychiatry, 148,* 10–20

Toman, S. M., & Rak, C. F. (2000). The use of cinema in the counselor education curriculum: Strategies and outcomes. *Counselor Education and Supervision, 40,* 105–114.

Tyson, L., Foster, L., & Jones, C. (2000). The process of cinematherapy as a therapeutic intervention. *Alabama counseling association journal, 26*(1), 35–41.

Ulus, F. (2003). *Movie therapy, moving therapy! The healing power of film clips in therapy settings.* Victoria, British Columbia, Canada: Trafford Publishing.

University of Connecticut. (2008). Course on *Movies and medicine: Using film to reflect on the patient, the family, and illness,* given by Catherine Weber, Ph.D. and Hugh Silk, M. D. (Family Medicine). Retrieved on May 3, 2008, from http://www.commed.uchc.edu/medicalhumanities /humanities.htm

Wagner, P., & Mongon, P. (1998). *Validating the concept of abuse. Women's perceptions of defining behaviors and the effects of emotional abuse on health indicators, 7*(1). Retrieved May 29, 2008, from Archives of Family Medicine database.

Wedding, D., Boyd, M. A., & Niemiec, R. M. (2005). *Movies and mental illness: Using films to understand psychopathology.* Gottingen, Germany: Hogrefe & Huber.

Wolz, B. (2003). *Using the power of movies for therapeutic process. The therapist.* San Diego, CA: The California Association of Marriage and Family Therapists.

Wolz, B. (2004). *The cinema therapy workbook: A self-help guide to using movies for healing and growth.* Cayon, CA: Glenbridge Publishing Ltd.

Wolz, B. (2005). *E-motion picture magic: A movie lover's guide to healing and transformation.* Centennial, CO: Glenbridge Publishing, Ltd.

Young, G. (1987). *Your TV twins.* New York: Fawcett Columbine.

International Cinema: An Abundant Mental Health Resource of Films for Education, Communication, and Transformation

Ryan M. Niemiec

The language of film is universal.
-Common expression

Abstract The purpose of this chapter is to consider what films from various countries say about mental health, strengths, and values; mental illness and psychopathology; and the portrayal of psychologists and psychotherapy. My hope is this will widen the reader's perspective of what international cinema offers and begin the assembly of a non-exhaustive resource of potential films to be considered for personal use, for education, and for client interaction.

Introduction

I recall some of my first exposures to world cinema during undergraduate film studies courses. I was mesmerized by such films as the merging of identities in Ingmar Bergman's *Persona* (1966, Sweden), the seemingly incomprehensible surrealism in Federico Fellini's *8½* (1963, Italy), the subtle use of two actresses to play the same character in Luis Bunuel's *That Obscure Object of Desire* (1977, France/Spain), and the blending of beauty, an unrelenting score, and horrific violence in Stanley Kubrick's *A Clockwork Orange* (1971, U.K.). The universality of the art of the cinema became clear to me. I realized that if viewers only view films from their own country, they miss a significant number of important movies – opportunities for inspiration, connection, and the deepening of our cultural awareness and understanding of human nature.

The purpose of this chapter is to consider what films from various countries say about mental health, strengths, and values; mental illness and psychopathology; and the portrayal of psychologists and psychotherapy. My hope is this will widen the

R.M. Niemiec (✉)
VIA Institute on Character and Hummingbird Coaching Services, Cincinnati, OH, 45202, USA
e-mail: ryan@viacharacter.org

M.B. Gregerson (ed.), *The Cinematic Mirror for Psychology and Life Coaching*,
DOI 10.1007/978-1-4419-1114-8_7, © Springer Science+Business Media, LLC 2010

reader's perspective of what international cinema offers and begin the assembly of a non-exhaustive resource of potential films to be considered for personal use, for education, and for client interaction.

While some might consider it ethnocentric to call "international cinema" anything that is not U.S.-made, in fact, it is generally accepted that the generic terms "international cinema," "world cinema," and "foreign films" refer to movies from a country other than your own. The focus of this chapter is from a U.S. vantage point or as is frequently reflected in film circles, the U.S. "gaze." Films from the United Kingdom, Canada, and Australia are included in this distinction as foreign films (i.e., outside the U.S.) even though most Americans would not reference them as foreign since they are not "foreign language films."

World cinema carries an implication of films that are artistic, independent, and stylistic. This is often true as these films are frequently character-driven and theme-driven which very much lend themselves to the psychology and spirituality of the characters and drive home important messages related to mental health, positive psychology, and personal inspiration and transformation. This is, of course, not always the case; just as films from the U.S. can be monotonous, created for mass appeal, and lack any kind of depth, meaning, or purpose, so can films from other countries. At the same time, films from non-U.S. countries can be both highly meaningful and commercial garnering mainstream appeal, such as *Amelie* (Jeunet, 2001, France), *Life is Beautiful* (Benigni, 1997, Italy), and *Hero* (Zhang, 2002, Hong Kong/China), the latter film being the first Foreign Language film to ever top the American box office.

Most of the film examples in this chapter are foreign language films. I make three exceptions to this rule by occasionally including international directors making U.S. films (e.g., German director Wim Wenders and his direction of the U.S. film, *Don't Come Knocking*; 2005), U.S. films with predominant non-U.S. locations (e.g., *Babel* [Iñárritu, 2006], *The Nativity Story* [Hardwicke, 2006]), and the inclusion of films from English-speaking countries (i.e., Canada, Australia, and U.K.). Nevertheless, the vast majority of the film examples included here are contemporary, non-U.S. produced films by non-U.S. directors in non-U.S. locations.

In most cases, I refer to the film's country/countries of origin as listed in the Internet Movie Database (www.imdb.com).

I recall a conversation I had many years ago with a film studies professor; he simplified the panoply of films and film genres into three categories: Hollywood, Third Cinema, and the auteur film.

The first refers to the blockbuster, special effects, happy-ending, simple plot stories that have become stereotypic from large production studios in Los Angeles. Action films and comedies are the genres that best fit this description. While we might not agree with the infamous film critic, Pauline Kael, when she said, "Kiss Kiss Bang Bang... movies are seldom more than that," it is an adequate description of how numerous people perceive Hollywood filmmaking today. This category also includes films from India's Bollywood (just as Hollywood does not nearly represent all of American cinema, Bollywood does not represent India's cinema, despite the stereotypes); Bollywood films tend to be melodramatic, with formulaic, predictable plots with an emphasis on song and dance. According to Wikipedia, they are exceedingly popular in Afghanistan, Bangladesh, Iran, and Pakistan, and are rising in popularity in Israel, Latin America, and much of the Arab World.

The Third Cinema category refers to films from developing (Third World) countries and often focuses on and describes the cultural and social plight of a village, city, or nation. Films from developing African countries (e.g., Senegal) fall into this category. These films have the most limited release and pose a tremendous challenge for students interested in the topic to attain them.

The auteur (from the French word for author) film refers to the film's director as the "author" and predominant force in the inception, creation, and final product of the film. American independent cinema and many international films fall into the auteur category. There is often a distinct narrative style that distinguishes a particular director's films, i.e., it is easily recognizable when "a Quentin Tarantino film" is playing or "an M. Night Shyamalan film," or international films by Zhang Yimou, Wim Wenders, Giuseppe Tornatore, or Jean Pierre-Jeunet. This perspective states it is the director, rather than the producers, who is mostly responsible for the final product. The bulk of this chapter refers to films that would be considered auteur cinema.

This chapter will first give a conceptual base, rationale, and relevant research for the use of films in counseling and education. This real-world usage of films in clinical and pedagogic settings leads into a discussion of international film examples of mental health and wellness. This will conclude with discussion and examples of how international cinema portrays the profession of psychology and the practice of psychotherapy.

Using Movies for Education

"Cinemeducation" – coined by Alexander, Hall, and Pettice (1994) – refers to the use of movies in the education setting. Movies provide a unique modality to educate students. A variety of student populations have benefited from the use of movies to facilitate learning about mental health and mental illness: Psychology students (Fleming, Piedmont, & Hiam, 1990; Nelson, 2002; Wedding, Boyd, & Niemiec, 2005), nursing programs (Raingruber, 2003), students in counselor education programs (Toman & Rak, 2000), and medical students (Alexander, 1995; Alexander & Waxman, 2000; Karlinsky, 2003). Mental health films have also been used for other professionals ranging from training clergy, police officers, pharmacy students, and occupational therapy. It seems that virtually any student group can potentially benefit from the use of films to accentuate the topics to be learned.

Teachers have taken advantage of the dynamism of cinema to teach a variety of specific topics, such as family systems theories (Alexander & Waxman, 2000; Hudock & Warden, 2001), psychodynamic psychotherapy with adolescents (Miller, 1999), group psychotherapy (Tyler & Reynolds, 1998; Brabender, 2006), personality theory (Paddock, Terranova, & Giles, 2001), marriage and family counseling skills (Higgins & Dermer, 2001), and teaching about countertransference to trainees and colleagues (Swift & Wonderlich, 1993).

While each of these programs is utilizing an innovative technique designed to reach a wider range of students, the majority of these programs only utilize American films in their curricula, occasionally including one or two token foreign films.

Due to the widespread use of films in the classroom it is not surprising that there are a number of benefits to using movies as an adjunct. Movies promote active learning, provide different points of view, apply complex concepts and theories directly to real-world situations, and illustrate psychological states not readily seen by students such as Dissociative Identity Disorder (Gregg, 1995).

In a phenomenological study, Raingruber (2003) examined 11 graduate level nursing students which revealed several common threads of meaning – that movies are effective in promoting reflection, are emotion-arousing and empathy-producing, and are a good way to introduce ethical dilemmas.

Wilt, Evans, Muenchen, and Guegold (1995) conducted a study that found that the combination of movies with an instructor-led discussion significantly increased the empathy of nursing students compared to controls; however, the empathy scores had decreased to baseline by the end of the semester.

Some texts are geared toward helping the instructor select and utilize movie clips for educating students (see Alexander, Lenahan, & Pavlov, 2005; Engstrom, 2004) while others provide an adjunct resource that can be used by both the student and the teacher (see Wedding et al., 2005).

Cinematherapy

The term "cinematherapy" – the use of movies in psychotherapy – was coined by Berg-Cross, Jennings, and Baruch (1990). Cinematherapy by psychologists is actually quite common. In a survey of 827 practicing licensed psychologists, 67% reported that they use movies to promote therapy gains, while 88% stated movies were effective in promoting treatment outcome (1% reported movies as potentially harmful) (Lampropoulos, Kazantzis, & Dean, 2004).

Although the media plays a large role in shaping the public's perception of people with mental illness, mental health, and the role of psychotherapy and psychologists, health professionals appear to ultimately have a one-up on the media. For example, MacHaffie (2002) found that patients are impacted far more by health promotion information provided by health professionals than by information provided by the media.

There is a significant amount of anecdotal and case report data indicating the benefits of cinematherapy; however, there is a paucity of controlled research studies indicating its effectiveness (Berg-Cross et al., 1990; Hesley & Hesley, 1998; Schulenberg, 2003; Sharp, Smith, & Cole, 2002; Wedding & Niemiec, 2003). In addition to the obvious benefits of rapport building and increased homework compliance, movies tap into the emerging fields of mindfulness and acceptance therapy. Movies can increase a client's mindfulness of their thoughts, emotions, interpersonal conflicts, and problematic habits while also building in levels of acceptance (e.g., characters to identify with, universality of suffering, and role models of characters accepting, trusting, and letting go) and providing options for change.

Sometimes movies – if they are properly set up by the therapist – can immobilize a client's "stuck" patterns and address sensitive issues as it is less threatening if the client sees their issue on the screen at a distance. Due to the educational benefits of movies mentioned above, there is little doubt that movies can provide important mental health and mental illness education about a disorder for the client and their family and, therefore, help the client/family in their coping. Berg-Cross et al. (1990) add that films can build optimism, provide alternatives previously not considered by the client, facilitate family communication, break through resistance, and give clients a deeper understanding of their own strengths and weaknesses.

Hesley and Hesley (1998) explain that films aid treatment planning by offering hope and encouragement, reframing problems, providing role models, identifying and reinforcing internal strengths, potentiating emotion, improving communication, and helping clients prioritize values.

Using International Films with International Clients

For a psychologist practicing psychotherapy in the U.S., having experience with world cinema is a handy tool to have in the clinical armamentarium. The greater variety of international directors and assortment of films from different countries that a therapist is familiar with, the more likely the application. International clients are typically impressed that a therapist practicing in the U.S. knows about films outside the U.S.; this often leads to a healthy sense of openness, curiosity, and satisfaction that bodes well for the therapeutic encounter.

The use of films with international clients has several benefits: Provides a jump start in rapport building or a leap in the therapeutic relationship; breaks down cultural barriers; enhances the therapeutic relationship as a way of connecting with the client; increases therapist credibility as someone that can understand them; increases compliance with suggestions and interventions; allows the therapist to temporarily speak the client's "language"; and indicates the therapist's own creativity and flexibility to which some clients will see as an advantage in addressing their unique cultural issues.

Moreover, in conceptualizing and planning treatment with an international client, the benefits noted by Hesley and Hesley (1998) above become magnified; the offering of hope and reinforcement of strengths standout as particularly significant. Wedding and Niemiec (2003) discuss success in using the films of legendary Swedish filmmaker, Ingmar Bergman, with a chronically depressed man, native to Sweden, and reflected therapeutic gains in rapport, insight, and a significant shift in perception.

In initiating any new intervention, a clinician should be aware of contraindications and potential negative consequences (see Hesley & Hesley, 1998; Schulenberg,

2003). A potential drawback for the international client is the misunderstanding of the intervention or its purpose; therefore, therapists must be very clear in their initial explanations and be sure to discuss the film with the client as closely as possible to the viewing time.

At its best, cinematherapy with international clients is a catalyst for change and at its least it is a fun, engaging tool that if done mindfully is unlikely to harm the client.

Portrayals of Mental Health (in International Films)

Mental health can be conceptualized in a variety of ways – from the absence of disease to the presence of feelings of contentment and balance. Mental health is intricately connected with physical health and extends to one's personal and social environments, namely family, friends, and other important relationships. The field of positive psychology, initiated by Martin Seligman (1999), has flourished around the world in research and clinical settings (Joseph & Linley, 2006; Seligman, 2003; Snyder & Lopez, 2002, 2007). Positive psychology initiates a careful study of strengths and virtues that provides a helpful system making up many of the components of good mental health and wellness.

Positive Psychology: Virtues and Strengths

In their groundbreaking manual, *Character Strengths and Virtues*, Peterson and Seligman (2004) compiled a comprehensive system of Positive Psychology, delineating six human virtues that can be found (nearly) universally in over 200 virtue catalogues spanning over 3,000 years across the globe ranging from the philosophy of Aristotle to Benjamin Franklin to the Boy Scouts to all the major religions; these six virtues are broken down into 24 core human strengths. This system has been referred to tongue-in-cheek as the anti-DSM or more accurately "The Manual of the Sanities" not only because to its scope, systematized typology, and data-driven analysis but also because of its focus on the positives of the human experience rather than pathologies.

What follows is a brief description of a strength (according to the Peterson & Seligman text) followed by important international films that represent this strength. Since some readers may become lost in the shuffle of film examples below, Table 1 provides a list of outstanding international movies that should be considered essential viewing for any clinician, teacher, or student interested in positive psychology, mental health, or wellness. For those not as familiar with world cinema, these forerunners provide an excellent starting point; viewers will likely find themselves getting immediately engrossed in the majority of these films. For an extensive list and discussion of American, independent, and international movies representing each of the 24 positive psychology strengths, see *Positive Psychology at the Movies* (Niemiec and Wedding, 2008).

Table 1 Fifteen essential international films and accompanying virtues and strengths

Film (Year) Director(s)	Country	Virtue	Strength(s) exhibited
To Be and To Have (2002) Philibert	France	Wisdom	Creativity Curiosity
The Chorus (2004) Barratier	France	Wisdom	Love of learning
Elling (2002) Naess	Norway	Courage	Bravery Integrity
To Live (1994) Yimou	China/HK	Courage	Persistence Vitality
Yesterday (2004) Roodt	South Africa	Humanity	Love
Amelie (2001) Jeunet	France	Humanity	Kindness/Generosity
Son of the Bride (2002) Campanella	Argentina	Humanity	Love Social Intelligence
Cinema Paradiso (1988) Tornatore	Italy	Justice	Citizenship/Loyalty
Gandhi (1982) Attenborough	India/U.K.	Justice	Fairness Leadership
The Motorcycle Diaries (2004) Salles	Argentina	Justice	Fairness Teamwork
No Man's Land (2001) Tanovic	Bosnia/Herz.	Temperance	Forgiveness/ Mercy
March of the Penguins (2005) Jacquet	France	Temperance	Self-regulation
Wings of Desire (1987) Wenders	West Germany	Transcendence	Appreciation of beauty
Life is Beautiful (1997) Benigni	Italy	Transcendence	Humor Playfulness
Run Lola Run (1998) Tywker	Germany	Transcendence	Spirituality

The virtue of wisdom/knowledge consists of the cognitive strengths of creativity, curiosity, open-mindedness, love of learning, and perspective.

Creativity refers to the production of original ideas and behaviors that are adaptive in that they make a positive contribution to the individual's life and/or the lives of others. *The Overture* (Vichialak, 2004, Thailand) portrays the creativity of a musician expressing his talents in a solid path of dedication as an expression of emotion, control, pride, sacrifice, love, and competition. In the magically practical film, *To Be and to Have* (Philibert, 2002, France) a teacher finds creative ways to educate a variety of young students, each with unique needs; this is one of the most inspiring, meaningful films about the impact of teachers and their creativity that one can see. The use of creativity as a coping strategy to manage or triumph over challenging times is displayed in *Right Now* (Jacquot, 2004, France) and *My Left Foot* (Sheridan, 1989, Ireland/U.K.). Other films that demonstrate this strength include those portraying creative artists, such as that of Sylvia Plath in *Sylvia* (Jeffs, 2003, U.K.) and Vincent Van Gogh in *Vincent* (Cox, 1987, Australia) and *Vincent and Theo* (Altman, 1990, The Netherlands). Legendary Japanese director Akira Kurosawa addresses creativity in *Dreams* (1990, Japan).

Curiosity means to take an interest in ongoing experience, often involving novelty seeking and an intrinsic desire for knowledge. One of the best films that taps into curiosity is *Mongolian Ping-Pong* (Ning, 2005, China), a story about children who come across an object they have never seen before – a ping-pong ball floating in the river. They display what Buddhists call beginner's mind – seeing things as if for the first time. They look at the ball from every angle, licking it, smelling it, shaking it, and then repeating the process. The boy most fascinated by the object sleeps next to it and examines it upon morning awakening. He curiously lifts the ball up to the moon to get a different look at it. His curiosity leads him to ask various people "What is this?" in his exploration. Other terrific portrayals of the curiosity strength include transcendent stories about angels who become human in the Wim Wenders' classic, *Wings of Desire* (1987, West Germany), and its follow-up *Faraway, So Close* (1993, Germany); the former angels overtly display curiosity as they explore their environment with fresh eyes, now able to experience all of their senses in ways they could not as angels. *Everything is Illuminated* (Schreiber, 2005, filmed in Ukraine & Czech Republic) displays a young man who is highly curious about his family history and decides to travel to the Ukraine for further investigation. In *Swimming Pool* (Ozon, 2003, France/U.K.) – a writer begins to take a curious interest in a young provocative woman who is living with her; this transforms her perspective and inspires her writing. In *Secrets of the Heart* (Armendáriz, 1997, Spain), a young boy, Javi, living with his mother, grandfather, uncle, and brother curiously explores his surroundings and incessantly (but not obsessively) asks questions of each of his family members. He displays a patient observation asking about which candle is his at church, why his grandfather wears his slippers on the wrong feet, whether a bee will escape or become captured by a spider web, about family history and secrets, and sex and relationships. Javi's curiosity and observation – visual and auditory – leads him to important conclusions that his family had been avoiding.

Open-mindedness means to examine things from all sides in a fair and balanced manner, especially the opposite view of one's beliefs, plans, or goals. While *Water* (Mehta, 2006, India) probably taps into all six human virtues, the virtue of wisdom seems to be predominant, especially the strengths of open-mindedness and curiosity. Female widows are sent off to live a life ostracized from society after their husbands die. One widow is an eight-year-old curious and clever girl. Three of the other widows in the isolated community insist on keeping an open mind seeing all perspectives despite extraordinary injustice, antiquated and harmful traditions, and immense social and economic challenges; each woman and girl's wisdom helps the others to transcend their situation in a unique way. In *A Pure Formality* (Tornatore, 1994, France), Roman Polanski portrays an investigator who must consider all angles in order to solve a complex mystery.

Love of learning means to cognitively engage in new information and skills, often referring to the process of mastering new topics or knowledge areas. In the beautiful film, *The Chorus* (Barratier, 2004, France), the teacher, Clement Mathieu, inspires this strength in his students despite overt adversity from the school administration and the students themselves. *Unknown White Male* (Murray, 2005, U.K./U.S.) tells the true story of Doug Bruce who awakens one day to complete retrograde amnesia.

His family and friends appear to be strangers to him; some question the legitimacy of the amnesia and fugue. Bruce shows a passion for self-expression and communication. He cries at his visit to the ocean. He displays a genuine eagerness to learn or re-learn everything. He attempts to not engage in clichés or stereotypes, and looks upon the world with originality as he views his new chance at life as an opportunity to re-invent himself and start afresh.

Perspective means a person has a high capacity of knowledge and ability to address challenging questions about the meaning of life to assist oneself or provide wisdom to others. *Antonia's Line* (Gorris, 1995, The Netherlands) portrays independent women who approach issues of life and death with perspective and wisdom. Antonia is a strong, assertive woman in this deeply integrated story of multiple generations of women. The strength of wisdom is clear when Antonia explains death to her granddaughter saying, "Nothing dies forever. Something always remains, from which something new grows. So life begins, without knowing where it came from or why it exists." "But why?," asks the inquisitive girl to which Antonia responds, "Because life wants to live." In the interesting, cinematically beautiful film, *Taste of Cherry* (Kiarostami, 1997, Iran), the protagonist, Mr. Badii, has decided to commit suicide and spends several hours attempting to track down one person who would be willing to help him in his quest. He eventually comes across a man who represents the "wise old man" archetype. The wisdom from this stranger seems to break through the rigid thinking and belief patterns of Mr. Badii who appears to have gained wisdom in the interaction. Although the ending is intentionally left ambiguous to allot for viewer interpretation, it can be argued that Mr. Badii has deepened his connection with the world around him and has reversed his decision. In the three films of the *Lord of the Rings* trilogy (Jackson, 2001, 2002, 2003, New Zealand), the Gandalf character is a wisdom figure providing perspective and good counsel to the hobbits along their tumultuous journey.

The virtue of courage refers to the emotional strengths of bravery, persistence, integrity, and vitality.

Bravery or valor involves a voluntary action for what is perceived to be right despite the presence of opposition, danger, loss, or injury. *Hotel Rwanda* (George, 2004, filmed in South Africa and Rwanda) portrays the heroic Paul Rusesabagina (Don Cheadle), a hotel manager who risked his life to save over a thousand Tutsi refugees from Hutu militia during the genocide of 1994. Rusesabagina represents all dimensions of courage, including physical, psychological, and moral courage. Other prominent themes of the film include unconditional love, sacrifice, resiliency, hope, and the representation of the human spirit to overcome evil. *Don't Tell* (Eaton, 2005, Italy), nominated for Best Foreign Film, displays the psychological courage of a woman who had previously repressed her sexual abuse to face her painful past. Her psychological journey is depicted: Everyday life in her relationships, her descent (nightmares of her experiences), her healing (getting the truth), and the return to her daily life. In a similar display of psychological courage, a man in *The Celebration* (Vinterberg, 1998, Denmark) confronts his father in front of extended family and friends on his father's birthday for the sexual abuse he endured many years ago. The timing and modus are questionable, but the valor to take such an action is courageous. *Emmanuel's Gift* (Lax, 2005, filmed in Ghana, West Africa) tells the story of a man born with a deformed leg in Ghana. While this typically leads to a fate of a lifetime of begging on the streets, Emmanuel displays tremendous courage to overcome the challenge by riding a bike across his country and ultimately competing in triathlons. He refuses to accept "no" or be brought down by the overwhelming odds. *The Constant Gardener* (Meirelles, 2005, Germany/U.K.) portrays characters who display the courage and resiliency to battle the corruption of the pharmaceutical industry. The incredibly artistic, visually encapsulating films, *Crouching Tiger, Hidden Dragon* (Lee, 2000, Taiwan), *Hero* (2002, Hong Kong/China), and *House of Flying Daggers* (Zhang, 2004, China/Hong Kong), portray the strength of bravery in an unforgettable way using breathtaking cinematography and extensive choreography as the characters fight with grace and intensity. *Babel* (Iñárritu, 2006, filmed in Morocco, Japan, Mexico, and U.S.) interweaves four poignant stories, each portraying the strength of valor at a time of crisis; the value of intimacy and touch as well as the problems of cross-cultural communication are prime motifs. It is clearly bravery depicted in the documentary *Seoul Train* (Butterworth, 2004, filmed in North Korea, South Korea, China, Poland, Switzerland, and U.S.), about the life and death of North Koreans as they attempt to escape their homeland and the people who risk everything to help them. A classic film that addresses the strength of bravery is Robert Bresson's *A Man Escaped* (Bresson, 1956, France).

Persistence involves the continuation of a goal-directed action despite obstacles and challenges. Zhang Yimou is the best-known contemporary Chinese filmmaker and is particularly gifted at portraying the strength of persistence, often the determination of a low, poor peasant character breaking out of a hopeless situation (Lu, 2002). *Not One Less* (Zhang, 1999, China) is about a young, 13-year-old teacher who substitutes for a month in a classroom at a remote village. She finds creative ways to teach her students in a way that is applicable directly to life. She stands strong with her goal of "not one less," meaning that there not be any less students when the former teacher returns; she persists through numerous challenges to maintain her goal. Yimou addresses the persistence and sufferings of a family in *To Live* (Yimou, 1994, China/Hong Kong) as the couple overcomes a number of significant tragedies over the decades.

The shocking film *Nobody Knows* (Koreeda, 2004, Japan), about a mother and her four children, each from a different father and living in a small apartment, is inspired by true events that occurred in Tokyo. The mother slowly abandons her four young children leaving them to figure out how to survive themselves. This is a challenge for the kids since they do not realize she has left them (she would routinely leave them for several days at a time) and they do not have any resources as the mother prevented them from attending school. The 12-year-old (the oldest of the four) is left to take responsibility for himself and his siblings. *Mountain Patrol: Kekexili* (Lu, 2004, China/Hong Kong) portrays the perseverance of the Tibetan people in the Himalayas as they defend their land to save the antelope from poachers. *Peace One Day* (Gilley, 2004, U.K.) is a documentary about a young man who is a clear example of perseverance, ingenuity, and industriousness as he travels around the world to lobby a cause of creating a cease-fire day of peace. He persists through various powerful obstacles and is a good example of how one man can make a difference. *Rabbit-Proof Fence* (Noyce, 2002, Australia) is based on the true story of the endurance of two young Aboriginal girls who escape from an official government camp that has been set up to integrate them into a White society. Sir Ernest Shackleton's incredible persistence and perseverance in his legendary expedition to Antarctica from 1914 to 1916 is portrayed in *The Endurance* (Butler, 2000, Germany/U.S.). Persistence is also seen in a psychiatrist in *Equus* (Lumet, 1977, U.K./U.S.) and a Holocaust survivor in *The Pianist* (Polanski, 2002, France, Germany, U.K., Poland). A classic film depicting the strength of persistence in daily life is Vittorio De Sica's *The Bicycle Thief* (De Sica, 1948, France).

Integrity means to speak the truth and to represent oneself in a genuine way that is consistent with one's values. In *Intimate Strangers* (Leconte, 2004, France) a woman intending to go to a psychiatrist goes to the wrong room and has sessions with a tax advisor. It is interesting to contrast the authenticity of the woman, honest and self-disclosing, with that of the tax advisor which, at first, is inauthentic, not revealing his true identity. He eventually learns to take responsibility for his actions, which she also learns through her sharing in "therapy" to become more authentic and integrated in her daily life. *Dirty, Filthy Love* (Shergold, 2004, U.K.) is an offbeat comedy that portrays the growing integrity of a man with obsessive compulsive disorder (OCD) and Tourette's Disorder who learns to take responsibility and face the reality of his OCD illness.

Vitality means to have a zest, energy, and enthusiasm for life in which one approaches life activities with vigor in body and mind. In *The World's Fastest Indian* (Donaldson, 2005, New Zealand), an aging New Zealander (Anthony Hopkins) refuses to let anything get in the way of his passion for riding his Indian motorcycle. Whether he is riding his motorcycle, introducing himself to a stranger, or joking with his neighbor, he displays an ongoing quality of zest and love of life that is contagious. *Touching the Void* (Macdonald, 2003, U.K.) depicts two mountain climbers who face incredible survival challenges and must make use of every morsel of energy in order to survive; in considering the challenges that one particular climber faces, it is the resiliency of his vitality that saves his life.

The virtue of humanity refers to the interpersonal strengths of love, kindness, and social intelligence.

Love means to value close relationships with others, particularly those in which there belies mutual sharing, caring, and connecting. *2046* (Wong, 2004, China/Hong Kong) is a story of romantic love in different time periods, directed by Wong Kar-Wai, who is known for his "cinema of poetry," fragmented storylines, flamboyant color schemes, and manipulation of spatial and temporal relationships (Stringer, 2002). The lead character in *2046* summarizes a major theme in the film via his voice-over, "Love is all a matter of timing – it's no good meeting the right person too soon or too late." *Yesterday* (Roodt, 2004, South Africa) tells the story of a woman named Yesterday dying of AIDS whose final goal in life is to see her daughter, Beauty, attend her first day of school. Although Yesterday has many positive attributes, it is her love for her daughter that is most significant in the film. She also displays love in her care-taking of her dying, at times abusive, husband,

and *philia* love for a teacher-friend in the local community. It is ironic that the protagonist's name is Yesterday since her strengths lie in how she treats people in the present and in her persistence and mind-set of setting forth her future. Powerful romantic love stories are portrayed in *The Postman/Il Postino* (Costner, 1994, France), *Like Water for Chocolate* (Arau, 1992, Mexico), and *Moulin Rouge!* (Luhrmann, 2001, Australia/U.S.). In *Eros* (Antonioni, Soderbergh, & Wong, 2004, Hong Kong/China/Italy/U.S.) three renown directors give their perspective on love and lust in three short films connected by images of nude drawings in between. The first, *The Hand*, directed by Wong Kar Wai, reflects the theme of eros in yearning and non-judgment. The second, *Equilibrium*, directed by Steven Soderbergh, explores eros as fantasy. The third, *The Dangerous Thread of Things*, directed by Michelangelo Antonioni, explores eros as letting go and being free.

The undying love of John Bayley for his wife, British novelist/philosopher, Iris Murdoch, who is dying of Alzheimer's disease, is movingly portrayed in *Iris* (Eyre, 2001, U.K.). *3-Iron* (Kim, 2004, South Korea) is a highly unconventional love story about a man who breaks into houses while people are away vacationing and encounters a mute woman who is routinely abused by her husband. They fall in love, engage in the house-breaking together, and confront the abusive husband; the love clearly transforms both characters into a newfound happiness that seems impenetrable. Eventually, the man is killed, but their love continues on as he becomes a ghost continuing to love her. *Under the Sun* (Nutley, 1998, Sweden) is a slow moving love story drama about a lonely, avoidant farmer and a compassionate woman whom he hires as his housekeeper. The film addresses themes of secrecy, trust, and naivete in relationship to love. *Reconstruction* (Boe, 2003, Denmark) is an artistic film about a man with a girlfriend who falls in love with a random woman and suddenly everyone he knows except this new woman begins to deny his existence. This story within a story addresses themes of being in love, with being in love, love in the fleeting moment, and loving another person. Sibling love is portrayed between a 66-year old woman with an intellectual disability and her sister in *Pauline and Paulette* (Debrauwer, 2001, Belgium) and between fraternal twin sisters split apart in early childhood in *Twin Sisters* (Sombogaart, 2002, Netherlands). Love is also a major theme and strength expressed in *Heaven's Bookstore* (Shinohara, 2005, Japan) and *The Road Home* (Zhang, 1999, China), the latter depicting a woman's dedicated love to maintain extensive rituals and tradition for her deceased husband.

Kindness means to care for others solely for the act of generosity, altruism, nurturance, or compassion in and of itself. In *Vera Drake* (Leigh, 2004, U.K.), a care-taking woman, who seems to care for everyone in her life – her family (homemaker), her ailing mother, her friends/neighbors, her position as housekeeper – takes a role of helping women have abortions at a time and place in which it was outlawed and unacceptable. Regardless of one's stand on abortion, her intention of "I help out young girls" is one of compassion, nurturance, and ultimately self-sacrifice. *The Accidental Hero* (Jaoui, 2002, France) portrays different types of care-giving, particularly the idiosyncratic but loving attempts of an awkward son for his head injured mother. *Tsotsi* (Hood, 2005, South Africa) portrays an African gangster who kills and steals as needed until he discovers an infant in the backseat of a stolen car and reluctantly decides to care for it. Via flashbacks we learn of Tsotsi's painful past, longing for connections. Caring and nurturing the child helps Tsotsi make a connection with a care-taking mother, renew a friendship with the man he brutalized, and return the baby to its parents. *Manderlay* (von Trier, 2005, Denmark) addresses the themes of human compassion, taking action with compassion to help a community change and adapt, and the pros and cons of altruistic intentions despite the community not wanting a change. *Son of the Bride* (Campenella, 2001, Argentina) is a tremendously touching film about changing habitual patterns geared toward overworking and neglecting those whom one loves and transforming to a perspective of nurturance. *Mostly Martha* (Nettelbaum, 2001, Italy) displays a woman's patience, precision, creativity, and care for food that she learns to translate into her relationship with her sister's daughter. Nurturance and compassion expressed through food is expressed in ways to enhance community relationships in the award-winning films *Chocolat* (Hallström, 2000, U.K./U.S.) and *Babette's Feast* (Axel, 1987, Denmark). The impact of simple acts of kindness, generosity, and altruism is terrifically well done in the short film *Right Here, Right Now* (2003, India).

Social intelligence means to be aware of patterns, similarities, and differences in the motives and feelings of others and within oneself. This leads to the individual knowing what to do to fit into a variety of social situations. German director, Wim Wenders in another successful film, *Don't Come Knocking* (2005, Germany/U.S.) creates a character who seems to lack all virtues, yet as he persists in facing his past he begins to listen more; this leads to a deeper awareness of the feelings of those around him and the impact his actions have had upon others. *Japanese Story* (Brooks, 2003, Australia) depicts a Japanese businessman and a rustic Australian woman who have very low awareness of one another's feelings, motives, and perspectives. As they overcome adversity in the dangerous outback they begin to connect on an interpersonal level and display significant changes in acceptance, patience, and love; these strengths are then immediately tested in the tragedy of a freak accident.

The virtue of justice refers to the civic strengths of citizenship, fairness, and leadership.

Citizenship or social responsibility refers to an individual's sense of duty, loyalty, teamwork, and obligation to a common good. Many international films will fall under the virtue of justice and fit under the strength of citizenship due to the frequent themes of nationalism, political and community activism, and the challenges, rigor, and at times, success of social and political change. A good example of a film that fits this rubric is the Oscar-winning political thriller, *Z* (Costos-Gravas, 1969, Algeria/France). *The Sea Inside* (Amenábar, 2004, Spain) raises issues and a number of questions about justice and social responsibility, such as what is the level of social justice or responsibility in situations of assisted suicide among the terminally ill or those almost completely immobile? This film advocates for the right of people to make their decision on this matter. The sense of duty, loyalty, and obligation of the North Korean people to their leader, Kim Jong Il, could not be more clear in the propaganda film, *North Korea: A Day in the Llife* (Fleury, 2004, North Korea). Dutch filmmaker, Pieter Fleury, was allowed by the North Korean government to shoot this film that gives a glimpse into the life of this culture and country. This frightening documentary short engenders provocative questions relating to the blurry boundaries between duty, obligation, and coercion and between healthy nationalism and unhealthy propaganda; this film should not be taken as a suggestion for how to build citizenship.

Fairness means to treat all people the same, in a non-discriminatory, respectful, moral manner. Mahatma Gandhi was an advocate and prototype for the strength of fairness; his activism, beliefs, and courageous actions are portrayed by Ben Kingsley in the eight-time Oscar-winning *Gandhi* (Attenborough, 1982, India/U.K.). *V for Vendetta* (McTeigue, 2005, U.K./U.S.) depicts a mysterious character acting as a vigilante and semi-superhero fighting against a corrupt system. *Black Rain* (*The Last Wave*; 1977, Australia) addresses themes of fairness in this Peter Weir film about aboriginal integration in society, the maintenance of their rituals and beliefs and secrets, and the breaking of tribal law. *The Motorcycle Diaries* (Salles, 2004, Argentina) is based on the journals and adventures of Ernesto "Che" Guevara, who later became the leader of the Cuban revolution, and his journey with his friend through Central America. Themes of inequality, fairness, integrity, and suffering abound in relation to encounters and observations of rich/poor, healthy/sick, and perseverant/deteriorating. In one scene, the asthmatic Guevara exerts himself heavily to do what no other had previously done and swims across a river (which divides the healthy care-takers and the sick); this is a powerful symbolic act representing fairness, equality, and crossing the divide. Che reflects that this infamous voyage changed him awakening a Latin American consciousness within him that contributed significantly to his later work.

Leadership refers to the ability to motivate, influence, and help others to achieve a common purpose or goal. The political leadership of Gandhi in *Gandhi* (Attenborough, 1982) and religious leadership through the ascetic example of Siddhartha in *Little Buddha* (Bertolucci, 1993, Liechtenstein/U.K.) are good examples of positive leaders. Certainly, we can learn from dangerous leaders who have an ulterior or self-serving agenda that is not in the name of justice or the good of the people. Films portraying charismatic yet dangerous leaders include the character of Adolf Hitler in *Downfall* (Herschbiegel, 2004, Germany) and the portrayal of Ugandan leader, Idi Amin, in *The Last King of Scotland* (Macdonald, 2006, U.K.). Oscar-winner Forest Whitaker plays Amin as the "father" of Uganda – fun-loving, friendly, teasing, and highly engaging as well as ruthless, explosive, unpredictable, and paranoid. Amin murdered over 300,000 Ugandans during his reign.

The virtue of temperance refers to the moderation strengths of forgiveness, humility/modesty, prudence, and self-regulation.

Forgiveness or mercy refers to accepting the shortcomings of others and engaging in the internal, pro-social changes of extending mercy and giving others a second chance. *In My Country* (Boorman, 2004, South Africa/U.K.) is an emotional film that explicitly addresses forgiveness. In 1994, South Africa's apartheid system was overthrown and the film tells us that President Nelson Mandela offered amnesty to those who committed human rights abuses, providing they told the whole truth and could prove they followed orders . . . the victims would have the chance to tell their stories and confront their persecutors; instances of these are reenacted in this film. The emphasis on perpetrators coming forth in honesty and telling the truth while the victims have an opportunity to tell their story, forgive, and bring healing to the deepest of pains; macro-cosmically this film is about a country healing itself through the forgiveness of one person at a time. Best foreign film Academy Award winner, *No Man's Land* (Tanovic, 2001, Bosnia-Herzegovina), displays the mutual mercies of a Bosnian and Serb who meet in the middle ("no man's land") of their enemy lines during wartime. The search for forgiveness and letting go is seen in a man dying of a brain tumor in *The City of No Limits* (Hernández, 2002, Spain).

Humility refers to maintaining a balanced view of one's achievements, allowing one's success to speak for itself while readily acknowledging one's mistakes. In *Charisma* (Kurosawa, 1999, Japan), the protagonist displays humility and persistence in saving a peculiar tree. The man summarizes his non-grandiose, balanced approach in that "An average man can only do average things . . . I'm fine just as I am, an average man. That's plenty."

Prudence means to be practical, deliberate, and reflective with one's daily life choices while resisting impulses, and finding balance with one's goals. Helen Mirren's portrayal of Queen Elizabeth in *The Queen* (Frears, 2006, U.K.) is a prototypical example of the strength of practical, non-reactive, prudence. *The Story of the Weeping Camel* (Davaa, 2003, Mongolia) is a fascinating story about a nomadic family in the middle of the Gobi Desert in Mongolia with several camels, one of which has just given birth to an albino colt and is rejecting it, refusing to allow it to feed from her despite repeated human attempts. The two young boys of the family go on a journey in a desert to find a musician who will perform a ritual to attempt to re-connect the camel and her albino colt. Rather than reacting hastily, the family portrays careful prudence in their patience and strategy to influence the natural bonding process between the mother camel and her colt. *The Road Home* (Zhang, 1999, China) is a wonderful, simple film directed by Zhang Yimou with profound messages of love and dedication. Following the death of her husband, the wife is insistent on maintaining the cultural tradition of having her husband's body walked home so "he can find his way." The mother's prudence and patience are striking and are symbolized in many of her actions in the film. A delightful Yimou film that parallels *The Road Home* (Zhang, 1999, China) is *Not One Less* (Zhang, 1999, China), a simple but profound story that places emphasis on teaching, tradition, and carefully following what one believes in.

Self-regulation means to exert control and balance over one's thoughts, impulses, emotions, and behaviors, often in a disciplined, goal-oriented way. The troubled adolescent boys in *The Chorus* (Barratier, 2004, France) learn to regulate their emotions through their singing, which dampens much of their acting out behaviors. This film taps into many strengths and resources within the young student, such as creativity, love of learning, persistence, vitality, love, teamwork, appreciation of excellence, and hope. Films like the breathtaking documentaries, *Winged Migration* (Perrin, 2001, France) and *March of the Penguins* (Jacquet,

2005, France), portray birds with incredible persistence and self-regulation abilities. Despite the anthropomorphism in making such comparisons, both films are incredible examples by which humans can learn an abundance of wisdom. *March of the Penguins* (Jacquet, 2005, France) is specifically about the mating life of penguins in Antarctica. To not only survive minus 50-degree temperatures but to survive as a species, the penguins display the (human) strengths of patience, prudence, resiliency, sacrifice, and self-regulation. In the allegorical *Warm Water Under a Red Bridge* (Imamura, 2001, Japan), Shohei Imamura tells the story of a woman who regularly experiences a build up of water in her body and the only way to release it is to exhibit an impulse such as sex or shoplifting, but mostly the former, to which the water then comes pouring out. With a plot like this, it would be easy to see this as ridiculous, but it is presented as an authentic struggle and challenging situation – not in a supernatural context other than via the film's score. This situation seems to represent one's vital essence, satisfying of one's desires, expression of free will, and the genuine struggle of self-regulation. In *The Queen* (Frears, 2006), Queen Elizabeth's character is one of tremendous temperance – poise, order, and self-control. In both the public and private arena she handles situations with measured control. The Hindi-language film, *The Warrior* (Kapadia, 2001, U.K.), tells the story of a ferocious warrior at the time of feudal India who renounces his sword to take up peace by practicing non-violence; this, of course, requires the strength of self-regulation. In *Spring, Summer, Fall, Winter . . . and Spring* (Kim, 2003, South Korea), a teacher instructs a monk on self-control. As the seasons turn, so does the landscape of the emotions and the challenges to self-control.

The virtue of transcendence refers to the meaning strengths of appreciation of beauty, gratitude, hope, humor, and spirituality.

Appreciation of beauty and excellence means to identify and take pleasure in the beauty of the visual environment or the skills or virtues of another; this often involves an active sense of awe and wonder. *Wings of Desire* (Wenders, 1987, West Germany) and *Faraway, So Close!* (Wenders, 1993, Germany) place emphasis on the beauty of each moment, love of life, and the desire to do good. The film's themes even characterize this strength in that it is about how our "seeing" transforms how we "look." *The Wind Will Carry Us* (Kirostami, 1999, Iran), directed by Abbas Kiarostami, exhibits one minor character, the village doctor, who is completely dedicated to the strength of the appreciation of beauty. He exclaims, "Death is the worst. When you close your eyes on this world, this beauty, the wonders of nature, and the generosity of God, it means you'll never be coming back." *Amelie* (Jeunet, 2001, France) places significant emphasis on the appreciation of the little things in life – skipping stones, a garden gnome statue, photographs of strangers' faces, or a box of nostalgic items from childhood – essentially revealing that these aren't "little" things. The film, *After Life* (Koreeda, 1998, Japan), an intermediary place where those who have died go to reflect on their life and discern one's memory that will then be re-created for them to experience throughout eternity. As each character considers their options, they are often driven to appreciate their lives and choose the best of the best memories; characters choose a range of experiences from one sensation (e.g., a taste) to a Disney World experience (most often chosen by children) to a participation in a loved one's happiness. This process, in turn, naturally brings the viewer to reflect on their own memories and deepen their appreciation of the beauty and positivity of their experiences. The well-known *And Your Mother, Too/Y Tu Mama Tambien* (Cuaron, 2001, Mexico) addresses this strength in a dying woman who attempts to make the most of her final weeks by appreciating the beauty of nature and human beings around her.

Some films significantly engender appreciation of beauty within the viewer, such as the non-verbal film, *Baraka* (Fricke, 2001), a visual masterpiece filmed in 24 countries on six continents; "baraka" is a Sufi word translating to "a blessing" or the breath or essence of life from which the evolutionary process unfolds. Other films that build upon this strength in the viewer are the mesmerizing insect documentary, *Microcosmos* (Nuridsany & Pérenou 1996, France), and *Genesis* (Nuridsany, 2004, France), a documentary that brings one to think about and care more deeply for the universe, animals, environment, and the elements of water, fire, and earth.

Gratitude is to be aware of and express thankfulness for the gifts, actions, or presence of another. *Rory O'Shea Was Here* (O'Donnell, 2004, U.K.) portrays two young men with physical disabilities befriending one another and finding ways to support one another. Rory, an angry rebellious man who has muscular dystrophy, cannot walk and has limited use of his hands while his speech is unaffected. Michael, a lonely man, often teased, has cerebral palsy and slurred speech yet maintains good control of his arms and hands. As the two befriend one another, Rory becomes Michael's voice while Michael becomes Rory's arms. They pursue independent living with one another and hire a care-taker. They begin to take the care-taking for granted as their expectations rise. They learn the strength of gratitude, in that they deepen their gratefulness for one another and for the efforts and energy of the care-taker, hence transcending some of the challenges of their illnesses. Gratitude is well represented throughout the film, *Amelie* (Jeunet, 2001, France), in which characters express gratitude, verbally and non-verbally, to those who have done good deeds.

Hope and optimism mean to take a stance that the future will be positive and good; hope refers more to a positive feeling while optimism is positive thinking and expectations. *Cape of Good Hope* (Bamford & Bamford, 2004, South Africa) reveals several intertwining stories revolving around a rescue shelter of a small town. Each of the main characters – a refugee from a war-torn Congo, a single mother/housekeeper battling an abusive, rapist employer, a young Muslim couple, a nice-guy veterinarian, and an emotionally guarded animal shelter founder – is a symbol of hope. The Oscar-winning *Pelle the Conqueror* (August, 1987, Denmark) begins with the high hopes of a man, Lasse, and his son, Pelle, as they leave Sweden with dreams of living a luxurious and happy life in Denmark. They quickly find a painful existence with great hardships. Pelle faces many challenges, environmental (stuck with poor living conditions in a fly-infested area), psychological (mother has died), emotional (abused by the staff and teased incessantly by classmates), and spiritual (hope of living a better life seems almost unreachable). Despite atrocious circumstances, Pelle keeps up hope for a better life. While the film has an ambiguous ending in which Pelle courageously leaves his father and his situation, the viewer sees that he is attempting to follow his dream for a better life, thus concluding with a message of hope. Jean Pierre-Jeunet's WWI film, *A Very Long Engagement* (2004, France), is an allegory of hope as a woman follows her feeling that her husband who has gone off to war is still alive, despite all accounts to the contrary.

Vodka Lemon (Saleem, 2003, Armenia) is a slow but engaging and interesting comedy of subtle vibrancy from exiled Iraqi Kurd director, Hiner Saleem. It is filmed completely in Armenia, post-USSR. A widowed man and woman romance after meeting along their daily trips to their spouses' gravesites. The man eventually has to sell all of his possessions due to poverty but his optimism and resiliency remain unaffected. Perhaps this film is an allegory on "attitude" since the viewer never gets a pessimistic feeling despite circumstances that would indicate this for most. This minimalist film exhibiting white vistas of beauty pleasantly mixes diegetic (sound internal to the film) and non-diegetic (sound external to the film) music, and captures tragic experiences within the backdrop of beautiful landscape. *Lighthouse Hill* (Fairman, 2004, U.K.) and *Danny Deckchair* (Balsmeyer, 2003, Australia) portray themes of hope and transformation following a character making a change in their environment. In both films, the lead character struggles with their current life in a number of ways, leaves the situation heading to a very different community and change of scenery (in the latter film, the man constructs a flying device of helium balloons attached to a deck chair and flies off), finds hope, healing, and connections in the new environment, and eventually must return to their past home to face the realities of their old life. While avoidance and escapism are clearly unhealthy and usually exacerbate current problems, there are redeeming values of these two films. *Blue Butterfly* (Pool, 2004, Canada) is based on a true story in which a terminally ill boy and his idol (an entomologist) travel to a remote jungle in search of a rare, magical, blue butterfly. The boy's hope to find the butterfly parallels the hope in continuing to live his life and recover from his illness. A classic film that addresses the strength of hope is Ingmar Bergman's *Wild Strawberries* (1957, Sweden).

Humor refers to having a sense of playfulness and/or having the ability to make others laugh and see the lighter side of things. *Life is Beautiful* (Benigni, 1997, Italy) portrays a compassionate father, Guido, who uses uncanny imagination, playfulness, and humor to help his son cope with conditions and avoid the realities of a concentration camp. *Marie Antoinette* (Coppolla, S., 2006, France/U.S.) portrays Kirsten Dunst as Austrian royalty who marries into French royalty and becomes queen. Despite an uptight, high-brow society, Marie maintains a playfulness that is kept within reason; she gives hugs to nobility surprising the receiver, giggles frequently, is good-humored with her friends, and breaks trends when she is the only one clapping at operatic performances. *Ridicule* (Leconte, 1996, France) overtly addresses and applies different types of humor, particularly wit, as a poor French lord is challenged in building this strength within himself. *Looking for Comedy in the Muslim World* (Brooks, 2005, filmed in India and the U.S.), a pseudo-documentary depicting comedian, Albert Brooks, who portrays himself in that he is asked by the U.S. government to help them better understand the Muslim culture. His task is to go to India and Pakistan to ask people, "What makes you laugh?" and write an extensive report on his findings. The film speaks to themes on the psychology of humor and laughter and shows a rare depiction of "laughing clubs," which have become widely popular in India; Hindus, Muslims, and Sikhs are in attendance on yoga mats raising their hands and laughing for therapeutic benefits. *Nothing* (Natali, 2003, Canada) is a transcendent comedy in its originality and message. The film itself is very playful in that each character can make various things they think about disappear, including themselves.

Spirituality refers to finding meaning and purpose in one's life and in something greater – God, a divine force, Higher Power, or the sacred – that transcends reality. *Run Lola Run* (Tywker, 1998, Germany), an intense, fast-paced creative film that follows protagonist, Lola, on three fast-paced journeys controlled by time and fate, shows the significant difference of small and large decisions we make in life; the film acutely addresses themes of life purpose and interconnectedness. The spiritual journey is a common motif in world cinema; a character's physical journey is often metaphoric for their psychological, emotional, and/or spiritual quest to face and overcome obstacles, find meaning and purpose in life, and transform that which is afflictive and limiting. *Travelers and Magicians* (Norbu, 2003, Bhutan), *James' Journey to Jerusalem* (Alexandrowicz, 2003, Israel), and *Breakfast on Pluto* (Jordan, 2005, Ireland) emphasize the universal spiritual journey humans face in their quest to find meaning, purpose, and acceptance in life. The latter is a different type of film from Ireland in that it defies the stereotypes of bleak, depressive, Irish tales and instead remains positive and uplifting. In *Children of Men* (Cuarón, 2006, U.K./U.S.), Mexican director Alfonso Cuaron addresses the role of faith and belief in miracles. One touching scene in this violent film depicts all sides of violence and warring in a cease-fire in which the protagonist (symbolized as a Jesus figure) helps guide a mother (symbolized as a Mary figure) and her infant out of a war-zone; the viewer no longer hears the incessant gunfire, rather operatic music resounds with white light glowing as soldiers pause, contemplate, or kneel down with the sign of the cross as the characters walk by. In the film, *God Is Great and I'm Not* (Bailly, 2001, France), a woman changes her faith each time she has a boyfriend with a different religion, readily shifting from Catholicism to Buddhism to Judaism. The film raises questions about not only identity but also what it means to be spiritual. *September 11* (Chachine, Gitaï, Iñárritu, Imamura, Lelouch, Loach, Makhmalbaf, Nair, Ouedraogo, Penn, & Tanovic, 2002, U.K./France/Egypt/Japan/MexicoU.S./Iran) is a wonderful collection of eleven short films by eleven talented directors from around the world in a tribute to the 9/11 tragedy. The films touch on a variety of human strengths, with perhaps "spirituality" as the most frequently occurring (and cinematically interconnecting) characteristic. One of the filmmakers, Alejandro Gonzalez Inarritu, leaves the viewer with the resounding rhetorical question, "Does God's light guide us or blind us?"

Films portraying the strength of spirituality can also be religious in that they portray a religious figure or a particular dogma or teaching that has important effects in the human experience. The spirituality of kindness and generosity via a path of Christianity is portrayed in *Mother Teresa* (Petrie & Petrie, 2003, Spain), while the spirituality of non-violence is portrayed in *Gandhi* (Attenborough, 1982,

India/U.K.). Films depicting religious figures as having spiritual and faith strengths, however, also falling victim to faith crises and other problems include *Priest* (Bird, 1994, U.K.), *The Crime of Father Amaro* (Carerra, 2002, Mexico), and *The Pact of Silence* (Guit, 2002, France).

Themes related to Christianity are clear in *The Nativity Story* (Hardwicke, 2006, filmed in Italy and Morocco), *Jesus of Montreal* (Arcand, 1989, Canada/France), and *The Gospel According to Matthew* (Pasolini, 1964, Italy). The latter is directed by Pier Paolo Pasolini, who is described as "contradictory, Marxist, mystic, Catholic, and atheist," as he gives an interesting and unique depiction of the gospel; the portrayal remains reverent and dramatic as he makes good use of light and dark contrasts, vast landscapes, and close-ups on Jesus and his disciples. This can be contrasted with the word-for-word gospel depiction, *The Visual Bible: Gospel of John* (Saville, 2003, Canada/U.K.), a version that is likely to appeal more to those with more traditional religious beliefs. Buddhist themes are apparent in *Little Buddha* (Bertolucci, 1993, Liechtenstein/U.K.) while Islamic themes are prevalent in the striking *Paradise Now* (Abu-Assad, 2005, Palestine), in which two Palestinian men prepare for a suicide mission in Israel that goes wrong. One of the men rationalizes his actions with, "I'd rather have paradise in my head than live in this hell. In this life, we're dead anyway."

The films listing the 24 strengths above can be utilized in the classroom or in the therapy room. After reviewing the film and assessing its appropriateness for a given student group or client, the teacher and clinician can maximize the benefits of this media. For example, a teacher might show the film, *Intimate Strangers* (Leconte, 2004), to raise discussion about the therapeutic relationship and ethical issues or *Yesterday* to demonstrate different categories of love. A clinician might recommend to a client *My Left Foot: The Story of Christy Brown* (Sheridan, 1989) to encourage the use of finding creative means to overcome significant challenges, *To Be and To Have* (Philibert, 2002) to a teacher who is suffering from job burnout, or *Wings of Desire* (Wenders, 1987) as an introduction to teaching mindfulness meditation.

Some international films utilize characters that are so dynamic that they represent several areas of mental wellness, exemplifying numerous strengths. Examples include Amelie who is a prototype for creativity, curiosity, persistence, vitality, kindness, prudence, gratitude, playfulness, and optimism in *Amelie* (Jeunet, 2001, France); Guido in *Life is Beautiful* (Benigni, 1997, Italy) who masterfully exhibits humor, creativity, open-mindedness, bravery, persistence, love, citizenship, and hope; and the teacher, Clement Mathieu, who exemplifies humility, appreciation of beauty, creativity, love of learning, integrity, kindness, and social intelligence in *The Chorus* (Barratier, 2004, France). Such films can be particularly useful teaching tools for dynamic discussion in the classroom and the therapy office. Of course, these and many other examples are invaluable resources for instructors of Positive Psychology courses.

A couple of recent quality international documentaries directly address positive psychology themes: In *How Happy Can You Be?* (Hatland, 2005), European filmmaker Line Hatland combines archival footage, scientific experiments, and interviews with leading figures in positive psychology to address the strengths, limitations, and profile of happiness. *Monte Grande: What is Life?* (Reichle, 2004) explores the key concepts and research of Chilean neurobiologist, Francisco Varela, namely spirituality, responsibility/autonomy, and the biology of the mind–body relationship.

Friendship

Friendship and relationship themes are prevalent in international cinema and vary by the culture. The exploration of unlikely friendships is a common theme. Two highly recommended films that reflect the development and mutual benefit of friendship between a man and a boy are *Monsieur Ibrahim* (Dupeyron, 2003, France) and the timeless classic, *Cinema Paradiso* (Tornatore, 1988, Italy). In the former, an elderly, Turkish deli owner teaches the spiritual and moral principles of the Koran to a young Jewish boy. *Cinema Paradiso* explores the transformation of a projectionist and an eager young boy as they discuss life and movies, as its tag-line appropriately reads, "A celebration of youth, magic, and the everlasting magic of the movies." Several lonely characters, each with different struggles and strengths converge in an Italian class that leads to friendship and transformation in *Italian for Beginners* (Scherfig, 2000, Denmark). *Strawberry and Chocolate* (Alea & Tabío; 1994, Cuba) explores the friendship between a cultured homosexual and a prejudiced, communist hetero-sexual. A classic film that addresses the complexities of a multi-layered friendship is Krzysztof Kieslowski's *Three Colors: Red* (1994, Poland/France).

Children and Mental Health

World cinema is replete with portrayals of the mental health and strengths of children. Children provide a wonderful avenue for the exploration of what Buddhists call "beginner's mind," which means to see things as if we are seeing them for the first time. Children tap into important strengths of playfulness, curiosity, creativity, and appreciation of beauty. *Born into Brothels* (Kauffman & Briski, 2004, India) is a documentary about the impoverished children of prostitutes in Calcutta's red light district. The film depicts the exuberance, hopefulness, creativity, and resiliency of children; they present as happy despite the dreadful circumstances that surround them. In *Ponette* (Dollion, 1996, France), a young girl bereaves the death of her mother in creative, touching, and spiritual ways. In the quirky yet brilliantly artistic and surreal sets of *The City of Lost Children* (Caro, 1995, France), several children team up with a circus performer to defeat criminals who are kidnapping children to steal their dreams. Although the film is dark in its presentation, it portrays team-work and facing one's fears. The mythological *Pan's Labyrinth* (del Toro, 2006, Mexico/Spain) portrays a young girl who must persevere through the challenges of life and fantasy. The realities and inherent resiliency of children in poverty are depicted in a number of films including *Ali Zoua: Prince of the Streets* (Ayouch,

2000, Morocco), *City of God* (Meirelles & Lund, 2002, Brazil), *Pixote* (Babenco, 1981, Brazil), and Mira Nair's *Salaam Bombay!* (1988, India/U.K.).

A sweet, simple yet profound film, *Children of Heaven* (Majidi, 1997, Iran) depicts the challenges children face day to day in a beautiful way, highlighting the resiliency of the children. *Long Life, Happiness and Prosperity* (Shum, 2002, Canada, 92 minutes) portrays a young adolescent girl living with her single, over-worked mother; the girl remains preoccupied and dedicated to helping her mother with magic, religion, and anything to bring happiness and contentment to the family. A film emphasizing the value of family and friends to children is *Eldra* (Lyn, 2002, Wales). The short film, *Little Daddy* (Horsten, 2003, Denmark) is a lighthearted story of a young girl staying with her father for the weekend and as he gets caught up in busyness she goes on her own adventures; much of the film reveals the world from her view through her thinking and taps into themes of childhood playfulness, sharing, independence, and discovery. A classic film about childhood is Francois Truffaut's *The 400 Blows* (Truffant, 1959, France).

Adolescents and Mental Health

Adolescents are often portrayed in "coming of age" films in which the adolescent is finding one's way in life and learning to face challenges on one's own.

The Chorus (Barratier, 2004, France) is a terrific film that taps into how adolescents can access their strengths and come to terms with acceptance. *Whale Rider* (Caro, 2002, New Zealand) depicts the great perseverance of an adolescent girl within the Maori culture standing up for herself and keeping focused on her faith in her destiny to have an impact on her future and the future of her community. *Not One Less* (Zhang, China) depicts a 13-year-old teacher in a remote rural village going to extremes in her commitment and care for her students. *Pelle the Conqueror* (August, 1987, Denmark) and *The Island on Bird Street* (Kragh-Jacobsen, 1997, Denmark, filmed in Poland) portray young adolescent boys in highly challenging situations that force them to utilize their strengths of creativity and resiliency in order to survive. In *Maria, Full of Grace* (Marston, 2004, Colombia), an adolescent, seeing her family's desperate financial situation, courageously sacrifices her pregnant body by becoming a drug mule, smuggling 62 pellets of cocaine in her stomach into the United States. Adolescent resiliency through abandonment, neglect, and abuse is depicted well in *The Return* (Zvjagintsev, 2003, Russia), *Ratcatcher* (Ramsay, 1999, Scotland), and the poignant *Lilya 4-ever* (Moodysson, 2002, Sweden). *In Orange* (Lürsen, 2004, Netherlands) explores an adolescent boy coming to terms with the reality of the loss of his father.

The short film, *Savior* (Antonijevic, 2003, Iceland), portrays the classic coming of age journey of an adolescent girl, Kaja, who is a latch-key girl with neglecting parents that gets sent off to a summer camp clearly not fit for her. She sneaks out of the camp one evening and attempts to find her way to her grandmother's home traversing the vast Icelandic landscape. She eventually makes it to her grandmother's home and is met with the exclamation, "I'll always be there for you, but I can't save you anymore." This tough love encourages deeper insights that culminate to her realization at the film's conclusion, "Now I know there is always someone there . . . me."

Mental Health and Recovery

Films that depict characters recovering from physical illness, addiction, mental disorders, or trauma are particularly inspiring. *Son of the Bride* (Campenella, 2002, Argentina) depicts a man who lives a life of work, and as a result has a heart attack; he then transforms his life and lifestyle by connecting more with those around him. A character with a severe anxiety disorder who appears shocked to see the real world as he is released from a hospital slowly begins to confront his fears and triumph over his condition in the inspiring film, *Elling* (Naess, 2002, Norway). *The Man Without a Past* (Kaurismäki, 2002, Finland) portrays a man, pronounced dead in the hospital room after suffering severe head trauma, suddenly getting up and walking out of the hospital. Despite his resulting amnesia, he is left to re-create his life (and re-discover what his life was) with his brain injury.

Portrayals of Mental Illness (in International Cinema)

We can learn a lot about health by learning about what is not health. Pirkis, Blood, Francis, and McCallum (2006) reviewed the literature of the impact of mental illness portrayals and found that there are positive effects and opportunities that open up when people with mental illness appear on screen, namely the education of trainee mental health professionals, the motivation of people with mental illness to seek help, and the potential adjunct to conventional therapy for people with mental illness and their families.

I believe we can learn a lot about mental health and wellness by understanding both what "isn't" mental health and the dimensions and dynamics of mental illness. This can help us recognize and appreciate mental health in a deeper way. Viewing movies that portray disorders can empower students and patients to a perspective or experience of health.

There certainly is not a paucity of examples of mental illness portrayals in international cinema. Some films provide stellar examples of the symptoms, course, functional impact, and even treatment of a psychological disorder, while other films do a great injustice perpetrating misconceptions and confusion for the viewer. In other instances, there are cinematic examples of characters overcoming or managing their mental illness in an admirable way. For an extensive list and discussion of American, independent, and international movies that portray each of the *DSM-IV*'s diagnostic categories see *Movies and Mental Illness: Using Films to Understand Psychopathology* (Wedding et al., 2005).

Anxiety Disorders

Elling (Naess, 2002, Norway) depicts a lead character with an anxiety disorder (unclear diagnostically whether it is agoraphobia or social phobia), while *Dirty Filthy Love* (Shergold, 2004, U.K.) is an exploration of obsessive compulsive disorder (OCD) in which a lead character learns how to manage and accept the symptoms and functional and interpersonal ramifications of OCD and Tourette's Disorder. *Walking on Water* (Ayers, 2002, Australia) depicts Acute Stress Disorder.

Mood Disorders

Depression is depicted in *Last Tango in Paris* (Bertolucci, 1972, Italy/France), *My First Wife* (Cox, 1984, Australia), and *Rain* (Jeff, 2001, New Zealand). The phenomenon of suicide is depicted and explored in *Suicide Club* (Sono, 2002, Japan), *The Hours* (Daldry, 2002, U.K./U.S.), and atrociously in *Wilbur Wants to Kill Himself* (Sherfig, 2002, Scotland). In the latter, stereotypes and misconceptions abound as an angry and depressed character persistently attempts suicide in multiple ways. Once he finds love, the mood disorder and severe suicidality disappear, which perpetrates the common cinematic misconception that "love alone can conquer mental illness" (Wedding et al., 2005). It is possible that clients who have recovered from mood disorders and are stable might find the film's dramatizations and exaggerations comical; however, it is not a good educational film.

Psychosis

Severe mental illness (e.g., schizophrenia, delusional disorder) that is portrayed in movies presents a particularly wonderful opportunity for patient and family education. The tag-line for David Cronenberg's slow moving yet striking film, *Spider* (Cronenberg, 2002, France/Canada), summarizes the implicit horror of the film – "The only thing worse than losing your mind . . . is finding it again" – in which a man with schizophrenia slowly pieces together the realities of his past and the pain of his previous actions. Schizophrenia is portrayed in the character of brilliant pianist, David Helfgott in *Shine* (Hicks, 1996, Australia), in patients at a psychiatrist hospital taken over by soldiers in *House of Fools* (Konchalovsky, 2002, Russia), and in a disturbed adolescent boy in *The Butcher Boy* (Jordan, 1997, Ireland). *He Loves Me, He Loves Me Not* (Colombani, France) engenders a brilliant cinematic technique to portray delusional disorder; the first half of the film depicts a high functioning woman in love which the viewer realizes later is a thick delusional framework with little reality base as the second half rewinds to the onset and unveils the perspective of the object of her affection. Psychoses can be seen in films by auteur directors Peter Greenaway and Wernor Herzog in *The Cook, the Thief, His Wife, and Her Lover* (Greenaway, 1989, France/Netherlands/U.K.) and *Aguirre: The Wrath of God* (Herzog, 1972, West Germany), respectively.

Alcohol and Drug Abuse

In *16 Years of Alcohol* (Jobson, 2003, U.K.), an alcoholic becomes sober and faces tensions of hope, desire, and fear as he attempts to put his life back together; one quote from the film indicating the delicacy of his mental status is "Hope is a strange thing. A currency for people who know they're losing. The more familiar you are with hope, the less beautiful it becomes." Alcoholism is also portrayed in films by auteur directors Louis Malle and Wim Wenders in *The Fire Within* (1963, France) and *Paris, Texas* (1984, France/West Germany), respectively.

Drug addiction is depicted in several popular films including *Christiane F* (Edel, 1981, West Germany), *The Last Emperor* (Bertolucci, 1987, Italy/Hong Kong/U.K.), *La Femme Nikita* (Besson, 1990, France/Italy), and *Trainspotting* (Boyle, 1996, U.K.), while the brutal effects of withdrawal are exquisitely captured in *Quitting* (Zhang, 2001, China). Addiction to opioids can be seen in *Indochine* (Wargnier, 1992, France), heroin abuse in *The Barbarian Invasions* (Arcand, 2003, Canada), and polysubstance abuse in *Naked Lunch* (Cronenberg, 1991, Canada). Drug addiction is also portrayed in films by legendary directors Rainer Werner Fassbinder and Bernardo Bertolucci in *Veronika Voss* (1982, West Germany) and *Luna* (1979, Italy), respectively.

Personality Disorders

Personality disorders abound in international cinema, particularly the Cluster B disorders. See Table 2 for a list of each of the ten Axis II personality disorders and a film that contains a character that portrays each condition. Antisocial personality disorder is fairly common; consider such films as Alex and his droogs in *A Clockwork Orange* (Kubrick, 1971, U.K.) and Johnny in Mike Leigh's *Naked* (1993, U.K.).

Table 2 International films portraying personality disorders

Film (Year) Director(s)	Country	Personality disorder portrayed
The Last King of Scotland (2006) MacDonald	U.K.	Paranoid
Bartleby (1970) Parker	U.K.	Schizoid
Wise Blood (1979) Huston	U.S./West Germany	Schizotypal
The Child (2005) Dardenne & Dardenne	France	Antisocial
Betty Blue (1986) Beineix	France	Borderline
La Cage aux Folles/Birds of a Feather (1978) Molinara & Nichols	France	Histrionic
The Barbarian Invasions (2004) Arcand	Canada	Narcissistic
I've Heard the Mermaids Singing (1987) Rozema	Canada	Avoidant
Mad Love (2001) Aranda	Spain	Dependant
Guy (1997) Lindsay-Hogg	U.K.	Obsessive-compulsive

Narcissistic personality disorder can be found in Aaron Eckhart's character in the film *In the Company of Men* (LaBute, 1997, U.K.) and John Turturro as an opera singer in *The Man Who Cried* (Potter, 2000, U.K./France). Borderline personality can be found in *Swimming Pool* (Ozon, 2003, France/U.K.) and *Betty Blue* (Beineix, 1986, France).

Adjustment Disorders

These disorders do not typically stand out in films as their typically mild nature does not warrant exciting cinematic viewing; for this reason a multitude of films could qualify. A couple of films that fall under this category are *Open Hearts* (Jensen, 2002, Denmark) and *The Eye* (Moreau, 2002, Hong Kong).

Portrayal of Treatment

Role of the Psychologist/Psychiatrist

Movies and psychiatry have a rich, intertwining history, albeit often not positive. Gabbard and Gabbard (1999) estimated that through 1998, over 450 films dealing with psychiatry have been created.

Out of the mental health professionals portrayed in film, it is perhaps the field of social work that is the least bleak. Valentine and Freeman (2002) studied 27 movies that portray social workers – child welfare workers – in a variety of settings and found they are usually placed in one of three roles: advocate, supervisor, or clinician. The film *Elling* (Naess, 2002, Norway) portrays a social worker assisting two adults who have recently been released from a psychiatric hospital and are attempting to integrate into society. The social worker, while authoritarian at times, helps the two patients with community services, clinically (leading them in exposure techniques to face their anxiety) and motivationally.

This is more hopeful than the typologies offered regarding the portrayal of psychologists and psychiatrists (Schneider, 1977; Gabbard and Gabbard, 1992; Wedding and Niemiec, 2003). Schneider's typology notes psychiatrists can be represented as Dr. Dippy, Dr. Wonderful, and Dr. Evil; Gabbard and Gabbard's system includes the psychiatrist as The Libidinous Lecher, The Eccentric Buffoon, The Unempathic Cold Fish, The Rationalist Foil, The Repressive Agent of Society, The Unfulfilled Woman, The Evil Mind Doctor, The Vindictive Psychiatrist, The Omniscient Detective, and The Dramatic Healer; Wedding and Niemiec's thematic layout includes those cinematic psychologists who are Learned and Authoritative, Arrogant and Ineffectual, Seductive and Unethical, Cold-hearted and Authoritarian, Passive and Apathetic, Shrewd and Manipulative, Dangerous and Omniscient, and Motivating and Well-Intentioned. Added together there are 21 categories with only 5 categories being positive; for those categories that are positive portrayals (e.g., The

Dramatic Healer), this does not necessarily mean the depiction is accurate, realistic, and balanced.

"Cold-hearted and Authoritarian," one of the most common international cinematic categories, can be seen in *Jesus of Montreal* (Arcand, 1989, Canada/France), Jane Campion's *Sweetie* (Campion, 1989, Australia), *An Angel at My Table* (Campion, 1990, New Zealand), *Heavenly Creatures* (Jackson, 1994, New Zealand), *Vera Drake* (Leigh, 2004, U.K.), *The Chorus* (Barratier, 2004, Switzerland), the group home leader in *Spider* (Cronenberg, 2002, France/Canada), and the psychometrist in *Noi the Albino* (Kári, 2003, Iceland). The psychiatrist in *The Chorus* (Barratier, 2004, Switzerland) has a brief but memorable role as he administers psychological tests (e.g., Stanford-Binet, Rorschach) to troubled kids at a boarding school. He gives the testing feedback in front of the staff and the client/adolescent: "He isn't actually mad, but I should warn you, according to his profile, he's a gregarious pervert . . . a tendency to be cruel, parasitic, destructive and above all . . . above all, a mythomaniac." There are also those portrayals that defy stereotypes and are in a category of their own as in the film *Control* (Corbijn, 2003, Hungary) in which the psychologist just sits there not saying a word – people dump their problems on him and he says nothing.

The Accidental Hero (Jaoui, 2002, France), a well-acted film about a son who has to take care of his mother who has sustained a severe head injury and has subsequent retrograde amnesia, contrasts various types of care-giving, from a strict, forceful group home leader to an all-business social worker, to a compassionate, advocating neurologist. The film shows how the approach and style of the health-care professional can make a significant impact.

Niemiec and Wedding (2006) report seven common misconceptions of psychologists in movies – role confusion (films referring to "psychiatrist" when the role is that of a "psychologist"); psychoanalysis is the dominant practice in psychotherapy; psychotherapists are patently unethical; psychotherapists are cavalier about boundaries; almost all psychotherapists are men; almost all psychotherapists are white; research is of little value. Most of these remain prevalent with some progress being made in the inclusion of more female psychotherapists and other races.

Research psychologists are rarely portrayed; an exception occurred in *The Experiment* (Hirschbiegel, 2001, Germany), an attempt to re-create the landmark Zimbardo Prison Study which not only falls short in accuracy but it perpetrates negative stereotypes about psychologist researchers as unilaterally minded, self-serving, unethical, and dangerous.

The unethical psychologists in *Wilbur Wants to Kill Himself* (Sherfig, 2002, Scotland) continuously cross boundaries as one licks a patient's ear, crosses sexual boundaries, and blatantly misinterprets and disregards rules of confidentiality while another therapist smokes during group, looks for ways to avoid performing his duties as a group clinician, and drinks Jack Daniel's with *his* patients. Other boundary crossing, sexual and otherwise, psychotherapists can be seen in *Princess and the Warrior* (Tykwer, 2000, Germany), *The Eye* (Pang Brothers, 2002, Japan), and *Asylum* (MacKenzie, 2005, U.K./Ireland). It is important to remember that without proper education, viewing films depicting therapist–client boundary crossing behavior can lead to increased acceptance of sexual behavior between a therapist and a patient (Schill, Harsch, & Ritter, 1990).

Balanced portrayals of psychiatrists and psychologists are hard to find in cinema. In terms of characters that play a major role in the film (e.g., lead actress, lead actor), I've yet to come across a "perfect" portrayal of a psychologist. Therefore, at the present time, we must settle for "somewhat balanced" portrayals of flawed characters; these include *Elling* (Naess, 2002), *Lantana* (Lawrence, 2001), *Intimate Strangers* (Leconte, 2004), *House of Fools* (Konchalovsky, 2002), and *Equus* (Lumet, 1997).

Although in considering these examples the outlook appears bleak, there is an overall trend in international films toward more positive portrayals. European feature films that deal with mental health issues are portraying psychiatrists in a more positive light – caring and humane (Kelly, 2006). Rosen, Walter, Politis, and Shortland (1997) reported a shift in Australian and New Zealand films to messages of hope, resilience, and self-determination.

Theoretical Orientation

The dominant portrayal remains psychoanalysis as can be seen in *Mortal Transfer* (Beineix, 2001, France) and *The Son's Room* (Moretti, 2001, Italy).

The interpersonal psychotherapy approach is portrayed in *Lantana* (Lawrence, 2001, Australia). The psychologist is shown as supportive, nurturing, and giving help, although as the film progresses, her personal issues begin to have an impact on the therapeutic encounter.

A supportive psychotherapy approach is represented in *Intimate Strangers* (Leconte, 2003, France), although the hitch is that the therapist is not a therapist at all but is a tax advisor. The patient walks into the wrong office (the tax advisor and a psychiatrist work in the same corridor) and begins talking about her struggles to which the tax advisor initially believes are related to her financial struggles; when he figures out what has happened he has become too fascinated to explain the truth and instead offers his listening as support.

Interventions

A variety of therapeutic interventions are portrayed in international films. Common depictions include listening, social skills training, and advise giving. Two notorious interventions portrayed in films include hypnosis and electro-convulsive therapy (ECT).

The portrayal of hypnosis in films has a history as long as movies themselves. Unfortunately, the portrayal is predominately a negative, stereotypic one. Barrett (2006) explores the role of hypnosis in over 230 films and finds the majority of the portrayals to be negative in which the application of hypnosis is to seduce the subject or to bring the subject to kill, to harm oneself, or to commit a crime. She reports very few realistic portrayals: two of particular relevance here are *Mesmer* (Spottswoodie, 1994, Austria/Canada) and *Equus* (Lumet, 1977, U.K./U.S.), the latter of which includes an accurate explanation of hypnosis by the psychiatrist using the method.

The portrayal of electro-convulsive therapy in American and non-American films has been discussed in detail elsewhere (Walter, 1998; McDonald & Walter, 2001). ECT is usually portrayed in films as negative, harmful, and dangerous. This is true in *An Angel at My Table* (Campion, 1990, New Zealand) and more subtly in *Shine* (1996, Australia). McDonald and Walter (2001) catalogue and examine the portrayal of ECT in movies from the middle of the 20th century to the onset of the 21st century and conclude that ECT was initially portrayed as a severe but helpful treatment but progressed to being represented as a cruel and negative treatment. All 22 film examples are American movies. The negative impact of ECT in movies is clear – after viewing ECT portrayed in movies, medical students were more likely to talk family and friends out of receiving the treatment and one-third decreased their support for ECT (Walter, McDonald, Rey, & Rosen, 2002).

International Cinema Resources

Websites: The internet is a great resource to learn about world cinema. Two of the most comprehensive databases include The Internet Movie Database (www.imdb.com) and The Movie Review Query Engine (www.mrqe.com).

Film festivals: These events are unique opportunities to see films from a variety of countries and occur throughout the year in most major cities in the United States and throughout the world.

Movie clubs: Movie clubs provide an opportunity to view and own international films. Typically, these are organizations you can join and pay a monthly fee to receive a DVD that contains three to five films on it; often these are films that would never be released in the theater and many can only be seen at certain film festivals. The Spiritual Cinema Circle (www.spiritualcinemacircle.org) is a movie club that addresses a variety of mental health themes such as love, hope, compassion, and life purpose/meaning. Ironweed Films (www.ironweedfilms.com) is a movie club whose films are likely to address mental health themes related to courage, tolerance, social justice, and resiliency.

References

Alexander, M. (1995). Cinemeducation: An innovative approach to teaching multicultural diversity in medicine. *Annals of behavioral sciences and medical education*, 2(1), 23–28.

Alexander, M., Hall, M., & Pettice, Y. (1994). Cinemeducation: An innovative approach to teaching psychosocial medical care. *Family medicine*, 26, 430–433.

Alexander, M., Lenahan, P., & Pavlov, A. (2005). *Cinemeducation: A comprehensive guide to using film in medical education*. Oxford: Radcliffe.

Alexander, M., & Waxman, D. (2000). Cinemeducation: Teaching family systems through the movies. *Families, systems, & health*, 18(4), 455–466.

Barrett, D. (2006). Hypnosis in film and television. *American journal of clinical hypnosis, 49*(1), 13–30.

Berg-Cross, L., Jennings, P., & Baruch, R. (1990). Cinematherapy: Theory and application. *Psychotherapy in private practice, 8,* 135–156.

Brabender, V. (2006). How Hollywood's myths about group psychotherapy can benefit beginning group therapists. *International journal of group psychotherapy, 56*(3), 383–388.

Engstrom, F. (2004). *Movie clips for creative mental health education.* Plainview, N.Y.: Wellness Reproductions and Publishing.

Fleming, M., Piedmont, R., & Hiam, C. (1990). Images of madness: Feature films in teaching psychology. *Teaching of psychology, 17*(3), 185–187.

Gabbard, G., & Gabbard, K. (1992). Cinematic stereotypes contributing to the stigmatization of psychiatrists. In P. J. Fink & A. Tasman (Eds.) *Stigma and mental illness* (pp. 113–126). Washington, D.C.: American Psychiatric Press.

Gabbard, G., & Gabbard, K. (1999). *Psychiatry and the cinema* (2nd ed.). Washington, D.C.: American Psychiatric Press.

Gregg, V. (1995). Using feature films to promote active learning in the college classroom. In: Teaching of psychology. *Proceedings of the 9th annual conference on undergraduate teaching of psychology.* Ellenville, OH, March 22–25, 1995.

Hesley, J. W., & Hesley, J. G. (1998). *Rent two films and let's talk in the morning: Using popular movies in psychotherapy.* New York: Wiley.

Higgins, J., & Dermer, S. (2001). The use of film in marriage and family counselor education. *Counseling education & supervision, 40,* 182–192.

Hudock, A., & Warden, S. (2001). Using movies to teach family systems concepts. *The Family Journal: Counseling and therapy for couples and families, 9*(2), 116–121.

Joseph, S., & Linley, A. (2006). *Positive therapy: A meta-theory for positive psychological practice.* New York: Routledge.

Karlinsky, H. (2003, February). Doc Hollywood north: Part I. The educational applications of movies in psychiatry. *CPA bulletin, 35*(1), 9–12.

Kelly, B. (2006). Psychiatry in contemporary Irish cinema: A qualitative study. *Irish journal of psychological medicine, 23*(2), 74–79.

Lampropoulos, G., Kazantzis, N., & Dean, F. (2004). Psychologists' use of motion pictures in clinical practice. *Professional psychology: Research & practice, 35*(5), 535–541.

Lu, S. (2002). Zhang Yimou. In Y. Tasker (Ed.), *Fifty contemporary filmmakers* (pp. 412–418). New York: Routledge.

MacHaffie, S. (2002). Health promotion information: Sources and significance for those with serious and persistent mental illness. *Archives of psychiatric nursing, 16*(6), 263–274.

McDonald, A., & Walter, G. (2001). The portrayal of ECT in American movies. *The journal of ECT, 17*(4), 264–274.

Miller, F. (1999). Using the movie *ordinary people* to teach psychodynamic psychotherapy with adolescents. *Academic psychiatry, 23*(3), 174–179.

Nelson, E. (2002). Using film to teach psychology: A resource of film study guides. Retrieved from http://www.lemoyne.edu/OTRP/otrpresources/filmresource.pdf on December 1, 2006.

Niemiec, R. M., & Wedding, D. (2008). *Positive psychology at the movies: Using films to build virtues and character strengths.* Gottingen, Germany: Hogrefe.

Niemiec, R. M., & Wedding, D. (2006). The role of the psychotherapist in movies. *Advances in medical psychotherapy and psychodiagnosis, 12,* 73–83.

Paddock, J., Terranova, S., & Giles, L. (2001). SASB goes Hollywood: Teaching personality theories through movies. *Teaching of psychology, 28*(2), 117–121.

Peterson, C., & Seligman, M. (2004). *Character strengths and virtues: A handbook and classification.* New York: American Psychological Association.

Pirkis, J., Blood, R., Francis, C., & McCallum, K. (2006). On-screen portrayals of mental illness: Extent, nature, and impacts. *Journal of health communication, 11,* 523–541.

Raingruber, B. (2003). Integrating aesthetics into advanced practice mental health nursing: Commercial film as a suggested modality. *Issues in mental health nursing, 24,* 467–495.

Rosen, A., Walter, G., Politis, T., & Shortland, M. (1997). From shunned to shining: Doctors, madness and psychiatry in Australian and New Zealand cinema. *Medical journal of Australia, 167*, 640–644.

Schill, T., Harsch, J., & Ritter, K. (1990). Countertransference in the movies: Effects on beliefs about psychiatric treatment. *Psychological reports, 67*, 399–402.

Schneider, I. (1977). Images of the mind: Psychiatry in the commercial film. *American journal of psychiatry, 134(6)*, 613–620.

Schulenberg, S. (2003). Psychotherapy and movies: On using films in clinical practice. *Journal of contemporary psychotherapy, 33*, 35–48.

Seligman, M. E. P. (1999). The president's address. *American psychologist, 54*, 559–562.

Seligman, M. E. P. (2003). *Authentic happiness: Using the new positive psychology to realize your potential for lasting fulfillment*. New York: Free Press.

Sharp, C., Smith, J. V., & Cole, A. (2002). Cinematherapy: Metaphorically promoting therapeutic change. *Counselling psychology quarterly, 15*(3), 269–276.

Snyder, C., & Lopez, S. (Eds.) (2002). *Handbook of positive psychology*. New York: Oxford University Press.

Snyder, C., & Lopez, S. (2007). *Positive psychology: The scientific and practical explorations of human strengths*. Thousand Oaks, CA: Sage.

Stringer, J. (2002). Wong Kar-Wai. In Y. Tasker (Ed.), *Fifty contemporary filmmakers* (pp. 395–403). New York: Routledge.

Swift, W., & Wonderlich, S. (1993). House of games: A cinematic study of countertransference. *American journal of psychotherapy, 47*(1), 38–57.

Toman, S., & Rak, C. (2000). The use of cinema in the counselor education curriculum: Strategies and outcome. *Counselor education and supervision, 40*, 105–114.

Tyler, J., & Reynolds, T. (1998). Using feature films to teach group counseling. *Journal for specialists in group work, 23*(1), 7–21.

Valentine, D. & Freeman, M. (2002). Film portrayals of social workers doing child welfare work. *Child and adolescent social work journal, 19*(6), 455–471.

Walter, G. (1998). Portrayal of ECT in movies from Australia and New Zealand. *Journal of ECT, 14*, 56–60.

Walter, G., McDonald, A., Rey, J., & Rosen, A. (2002). Medical student knowledge and attitudes regarding ECT prior to and after viewing ECT scenes from movies. *Journal of ECT, 18*(1), 43–46.

Wedding, D., Boyd, M., & Niemiec, R. M. (2005). *Movies and mental illness: Using films to understand psychopathology*. Gottingen, Germany: Hogrefe & Hubor.

Wedding, D., & Niemiec, R. M. (2003). The clinical use of films in psychotherapy. *Journal of clinical psychology, 59*(2), 207–216.

Wilt, D., Evans, G., Muenchen, R., & Guegold, G. (1995). Teaching with entertainment films: An empathetic focus. *Journal of psychosocial nursing and mental health services, 33*(6), 5–14.

Trauma and the Media: How Movies can Create and Relieve Trauma

Ani Kalayjian and Lisa Finnegan Abdolian

Abstract Any movie producer will tell you that action and violence will almost guarantee an international audience .This chapter discusses how the mass media affect the social understanding of traumatic events, how they influence individuals who have experienced a trauma in both positive and negative ways and how carefully chosen movies can be used to help clients reframe negative experiences and/or perceptions. The authors have enlisted several movies throughout the chapter that in their opinion can be therapeutic for trauma survivors if used appropriately. Films can help facilitate understanding; they can help the survivors realize that they are not alone in their suffering and that their thoughts and feelings are normal reactions to an abnormal event. Films also can be used to instill hope, can illustrate the importance of practicing forgiveness; and can provide information about how to heal, including role models who use healthy coping modalities. Films can also introduce integrative approaches such as psychotherapy, counseling, energy work, Reiki, acupuncture, deep tissue massages, flower remedies, and homeopathic remedies.

Introduction

Any movie producer will tell you two things: action and violence travel well and will almost guarantee an international audience; and unless your target viewers are pre-teens, a PG rating is a death knoll. Action movies are in a word, easy. They require little plot, dialogue or character development. However, testosterone, adrenaline and violence prevail over sensibilities on the big screen.

Such attitudes hold true in the mass media as well. An old news adage says, "If it bleeds, it leads." The prevailing belief is that trauma sells and the more lurid the story, the better chance it has of reaching the public. Unfortunately, sensationalizing

A. Kalayjian (✉)
Fordham University, New York, NY 10023, USA
e-mail: drkalayjian@gmail.com

M.B. Gregerson (ed.), *The Cinematic Mirror for Psychology and Life Coaching*,
DOI 10.1007/978-1-4419-1114-8_8, © Springer Science+Business Media, LLC 2010

155

traumatic events and glorifying violence does not help the healing process. In this chapter we discuss how the mass media affect the social understanding of traumatic events, how it influences clients who have experienced traumas and how movies can be used to help clients reframe events and/or perceptions so they can cope in a psychologically healthy way and ultimately lead a happier life.

What Is Trauma?

Interest in trauma and stress reactions has increased over the twentieth century. However before recently, there was little agreement as to how to define trauma and what its causes are. Scholarly research and writing in the field of psychology has greatly increased over the past two decades, with numerous books published on the subject, the creation of the *Journal of Traumatic Stress*, as well as a host of related articles. The 1990s saw the advent of more than one international volume bringing together the research of traumatologists from around the globe. Veith (1965) observed that the earliest known records of trauma are the ancient Egyptian physicians' reports in the Kunya Papyrus, dating back to 1900 BC. These records describe hysterical reactions to highly stressful situations, and may have served as the world's first medical textbook on trauma.

Emotional negative reactions to highly stressful events have been well documented in every century for which records of human behaviour exist. However, the theories, explanations, analysis and clinical interventions have varied. In addition, symptoms of flashbacks, dissociation and startle responses have variously been interpreted as works of God, evil, the devils, and spirits (Ellenberger, 1970).

According to research conducted by Elliott (1997) 72% of his subjects experienced some form of childhood trauma. Further, Herman (1992), purports that to study psychological trauma is to come face to face with both human vulnerability and the capacity for evil. In other words, the study of psychological trauma requires one to bear witness to horrible events that expose the frailties and vulnerability of humanity.

For the purpose of this chapter, trauma is defined as a mass bio-psychosocial and spiritual wound that needs attention and that, in many cases, may benefit profoundly from an integration of a variety of professional interventions (Kalayjian, 2002).

Clinical Symptoms of Trauma

There are many psychosocial and spiritual disturbances associated with exposure to traumatic events. Although posttraumatic stress disorder (PTSD) has been the most prevalent or widely discussed traumatic disorder in recent years, it is essential to note that it is not the only psychiatric disorder that can result from witnessing traumatic events. Clinical disorders such as major depression, generalized anxiety disorder, substance abuse, phobic disorders as well as others are well-documented syndromes that may eventuate.

On a more spiritual level, the following symptoms may follow: Loss of faith, ambiguity in spiritual practice, existential vacuum, helplessness and hopelessness (Kalayjian, 2007). Survivors have frequently expressed, "Where was God when the genocide was taking place?" and "Where was God when terrorists attacked the World Trade Center?" indicating that such disasters should not happen to "good people." These questions often give rise to feelings of helplessness and hopelessness in humanity.

Yet, the most frequently expressed symptomatology after disasters and mass trauma is PTSD. Therefore, it is useful to review what causes and constitutes PTSD. According to Schiraldi (2000), PTSD results from exposure to an overwhelmingly stressful event or series of events, such as war, genocide, rape, abuse, natural disasters, or accidents. PTSD is a normal response by normal people to abnormal situations (Kalayjian, 2002). The symptoms, if viewed apart from the traumatizing context, may appear strange and inexplicable at best, or pathological at worst, to the naïve observer. However, they make perfect sense when considered within the context of trauma. Since what has happened is out of the ordinary, it has overwhelmed the traumatized person's customary coping responses.

Trimble (1985) uses anecdotal accounts from the diary of nineteenth-century British novelist Charles Dickens to illustrate the psychological impact of trauma. Dickens was involved in a railway accident in June 1865, and was quoted saying, "the scenes amongst the dead and dying rendered his hand unsteady," and "I am not quite right within, but believe it to be an effect of the railway shaking . . . I am weak-weak as if were recovering from a long illness" (Trimble, 1985, p. 7).

B. Warheit (1985) offers a more dynamic model of posttraumatic outcomes, encompassing the systematic relationships of life event coping resources, stress and stress outcomes. Warheit emphasizes five sources that cause stressful events: (1) an individual's biological constitution, (2) an individual's psychological characteristics, (3) the social structure, (4) the culture and (5) the geophysical environment. Kalayjian adds a sixth element: the spiritual component – survivors' spiritual development. After trauma, there is a time of reflection, re-examination of faith-based values, global meaning and purpose of life. According to Frankl (1965), there is a meaning or a positive lesson learned from any and every incident, trauma, or accident. Just as Buddhists believe that there are no mistakes, only lessons to learn from and integrate into our psyche, soul and spirit.

Historic or Generational Transmission of Traumas

Many articles addressing the generational transmission of Holocaust trauma have been published in the past three decades. In contrast, articles addressing the generational transmission of the Genocide of the Armenians only began to be published in the early 1980s. Research conducted with the offspring of Armenian survivors of the Ottoman Turkish Genocide (Kalayjian and Weisberg, 2002) revealed the following: Deep sadness, helplessness, a sense of being overwhelmed, paralyzed, and in intense psychic pain. When asked how their own memories affected them personally, responses ranged from such violence being a major factor in shaping their identity to making them cynically angry and intensely curious about the tragic past.

In addition they expressed mixed feelings regarding their relationship to the larger Armenian community. On the one hand, they felt closer to the Armenian-American community, hoping to keep the memories alive; on the other, there were feelings of being burdened and wishing to distance themselves from the community. In response to the impact of the Genocide on the survivors, responses ranged from it having a devastating effect on their ability to live a normal emotional life, burdening them with sadness, being forced to live in the past, to living in a continuous state of trauma. In reference to the impact of the Genocide on the Armenian people in general, responses included protracted suffering, deep sadness and distrust of outsiders, especially in the light of the continued denial of the Genocide. When asked if there were things they did or avoided regarding the Genocide that caused any feelings of guilt, the following was expressed: There was general paralysis and a deep sense of helplessness, especially in regard to the Turkish denial and the search for finding a proactive stance (Kalayjian and Weisberg, 2002).

How People React to/Cope with Trauma

People often react by feeling uncertain, fearful, helpless and hopeless. An individual may have an acute stress disorder (308.3), which includes characteristic anxiety, dissociation, and other symptoms that occur within one month of exposure to an extreme traumatic stressor (Criterion A). In addition, the individual usually has at least three of the following dissociative symptoms: a subjective sense of numbing, detachment or absence of emotional responsiveness; a reduction in awareness of his or her surroundings; derealization; depersonalization; or dissociative amnesia (Criterion B). Following the trauma, the traumatic event is persistently re-experienced (Criterion C), the individual displays marked avoidance of stimuli that may arouse recollections of the trauma (Criterion D) and has marked symptoms of anxiety or increased arousal (Criterion E) (APA DSM-IV, 1994).

Posttraumatic stress disorder can also develop the following exposure to an extreme traumatic stressor. This stressor may include direct personal experience of an event or witnessing an event that involved death, injury or violent death, serious harm that involves a loved one, a family member or others. PTSD may be severe and long-lasting when the stressor is of human design, such as torture, killing, and or rape. The closer the intensity of the trauma, the more severe the disorder is.

Common symptoms of PTSD include experiencing recurrent and intrusive recollections of the event or recurrent distressing dreams during which the event is replayed. In rare instances, there may be dissociation. It is also common for the individual to experience a "psychic numbing" or "emotional anaesthesia," with a diminished responsiveness to the external world; diminished interest or participation in previously enjoyed activities or hobbies; feeling detached or estranged from others; decreased ability to feel normal emotions without reactivity; and sense of foreshortened future.

Incorporating film into counselling/therapy sessions can help relieve some of the aforementioned psychic numbing by allowing clients to understand that they are not alone in their suffering; that they are not at fault for what happened, and that their thoughts and actions are normal under the abnormal circumstances. If the client can relate to a character in the movie it can help facilitate understanding and resolution. However, it is very important to choose films carefully, as not every portrayal is helpful.

Media Depictions of Trauma and the Impact on Survivors

In a very real sense, the mass media (the film industry included) direct public opinion about an issue, crime or traumatic event by placing emphasis on one perspective rather than another (Finnegan, 2006). For example, one could be forgiven for thinking that prostitution is a stepping-stone to a better life after watching Julia Roberts being rescued by a handsome millionaire in *Pretty Woman*.

More recently, the news media portrayed prostitute Ashley Alexandra Dupré as a celebrity for accepting money in exchange for sex from then New York Governor Eliot Spitzer. Rarely mentioned is the fact that Ashley left her broken home at age 17 to move to New York City in hopes of becoming a musician. Instead, she was forced into prostitution because she needed the money to survive. Thus, her story is very tragic, not glamorous.

While members of the media were well aware of all of this, it did not prevent them from sensationalizing the life of a "call girl." For instance, CNN's Anderson Cooper wrote this in his blog:

> Standing in front of Ms. Dupré's apartment last night, I got that awful feeling that I was contributing to the glamorization of prostitution. A fancy address, a doorman, young fashionable people walking in and out, with the implicit message: 'all this could be yours if you enter the world of so-called high end hookers' . . . Read between the lines of her MySpace story and I see a young girl, confused and simply used by so many in her life. She even told the NYTimes she doesn't know how she can pay for her apartment since a man she was living with walked out. All of it tragically sad, and sadly glamorous in a spotlight that I feel will leave Ms. Dupré in a dark shadow once we in the media focus our lights elsewhere.

What the press and the films neglect to mention, is that prostitution often leads to posttraumatic stress disorder. More than half of all working prostitutes report that they have been raped, assaulted, or threatened with a weapon. Despite his reticence, Cooper did the interview with Dupré without a discussing the "down sides" of prostitution, essentially influencing thousands of impressionable girls.

The manner in which an issue is presented by the media is called framing. Political scientist Robert Entman explains it this way: "Framing entails selecting and highlighting some facets of events or issues, and making connections among them so as to promote a particular interpretation, evaluation and/or solution" (Entman, 2003).

Such framing occurs on a daily basis, both in the news media and in the entertainment arenas of television and film. The manner in which something is framed influences public attitudes and creates a social reality (Herman and Chomsky, 1988). This can be either helpful or harmful, depending on the way in which a trauma and its survivors are portrayed. Domestic violence, murder, rape, war and terrorism are frequent subjects of television news, docudramas and films, and each episode is presented in a way that is meant to influence opinion about the victim, the perpetrator and the crime.

Unfortunately, as noted earlier, while trauma sells, sensationalized accounts rarely help real-life survivors. Depictions that blame the victim, e.g., portrayals that frame women who have been raped as having "invited" the attack or present abusers as sympathetic innocents, can cause pain and confusion as well as distort societal opinions.

For example, years ago CBS aired a movie called Cry Rape (Allen, 1974) in which a woman raped by an influential man was convinced that if she pressed charges she would be publicly humiliated and would relive the traumatic event in court. As a direct result, rape reports nationwide dropped significantly in the weeks that followed the airing (Aronson, 1999). There are still examples of women being re-victimized or belittled during high-profile rape cases where her past sexual history is used to confuse the jury about the validity of her claims. In fact, many victims describe their assault as threefold: the initial assault, the secondary attack from the criminal justice system and a third from the media.

The OJ Simpson case is another example of how public perceptions are shaped by the media. An entire nation was transfixed as television stations aired live footage of dozens of police cars slowly following a white Ford Bronco driven by OJ Simpson. People gathered along the highway shouting, "go, go, go" to the alleged perpetrator of a brutal murder. It was a bizarre scene that was followed by an equally bizarre trial that could not have brought comfort to the survivors' family members or anyone who had suffered a violent crime.

One of the most traumatic events in U.S. history, the 9/11 attacks and their aftermath, was also portrayed in a very cinematic manner. Viewers repeatedly saw the planes hit the World Trade Center (WTC) buildings; the buildings crumble and terrified people run through the streets of Manhattan. A national survey conducted the weekend after the attacks found a strong correlation between stress symptoms and television viewing habits. Those who watched more news about the attacks were angrier and more anxious than those who watched less (Kanihan & Gale, 2003).

These findings are similar to those of an earlier study conducted after a devastating earthquake in California's Santa Cruz Mountains. Researchers found that "increased exposure to television news [about the Quake] corresponded to higher levels of fear for respondents in the affected area. Increased viewing also corresponded to higher estimates of damage and destruction" (Newhagen, 1998).

However, correlation does not imply causation and it is very possible that those who were more fearful were compelled to watch more television. Yet, sensationalized coverage heightens certain emotions, most notably fear, anxiety, and guilt. For those directly touched by the event it may also prolong the grieving process and lead to feelings of isolation (Shapiro, 2002). This is only exacerbated by the fact that those involved in the traumatic event focus on it longer than the news media, the general public, family, and friends (Attig, 2001). As firefighters and volunteers sifted through the rubble of the Trade Center, searching for survivors and then later worked to recover the remains of victims and restore order after the attacks, the media had already turned its attention to the call for war and the administration's political manoeuvres. The victims had been reduced to symbols by the nation, yet survivors and victims' family members struggled to go on with their lives and to understand what had happened.

In a sense, the pain and suffering of those left behind were minimized and the loss of lives sensationalized. Interestingly, some of those directly affected by the attacks turned to film as a way to regain public attention and to heal. The work of the Jersey Girl (Smith, 2004), the wives of men killed in the WTC, was highlighted in a documentary called 9/11 Press for Truth (Nowoseleski, 2006). And, the mass media was their chosen outlet. These women made the talk show circuit and worked to garner support for their desperate need to find answers about why anyone would perpetrate these terrible attacks.

Patty Casazza, who lost her husband in the attacks, was quoted in the documentary as saying: "Our families didn't want us to ask these questions. That was painful, you know, [they believed] we should just be grieving and healing. No – part of our healing process is finding out exactly what happened."

These widows struggled to "heal" by "banding together" and attempting to make sense of what had happened and why. They strove to make their daily reality, with all its pain and confusion, understood by the American public. Transition: "We are asking you, America, to stand behind us," Jersey Girl (Smith, 2004) Mindy Kleinberg said at a rally. However, others felt that such public grieving was inappropriate and were upset by their efforts.

This supports the notion that the experience of trauma is unique to the individual who is experiencing it. Our personality types, learning experiences, temperament, education, culture, religion, previous traumas, meaning in life, generational inheritance of trauma, as well as other influences will contribute to that uniqueness.

Like the Jersey Girls (Smith, 2004), Cindy Sheehan became a public face of the peace movement after her son Casey was killed in Iraq. She also chose to grieve very openly and faced criticism for it. In her "resignation letter" from the peace movement she said: "I have sacrificed a 29 year marriage and have traveled for extended periods of time away from Casey's brother and sisters and my health has suffered and my hospital bills from last summer (when I almost died) are in collection because I have used all my energy trying to stop this country from slaughtering innocent human beings. I have been called every despicable name that small minds can think of and have had my life threatened many times. The most devastating conclusion that I reached this morning, however, was that Casey did indeed die for nothing. I am going to take whatever I have left and go home. I am going to go home and be a mother to my surviving children and try to regain some of what I have lost."

The framing of 9/11 and its aftermath shifted public attention from the very painful human reality of the traumatic event experienced by people like Patty Casazza and Cindy Sheehan, to more generalized concepts, like a "war against terrorism" and the preservation of "freedom and democracy" that were deemed more acceptable to the American public. This shift relieved some of the cognitive dissonance experienced after the attacks and allowed people to continue with their daily lives as normally as possible. However, it did not help the survivors who struggled to recreate a life without their husbands, wives, partners, sons, daughters or siblings.

This move away from the reality of the senseless death of innocent people is reminiscent of the 1999 Columbine school shooting in Colorado. (Finnegan, 2006) In the aftermath of Columbine, media attention quickly switched from the school shooting and the student deaths to the cause of the shootings and the community's reaction. This led to an irrational yet widespread belief that schools were unsafe. However, the reality was that a student was far more likely to be victimized at home, involved in drugs or be killed by a drunk driver than be shot in school. School killings such as Columbine are so rare that it is difficult to statistically calculate whether they are even on the rise or decline.

However, the debate that followed the Columbine incident focused on gun control laws, school safety, high-school cliques and violence in movies. The U.S. Senate Commerce Committee (2000) held a series of hearings on the "marketing of violent entertainment to children." Senator Sam Brownback (R-KS.) opened the investigation by saying, "We are not here to point fingers but to identify the causes of cultural pollution and seek solutions." The "solutions" he sought were ones that would restructure or reframe what constituted acceptable portrayals of violence on television, in film, and in music.

"We are having endless debates about First and Second Amendment rights while our children are being killed and traumatized," he said. "I am willing to bet that there aren't many adults who are huge fans of teen slasher movies or the music of Cannibal Corpse and [singer] Marilyn Manson." Other speakers urged that distinctions be made between works that they believed used violence to illustrate a point, such as *Braveheart* (Gibson, Rogers, & Beesley, 1995), *Saving Private Ryan* (Spielberg, 1998) or *Clear and Present Danger* (Noyce, 1994), and those that "gratuitously" use violence, such as *The Basketball Diaries* (Kalvert, 1995), *Cruel Intentions* (Kumble, 1999) or *Scream* (Craven,1996) (Jenkins, 2000)

Brownback later stated, "Movies have great power – because stories have great power. When that power is used responsibly, their works can edify, uplift, and inspire. But all too often, that power is used to exploit. I've seen some movies that are basically two-hour long commercials for the misuse of guns."

This tragic event also led to the making of *Bowling for Columbine* (2002), a documentary film directed by Michael Moore. Brownback is correct about the power of film, however he is wrong in his belief that there is a simple way to understand or define exploitation. What constitutes exploitation to one individual may be healing to another, and this is precisely why film can be such a powerful therapeutic tool.

In 2006, a movie trailer about hijacked *Flight 93* was received very differently by those directly affected by the 9/11 attack and those who were affected peripherally. According to news reports, "horrified audience members shouted: 'Too soon!' " when the trailer premiered in LA and in New York, the movie trailer sparked fury among audiences still traumatised by the events of September 11, 2001. Cinema manager Kevin Adjodha said: 'One lady was crying. She was saying we shouldn't have played the trailer, that it was wrong. I don't think people are ready for this' " (Usborne, 2006).

Conversely, family members of those who perished in the attack supported the film because it focused on what they had struggled with – their desperate desire to know what happened on that plane, and the day-to-day reality that those they loved were dead. The film made it impossible to maintain the sanitized image of the faceless, anonymous "heroes" of 9/11 or the "evil doers" who perpetrated the attacks. The trailer brought humanity to the forefront, something that the public found deeply disturbing.

A woman who lost her sister on 9/11 put it this way: "We have been dealing with it and thinking about it and imagining what happened that day for four years now, but the public might not always be thinking about it. I'm grateful this project is going on." In addition, a man whose brother died on the plane said the film would "help permanently memorialise the bravery of the 40 passengers and crew of Flight 93 who chose to fight back." The film's director said he had been surprised by the "unanimity" of the families in their support of the film (Usborne, 2006).

The divergent reactions to the trailer can be partially explained by the misconception that discussing traumatic events causes increased distress (Goldsmith, Barlow, & Freyd, 2004). Five years after the attacks, victims' family members understood that discussion was healing and necessary. Members of the general viewing audience had not had the opportunity to learn this difficult lesson and believed that viewing a movie about the realities of what happened on that plane was dangerous. In fact, several studies have shown that allowing discussion helps survivors to validate their loss and work towards reinvesting in life (DeRanieri, Clements, Clark, Kuhn, & Manno , 2004).

The words of those who defended the "Flight 93" film perfectly illustrate what one can hope to accomplish by using film to guide clients suffering from trauma towards acceptance and renewal. Oftentimes the acknowledgment that something happened and an understanding that others have had similar experiences is enough to facilitate behavioural changes. Very often, the perception of trauma plays a key role in the development of symptoms following the event. Film can be used, for example, to help children who have lost a parent come to terms with the death and feel more comfortable with their loss. Victims of PTSD can learn to reshape their perceptions of events and come to terms with what happened by identifying with a character in a film. Also, film can help a client better understand his or her feelings and can help end the cycle of re-experiencing, avoidance, and hyper-vigilance.

Using Film to Treat Trauma

While it is essential to be extra vigilant when assigning movies as homework to individuals who have experienced a traumatic event, it is possible to use film to facilitate dialogue, introduce options that have not been considered previously, and to and assist the therapeutic process. However, it is critical that you have a thorough understanding of the film and a good working relationship with your client before using movies to explore situations. Additionally, it is important that the client feels safe knowing very specifically what happens in the movie. Therefore it is essential to explain in detail the disturbing scenes and discuss emotions that might arise and how he or she can cope until the next session. It is also helpful to let your client know that you are available if necessary and that they do not have to watch the entire movie if it is too difficult. If your client is willing to watch the movie with a family member, encourage this as they can process their emotions together. Remind your client to note which characters or actions they agreed with or enjoyed and those they disagreed with and to consider any modelled behaviour they would like to emulate.

Films to Consider

Groundhog Day (Ramis, 1993; Negative Behaviour Patterns, Depression)

Non-threatening and humorous in its presentation, *Groundhog Day* is about an unhappy, unfulfilled man who falls into a time warp and relives the same day over and over again. At first he is horrified, cynical, desperate and suicidal. However, in time he changes his behaviour and learns the value of patience, people, and putting others before himself. In short, he begins to focus on the good things in life and the pursuit of knowledge.

This film provides discussion points about negative behaviour patterns and possible ways to reverse them. In a sense, like many clients, the main character feels condemned to repeat the same day even before he slips into the time warp. He is depressed, suspicious of happiness, and dislikes himself and humanity in general.

Born on the 4th of July (Stone, 1989; PTSD, War, Death, Loss of Independence)

Like many vets who return from war, the primary character of this film goes from being an idealist who believes he can best serve his country by going to war, to a man who has seen first-hand the horrific realities of war and must live with the consequences. He struggles with the knowledge that he killed innocent people, including a fellow soldier. Eventually, he is wounded and sent home where he learns that he is paralyzed from the waist down. His guilt and confusion regarding what happened in Vietnam is further exacerbated by his anger over how the country had changed and people's indifference to what was happening in Vietnam. The main character spirals downward, self-medicating with drugs and alcohol before ultimately finding his way as an activist.

This is a powerful and realistic portrayal of some of the issues that war veterans struggle with upon re-entering "civil" society. It is brutally honest and therefore should be thoroughly discussed before it is assigned. The primary lesson of this film is that there is life after war, but it takes work and perseverance. It also makes it clear that issues and feelings must be explored, understood, and resolved.

Coming Home (Ashby, 1978; PTSD, War, Infidelity, Loss of Independence/War Injury)

In the film *Coming Home*, a military housewife is left alone for the first time after her husband goes to fight in Vietnam. She slowly grows more independent and volunteers at a veterans' hospital, where she meets a high-school acquaintance who is paralyzed as a result of a war injury. He is very angry and difficult to manage, therefore, the hospital staff keep him medicated most of the time. However, as his relationship with the newly independent wife develops, he begins to redirect his anger toward the war itself and regains a sense of hope. The two eventually have a sexual affair, which ends when her husband, himself wounded, returns from war.

This is a realistic and heartbreaking film that reminds us that no one is untouched by war. It focuses on similar issues as *Born on the 4th of July* (Stone, 1989) yet has the added character of the confused wife who ultimately learns important lessons about herself.

Life as a House (Winkler, 2001; Chronic Illness, Death, Self Destructive Adolescent, Divorce, Negative Behaviour Patterns)

A man who has spent many bitter and unhappy years learns he has cancer and sets out to transform his life in the wake of death. During his last months, he reconnects with his ex-wife and son, and builds a house. While the transformation is seemingly unrealistic, the film provides good discussion points about what is really important, how he or she would change his or her life if given an opportunity, and why we make the choices we do.

Good Will Hunting (van Sant, 1997; Abuse, Insecurity, Death)

A mathematical genius working as a janitor in a university comes to terms with the abuse he suffered as a child. He works through his defence mechanisms with a psychologist and is able to move forward with his life. The primary theme is healing, the importance and difficulties of allowing oneself to be vulnerable, and the value of taking chances in personal relationships.

Steel Magnolias (Ross, 1989; Family Conflict, Death, Grieving, Friendship, Healing)

This film focuses on a group of women and how their relationships develop as they struggle with life's difficulties, including marital discord, infidelity, and the death of loved ones.

Ordinary People (Redford, 1980; Death, Family Conflict, Suicide)

A deeply moving and disturbing film about a family that falls apart after a child dies. Each character is troubled and is given the opportunity to improve her/his own ways of dealing with a troubled situation. Some are able to change, while others are not.

Truly, Madly, Deeply (Minghella, 1990; death, grieving)

This film depicts the story of a woman who loses her husband and as a result her sense of purpose in life. Her grief is very realistic and she expresses anger towards her husband for leaving her. As she begins to drown in grief, he returns as a ghost to help her through the grieving process and to convince her that she should leave the past behind and live for today.

The Son's Room (Moretti, 2001; death, grieving process, family conflicts)

A psychoanalyst lives with his wife, son, and daughter. One Sunday morning, he gets a call from a client newly diagnosed with cancer and decides he must attend to his patient and cancels a family outing. That day his son dies in a diving accident. The film deals with family bereavement and the father's feelings of guilt.

Three Colors: Blue (Kiewslowski, 1993; Death, Betrayal)

A woman loses her husband and only child in a car accident. Afterwards, she learns that her husband was having an affair and that the woman is pregnant with his child. The film provides good example of posttraumatic coping styles and life choices.

Hotel Rwanda (George, 2004; Genocide):

This story about the genocide that occurred in Rwanda and how the actions of one man saved thousands; tells how in the midst of evil and chaos there can still be hope.

Summary and Conclusions

There is little doubt that mass media – film, television and news media – have a significant impact on public perception and opinion. While caution must be used when a film is introduced as a tool to foster healing and forgiveness in trauma survivors, it can be extremely beneficial if done properly. Films can help facilitate understanding; films can help the victims realize that they are not alone in their suffering and that their thoughts and actions are normal.

Healing movies, such as the ones introduced in this chapter, can provide information about how to heal, including role models who use healthy coping modalities. Films can also introduce integrative approaches such as psychotherapy, counselling, energy work, Reiki, acupuncture, deep tissue massages, flower remedies, homeopathic remedies, etc.

However, it is critical that before movies are assigned as "homework," the issues and problems are well understood by the counselor. Trust must be established and the person must feel safe and secure with the therapist in order for the film to be used to promote healing and understanding. Find a character that you think the client will relate to and use it to facilitate a discussion. Work toward a specific goal such as a dialogue about fear of intimacy or death. Reinforce what is learned and help your client incorporate this new reality into his or her daily life.

Healing movies would be enhanced by including transitional justice and forgiveness as modalities of healing. By practicing forgiveness, victims become survivors and empower themselves by disconnecting from the perpetrator. These survivors then can prevent re-victimization, while the perpetrators are busy denying that the event occurred. Such is the case of the survivors of unresolved trauma, including the Ottoman Turkish Genocide of the Armenians and other Christian populations during 1914–1923 or a misjudged case such as OJ Simpson's. Forgiveness allows the survivor to be at peace with him/herself (Kalayjian, 1999). This is something that the survivor has to actively work on in conjunction with a counselor. Very often forgiveness is misunderstood as benefiting the "enemy," "perpetrator," or "the other." Survivors have told the authors "I am not going to forgive him; he should come and ask for forgiveness." Of course, we would enjoy a healthier existence if individuals came forth and acknowledged their wrongdoings; however this is not the reality we live in. Explain that forgiveness is for-giving to oneself. Sometimes, it is helpful to write it as 4-giving to self, in order to shift the focus and help the client see the direction of the giving toward oneself and not the other way around (Kalayjian, 2009).

Additionally, film producers and directors who tackle the difficult issues related to trauma would benefit greatly by creating an inter-disciplinary team of physicians, psychologists, educators, anthropologists and spiritual practitioners to help create accurate portrayals of victims and events that can be used to foster healing and forgiveness rather than revenge and hate.

Achnowledgement We express special gratitude to Elissa Jacobs and Miryam Nadkarni for their generous and kind editorial comments.

References

American Psychiatric Association. (1994). *Diagnostic and statistical manual for mental disorders.* Washington, DC: American Psychiatric Association.

Aronson, E. (1999). *The social animal* (8th ed.), 58pp, New York: Worth Publishers.

Attig, T. (2001). "Relearning the world: Making and finding meanings," In R. A. Neimeyer (Ed.), *Meaning reconstruction and the experience of loss,* pp. 33–53. Washington, D.C.: American Psychological Association.

DeRanieri, J. T., Clements, P. T., Clark, K., Kuhn, D. W., & Manno, M. S. (2004). War, terrorism and children. *Journal of school nursing, 20*(2), 17–23.

Ellenberger, H. F. (1970). *The discovery of the unconscious.* New York: Basic Books.

Elliott, D. M. (1997). Traumatic events: Prevalence and delayed recall in the general population. *Journal of counseling and clinical psychology, 65,* 811–820.

Entman, R. M. (2003). Cascading activation: Contesting the White House's frame after 9/11. *Political Communication, 20*(4), 415–432(18).

Finnegan, L. (2006). *No questions asked, news coverage since 9/11.* Wesport, Conn: Praeger.

Jenkins, Henry, "Lessons from Littleton. What Congress doesn't want you to hear about youth and the media," *National association of independent schools,* Winter 2000.

Frankl, V. (1965). *Man's search for meaning.* New York: Simon & Schuster.

Goldsmith, R. E., Barlow, M. R., & Freyd, J. (2004). Knowing and not knowing about trauma: Implications for therapy. *Psychotherapy: Theory, research, practice, training, 41*(4), 448–463.

Herman, E. S., & Chomsky, N. (1988). *Manufacturing consent: The political economy of the mass media.* New York: Pantheon Books.

Herman, J. (1992). *Trauma and recovery.* Newyork, NY: Basic Books.

Kalayjian, A. (1999). Forgiveness and transcendence. *Clio's psyche, 6*(3), 116–119.

Kalayjian, A. (2002). Biopsychosocial and spiritual treatment of trauma. In R. Massey, S. Massey, & F. Kaslow (Eds.), *Comprehensive handbook of psychotherapy* (pp. 615–637).New York: John Wiley & Sons.

Kalayjian, A. (2009). Forgiveness in spite of denial, revisionism, and injustice. In A. Kalayjian and R. F. Paloutzian (Eds.), *Forgiveness and reconciliation: Psychological pathways to conflict transformation and peace building.* New York, NY: Springer Publishing.

Kalayjian, A. (2007). Family challenges for post tsunami survivors in Sri Lanka: The bio-psychosocial, educational and spiritual approach. *The family psychologist, 23*(2), 8.

Kalayjian, A., & Weisberg, M. (2002). *Generational impact of mass trauma: The post-Ottoman Turkish genocide of the Armenians.* Paper presented at the Annual Meeting of the American Psychological Association, Chicago, IL.

Kanihan, D., & Gale, S. F. (2003). Within three hours 97 percent learn about the terrorist attacks. *Media studies of September 11, newspaper research journal, Winter,* 78.

Newhagen, J. E., (1998). TV news images that induce anger, fear, and disgust: effects on approach-avoidance and memory. *Journal of broadcasting & electronic media, Spring,* 265pp.

Schiraldi, G. R. (2000). *The post-traumatic stress disorder sourcebook.* New York: McGraw-Hill.

Shapiro, E. R. (2002). Family bereavement after collective trauma: Private suffering, public meanings, and cultural contexts. *Journal of systemic therapies, 21,* 81–92.

Trimble, M. R. (1985). Post traumatic stress disorder: history of a concept. In C. R. Figley (Ed.), *Trauma and its wake* (p. 7). New York: Brunner/Mazel.

US Senate Commerce Committee meeting transcript. (2000). *Sen. Sam Brownback statement on marketing violent movies to children.* Wednesday, September 27.

Usborne, D. (2006). US cinemas pull harrowing movie about 9/11. *The independent online,* April 4.

Veith, I. (1965). Retrieved April 17, 2009, from the OLPC Wiki: http://www.wrongdiagnosis.com/p/post_traumatic_stress_disorder/wiki.htm#wiki_Background

Warheit, B. (1985). A propositional paradigm for estimating the impact of disasters on mental health. *Mass emergencies and disasters, 3,* 29–48.

The Myth of Mental Illness in the Movies and Its Impact on Forensic Psychology

L.E.A. Walker, M. Robinson, R.L. Duros, J. Henle, J. Caverly, S. Mignone, E.R. Zimmerman, and B. Apple

Abstract This chapter will attempt to expose and discuss various false depictions of mental illness, while explaining how this can have devastating consequences for forensic psychologists who work in our justice system because they create erroneous public opinion. The media can be a very powerful tool but when inaccurate knowledge about mental illness is portrayed, people become less able to decipher truth from entertainment.

Introduction

> ......*I am going to show you why we insist on such precautions. On the evening of July 8th, 1981, he complained of chest pains and was taken to the dispensary. His mouthpiece and restraints were removed for an EKG. When the nurse leaned over him, he did this to her. [Pulls out photo showing the results of the brutal beating]. The doctors managed to reset her jaw more or less. Saved one of her eyes. His pulse never got above 85, even when he ate her tongue*.......
>
> (Dr. Frederick Chilton, *Silence of the Lambs* [Demme, 1991]). This film grossed $272 million worldwide and received several awards. (Wikipedia, 2007).

> *Our daddy may have advanced delusionary schizophrenia with involuntary narcissistic rage. But he is a very gentle person!*
> From *Me, Myself, and Irene* (Farrelly & Farrelly, 2000). This particular movie grossed $83 million (IMDb, 2007) and was nominated for four awards (IMDb, 2007).

These are just two examples of the countless number of films that depict inaccurate and exaggerated behaviors of mentally ill people. The first quote from *Silence of the Lambs* is the typical media view of mentally ill persons as extremely violent,

---

L.E.A. Walker (✉)
Nova Southeastern University Center for Psychological Studies, Ft. Lauderdale, FL 33314, USA
e-mail: walkerle@nova.edu

This chapter is based, in part, on a symposium presented at the American Psychological Association 2006 Annual Meeting in New Orleans, LA.
Chapter prepared for Gregerson, Mary (Ed.). "The Cinematic Mirror for Psychology and Life Coaching."

M.B. Gregerson (ed.), *The Cinematic Mirror for Psychology and Life Coaching*,
DOI 10.1007/978-1-4419-1114-8_9, © Springer Science+Business Media, LLC 2010

clever, and dangerous people. The second quote portrays behavior that is not known to be part of any one diagnosis as is stated. However, to the general public it may appear to be a legitimate diagnosis characterized by violence, anger, and unpredictable behavior adding to their fears of the mentally ill. Sadly to say, these movies are not an exception and only further contribute to misconceptions about mental illness (e.g., Wedding, Boyd, & Niemiec, 2005).

This chapter will attempt to expose and discuss various false depictions of mental illness, while explaining how this can have devastating consequences for forensic psychologists who work in our justice system because they create erroneous public opinion. The media can be a very powerful tool but when inaccurate knowledge about mental illness is portrayed, people become less able to decipher truth from entertainment.[1]

What Do Insane People Really Look Like?

Theoretical Implications

The two above examples of how mentally ill persons are portrayed in movies demonstrate how these inaccurate and false portrayals can have damaging effects on the formation of public perceptions. Social psychology theories explain how the presentation and exposure of material can help shape persons' beliefs, how these shaped beliefs can form the basis of ideology of mentally ill persons, and how these ideas formulate attitudes. These theories also help to explain how these misattributed portrayals can cause great harm in the courtroom. This is especially true when lay persons on juries, but also untrained judges, must make decisions about the behavior and level of responsibility of mentally ill defendants in a legal proceeding.

Exposure

Although the magic that takes place on the big screen may be seen as mere entertainment by the movie industry, there are consequences, as was mentioned, and the exaggerated and false portrayals of the mentally ill in movies and news coverage may be dangerous. George Gerbner (as cited in LeAmm, 2006), a Hungarian communication researcher, developed the "cultivation theory" to theorize how public

---

[1] This chapter is based, in part, on research undertaken by graduate students in the clinical forensic doctoral psychology program at the Center for Psychological Studies at Nova Southeastern University in Fort Lauderdale, Florida, and presented at the American Psychological Association's Annual Meeting, Washington, D.C., August 2005. Copies may be requested from Dr. Lenore Walker, walkerle@nova.edu.

perceptions can be formulated by heavy exposure to television. Gerbner believed that heavy exposure to television and other forms of media will shape the view that persons have about reality (Greunke, 2000). The more people are exposed to imagery through media, the more likely they are to accept that portrayal as real, whether or not it matches the actual reality. In applying this theory to the portrayal of mentally ill persons in the media, we concluded that the more inaccurate these portrayals are, the more likely the average person (who is the average juror) will come to accept these false images of truth. Judges who do not have special training in diagnosis and treatment of mental illness can be expected to respond as would a lay person. Therefore, they will be unable to accurately recognize someone who is truly mentally disordered unless they behave just like the media characters.

Another important theory that applies to this phenomenon is the "mere exposure" theory. In the late 1960s a researcher by the name of Zajonc formulated a theory that the more a person is exposed to a stimulus, the more likely they are to attribute positive traits to the stimulus (Wikipedia, 2007). In applying this theory to media and mental illness, an exaggerated or false portrayal of a person with schizophrenia will more likely receive favor from jurors and lay persons than a person not displaying those characteristics.

Why are these exposure theories alarming to us? First of all, because portrayals like the ones in *Girl Interrupted* (Mangold, 1999), *Hannibal* (Scott, 2001), *Primal Fear* (Holbit, 1996), and *Me, Myself and Irene* (Farrelly & Farrelly, 2000) are usually not true. In fact, they are more often inaccurate than accurate. Portrayals such as these would lead the average juror to believe that if defendants seem calm and coherent during their trials, then they must be sane even if they are medicated or otherwise trained to conform to proper courtroom demeanor. If defendants cannot follow these rules, they may be declared "Incompetent to Proceed to Trial" and sent to the state hospital to be restored to competency before proceeding to the courtroom. Therefore, it is rare that a defendant with impulsive or otherwise disruptive behavior would go to trial.

In most jurisdictions, to meet the standards for the insanity defense, a person must demonstrate the inability to understand the difference between right and wrong or the consequences of one's behavior (often called the McNaughten rule as it came from judicial opinions in a British case by the same name). In some areas, there may also be a behavioral component such as the inability to conform one's conduct to the correct standard, even when knowing what it is. As these definitions are determined by the legislative or judicial systems and are not based on mental health diagnoses, those trying to judge the defendant's behavior must rely on their own beliefs about what an insane person would look like. These inaccurate images suggest that a person with a Not Guilty by Reason of Insanity (NGRI) defense would have to look and act "crazy" in front of the jurors, as well as having had to commit the crime irrationally, without the requisite mental state of knowing right from wrong. Obviously, this is rarely true. By the time most defendants go to trial the behavior associated with a serious mental disorder may have been mitigated by medication or modified by some form of treatment. Even so, it is the person's cognitive behavior or thoughts that will meet the insanity standards, not their courtroom behavior.

Ideology Formation

In order to extend the argument of exposure, it is important to look at how this affects the average person. Philosophers such as Marx and Destutt de Tracy hypothesized that our ideas are simply a collection of the greater society (Fluxman, 2005; Larraine, 1979). Whatever the majority or ruling class deems as an idea, or a way of thinking, all members of that society will fall in line and also form ideas in the same manner. When applying the theory of ideology to the silver screen, it would mean that people would formulate their ideas about how mentally ill defendants should present themselves in court before learning all of the factual information presented during trial.

The field of psychology is always concerned with public perception because we know the extent to which ideas will affect behavior and thought processes. Therefore, watching a movie about violent schizophrenics is not just entertainment; it is exposing society to the idea that persons with a serious mental illness are violent, which is simply not usually true, as has been noted. Therefore, as a public policy, it is critical that the images that are portrayed in these movies are as accurate as possible so as not to skew the public's ideas of the mentally ill. Although most movie producers understand the benefits of portraying psychological disorders appropriately, as they utilize consultation with psychologists as reported in screen credits, there are those that still portray the seriously mentally ill as violent to enhance their story.

Theories of Attitude

Research indicates that public attitudes often overpower private attitudes (Wood, 2000). These private attitudes influence the way in which we evaluate a person, situation, or stimulus – whether positively or negatively (Ajzen & Fishbein, 1982). Attitudes help to serve the way in which we are willing to listen and understand information presented to us.

Preconceived notions may exist about how a mentally ill person should behave based loosely from exposure to movies and the ideas that we have formulated; this stereotypy can have damaging effects for defendants pleading NGRI, especially if their behavior does not conform to these stereotypes.

It is clear from this brief theoretical overview that exposure, ideas, and attitudes all can affect the mentally ill populations. Now let's take a closer look at the types of mentally ill frequently portrayed by the media and enjoyed by the general public who pay to watch these movies.

Formulating Public Perception

Media Consumption

Whether through television, movies, newspapers, magazines, or the Internet, our worlds are encompassed by the media. According to the National Association of Theater Owners (2007), there were 1.4 billion admissions to movies, nationally, into movie theaters in 2005 with total sales of $8.99 billion (MPAA, 2005). The average American is said to watch more than 4 hours of television per day (TV website). But it is not only television and movies that contribute to our media exposure. Approximately, 210 million people in the United States utilize the Internet, a vast source of information (both accurate and inaccurate), with a potentially endless amount of information that can be shared (interview world stats.com, 2006). Also, newspapers provide about 216 million people with information (NAA, 2006).

Media Portrayal and Public Perception

Through these media outlets, we are exposed to many different ideas and viewpoints. We are exposed to truths, and unfortunately, we are also exposed to many misconceptions. Media has a tendency to over-sensationalize stories and provide information about only the most outrageous events with the hopes of having more viewers or selling more copies. This also holds true for their portrayal of mental illness so it is not surprising that the mentally ill are sensationalized and attention drawing events are featured rather than focused on the everyday difficulties that they bear, including the discrimination and abuse from others who do not understand their illness.

All of the media outlets, not just movies, affect public perception of mental illness when it comes to the accuracy of portraying the types and symptoms of mental illness. Many people receive their information and informal education through media outlets, especially movies and television (Wedding et al., 2005). These media influence the perceptions of mental illness and assist in the formation of ideas and beliefs about persons with mental illness, including themselves. Those with emotional problems also are impacted by misperceptions of mental illness, often causing them to shy away from seeking treatment as they simply cannot identify with the media characters. According to Otto Wahl, a prominent figure in media psychology, "Overall, the mass media do a poor job of depicting mental illness, with misinformation frequently communicated, unfavorable stereotypes of people with mental illness predominating, and psychiatric terms used in inaccurate and offensive ways" (Wahl, 1995, pp. 12–13).

Sometimes, the media go so far as conveying the message that people with mental illness foam at the mouth and their eyes roll to the back of their head. Although this sounds more like a person with rabies, or having an epileptic seizure, perhaps minus the rolling of the eyes, uninformed consumers may incorporate this image into their views of the mentally ill. At other times, there are more accurate portrayals of mental illness, such as in the movies *As Good as It Gets* (Brooks, 1997) or *K-Pax* (Softely, 2001). The former takes the viewer into the life of a person suffering from Obsessive Compulsive Disorder; the latter takes the viewer into the realm of a person who is either suffering from Post Traumatic Stress Disorder (PTSD) or a delusional disorder (the diagnosis seems to be left to the viewer). Other movies such as *Me, Myself, and Irene* (Farrelly & Farrelly, 2000) and *Primal Fear* (Holbit, 1996) are at the opposite end of the spectrum and grossly exaggerate and falsely portray various disorders. For example, as mentioned earlier, in *Me, Myself, and Irene* (Farrelly & Farrelly, 2000) the main character is diagnosed with "advanced delusionary schizophrenia with involuntary narcissistic rage" following the breakup of his marriage after he discovers his new wife was having an affair with another man. As mental health professionals, we know that no such diagnosis exists. At the very best, the character may be exhibiting signs of Dissociative Identity Disorder (DID), as he switches between two personalities. As well as making up diagnoses, this film also contributes to a stereotype that mental illness is always a product of some traumatic life event (Wedding et al., 2005). The character is seen as a violent individual who "snaps" in an instant, but real people diagnosed with DID, which used to be called Multiple Personality Disorder, rarely are violent and switch personalities in a much more subtle manner. Those who do have a Delusional Disorder, which used to be called Paranoid Delusional Disorder, also do not usually become violent as the movie portrays this character.

Mental illness is frequently portrayed in children's films as well. In a recent study of Disney movies, a majority of the films making reference to mental illness did so to disparage and belittle the characters (Lawson & Fouts, 2004). People with psychological problems are usually shown with poor speech and hygiene as well. Whereas it may be true in some cases, particularly with the homeless or those who are hospitalized, this is not true for everyone with mental illness. In fact, there are people who are not considered mentally ill and who have those issues with speech and hygiene as well.

Violent Portrayals

The mentally ill are also usually portrayed as violent. For example, Hannibal Lechter from *Silence of the Lambs* (Demme, 1991) is considered the epitome of this portrayal. He is so violent that his face has to be bound so he will not use his mouth to cause destruction and harm. Images such as this one feed into the perception that all mentally ill persons are violent and dangerous. Current research has shown the rate of violence among people with mental illness is only moderately higher than in the general population. The majority of people identified as being mentally ill do not use violence and when they do, it is in response to situations that are avoidable. In fact, studies show that substance abuse is more of a factor when considering causes of violent behavior (Steadman et al., 1998). Persons with

Schizophrenia, DID, and various personality disorders are depicted as violent in movies. This enhances stereotypes and public fear of people with these disorders.

Effects and Consequences in the Courtroom

When a person with a mental illness, especially with the aforementioned disorders, is on trial for committing a crime, the lay public serves as their jury. The jurors take with them the biased attitudes regarding the mentally ill. Beliefs such as those about mentally ill people being extremely violent and dangerous will influence jurors' decisions. Therefore, the person on trial is punished by these myths of mental illness, and may spend their lives in jail, or worse, on death row, because of a lack of information and misunderstanding. Judges are rarely trained to understand the mentally ill, so they cannot be of any assistance in making sure that true facts rather than myths are put in front of the jury. In essence, the mental illness serves as a reason in and of itself to keep someone locked up, rather than place them in a facility where they could receive treatment. Given the scarcity of beds in mental hospitals today, it is far more likely that a mentally ill person will spend time in the jails and prisons. In the U.S., reports indicate that 25–66% of the jail and prison population have been diagnosed with mental illness (BJS, 2007).

A Successful Insanity Defense Means Everyone Will Escape Responsibility, Right?

Society at large is consistently bombarded by many different types of media including books, television shows, newspapers, magazines, tabloids, the Internet, and nightly news as well as movies. These forms of mass information and communication continue to report or depict murderers faking "insanity" in order to avoid the consequences of their actions. Often, the news portrays information in such a way that creates public concern or outrage. Unfortunately, media needs sensation to generate sales and therefore may not always print the whole story.

In popular fiction, whether literature or movies, it is commonplace to come across stories in which an offender is trying to get off "scot-free" for their crimes by pleading NGRI because of mental illness or mental defect. Usually it is portrayed and reported in the media as "temporary" insanity, and then the defendant claims that he or she is no longer afflicted by this "temporary" mental illness and should go free. The story line follows that the court finds them NGRI and the defendant is immediately released, only to murder and pillage once again. Nothing can be further from the truth in most cases. In fact, it is rare that someone is found "temporarily insane" by judges or juries and even less likely that if that should happen, they will go free.

While the "temporary" insanity defense is a phrase that is commonly used in many movies and fictional novels, it is a myth. That being said, there is a caveat to this point. Temporary breakdowns or decompensation of one's mental health do occur. Situations in which a person is driven by a completely unstoppable rage are unlikely and this type of occurrence is rarely seen (Woodmansee, 1996).

The truth is that even if they are found insane, they will be sent to the state hospital until doctors and the judge find them no longer insane. Even if they claimed that they were no longer insane at the time of the trial, they are usually kept in the hospital for a longer time than they would have been had they been sentenced to a determinate prison term.

Unfortunately, many people believe the media suggestions that it is easy to commit a crime and get away with it through the use of the insanity plea. In actual fact, the scenario of someone attempting to be found not guilty on these grounds is so rare that members of the criminal justice system could easily go their entire careers without coming across a single case of this type. In fact, most of the criminal justice system only sees these pleas when they are watching a movie or reading a fictional novel. Perhaps, even more damaging is that few attorneys or judges are willing to consider the insanity defense even when it provides a legitimate understanding of the defendant's actions. They fear the public will be unable to understand how the person's mental illness impacted his or her state of mind at the time of the commission of a criminal act because they do not look as mentally ill as the movies depict.

Media Depictions of Mentally Ill Defendants

The media has a tendency to focus on cases such as Lorena Bobbitt, and portray this type of case as the norm. Lorena Bobbitt was a woman who received national coverage when she cut off her husband's penis. As a result of this widespread media coverage with speculation as to what actually happened and why she did it, there was inevitable misreporting of the story and the facts behind the case. The facts of the case indicate that Lorena Bobbitt cut off John Wayne Bobbitt's penis after being repeatedly raped and beaten by her husband. She ran out of the house afterwards with the part of the penis she had cut off still in her hand. Terrified that he was following her, she got into her car and drove away. When she finally saw it in her hand, she threw it out of the car window while she was driving. She felt so badly afterwards that she drove around to help find where she threw it and the doctors were able to reattach it to his body.

Ms. Bobbit was arrested and sent to the local mental hospital when her attorney announced that she would plead NGRI. Unfortunately, at that time the state of Virginia did not have a self-defense statute that would permit the defense of a battered woman who used a knife to defend herself against the man's use of parts of his body with which to batter her. So, there was no choice but to use the insanity defense, which was consistent with "temporary insanity" as her description indicated she went into a dissociative state that prevented her from knowing the difference between right and wrong at that time. Obviously, when she recovered, some time during the drive when she fled the scene, she realized what she had done was wrong and went back to find the severed penis.

However, the public remembers the parts of the media coverage that tends to stir interest and make it to the headlines. Shortly after her trial where she was found NGRI, she was sent back to the hospital, and within a few days she was released as the doctors had testified she was no longer in a dissociative state. It was reported that she was "cured" and subsequently released, to the fear of many people that she would do it again, which of course, she has not.

Interestingly, at that same time John Wayne Bobbitt was also arrested and prosecuted for physically and sexually abusing Lorena. His criminal behavior, which is much more common for men to batter women, and his subsequent trial, received little media coverage as compared to her daring but rare behavior. In fact, John Wayne Bobbitt has been arrested and convicted of domestic violence on other women subsequent to his abuse of Lorena Bobbitt (personal communication, Judge Brown, Las Vegas, NV). Again, the media did not tie the woman abuse together with the self-defense behavior of Lorena Bobbitt and instead continued to portray her as the mentally ill and dangerous one and raised the fear that other women would copy her crime and cut off men's penises, believing that like Lorena Bobbitt, they then will go free.

The fact is that this entire case was an anomaly and not the norm for our society. What is far more common is that an individual who is convicted of an offense is hospitalized in a psychiatric facility for an extended period of time. The most disturbed offenders (e.g., murderers) or defendants found either incompetent to proceed to court or NGRI can technically be hospitalized for decades.

In the past there have been criminals who reported that they committed offenses that were inspired by media coverage. Movies have been cited by suspects as diverse as John Hinckley Jr., who said he tried to assassinate President Reagan after watching *Taxi Driver* (Scorsese, 1976), to the accused young DC sniper, Lee Malvo, who reportedly cited *The Matrix* (The Wachowski Brothers, 1999) in his statement to police. More recently, some media have blamed video games for the crimes committed by teenagers. For example, allegations about video games increasing teenage violence were reported immediately after the Columbine High School massacre. Interestingly, in the Columbine High School case the two high school teens who committed the violence had not been previously diagnosed with a mental illness. However, they had created an extremely violent movie for a class that described some of the explosives they had stockpiled in one of the youth's garage and demonstrated via the media how they might blow up buildings such as the school and even New York City. Instead of viewing the movie as a possible portent of things to come, their teacher simply graded it on the technical qualities.

Dispelling the Myths

The Insanity Defense

There have been many well-publicized court cases (at the turn of the century) involving the insanity defense. These cases include people such as John Hinckley Jr.,

Russell Weston Jr., and more recently Andrea Yates (whose story will be explored later in this chapter). These cases involved individuals who had been diagnosed with a mental illness and who committed crimes resulting in tragedies or near tragedies.

Is the public perception of the insanity defense leaning toward it being overused and exploited by defendants with their "shady over priced" lawyers? If so, what, if anything, about the media coverage of these crimes lends itself to this erroneous myth? What makes trying to understand violent behavior so interesting and so intertwined with our concept of mental illness?

Since the insanity defense is seldom used (less than 1% of all murder cases according to the American Bar Association), it appears that the publicity the insanity defense receives is far out of proportion in comparison to its use. It has become part of the promotional apparatus of high profile criminal cases in modern times. The trials of Jeffrey Dahmer, David Berkowitz (*The Son of Sam Killer*; Lee, 1999) and the Lorena Bobbitt mutilation case, are simply not typical of most criminal trials held in America any more than O.J. Simpson is a typical murder defendant. However, these are all fascinating cases because they permit a glimpse into behavior that few of us would ever be capable of thinking about much less undertaking.

The insanity defense received a lot of attention when John Hinckley, the man who shot President Reagan, allegedly to impress the actress Jody Foster, used it as part of his defense strategy. Obviously, this case created such an impact on the way people in the United States looked at the insanity plea that in the aftermath of Hinckley's trial, many states as well as Congress sought ways to restrict use of the insanity defense. The media reported that many people became nervous that defendants who were to be found NGRI might be released too easily from secure hospitals and therefore given the chance to cause harm again. The outcome of the Hinckley case sent shockwaves throughout the nation's courts. How could a man who shot the President, his aide, and a police officer in front of millions of people be found not guilty?

With the help of the media, John Hinckley's acquittal of murder but guilty verdict for NGRI in 1982 set off a groundswell of criticism against the insanity plea and legislatures across the U.S. tightened up the restrictions even further, making it one of the least likely defenses. It was thought that lawyers and psychiatrists had manipulated the courts and abused constitutional protections in order to set a guilty man "free." Many people, lawyers, legislators, and newspaper editors called for the abolition of the insanity defense. Despite peoples' outrage and beliefs that he was going to go free after being found NGRI, he is still confined at St. Elizabeth's Hospital in Washington, D.C., over 25 years after the incident. His therapists and forensic experts all have testified at release hearings that he will never be cured from his severe mental illness, but it is under control with medication and it is unlikely that he will commit violence against himself or others. He has been released for a weekend under his parents' supervision and he has not committed any violent acts. Under the laws that were in place in 1982, he might well have been released from a prison sentence already, but without having any treatment, making it easier for him to repeat his criminal behavior. The fact that people perceive the insanity defense as both commonplace and abused suggests that they may give it a great deal of weight in shaping their views of the legal system as a whole (Bailis, Darley, Waxman, & Robinson, 1995).

The Hinkley case demonstrates how much more the risk of danger to public safety would have been had he not been sent for treatment and released into the community. Perhaps changing the misinformation provided to the general public about the benefits of treatment for the mentally ill versus a determinate prison sentence would make it safer for the general public and the almost two-thirds of prison inmates who are currently diagnosed as mentally ill but not receiving adequate treatment prior to their release back into the community.

Not Guilty by Reason of Insanity

After the Hinckley verdict, some states adopted a different standard for criminal responsibility called Guilty But Mentally Ill. Here a person is first tried on the merits of the case and if found guilty, then he or she is sentenced to the state hospital until such time as the person is no longer mentally ill. It has been suggested that journalists and politicians also have a tendency to abuse the NGRI plea for their own personal gains, while capitalizing on people's fears that someone so mentally ill that they could kill another person might someday be released from the hospital. Politicians have used NGRI plea as a vehicle to capture the public's attention while journalists write dramatic stories about it because they are aware that there is a great deal of public interest in the subject. Thus, they create sensational headlines that stir interest which in turn leads to sales and increased profits.

Statistics confirm that the NGRI plea is vastly exaggerated as a "loophole" and rarely does it get anyone off a criminal charge when it is used (Zonana, Wells, Getz, & Buchanan, 1990). But, the common understanding of the plea is exactly the opposite. Circincoine and Steadman (1994) found that the majority of people believe that those who claim to be insane at the time of a crime actually get off and do not go to prison or the hospital. Table 1 demonstrates the public opinion in their study.

According to Siegel (2000), in fact, approximately 70% of insanity acquittals result from opposing attorneys' agreements, in which the prosecution agrees that

Table 1 Public perception compared with the actual use of the insanity defense

	Public perception (%)	Reality (%)
(A) Use of the insanity defense		
Percentage of felony defendants pleading insanity	37	0.9
Percentage of acquittals when using insanity plea	50–80	26
(B) Outcome for successful insanity defendant		
Percentage of insanity acquittees sent to a mental hospital	50.6	84.7
Percentage of insanity acquittees set free	25.6	15.3

Source: Circincoine and Steadman (1994).

society would be better served by placing the defendant in treatment, rather than in prison. Yet this is rarely if ever portrayed by the media.

How Media Portrayals Effect the Courtroom

Lawyers have the tendency to utilize the media when possible in order to persuade the public perception in their favor of the insanity plea. "When lawyers present an insanity defense, they look very hard for everyday ways of showing jurors the degree of the defendant's disorder" (Siegel, 2000).

In a 1983 case (*Jones v. United States*), the U.S. Supreme Court held that a person with an NGRI acquittal "could be confined to a mental hospital for a period longer than he could have been incarcerated had he been convicted" (Siegel, 2000). This shows the extent to which defendants who are successfully found NGRI lose all rights with the possibility that they may remain confined for longer periods of time if accepting a guilty plea and completing their prison sentence.

When the insanity defense is finally used, it is typically with an individual who has a documented history of a profound mental illness (e.g., such as a long history of paranoid schizophrenia). There is usually a lot of documentation of these individuals' mental health histories over the years, portraying how they have been out of touch with reality on several occasions.

For the skeptics, bashing the NGRI plea is a necessity of our society. They have a way to express their frustration with a system that does not protect society from crazy killers. It may also help people believe in a just world where you can stay safe except in very rare cases, and, then society will lock up those people who can harm us. For others, it may be a way to hide our mentally ill much like societies in the Middle Ages used to do – throw them down into the caves and forget about them. However, today we do have ways of treating most seriously and persistently mentally ill individuals through medication that permits them to function at their own level in society. It is no longer necessary to fear the mentally ill nor should people fear this poorly publicized plea and verdict, or see it as a way for criminals to get off free for their crimes, only to be allowed to harm again. As seen in the past, fiction, movies, and media publications have clearly misguided and misinformed the public.

"Faking" Insanity and Multicultural Issues

> To tell you the truth, I'm glad you figured it. 'Cause I have been dyin' to tell! I just didn't know who you'd wanna hear it from. Aaron or Roy or Roy or Aaron ... Well I'll let you on a lil' secret, a client-attorney kind of secret. It don't matter who you hear it from, it's the same story!
>
> Aaron Stampler, played by Edward Norton, *Primal Fear* (Hoblit, 1996)

The Effect of Media on Public Perceptions

As has been described above, the effect of media on laypeople's perceptions of legal issues has had an extensive history. In the more recent, well-publicized case of Andrea Yates, the infamous mother who drowned her five children in the bathtub, media influence was originally alleged to have played a major role in the crime. Psychiatrist, Park Deitz, the expert witness for the prosecution and a consultant for the television drama *Law and Order* (Makris, Alexander, Dobbs, Sherin, Platt, Penn, Scardino, Mitchell, Misiano, Quinn, Forney, Gould, de Segonzac, Swackhamer, Sackhelm, Pressman, Gerber, Muzio, Frawley, Misiano, Gillum, Wertimer, Watkins, Whitesell, Robman, Florek, Mertes, Correll, Arner, Hayman, Shilton, Ellis, Shill, Martin, Chapples, Hunter, & McKay, 1999 to present), testified that a story of a mother drowning her children and being found NGRI had been portrayed on the television series. Deitz testified that Yates had told him during the evaluation that she watched that *Law and Order* (Makris et al., 1999 to present) episode and replicated the events with the expectation of "getting away" with murder. After the jurors rejected the NGRI verdict and convicted Yates of first degree murder, her lawyers discovered that no such episode had ever been televised, and filed an appeal with the Texas State Court of Appeals who agreed that the testimony wrongly influenced the jury's verdict. Yates, who appeared as profoundly schizophrenic as she had always been by the time of her retrial, was found NGRI this time. She may never be released from the mental hospital.

The concern of media effects on jurors has a long track record, and has historically brought about requests for either relocation or rescheduling a trial–or that the jury be sequestered throughout the duration of trial. A large body of evidence indicates that jurors' decisions can be influenced by many types of media (e.g., newspapers, radio and television news, advertising, televised shows of legal content or courtroom T.V., and movies). However, the effects of such exposure are believed to be incremental, not ultimately decisive (Greene, 1990). Therefore, social psychologists may be used to survey the community opinions prior to trial, and testify at a motion to change the venue in order to try to persuade the judge that the defendant could not get a fair trial in the present community. Rarely will the judge grant such a request, often weighing the cost of moving a trial against the potential damage from undue media publicity.

With this legal concern in mind, it is reasonable to expect that the general public also develops a certain bias from exposure to different types of media. Steadman and Cocozza (1977–1978) investigated the public perception of the "criminally insane," and found that it is heavily stereotyped and inclusive of elements of both fear and danger. The authors also emphasized that out of the 413 respondents, most named highly publicized offenders as their source of reference, with Robert Garrow and Charles Manson at the top of the most frequently cited "poster children" for criminal insanity. Alarmingly, the literature also indicates negative, stereotyping attitudes toward mental illness in general (i.e., outside of forensic settings), and it is clear that these attitudes have a persuasive effect on mental health policy in different parts of the world (Hannigan, 1999; Hallam, 2002).

Insanity and Malingering

Confusion and potential communication difficulties arise when legal terms are used interchangeably with clinical terms. The media does not always get it right; however, legal and psychology scholars are frequently just as erroneous. Indeed, as human beings we are constantly in the midst of trying to make sense of the outside world. We sometimes change our beliefs based on contradictory evidence from that outside world, but most of the time we will save our energy and simply make the outside world fit our needs. Understandably, legal scholars may attempt to make sense of a given psychological construct by comparing it to a legal concept they more clearly comprehend – and vice-versa for the psychology scholars. Furthermore, if we escape the minute scholarly circles, we must consider yet another complication: the popular language. For a layperson, someone described as "insane" is equivalent to someone being "mentally ill."

We are faced with a popular belief that "insanity" means "mental illness," and "faking insanity" means "malingering." In fact, these words, frequently used inter-changeably, are divergent constructs specific to the context of their discipline. The *Diagnostic and Statistical Manual of Mental Disorders: DSM-IV-TR*; (APA, 2000) describes mental illness as

> A clinically significant behavioral or psychological syndrome or pattern that occurs in an individual and that is associated with present distress (e.g., a painful symptom), or disability (i.e., impairment in one or more important areas of functioning), or with a significantly increased risk of suffering death, pain, disability, or an important loss of freedom. In addition, this syndrome or pattern must not be merely an expectable and culturally sanctioned response to a particular event, for example, the death of a loved one. Whatever its original cause, it must currently be considered a manifestation of a behavioral, psychological, or biological dysfunction in the individual. Neither deviant behavior (e.g., political, religious, or sexual) nor conflicts that are primarily between the individual and society are mental disorders unless the deviance or conflict is a symptom of a dysfunction in the individual, as described above.

On the other hand, legal insanity occurs if, "at the time of the committing of the act, the party accused was labouring under such a defect of reason, from a disease of the mind, as not to know the nature and quality of the act he was doing; or, if he did know it, that he did not know he was doing what was wrong" (Queen v. McNaghten, 1843). In other words, the defendant would have to be suffering from a mental illness which directly affected his ability to know right from wrong or to understand the consequences of her/his actions at the time of the offense.

Finally, malingering is a psychological construct defined by "the intentional production of false or grossly exaggerated physical or psychological symptoms, motivated by external incentives such as . . . evading criminal prosecution" (p. 739; APA, 2000). In 1986, Rogers reported a 21% base rate of suspected or definite malingering in sanity evaluations. Currently, the prevalence of malingering in forensic cases is generally estimated in the 15–18% range (Rogers and Cruise, 2000; Rogers, Salekin, Sewell, Goldstein, & Leonard, 1998; Rogers, Sewell, & Goldstein, 1994).

The assessment of malingering, which is sometimes described as the amount and type of effort a person puts into the evaluation depending upon self-interest, takes into account many components, including direct clinical observation, psychological testing, and a review of both historical records and collateral information. In addition to reviewing an array of records and obtaining third party interviews, the evaluator also spends time examining the defendant for potential atypical or implausible symptom reports, contradictions or evasiveness, and inconsistencies (e.g., inconsistency between reports and behavior; and inconsistency between reports and collateral information/sources, including the details of the crime).

A thorough malingering assessment also includes the use of standardized objective measures. Some of the more widely used and validated instruments for this purpose include the *Minnesota Multiphasic Personality Inventory-2 (MMPI-2)*, the *Structured Interview of Reported Symptoms (SIRS)*, the *Miller Forensic Assessment of Symptoms Test (MFAST)*, the *Test of Memory Malingering (TOMM)*, the *Rey 15-Item Memory Test (MFIT)*, and the *Validity Indicator Profile (VIP)* to name a few. These instruments range from structured interviews designed to detect malingering of certain psychiatric symptoms to psychological tests used to identify malingering of memory problems. In addition, the forensic psychologist may also use assessments of violence risk based on actuarial tables of the recidivism of those physically or sexually violent prisoners who are released back into the community. The tests include *Violence Risk Assessment Guide (VRAG)*, *Sexual Offender Risk Assessment Guide (SORAG)*, *Minnesota Sex Offender Screening Tool (MSOST)*, *Historical Clinical Risk – 20 (HCR-20)*, and the *Psychopathy Check List, Revised Edition (PCL-R)*.

With all of these components in mind, it is extremely unlikely that a defendant will be able to "fake" a mental illness and successfully "fool" the evaluator. Furthermore, once it is determined that the defendant is not feigning mental illness, the evaluator has answered only a small portion of the ultimate question of legal insanity and criminal responsibility. Once it is determined that the defendant is indeed suffering from a mental illness, the role of that mental illness at the time of the crime still remains to be addressed, as does its effect on the defendant's ability to know right from wrong or to understand the consequences of her/his actions.

A Closer Look at Media Influence

When taking a closer look at the many types of media, it is not difficult to realize the vast extent of the media industry's influence on its massive audience. Several movies which portray individuals who "fake" insanity have won the hearts of Hollywood's audiences and awards. Creating films to show individuals feigning insanity is no new idea. As early as 1965, the film *Brainstorm* (Natali, 2002) featured a character who attempted to "get away with murder" by pleading insanity. Negative portrayals of individuals with mental illness are also present in *Girl, Interrupted* (Mangold, 1999) and *One Flew over the Cuckoo's Nest* (Forman, 1975). These movies have captured the minds of viewers and, in turn, have helped to shape viewers' ideas about the outside world. Distorted ideas about what mental illness is, and how it can be used to justify and get away with violent criminal behavior, are portrayed in *Final Analysis* (Joanou, 1992) and *Primal Fear* (Hoblit, 1996). Such films have introduced the public to areas in which psychology and law intertwine. It is important that the general public be educated about how different fields such as these can work collaboratively; however, these films do not necessarily present a positive, unbiased, or even an accurate view of this collaboration.

In the film *Primal Fear* (Hoblit, 1996) the character Aaron Stampler, played by Edward Norton, is charged with murdering an archbishop. Norton's character, who pleads insanity, portrays himself as someone with DID. While on the witness stand, this usually calm character displays overt symptoms of this disorder in an attempt to sway the jury. The problem with this portrayal is that it suggests a number of myths to the audience. This film's depiction of pleading insanity suggests that in order to "get off" on the insanity defense, one must act unstable and "crazy", when in fact the insanity defense is interested more with the individual's mental state at the time of the offense, not how the individual acts on the stand at the time of trial.

However, the media does not limit its delivery to movies or other televised content. Instead, there are many additional forms of media influence present in our everyday lives, including (but not limited to) magazines, billboards, and the Internet. Here we will focus on the Internet.

The Internet is an easily accessible tool that can be used to learn about a broad range of topics. This amazing tool can give us both positive and negative, both accurate and inaccurate information. Some of the information available may even claim to help individuals fake insanity in order to obtain some secondary gain. Criminal offenders have used the Internet as a tool to help them feign symptoms of mental illness as well as to identify assessments that mental health professionals may use to "test their insanity." In the recent trial of a man accused of killing seven co-workers, the defendant, Michael McDermott, was found to have researched the topic "how to fake a mental illness" on the Internet. In an attempt to explain this search, he claimed that he suffers from schizophrenia, and was actually researching how to fake being sane in order to avoid having to go to a mental hospital. This is a prime example of how media can influence someone's behavior.

Just as the Internet is being used by individuals who try to find ways to feign a mental illness, it is also instrumental in maintaining stigmas about mental illness. With the use of an internet search engine, it is easy for the public to locate information about insanity. One just needs to type in the keywords and an array of websites emerge, boasting their ability to test for insanity, while reinforcing the myth that insanity can be tested by a simple yes/no questionnaire. Although insanity is used in a legal context, when searching this term on the Internet, it assumes a very loose definition. A particular "insanity test" located on the Internet claims to assess one's insanity via questions such as, "Do you always keep to 30 miles per hour speed limits? [While driving a car]" and "Are you an alien?" These types of internet sites portray what they call *insanity* as a joke; in doing so, they minimize the reality of severe symptoms that some mentally ill individuals live and struggle with. Maintaining stigmas such as these damages the field of psychology and ridicules those affected by mental disorders.

Media as an Agent of Discrimination via Myths Dispersal about Mental Illness

In addition to stereotypes and prejudices based on gender, race, ethnicity, and sexual preference, mentally ill individuals suffer from discrimination aimed at certain characteristics (based on popular myths) with which they are associated. People are afraid of mentally ill people especially if they act different from others. One of the most prominent myths proliferated by the media is that mentally ill individuals are dangerous, out-of-control individuals as mentioned earlier. In reality, the scientific literature indicates that there is no causal relationship between mental illness and dangerousness. Furthermore, contrary to popular belief, criminal activity does not occur at a higher rate in people with mental illness than it does in the general population.

Another popular myth is that dangerous, mentally ill individuals cannot be rehabilitated. This belief fosters societal animosity toward this minority group and leads to their being outcasts. To enable an artificial sense of protection from these individuals, the legal setting has become one of society's primary modes of segregation. Mentally ill individuals become easy preys within the correctional setting, and further deteriorate due to lack of treatment and/or exploitation by other inmates. While the public clings to a spurious sense of safety, the mentally ill rarely receive the protection they need.

If we apply what we know about other types of discrimination, the key to societal tolerance is to develop a better understanding of individuals who have mental disorders. Increased contact and familiarity with this group of people may help develop a more accurate understanding of their needs, struggles, and hopes. It would surely humanize them and cultivate more positive attitudes toward that group. In many communities today, the mentally ill are integrated with others, often through the auspices of peer support groups sponsored by the National Alliance for the Mentally Ill (NAMI). A majority of individuals experience this increased contact with the unfamiliar through media depictions, televised or in other forms. This is another reason why it is crucial that the mentally ill be represented accurately, and that the myths surrounding dangerousness, criminal intent, and "faking insanity" be abolished.

The Role of the Psychologist in Extinguishing the Myths Surrounding Mental Illness

Advocacy to the Public

Psychologists have a moral if not ethical obligation to help change the public's misperceptions about the mentally ill. Popular movies often portray the mentally ill as highly violent, unpredictable, and unable to be helped by mental health professionals as discussed earlier in this chapter. These same popular movies provide the viewers with humorous, but inaccurate portrayals of how a psychologist works with the mentally ill.

For example, in the 1998 blockbuster *There's Something About Mary* (Farraelly & Farralley, 1998) starring Ben Stiller and Cameron Diaz, there is a scene where Ben Stiller's character, Ted Stroehmann, visits a psychiatrist. During the session the psychiatrist becomes bored and sneaks out of the room while Ted discusses the issues that are pertinent to him. The psychiatrist is absent from the room for an extended period of time while Ted is reclined on the couch and does not know that his psychiatrist has left. At the end of the session the psychiatrist sneaks back into the room, takes his bib off, and cleans his hands from his recently eaten lunch. This leaves the audience with a very negative view of the psychiatrist as well as mental health professionals in general. Someone who has never interfaced with a mental health professional may be left with the impression that they do not care about what their patients tell them. They may feel that the mental health professional is only concerned with collecting a fee and has little ability or interest in helping the patient. This same view has been promulgated by Woody Allen's movies where he portrays characters who are what used to be called, "neurotic" or mildly mentally ill so that life is always a struggle.

The obvious question is "What can a psychologist do to help extinguish the myths surrounding mental illness?" There are several things that a responsible psychologist can and should do to extinguish this myth. The first and most crucial step is normalizing mental illnesses. The second way that a psychologist can help is by pushing for advocacy in large organizations. The final way that a psychologist can help is endorsing and reinforcing accurate portrayals of the mentally ill in the media. Each step will help the public understand what it means to suffer from a mental illness and what can be expected from a qualified mental health professional.

Normalizing Mental Health

Let's first look at normalizing mental illnesses. The National Institute of Mental Health (NIMH) estimates that 26.2% of Americans aged 18 and older suffer from a diagnosable mental disorder in any given year. Approximately 6% or 1 in 17 people suffer from a serious mental illness (NIMH Statistics, 2007). These statistics highlight the fact that mental illness is a rather common occurrence that many people deal with on a normal basis. In fact, these disorders know no bounds. They affect the affluent, famous, successful, and sophisticated at similar levels to the rest of society. History has provided us with several examples of famous people who have suffered from a myriad of mental illnesses. For example, actress Tracy Gold and musician Karen Carpenter both reportedly struggled with anorexia nervosa. Singer and popular television personality Paula Abdul was rumored to struggle with bulimia; actor Robin Williams has sought treatment for alcoholism; and Ernest Hemingway reportedly dealt with depression throughout his life. This is a partial list of well-known individuals who have allegedly suffered from some type of mental illness.

Making the general public aware of others who suffer from similar disorders is helpful in normalizing mental illness. It is helpful for the general public to recognize that people are able to function in society despite the fact that they suffer from a mental illness. In fact, several popular websites list mental health diagnosis of several famous people. For example, the following websites offer a comprehensive list of famous people who allegedly suffered from a mental illness:

- www.naminh.org/action-famous-people.php
- www.schizophrenia.com/famous.htm
- www.nami.org/Template.cfm?Section=Helpline1&template=/ContentManagement/ContentDisplay.cfm&ContentID=4858

Getting the message to the masses is often very difficult, but psychologists must think of creative ways to reach the public. One effective way to reach the public is through public service announcements (PSAs). Psychologists can approach individuals in the public eye who have themselves suffered from a mental illness or had a loved one who has struggled. These announcements would need to appeal to a large audience and be delivered in a manner that is interesting. The PSAs could run in movie theaters at the end of movies or during commercial breaks of television shows. These announcements might even be replayed in audio form over the radio during commercial breaks. Again, getting the word out to the public is essential to normalizing the experience of the mentally ill.

Another way to normalize the public to mental health is through the media. The media is perhaps the most persuasive tool in American society, and, when used properly, can influence millions of people. Psychologists should encourage the writers and producers of television shows to showcase characters from time to time who suffer from a mental illness. This portrayal should focus on the particular symptoms the patient suffers. The overall message of the program should focus on the ability of the patient to overcome the illness and function in society and the ability to accurately portray mental illness.

Finally, an additional way to normalize the public is through daily news reporting. The evening news often deals with issues of mental illness; however, this portrayal is often not an accurate one. The news tends to glamorize and distort the mental illness issues of both celebrities and non-celebrities alike. All too often news reports seem to discuss the substance abuse habits of the famous, but do not show their struggles. They seem to focus on the failures that these people experience or the legal troubles that they have because of their mental illness or substance abuse.

Advocacy

Another way to extinguish the myths surrounding mental illness is by psychologists becoming involved in nationally recognized organizations concerned with the rights of the mentally ill. The American Psychological Association (APA) is organized into specific divisions concerned with various mental health issues. Among those is Division 46 or the Media Psychology Division. This division focuses on the roles that psychologists play in various aspects of the media. Psychologists should be encouraged to join this division of the APA and become active in their pursuits. Division 46 should identify senior psychologists who are willing to work with the popular media. These psychologists would form a work group that would brainstorm and develop a plan to interface more effectively with those in positions of power in the media.

The organization as a whole would provide new ideas of how to show the mentally ill. The goal is to portray the mentally ill differently than they have been portrayed in the past. All too often the mentally ill have been shown to be violent, unpredictable, and incapable of functioning within society. Writers and producers of movies and television shows likely have little experience with the mentally ill. They are not likely to understand the course and treatment of a mental illness. A seasoned psychologist would be able to give some guidance to the writers so that the mentally ill can be portrayed accurately. The consulting psychologist might be able to actually do some of the writing himself or herself.

Endorsing Accurate Portrayals

The final way for psychologists to help extinguish the myths surrounding mental illness is through reinforcing or endorsing the accurate portrayals of the mentally ill that currently exist. Division 46 of APA should be encouraged to develop a list of television programs, media outlets, and popular movies that are particularly sensitive to the needs and experiences of the mentally ill. The division should develop a set of criteria that must be met in order to be included on the list. This list would then be sent out to media outlets, producers, writers, as well as others involved in the media. Programs that meet the minimum requirements would be recognized both by the APA website and an endorsement in the closing credits of the movie or television show.

Television shows and movies such as *Law and Order* (Makris et al., 1990 to present) and *A Beautiful Mind* (Howard, 2001) have long provided accurate portrayals of the mentally ill as well as the work of a mental health professional. For example, psychiatrist Dr. Park Dietz has consulted on many episodes of *Law and Order* (Makris, et al., 1990 to present) and has insured that mental illness is portrayed in an accurate manner. Dr. Marianne Gillow also consulted with writers and producers of *A Beautiful Mind* (Howard, 2001) in order to portray the struggles of the John Nash character accurately. These particular shows should be further recognized for their hard work in extinguishing the myths around mental illness. Perhaps organizations such as the APA, the NAMI, or the NIMH could offer some type of award for the television show, movie, producer, actor, and writer that best portrays the mentally ill in the media. These awards could be presented annually at national conventions as to attract the attention of media and draw more attention to the issues.

The goal is to make the endorsement of psychologist and accurate portrayals of the mentally ill the standard for media persons to reach. This initiative must be undertaken by psychologists with the help of others in positions of power. The only way to effect change is by advocating for the rights of the mentally ill in a public forum.

References

Ajzen, I., & Fishbein, M. (1982) Understanding attitudes and predicting social behavior. Reprinted in *Contemporary issues in social psychology* (4th ed.). In J. C. Brigham & L. S. Wrightsman. Monterey, CA: Brooks/Cole Publishing Company.

American Psychiatric Association. (2000). *Diagnostic and statistical manual of mental disorders* (4th ed.). Washington, DC: Author.

Circincoine, C., & Steadman, H. L. (1994). Demythologizing inaccurate perception of the insanity defense. *Law and human behavior, 18,* 67.

Famous People and Schizophrenia. (n.d.). Retrieved February 20, 2007, from http://www.schizophrenia.com/famous.htm

Farrelly, B., & Farrelly, P. (2000). *Me, myself, and Irene.* Universal City, CA: 20th Century Fox Home Entertainment.

Fluxman, T. (2005). *Marx and the theory of ideology.* Paper to be presented to the philosophical society of southern Africa conference.

Greene, E. (1990). Media effects on jurors. *Law and human behavior, 14,* 439–450.

Hallam, A. (2002). Media influences on mental health policy: Long-term effects of the Clunis and Silcock cases. *International review of psychiatry, 14,* 26–33.

Hannigan, B. (1999). Mental health care in the community: An analysis of contemporary public attitudes towards, and public representations of, mental illness. *Journal of Mental Health, 8,* 431–440.

Larraine, J. (1979). *The concept of ideology.* London: Hutchinson

Lawson, A., & Fouts, G. (2004). Mental illness in Disney animated films. *Canadian journal of psychiatry, 49*(5), 310–314.

LeAmm, G. (2006). *Cultivation theory. George Gerbne. Cultivation theory.* Retrieved on March 1, 2007, at: http://www.colostate.edu/Depts/Speech/rccs/theory06.htm

Motion Picture Association of America. (2005). *U.S. theatrical market: 2005 statistics.* Retrieved on February 28, 2007, from http://www.mpaa.org/researchStatistics.asp

Newspaper Association of America. (2006). *Daily and Sunday newspapers 2006 readers per copy.* Retrieved on March 1, 2007, from http://www.naa.org/trends-and-numbers/market-databank/2005-daily-and-sunday-readers-per-copy-.aspx

NIMH statistics. (2007). Retrieved February 20, 2007, from http://www.nimh.nih.gov/healthinformation/statisticsmenu.cfm

People with mental illness enrich our lives. (n.d.). Retrieved February 20, 2007, from http://www.nami.org/Template.cfm?Section=Helpline1&template=/ContentManagement/ContentDisplay.cfm&Content

Queen v. M'Naghten (1843). Retrieved February 15, 2007, from http://www.answers.com/topic/insanity-defense

Rogers, R. (1986). *Conducting insanity evaluations.* New York: Van Nostrand Reinhold.

Rogers, R., & Cruise, K. R. (2000). Malingering and deception among psychopaths. In C. B. Gacono (Ed.), *The clinical and forensic assessment of psychopathy: A practitioner's guide* (pp. 269–284). Mahwah, N.J.: Lawrence Erlbaum Associates, Inc.

Rogers, R., Salekin, R., Sewell, K., Goldstein, A., & Leonard, K. (1998). A comparison of forensic and nonforensic malingerers: A prototypical analysis of explanatory models. *Law and human behavior, 22,* 353–367.

Rogers, R., Sewell, K., & Goldstein, A. (1994). Explanatory models of malingering: A prototypical analysis. *Law and human behavior, 18*, 543–552.

Siegel, L. (2000). *Criminology* (7th ed.). Belmont, CA: WadsworthlThomson Learning.

Steadman, H. J., Mulvey, E. P., Monahan, J., Robbins, P., Appelbaum, P., Grisso, T. et al. (1998). Violence by people discharged from acute psychiatric inpatient facilities and by others in the same neighborhoods. *Archives of General Psychiatry, 55*, 393–401.

Steadman, H. J., & Cocozza, J. J. (1977–1978). Selective reporting and the public's misconception of the criminally insane. *The public opinion quarterly, 41*, 523–533.

Take action – famous people with mental illness. (n.d.). Retrieved February 20, 2007, from http://www.naminh.org/action-famous-people.php

Wahl, O. (1995). *Media madness: Public images of mental illness.* New Brunswick, N.J.: Rutgers University Press.

Wedding, D., Boyd, M., & Niemiec, R. M. (2005). *Movies and mental illness: Using films to understand psychopathology* (2nd Ed.). Cambridge, M.A.: Hogrefe & Huber.

Wood, W. (2000). Attitude change: Persuasion and social influence publication (539), *Annual review of psychology.* Florence, KY: Annual Reviews, Inc., Gale Group.

Zonana, H. W., Wells, J. A., Getz, M. A., & Buchanan, J. (1990). Part i: The NGRI registry: Initial analyses of data collected on Connecticut insanity acquittees. *Bulletin of the American academy of psychiatry and the law, 18*, 115–128.

Looking at Disability Through a Different Lens: Reinterpreting Disability Images in Line with Positive Psychology

Rochelle Balter

Abstract The media annals for the last 75 years form a veritable social history with values, attitudes, habits, and prejudices evolving over this time span. Movies have been especially powerful when portraying stereotypes, especially those of stigmatized groups including people with disabilities. If we look at films conceived after the passage of the Americans with Disabilities Act (ADA; 1990), we find that people with disabilities are now portrayed in cameo and background roles that do not lead to inspiration as they did previously (e.g., Helen Keller in *The Miracle Worker* and Don in *Butterflies Are Free*). Older films reveal an interesting phenomenon, that is, many of the films discussed in this chapter do have the positive psychology approach of offering a balanced portrayal of a character overcoming obstacles in an uplifting or inspirational manner. Reasons for this seeming paradox are discussed; whereas the law now protects the civil rights of those with disabilities, these people seem to have lost their interest as major dramatic personae.

Media, including television and movies, have traditionally reflected and molded societal attitudes. If we were to examine the media annals for the last 75 years, we would find a veritable social history and would see how our values, attitudes, habits, and prejudices have evolved over this time span. Movies have been especially powerful when portraying stereotypes, especially ones of stigmatized groups including racial and ethnic stereotypes, gender orientation stereotypes, those regarding aging or elderly, and people with disabilities.

Norden (1994) summarized how those with disabilities had historically been depicted in the movies. Those with disabilities are shown as:

> "extraordinary (and often initially embittered) individuals whose lonely struggles against incredible odds, make for what is considered heart warming stories of courage and triumph;...comic characters who inadvertently cause trouble for themselves and others,

R. Balter (✉)
Department of Psychology, John Jay College of Criminal Justice, New York, NY, 10019, USA
e-mail: rbalt@aol.com

Dedicated to the memory of Betsy Zabarowski, Ph.D., a true advocate in the field of blindness rights.

saintly sages who possess the gift of second sight, and sweet young things whose goodness and innocence are sufficient to escape isolation in the form of a miraculous cure" (p. 3).

Norden (1994) also opined that film makers have used their various tools, techniques and story lines to separate their characters with disabilities from those who are non-disabled (p. 1). The purpose is to allow non-disabled audience members to associate themselves with non-disabled characters, "thereby enhancing the disabled charac-ter's isolation and 'Otherness' thus reducing them (characters with disabilities) to objectifications of pity, fear and scorn" (p. 1).

Are these portrayals a form of stigma and discrimination . . . that depends on who you ask. Some (for quotes see Norden, 1994) say that it is a matter of the person with a disability's emotional acceptance of his/her condition or the per-son's emotional coping skills. Others (for quotes see Norden, 1994) look at it in terms of dramatic construction . . . will this condition or circumstance make a salable story?

Elliott and Byrd (1983), who wrote about this topic in the context of Rehabilitation Psychology 10 years before Norden, described portrayals of charac-ters with disabilities in the context of social distance, also a form of isolation. Elliott and Byrd (1983) pointed out that dramatic stereotypic characterizations "may be ideal for ratings, but provide inaccurate information for the formulation of attitudes" (p. 349) toward the disabilities that are being portrayed.

Both Norden (1994) and Elliott and Byrd (1983) looked at the media stereotypes as only having negative connotations although they stated that television portrayals could be used for positive attitude change. Balter (1999) discussed various stereo-typic portrayals such as the blind hero in *Butterflies Are Free* (Kastelas, 1972) and Jill Kinmont, the skier with quadriplegia in *The Other Side of the Mountain* (Peerce, 1975). Balter (1999) also pointed out how these images are used to isolate and dis-tance from those with disabilities rather than including persons with disabilities in the mainstream. This was thought to be necessary in order to insure the viewer's sense of safety and security.

Both Norden (1994) and Balter (1999) stated that *The Miracle Worker* (Penn, 1962) portrayed some of the stronger stereotypes of disability. Helen, although beloved, shows the signs of a beast. She is undisciplined, unruly, slovenly, and lacks all manners and characteristics of human civility. Her parents are at a loss as to how to handle her, but at the same time, feel pity and contempt for her. Annie Sullivan, a teacher who also has a visual impairment, is brought in to help tame Helen. At first, she too is frustrated; however, her efforts eventually meet with success since only another similarly challenged individual can help to transform Helen (Norden, 1994). Helen becomes more of a sweet innocent; however, she does not merit a miraculous cure, but instead goes on to help others as a disabled superhero.

Jill Kinmont, a true life skier who had an accident while skiing which resulted in quadriplegia, is another dramatized autobiography. Norden (1994) would probably describe Jill as a sweet innocent. She does not receive a miraculous cure, but instead struggles, and never quits. Even as she adapts to her disability, and grapples with unfair societal requirements, she meets with tragedy. Thus her goodness does not save her.

Positive Psychology and Film

In 2000, Seligman and Csikszentmihalyi published their theory of positive psychology. Seligman (2003) and others (Frederickson, 2001) noted that psychology and psychotherapy tended to focus on symptoms and psychopathology rather than individual strengths and resilience.

Seligman and Csikszentmihalyi (2000) asked how strengths, optimism, and resilience contribute to a good life and what positive attributes contribute to mental health. Seligman (2003) theorized that positive qualities such as "confidence, optimism, hope, and trust serve us best . . . when life is difficult" (p. 306).

Seligman realized that he needed to validate his findings through research and therefore attempted to quantify the components of a "good life," among which are wisdom, knowledge, courage, humanity, justice, temperance (which includes forgiveness, humility, and self-regulation), and transcendence (Peterson & Seligman, 2004). These are broad categories which include qualities such as creativity, open-mindedness, bravery, persistence, kindness, forgiveness, hope, and humor among others (p. 412).

The above-mentioned researchers (Seligman, Peterson, Aspinwall, & Staudinger, 2003) also stated that the strengths involved had to be stable across time and had to be generalizable across situations; were celebrated when present but mourned when absent; were strengths that parents wanted to develop in their children and that the larger society also values these strengths (pp. 307–308). Seligman added that the strengths also had to be recognized and valued "in almost every subculture" (p. 308).

Niemiec (2007), in writing about what makes a positive psychology film, listed four elements that he felt had to be present for a film to be characterized as a positive psychology film. These are the following: (1) "a balanced portrayal of a character displaying at least one of the 24 strengths . . . " listed by Seligman and Peterson (2004) including humility and creativity; (2) "depiction of obstacles, struggles/conflicts that the character faces or copes with;" Niemiec (2007, 8/29) points out that the struggle may be metaphorical. (3) the character portrayal illustrates how the obstacles are overcome or the strengths are built; and (4) the film itself has an uplifting or inspiring tone. He applied these to the *Pursuit of Happiness* (Muccino, 2006), a film about a man and his son who are down-and-out, a marriage that dissolves and how the hero overcomes these obstacles to be both successful and bring himself and his child success and fulfillment.

If we apply these principles to films about disability that up to this time have been considered isolationist and stereotypic, where does it leave us? If we look at films conceived after the passage of the Americans with Disabilities Act (1990), we interestingly find that people with disabilities are now portrayed in more minor roles and roles that do not lead to inspiration. If we go back and look at the older films discussed by Norden (1994) and Balter (1999), we find an interesting phenomenon, that is, many of the films mentioned do have the characteristics delineated by Niemiec (2007) that make a film a positive psychology film.

If we examine one to two films for each physical disability category that both Norden (1994) and Balter (1999) discussed, we find the following.

Blindness and Visual Impairment

Butterflies Are Free (Kastelas, 1972): As discussed before, this film follows Don Baker's attempts (sometimes successful, sometimes frustrating) to live alone and shape a normal life for himself despite his blindness. His neighbor, Jill, plays the foil who does not believe that Don cannot see and does not see how he can function when she finally does understand that he is blind. Jill has her own emotional disability (she is commitment phobic). How could this film fit a positive psychology paradigm? It has all four of Niemiec's elements. Don demonstrates creativity, humility, tenacity, and optimism. He is not unrealistic and his sometimes lonely struggles to overcome adversity, especially, functional limitations, are documented throughout the film. His mother's children's book series about Little Donny Dark, the blind boy superhero, adds an extra inspiring element; however, not for Don since he always believed that his mother wanted him to act this way and he, in his mind, could never measure up (Norden, 1994). Little Donny Dark was created to inspire Don and to keep him hopeful rather than fearful when dealing with the challenges he must face and her books became a commercial success. Although Mrs. Baker originally comes across as overprotective, she does end up encouraging him not to come home, but to face his life. Even Jill demonstrates humor and hopefulness. The film has a very uplifting and inspiring atmosphere.

The second film on blindness that must necessarily be examined is *The Miracle Worker* (Kastelas, 1962). Helen Keller is both blind and deaf and when first seen in this story that is both hopeful and inspirational (one of Niemiec's four elements) bears little resemblance to a civilized child. Her parents' attitudes toward her shift back and forth between pity, frustration, guilt, and hopelessness. When Annie Sullivan is hired (a teacher of the deaf and blind) who herself has a visual impairment, Helen's parents express little hope of success but are willing to try anything. Helen undergoes a series of trials before she finally learns to learn from her teacher. She definitely faces struggles and overcomes obstacles and demonstrates a number of the Seligman qualities that typify positive approaches including tenacity, hope, and creativity, and both Annie and Helen are icons of persistence. The story is both uplifting and touching and is a real-life dramatization. Helen Keller, as we know, went on to help many other individuals who were blind and deaf/blind.

Deafness and Hard of Hearing

When we look at movies about people who are deaf or hard of hearing, *Children of a Lesser God* (Hanes & Palmer, 1986) stands out from the rest. This is a complex story of Sarah Norman who is deaf and a former honors student who works at the deaf school at which she was trained. She communicates by signing rather than speaking, even though she has some limited speech. She works in a custodial type position and hides her competence from James Leeds, a new teacher who is hearing, works at the school, and falls in love with Sarah despite her disability or maybe because of it. The story centers about their relationship and how James tries to "fix her" when Sarah does not want to be changed. Both lead characters are strong. Sarah constantly demonstrates how she has conquered the challenges she has met and still has found happiness, whereas James, the non-disabled character, is often angry and frustrated. Does this conflict meet Niemiec's (2007) positive psychology requirements? It probably does. The female, played by Marlee Matlin, is determined, tenacious, and very sure of what she wants from life and how to get it. She has a strong sense of humor and is self-confident. She is far from dependent. James leaves doubts as to whether the relationship will survive, but there is no doubt that the female lead will survive and prosper.

Marlee Matlin, a talented and personable actress who is deaf, has also played deaf roles on television series. She played an attorney who is deaf in the short-lived series, *Reasonable Doubts* (Singer, 1991–1993), and also played a spin expert on *The West Wing* (Misiano, Graves, Schlamme, Glatter, Innes, Misiano, D'Elia, Barclary, Olin, Yu, Hébert, Bernstein, Taylor, Kagan, Berlinger, Coles, Schiff, McCormick, 1999–2006). These were not inspiring roles, but normal roles where deafness was ancillary, not central to the role, but roles which still could be used to inspire people with disabilities toward full participation.

Another, more modern film, featuring a deaf character is *Four Weddings and a Funeral* (Newell, 1994). The story is that of a group of friends who see each other through their eventual couplings and weddings; however, Charles, the protagonist, who falls for Carrie, does not see himself as the marrying kind. Charles' deaf brother, David, is around throughout the action but does not play a central role, until Charles decides it is time to marry and goes to the altar to marry Henrietta, someone he does not love. When the minister asks if anyone knows why the couple should not be wed, David stands up and in sign language states that Charles does not love Henrietta. He thus moves the plot along. Does this meet Niemiec's positive psychology requirements . . . probably not; however, it is uplifting and shows David's inherent strengths and regard for his brother and is more typical of post ADA movies, even though it is British. In these movies, as previously mentioned, those with disabilities often play smaller, less visible roles, but ones that are less stereotyped or discriminatory.

Orthopedic Disability/Mobility Impairment

There are different genres of movies that have addressed paralysis, limited mobility, traumatic brain injury, and other mobility-impairing conditions. Most of the older ones are isolationist or speak to evil such as *Dr. Strangelove* (Kubrick, 1964). The Jill Kinmont story, *The Other Side of the Mountain (Parts I and II*; Peerce, 1978), is typical of such a true story that can be looked at either through the eyes of separation, pity and "dis" ability or as a positive psychology film. As discussed previously, Jill, a professional skier, is injured in a sports accident. She ends up paralyzed and needs to relearn even the simplest "activities of daily living" (ADL) skills. Whereas she is optimistic and pleased with each advancing step she takes, others, such as her fiancé, walk away in disgust. How can this be a positive psychology film? It is. Jill meets all four of the requirements. She possesses many of the characteristics of the portrayal of a positive character. She is optimistic, determined, has a goal to teach others, and fights on with dignity to reach that goal. She overcomes major obstacles such as learning to get around, learning how to fight for her rights as a teacher, and losing those important in her life but still being able to prevail and find fulfillment in her life. Her fight is both practical and metaphysical. She is an excellent role model. Her true story is definitely inspiring. Norden (1994) commented on how the protagonist had discussions with the script writer who tended to downplay the roles of those around Jill rather than showing them realistically. Norden (1994) also notes a factor that is true of Don Baker in *Butterflies Are Free* (Kastelas, 1972), that is, much of Jill's and Don's struggles are against ableist attitudes, rather than disability.

A truly unique depiction of multiple orthopedic and neurological disabilities can be found in *My Left Foot* (Sheridan, 1989). This film, shot in Dublin, Ireland, presents the life story of author/painter Christy Brown (Norden, 1994) who had cerebral palsy. The only part of his body that Christy could dependably use was his left foot with which he learned to write and paint, astounding his father and mother. The script, as Norden (1994) points out, is realistic and earthy, not purposely meant to inspire, yet it does.

The film, or maybe just Christy, meets all of the requirements that Niemiec (2007) set forth. Christy himself demonstrates many of the qualities delineated in Seligman and Peterson's (2004) list including creativity, tenacity, hope, and perseverance. He overcomes numerous struggles both within his large, poverty-stricken family and with the outside ableist world. His struggles are both practical and metaphysical. He shows these are overcome and the film is uplifting despite its realistic tone.

A more modern film with a character with an orthopedic disability who plays a major role is *Notting Hill* (Michell, 1999). The film, in this case, is not about the character with the disability, Bella, even though she plays a major role and moves the action forward. The story is about an American film star, Anna Scott, who meets a London bookseller, William Thacker, and about their love story. The character who has paralysis is Bella, the wife of William's good friend Max. Her disability is handled realistically and not dramatized; but in its visibility and lack of pathos, it plays an important role as does Bella in the concluding part where she uses her disability to help William gain access to a press conference that is pivotal to resolving the relationship. She is witty, engaging and leaves no doubt about her abilities. *Notting Hill* (Michell, 1999) is not a positive psychology film, yet Bella's role can be seen as a very underplayed, but very realistic positive psychology role and can be used in rehabilitation and psychotherapy as a role model.

Using Positive Psychology Films in Clinical Settings

Many people live with some type of physical disability. Some estimates are that nearly 20% of the population has a visibly discernible disability at any time (Cornell University, 2004). This statistic does not include millions who live with invisible disabilities or chronic illnesses. Many discernible disabilities are the results of automobile accidents or sports accidents. Presently, a large number of returning veterans have disabilities acquired as a result of the Iraqi War. Some of these are amputations; other are traumatic brain injury while still others result in paralysis, blindness, and deafness.

Vision and hearing decrements are also a result of people having a longer life span.

The role of the rehabilitation psychologist working with these patients is to help the person with the newly acquired disability to accommodate to a new lifestyle often filled with new ways of doing everyday tasks and with assistive devices that are employed to facilitate tasks that heretofore were automatic (e.g., using an assistive animal to help with dressing and fetching).

When psychotherapists and rehabilitation psychologists work with these patients, a picture (albeit a film) often has a large impact on the patient who may need a role model. The patient needs to see that someone in similar circumstances can lead a relatively normal and fulfilling life. Bella, in *Notting Hill* (Michell, 1999), would serve this purpose.

One of the challenges of working with someone with a physical disability is a lack of trust that the person with the disability develops toward medical/psychological professionals because the professional lives in the "normal world" (Balter, 2006).

Often the individual with the newly acquired disability needs help in understanding and not incorporating ableist attitudes, which a film such as *Notting Hill* (Michell, 1999) or *Four Weddings and a Funeral* (Newell, 1994) can assist with by normalizing the person with the disability, in a way that most non-disabled mental health professionals cannot.

References

Balter, R. (1999). From stigmatization to patronization: The media's distorted portrayal of physical disability. In L. L. Schwartz (Ed.), *Psychology and the media: A second look* (pp. 147–171). Washington, DC: American Psychological Association.

Balter, R. (2006, June/July). Psychotherapy with persons with disabilities. *The New York state psychologist, 8* (4), 67–73.

Cornell University (2004). *Rehabilitation Research Center on disability demographics and statistics: 2004 disability status report.* Retrieved 12/05 from http://www.disabilitystatistics.org.

Elliott, T., & Byrd, E. (1983). Attitude change toward disability through television portrayal. *Journal of applied rehabilitation counseling, 14* (2), 35–37.

Frederickson, B. L. (2001). The role of positive emotions in positive psychology: The broaden-and-build theory of positive emotions. *American Psychologist, 56,* 218–222.

Niemiec, R. (2007). What is a positive psychology film? *PsycCRITIQUES, 52*(38).

Norden, M. (1994). *The cinema of isolation: A history of physical disability in the movies.* New Brunswick, NJ: Rutgers University Press.

Peterson, C., & Seligman, M. E. (2004). Hope (optimism, future-mindedness, future orientation). In C. Peterson & M. E. Seligman, *Character strengths and virtues: A handbook and classification* (pp. 569–582). Washington, DC: American Psychological Association, xiv, 800pp.

Seligman, M. E. (2003). Positive psychology: Fundamental assumptions. *The psychologist, 16* (3), 126–127.

Seligman, M. E., & Csikszentmihalyi, M. (2000). Positive psychology: An introduction. *American psychologist, 55* (1), 5–14.

Seligman, M. E., Peterson, C., Aspinwall, L., & Staudinger, U. (Eds.). (2003). *A psychology of human strengths: Fundamental questions and future directions for a positive psychology* (pp. 305–317). Washington, DC: American Psychological Association, (203) xvi, 369pp.

Cinema as Alchemy for Healing and Transformation: Using the Power of Films in Psychotherapy and Coaching

Birgit Wolz

> *No form of art goes beyond ordinary consciousness as film does,*
> *straight to our emotions, deep into the twilight room of the soul.*
> –Ingmar Bergman

Introduction

As clients respond to movies emotionally, their reactions reflect their inner world. Using Cinema Alchemy, psychotherapists and coaches make use of this reflection by using movies as an adjunct to traditional methods. Films draw a client into the viewing experience, but at the same time – often more easily than in real life – afford a unique opportunity to retain a perspective outside the experience, the observer's view. This allows the viewing experience to become a catalyst for the therapeutic or coaching process.

"Movies affect us powerfully because the synergistic impact of music, dialogue, lighting, camera angles, and sound effects enables a film to bypass ordinary defensive censors in us" (Fischoff, 2006). As one measure of just how powerful motion pictures have become, we should consider how some sociologists, psychologists, politicians, and clerics complain that movies are changing the way society, especially children, view themselves and their world (Mitry, 2000).

Such critics point out that in an effort to appeal to the basest elements of human nature, many movies overemphasize graphic violence and sex. The classic Bandura experiment with a Bobo doll showed how imitation on a screen is powerful in changing behavior. Eighty-eight percent of the children, who watched a video where a model would aggressively hit a doll, subsequently imitated the aggressive behavior. Eight months later, 40% of the same children reproduced the violent behavior observed in this experiment (Bandura, 1973, p. 72).

B. Wolz (✉)
Oakland, CA 04611
e-mail: bwolz@earthlink.net

M.B. Gregerson (ed.), *The Cinematic Mirror for Psychology and Life Coaching*,
DOI 10.1007/978-1-4419-1114-8_11, © Springer Science+Business Media, LLC 2010

It is true that many films play to the lowest common denominators – the base human instincts and desires. These movies can end up serving as a catalyst for personal insight into the darker side of the soul. When those dark aspects are brought into the light of conscious awareness in the therapeutic process, true inner freedom is possible.

It is practically impossible to number the movies that seek the opposite pole, that strive to inspire the highest human values. Like no other medium before it, the popular movie has the potential for illuminating the depth of human experience.

The Inner Landscape Fertile for Cinema Alchemy

Roots of Cinema Alchemy
As with most "new" ideas, many aspects of Cinema Alchemy are not really new. The use of movies for personal growth and healing carries forward a long-standing connection between storytelling and self-reflection that in all probability dates back to the beginnings of spoken language.

Cinema Alchemy can be traced back to bibliotherapy, which is the use of engaged reading of novels and short stories in order to gain insight into one's psyche (Mellon, 2003). The practice of bibliotherapy may go back as far as the ancient Greeks where the door to the library at Thebes bore the inscription: The Healing Place of the Soul (Riordan & Wilson, 1989).

The Greeks used drama in their visual and performance arts as a means of dealing with their emotions. Up to this day the Greeks do not sit passively in their seats and clap politely at the end. In both ancient and modern Greek theaters, people yell, scream, cry, and become quite expressive. The ancient Greeks had developed poetic ways to heal the emotional wounds caused by war. Tragedy was performed for this "catharsis" essentially cleansing disordered emotions and healing trauma. Aristotle theorized "tragic plays have the capacity to purify the spirit and aid us in coping with aspects of life that cannot be reconciled by rational thought" (Murnaghan, 1951).

How the Effect of the Movie Experience in the Context of Psychotherapy and Coaching can be Explained
Recent Theories of Learning and Creativity
Research about accelerated learning indicates that acquisition and retention are enhanced when, in addition to the use of stories and metaphors, multiple senses are engaged during the learning process. Howard Gardner suggests that we have multiple "intelligences" (Gardner, 1993a,b). The more of these intelligences we access, the faster we learn, because by doing so we employ different methods of information processing. Sturdevant hypothesizes that watching movies can engage most of these intelligences (Sturdevant, 1998):

- The film's plot engages our *logical intelligence*.
- Script dialog engages the *linguistic intelligence*.

- Pictures, colors, and symbols on the screen engage the *visual–spatial intelligence.*
- Sounds and music engage our *musical intelligence.*
- Storytelling engages the *interpersonal intelligence.*
- Movement engages the *kinesthetic intelligence.*
- Self-reflection or inner guidance, as demonstrated especially in inspirational films, engages the *intrapsychic intelligence.*

The viewer accesses the last three intelligences not directly but through identification with the characters.

The above demonstrates how movies can speak to a client on a variety of psychological and physiological channels; and the effect is synergistic, all of which further elevates cinema's potential for growth, healing, and transformation. Film characters often model strength, courage, and other positive qualities, helping a client through life's difficult times.

The Power of Metaphors and Symbols

Many films, like dreams, are full of metaphors and symbols. Metaphors and symbols can affect us on a deep level (Gordon, 1978). Carl G. Jung wrote: "As the mind explores the symbol, it is led to ideas that lie beyond the grasp of reason" (Jung, 1964, p. 35).

This concept has similarities to the theories of learning and creativity, though both are coming from a very different theoretical background. Metaphors and symbols, in a therapeutic context, are especially useful for Cinema Alchemy because they

- stimulate bi-lateral thinking and creativity, since both parts of the brain get engaged,
- carry multiple levels of information,
- pass suggestions to the subconscious mind,
- bypass normal ego defenses with therapeutic messages, and
- facilitate retrieval of resource experiences.

The Power of Myths and Stories

Voytilla emphasizes that "moviemaking can be considered the contemporary form of mythmaking, reflecting our response to ourselves and the mysteries and wonders of our existence" (Voytilla, 1999, p. 1).

Carl Gustav Jung said that mythic stories make up a collective "dream." The whole of mythology can be taken as a sort of projection of the collective unconscious (Jung, 1927). Movies are a significant part of our evolving mythology. The individual is linked to the past of the whole species and the long stretch of evolution of the organism.

The patterns of myth are used in many fairy tales, novels, theater plays, and screenplays for movies. Therefore, our responses to certain movies demonstrate recognition of these deep layers of our unconscious. Films, like myths, tap into patterns of the collective unconscious. Their stories have such a powerful effect on us because they speak directly to the heart and spirit, avoiding the resistance of the conscious mind. In doing so they help us in our personal process of healing and transformation.

Milton Erickson constructed metaphoric tales with a series of embedded commands (Erickson & Rossi, 1980). He used these *Teaching Tales* in formal trance states, as well as in open-eye-trance when he told the story without formal induction (Rosen, 1982).

The Power of Projection

Projection is an interesting concept in this context. According to the *Merriam-Webster's Dictionary* the verb "project" stems etymologically from Middle and Old French, as well as Greek and Latin for "throwing forward." Among others, the dictionary lists the following meanings for projection (Merriam-Webster's, 1998):

> The display of motion pictures by projecting an image from them upon a screen and the act of perceiving a mental object as spatially and sensibly objective; also something so perceived or the attribution of one's own ideas, feelings, or attitudes to other people or to objects.

All three meanings are relevant here. First, the movie is projected onto a white screen; then, everyone who watches these images projects a different meaning on what he or she sees. How and what we project depend on our view of the world, our history, and our personality.

Clients go through the following process of identification through projection as they watch a movie.

Stages of Cognitive and Emotional Interpretation Through Identification and Projection

Going through the following stages, clients can examine and work with their issues, which are first safely "outside," and subsequently are identified as their own.

1. *Disassociation*: Client watches character(s) outside their internal frame of reference.
2. *Identification Through Projection*: Client begins to identify with character, situation, etc.
3. *Internalization*: Client develops sense of ownership of what was felt through character, scene, and situation and feels less alone.
4. *Inquiry into transference or projection.*

These stages can be described to clients in the following way:

1. Watching a character outside yourself in a movie.
2. Beginning to identify with a character, scene, etc.–"I feel like a character," or "I hate what he is doing."
3. Examining whether a character, their behavior, or attributes might be part of your not-yet-fully-recognized positive qualities or repressed "shadow" self.

4. Exploring ways to become more whole by embracing the projected positive qualities, in order to realize your full potential as well as acknowledging your repressed "shadow" self, to move toward emotional healing and inner freedom.

Clients are usually more open to acknowledging their projections on movie characters than projections on people in their life, especially on their therapist. After they understand the projections on film characters, they are sometimes more ready for transference work.

Stages of Cognitive and Emotional Interpretation Through Projection of Disowned Parts of Self

Going through the following stages, clients can examine and work with previously disowned parts of their psyche.

Disassociation
Client watches character(s) outside their internal frame of reference.

Projection of Disowned Parts of Self
Client begins to dislike or disapprove of character(s), their behavior,or certain attributes .

Inquiry into Transference or Projection
Client examines whether rejected character(s), their behavior, or attributes could be part of repressed self.

Acknowledgement of Disowned Parts
Client explores ways to become more whole by embracing their repressed shadow self and therefore move toward emotional healing and inner freedom.
These stages can be described to clients in the following way:

1. Watching a character outside yourself in a movie
2. Beginning to like or dislike a character, their behavior, or certain attributes that you do not recognize in yourself.
3. Examining whether a character, their behavior, or attributes might be part of your not-yet-fully-recognized positive qualities or repressed "shadow" self.
4. Exploring ways to become more whole by embracing the projected positive qualities,in order to realize your full potential as well as acknowledging your repressed "shadow" self, to move toward emotional healing and inner freedom.

Clients are usually more open to acknowledge their projections on movie characters than projections on people in their life, especially on their therapist. After they understand the projections on film characters, they are sometimes more ready for transference work.

The Alchemy Process

Four Ways of Cinema Alchemy

The Evocative Way

Films can be seen as the "collective dreams" of our times. Therefore, the *Evocative Way* utilizes movies in a therapeutic and growth-provoking manner by borrowing from dream work. As it is possible to gain insights from any dream, emotional responses to almost any kind of movie scene or character can help clients to understand themselves better. When certain movies resonate with clients, they tap into an unconscious or preconscious part of their psyche. A film may move them deeply. A character or a scene might also upset them intensely. Understanding their emotional responses to movies, just as understanding their nighttime dreams, can serve as a window to their unconscious. Both dream work and *The Evocative Way* of Cinema Alchemy are ways to bring their unconscious inner world to a conscious level.

The following therapeutic methods are especially conducive to a combination with the movie watching experience when Cinema Alchemy is practiced in *The Evocative Way*:

- Parts work;
- Couples, family, and group therapy;
- Interactive hypnotherapy or imagery work;
- Suggestive hypnotherapy;
- EMDR – resource installation, and positive psychology EMDR.

There is no need to recommend specific movies to clients *in The Evocative Way*. For this approach, it usually does not matter whether the therapist has not seen the movies that clients might bring up in their sessions. Sometimes being unfamiliar with a film can even be an advantage because the therapist is forced to see the movie through the clients' eyes, like their dreams. When clients see themselves as experts in knowing certain movies, greater rapport is possible and there is an increased likelihood for more independence in the relationship.

The Prescriptive Way

In *The Prescriptive Way*, specific films are prescribed to model specific problem-solving behavior. "Psychotherapists continually strive to find stratagems to help their patients 'see the obvious'. What tools we have in movies for our armamentarium! Precious images of sight and sound, imagined and acted truly, and now thanks to new technologies, readily accessible through rental from the local video store. ... Patients can be pointed to key scenes, which they can watch easily over and over as they practice their own new skills" (Kalm, 2004, p. iii). In order to choose a movie for prescription, categorized film indices can be found in the literature (Hesley & Hesley, 2001; Horenstein et al., 1994; Solomon, 1995, 2001; Sturdevant, 1998; Wolz, 2005) and on the Internet (www.cinematherapy.com).

The Prescriptive Way is based on the same concept as Milton Erickson's *Teaching Tales* with their embedded suggestions (Rosen, 1982). Listening to stories and watching movies in a focused way create a form of trance state, similar to the state often achieved via guided visualizations. This kind of trance work is designed to help clients get in touch with a mature and wise part of themselves that helps them overcome problems and strengthen positive qualities.

Movies can also help clients to learn "by proxy" how not to do something or not to behave in pursuit of their goals, because they see the negative consequences of a character's action (Solomon, 2001). It is often helpful to use movies in this way, for clients who struggle with addictions, or when a couple works on their communication. Here films are used as cautionary tales.

The following methods are especially conducive to a combination with the movie watching experience when Cinema Alchemy is practiced in *The Prescriptive Way*:

- Cognitive therapy;
- Behavior modification therapy;
- Couples and family therapy;
- Coaching.

The Cathartic Way

Our cultural preference for processing emotions cognitively instead of feeling them in our bodies tends to maintain and prolong distress (Nichols & Zax, 1977).

Emotions are stored in the body as well as the mind. Cathartic therapeutic techniques allow therapists to help clients access these stored emotions and release them. These methods are based on the assumption that the more catharsis clients experience, the faster they move through the healing process (Nichols & Bierenbaum, 1978). Painful emotions have been proven to create stress chemicals in our bodies. Catharsis helps to counter these by releasing buried feelings. Nature has provided us natural cathartic processes like laughing and crying to move us through and beyond our pain.

Because many films transmit ideas through emotion rather than intellect, they can neutralize the instinct to suppress feelings and trigger emotional release. By eliciting emotions, watching movies can open doors that otherwise might stay closed. For many of our clients it is safer and therefore easier to let go of their defenses while watching a movie than it is in real life with real people. By identifying with certain characters and their predicaments, they can experience emotions that lie hidden from their awareness.

Sometimes tears flow over a sentimental film but not in real life, especially under duress. Watching and empathizing with a movie character who experiences tragedy can stimulate the desired emotional release. This release usually lifts a client's spirits for a little while as the overwhelming emotion diminishes. Energy that was drained by depression or grief can reemerge at least temporarily. Often this "break" allows a depressed person to start exploring and healing the underlying issues that caused the depression originally. Grief can be processed more easily.

Cathartic psychotherapy tells us that laughter too releases emotion (Klein, 1988). It provides the physical process that releases tension, stress, and pain, physically as well as emotionally. Laughter decreases stress hormones, increases pain-relieving hormones, and activates our immune system.

Laughter can relieve anxiety as well as reduce aggression and fear. Often clients are able to approach a solution to a problem with less emotional involvement and a fresh and creative perspective after watching a humorous movie. Even light depression can lift for a while.

Specific movies or types of movies are recommended in the Cathartic Way. Clients respond differently to different kinds of humorous or sad movies. With their unique sensibilities, some of them like intellectual humor, some gallows humor, some slapstick, etc. A "one-hanky" film for one person might be a "five-hanky" movie for somebody else. Therefore, clients will find the best emotional release when they choose a movie using their own experience of typical emotional responses.

Cinema Coaching

The field of coaching is still evolving and branching out. The main focus of coaching is to support clients to achieve their goals with encouragement and questions. Watching movies in conjunction with the coaching process can be especially effective if *The Prescriptive Way* is applied. Specific films, in which a character successfully pursues a goal, are prescribed to guide the clients through the coaching process by helping them access and develop their potential.

According to Leonard and Robin, a movie can be a complex and powerful learning tool in the coaching process, because the gestalt of the film acts on many levels of the psyche. "The appropriate movie can illustrate a concept, skill set or growth experience in a three dimensional way. Since the viewer tends to identify with the characters, the doors of transformation are wide open" (Leonard & Robin, 2004).

The Evocative, The Prescriptive, and *The Cathartic Way* as well as *Cinema Coaching* can be used in various combinations.

Watching Movies with Conscious Awareness

Many therapeutic and spiritual orientations recognize the healing power of awareness. For example, the Jewish Talmud points out that normally we do not see what we think we see, that what we perceive is more a reflection of *us* than it is objectively *it*. Everything we experience is altered and shaped by our minds. Our desires filter our selection of the items that we perceive. Our emotions color those perceptions. And finally, our attention wanders from perception to perception, virtually guaranteeing that what we see of the world and ourselves is mostly inaccurate.

Buddhism makes the same basic observation and gives it a name: *mindlessness*. In this usage, the term includes the *absentmindedness* that we mean when we say "mindless," but it encompasses more, too – that our awareness is clouded, that we are *spiritually* asleep. Poets, storytellers, and philosophers have echoed this idea throughout the ages. Today, many psychologists agree with the idea that mindlessness, in the Buddhist sense, is very common. Mindlessness conditions us to replace authentic experience with habitual responses.

Daniel Goleman provides a commentary on meetings he had with the Dalai Lama and world-class scientists and philosophers (Goleman et al., 2003). They discuss new findings with high-tech devices that permit scientists to peer inside the brain centers responsible for calming the inner storms of rage and fear. Experiments have demonstrated that awareness training strengthens emotional stability and greatly enhances our positive moods.

With the technique *of watching movies with conscious awareness*, I introduce a new way of creating a state of dual awareness as it is found in many and varied psychotherapeutic modalities, such as *Somatic Experiencing*, developed by Peter Levine (Levine & Frederick, 1997); *Focusing*, developed by Eugene Gendlin (Gendlin, 1982); *Sensorimotor Sequencing* (Ogden & Minton, 2000); or the Buddhist's *mindfulness*. The above-mentioned research by Daniel Goleman has shown that dual awareness helps process previously unprocessed psychological material.

When clients start watching movies with *conscious awareness*, they experience a psychological strengthening process and create a "larger inner container" for their undesired emotions, so that they can hold them consciously. The more they learn to be able to tolerate unwanted feelings while watching a movie, the less they feel compelled to suppress them or act out against themselves or others in their real life. Instead, they become strong enough to resist acting out. And the more they practice, the more confident they will be.

Guidelines for Therapists to Give to Clients to Introduce Watching Movies with Conscious Awareness

In preparation for each viewing session, sit comfortably. Let your attention move effortlessly, without strain, first to your body, then to your breath. Follow your breath in a watchful way for a while. Notice any tension or holding. To release tension you may experiment with "breathing into" any part of your body that feels strained.

As soon as you are calm and centered, start watching the movie. Pay attention to the story and to yourself. Do not continue to create a particular state, such as relaxation, but rather be a compassionate witness of what is. Observe especially how the movie's images, ideas, conversations, and characters affect your physical sensations. What happens when these throw you off balance because they trigger undesired emotions? Just put your attention on that experience while you are watching. In all likelihood, a film's stimulants are similar to whatever unbalances you in daily life. (Sinetar, 1993)

After watching the movie, reflect on the following questions. (It is helpful to write down your answers):

1. Do you remember your feelings and sensations, or whether your breathing changed throughout the movie? In all likelihood, what affects you in the film is similar to whatever influences you in your daily life.
2. Notice what you liked and what you did not like or even hated about the movie. Which characters or actions seemed especially attractive or unattractive to you?
3. Did you identify with one or several characters?
4. Were there one or several characters in the movie that modeled behavior that you would like to emulate? Did they develop certain strengths or other capacities that you would like to develop as well?
5. Notice whether any aspect of the film was especially hard to watch. Could this be related to something that you might have repressed?
6. Did you experience something that connected or reconnected you with certain values, virtues, capacities, inner wisdom, or your higher self as you watched the film or immediately after?

7. Did anything in this movie touch you? The fact that a character or a scene moved you might indicate that your subconscious mind is revealing information that might guide you toward healing and wholeness. Dreams have the same capacity. What might this guiding "message" be?

As you examine your reaction to the film, try to avoid focusing on the artistic merits of the movie or even the story. It is you, the film viewer, who should remain at the center of attention.

If some of the guidelines in the exercise turn out to be useful, you might consider adapting them to scenes in your real life after you have practiced in "reel" life. These guidelines are intended to help you become a better observer. As observing helps you to step back, the bigger picture becomes more obvious. Such practice will help you learn to understand yourself and others more deeply in the big "movie" of your life and to see yourself and the world more objectively. Learning more conscious awareness while watching movies can create a bridge to more awareness and therefore more control over your real life.

Doubting Voices
The most frequent arguments against the use of movies in therapy are

— *Cinema Alchemy is too simplistic and unscientific a tool with little research to account for therapeutic value; one cannot treat serious psychological problems just by letting clients watch movies.*

Movies are best used in combination with a traditional modality, like depth psychotherapy, parts work, cognitive, behavioral therapy, EMDR, hypnotherapy, narrative therapy, couples, family, and group therapy, coaching, etc. Cinema Alchemy is meant to be a supportive, adjunct tool for these approaches. Therefore, its therapeutic value depends on the therapeutic efficiency of these other modalities. If the main modality helps treat serious problems, the use of films can only increase this effect.

— *Most movies are bad in quality and bad for the psyche, especially the violent or depressing ones.*

Like the proverbial hammer, which can be used to harm or to serve us, movies can be damaging or they can be used to our clients' benefit. Using *The Prescriptive* and *The Cathartic Way*, it is important to choose an appropriate film for a specific treatment goal. A thorough assessment is required before assigning a movie. In order to assess correctly, clients must be asked how they responded to certain types of films in the past.

Violent films can be re-traumatizing if they reactivate previous psychological trauma. On the other hand, clients who have suffered from trauma can find a sense of resolution and healing when the "bad guy" in a violent movie gets beaten up at the end. Movies that trigger fear, anger, or sadness might help clients become more conscious of these emotions, if these had been repressed. In work with psychological trauma, several treatment methods help to process trauma within a so-called therapeutic window. Interventions are done within this "window," as they create sufficient therapeutic challenge but avoid an overwhelming internal experience. Emotional overwhelm could create an avoidance response, like dissociation, etc. Certain films, even those with violent elements – used carefully and creatively – can help clients get in touch with unresolved trauma and therefore serve as an intervention that provides sufficient therapeutic challenge to enter the "therapeutic window."

Certain movies that portray depressed characters can – almost like support groups – help clients feel isolated with their experience. These films can serve as a psycho-educational tool in cognitive work with depression or be used if the therapist considers it appropriate to normalize depression or grief.

— *Most people want to be entertained by films instead of analyzing them for therapeutic purposes; they don't want to spoil their fun of watching movies.*

A psychotherapist or coach does not ask a client to analyze movies but to watch them with *conscious awareness*. Besides, people who seek therapy or coaching are usually receptive to interventions. Watching a movie is considered one of the more pleasurable ones.

We usually remember our experiences better when we have them under two distinct circumstances: pain and pleasure. We also learn well when we are relaxed. Since entertainment can create pleasure and relaxation, a movie with high entertainment value can also have a high therapeutic value if it conveys therapeutically relevant messages. Enjoying a movie might give clients a "vacation" from their troubles and consequently allow them to approach a solution with less emotional involvement and a fresh and creative perspective.

Alchemy and the Psychotherapist or Couch

Ways Films Aid the Therapeutic and the Coaching Process
Supporting Process of Diagnosis and Assessment

In addition to questions regarding family history, presenting problem, lifestyle, overall goals, and objectives, clients are asked to name a few films they have found to be personally meaningful or the kind of films they prefer. It can also be fruitful to ask which characters had a personal impact on them and how their own attitudes and behaviors are mirrored by the characters in these movies. Learning about the clients' identifications and projections in this way can be a very helpful tool to understanding their psyche early. Many clients reveal more about themselves this way than when they are asked more directly (Hesley & Hesley, 2001).

For the purpose of diagnosis and assessment it usually does not matter whether the therapist has seen the movies the client describes. Being unfamiliar with a film can even be an advantage because the therapist is forced to see the movie through the client's eyes.

Helping to Overcome Resistance

Milton Erickson was able to circumvent resistance in clients by telling stories (Erickson & Rossi, 1980). Using movies can do the same. Erickson called his teaching tales a form of indirect suggestion, in which "subliminal commands" are conveyed. He used this method to circumvent resistance through "unconscious learning" (Hudson & Martin, 1992). Unconscious learning is seen as a state wherein clients intuitively understand the meaning of symbols, metaphors, and allegories. They enter this state, while listening to stories, in which they are less involved with thoughts and issues. They accept suggestions with a reduced critical sense. Erickson emphasized that people resist commands, but they do not resist descriptions.

Additional reasons why resistance can dissolve when movies are used are

1. Clients become curious when the therapist or coach suggests that they watch a movie, especially if they do not expect this kind of intervention.
2. Rapport develops faster and stronger because films speak a language they are familiar with; this is less intimidating than psychological terms.
3. Watching a movie with subsequent discussion helps clients to see their situation from a bird's eye perspective. Resistance often results from a feeling of helplessness. Many movies demonstrate behavior change, and clients start to envision how their own problems might be solved (Hesley & Hesley, 2001).

Eliciting Emotions

This aspect is particularly important for clients who tend to intellectualize or otherwise suppress their emotions. By triggering emotions, movies can open doors that otherwise might stay closed. For some clients, it is safer and therefore easier to let go of their defenses when feelings arise while watching a movie than when they arise in "real life" with "real people." They experience emotions that they are often not in touch with through identification with certain characters and their predicaments (Hesley & Hesley, 2001).

The above-described *Cathartic Way* makes use of the capacity of movies to elicit emotions through laughter and crying. Besides, scary films can make viewers feel alive, "on the edge of their seats." They are fully present with their experience, just like they would be to challenging moments of extreme sports such as mountain climbing, surfing, or skiing. Clients need to be encouraged to be consciously aware of these emotional responses while they watch the movie. Talking about these feelings after the viewing experience helps to integrate them and prepares for an inquiry into the possibilities to access aliveness and presence in their own lives.

Identifying and Reinforcing Inner Strength

Remembering Internal Resources: When clients struggle with low self-esteem, they are usually not aware of their assets and the means by which they can access them. They need guidance to recall forgotten and discounted resources and to become aware of opportunities for those resources to be applied (Hesley & Hesley, 2001). Therapists or coaches need to encourage these clients to see how the film characters find solutions to their problems and help them recognize which of the character's skills are familiar and accessible to them. If they discount the skills and strengths that they have in common with the movie characters, this needs to be pointed out. A shift in the clients' perspective has happened when they acknowledge and appropriate resources from their own repertoire.

Gaining Hope and Encouragement: Many movies begin in despair and end in triumph. If clients can identify with characters trapped in their circumstances and share their disappointments as well as steps toward liberation, they often find reason for optimism in their own situations (Hesley & Hesley, 2001). In this process, they get in touch with the courage to do what is necessary to change their situation.

Validation: By watching the movie characters, who go through similar experiences, clients can develop compassion with their own predicament and feel less isolated. This often helps them gain new strength.

Self-discovery, Healing, and Growth Through Work with Matrices
Using *The Evocative Way*, the *Film, Self, and Growth Matrices* offer tools for clients to understand their projections and use this understanding for their healing and personal growth.

The Film Matrix
The following guidelines are given to clients when working with the *Film Matrix* after they watched a specific movie or while reflecting on several films.

The Film Matrix

Character you	Like most	Like least
Identify with strongly or in some ways	I	II
Identify with less or not at all	III	IV

Guidelines for Questions and Instructions for Clients
Quadrant I: Has there been one character that you especially liked and with whom you especially identified? Was there a character who sometimes acted, felt, or viewed the world in a similar way to your own? This character may also have shown some behaviors that are different from yours, but focus only on the similarities you liked. Write the name into Quadrant I. If you can think of several characters, choose the one you identified with most.

Quadrant II: Write down the name of a different character in which you saw yourself, but for this quadrant choose a character you disliked overall. He should have aspects of his personality or should have behaved and expressed himself in ways of which you do not approve. And again, if you can think of several characters, choose the one you identified with most.

For Quadrant III: Choose a character that strikes you as being different from yourself but whom you liked or admired, either for their innate qualities or possibly for the way they related to others. If you can think of several characters, choose the one about whom you feel most positively.

In Quadrant IV: Write the name of a character you could not identify with, or could only identify with very little and about whom you had negative feelings perhaps because of their demeanor, expressions, or actions. If in doubt, choose the one you identify with the least and toward whom you felt most negatively.

The Self Matrix

The Self Matrix

Qualities or capacities you	Like in yourself	Dislike in yourself
Are aware of	I	II
Are not always fully aware of	III	IV

In this matrix, clients are asked to identify their own characteristics that the characters in the *Film Matrix* remind them of.

The upper left square of the *Self Matrix*, Quadrant I, reflects their own realized or unrealized potentials that they are conscious of; the upper right, Quadrant II, represents their conscious shortcomings.

Quadrant III shows positive qualities that clients are not usually aware of.

Quadrant IV illuminates the shortcomings the client does not like in others. The therapist explains to clients that they are often not conscious of the fact that they carry these traits deep inside themselves (repression), and therefore project them onto others. Clients need to learn about the possibilities of becoming more whole and to find emotional healing as well as inner freedom by starting to embrace their repressed shadow self.

The Growth Matrix

With help of the *Self Matrix*, clients are able to identify aspects in themselves, which the movie characters reminded them of. Now they explore together with the therapist how they can make use of this new understanding for healing and growth. The *Growth Matrix* provides a structure for this process.

The Growth Matrix

	How can you enhance and strengthen your positive qualities and capacities?	How can you learn to have compassion with your real or perceived shortcomings and grow beyond them?
Qualities you are fully aware of	I	II
Qualities you are not always fully aware of	III	IV

Many therapeutic interventions or exercises from the therapist's toolbox are helpful here if they fit into the categories of this *Growth Matrix*. They can be applied in session or given as homework. Examples of such interventions and exercises are listed in *E-Motion Picture Magic* (Wolz, 2005).

On the left side of the *Growth Matrix* (Quadrant I and III), clients usually note exercises such as affirmations and self-hypnosis, which help develop and strengthen their potential.

On the right side (Quadrant II and IV), clients note tools that help them to either accept or overcome shortcomings and deficiencies. For example, exercises to help develop compassion with deficiencies they do not have control over, such as "Working with the Inner Critic," are introduced here. Exercises and interventions that strengthen endurance and determination often help clients reduce or overcome shortcomings that are in their control.

Ways to Integrate Movies in the Therapeutic and the Coaching Process
Depth Psychotherapy and the Movie Experience
   Therapeutic Reasoning for Working with the Unconscious
Psychodynamic therapy recognizes the significant influence that emotions and unconscious motivation can have on human behavior. Our unconscious is often in conflict with our conscious ideas, intentions, and goals. Inquiring into the symbolism and the effect of a movie can break down the barriers between these two levels of the psyche and set up a genuine flow of communication between them; unconscious material can start to become more conscious. This helps to resolve some of our neurotic conflicts with the unconscious and thus learn more about who we really are as authentic human beings.

   Viewing Films as Doorways to the Unconscious
The unconscious communicates its content in symbols. Clients can become aware of this "communication" through dreams and active imagination, which are "windows" to the unconscious: both convert the invisible forms of the unconscious into images that are perceptible to the conscious mind. Another "window" can be the emotional response to a movie scene or character. Such a response often indicates that a pathway to the unconscious is activated. Therefore, depth psychologists can use responses to movies, as they use responses to dreams or active imagination.

Cognitive Therapy and the Movie Experience
Cognitive therapy aims to identify and correct distorted thinking patterns that can lead to feelings and behaviors that may be troublesome, self-defeating, or even self-destructive. The goal is to replace such thinking with a more balanced view that, in turn, leads to more fulfilling and productive behavior.

   Support in Understanding the Cognitive Model
The cognitive model says: A situation is a situation. It is how a person thinks about or interprets the situation that determines how he or she feels. Therapists teach the cognitive model to give clients a framework and give them some sense of control

over their emotional reactions. Movies can be a very useful aid in this teaching process. For example, if a character seems depressed, therapists can ask the client what negative beliefs this character might hold about him or herself. Clients often come up with an answer right away, even if it was hard for them to make the same connection for themselves.

Identifying Cognitive Distortions and Schemas

The therapist can give clients the list of negative distortions (Burns, 1999) and ask them which ones possibly apply for the film character. They usually enjoy this process because they experience it like a game. After that, when the therapist asks clients to turn their attention to their own process and asks about *their* cognitive distortions, they feel less alone with their experience and less judgmental about themselves. Since depressed clients usually have cognitive distortions and tend to be self-loathing, it helps that the work with movies often introduces some lightness because they are designed to entertain.

Behavior Modification Therapy and the Movie Experience

Behavior modification therapy focuses on behavior – changing unwanted behaviors through rewards, reinforcements, and desensitization.

Assertiveness Training
Overt Modeling

Overt modeling techniques are used to train assertion skills. First, clients are shown examples of appropriate assertive behavior. Then they are asked to imitate the behavior, called behavioral rehearsal. Characters who demonstrate such behavior in movies or certain movie scenes can very well serve as examples.

Covert Modeling

Covert modeling requires the client to imagine assertive responses. The therapist provides suggestions about what to include in the imagined scene. This imagination can draw from characters in films the client has seen.

Exposure Methods
Preparing Systematic Desensitization

Systematic desensitization is based on counterconditioning and involves the attempt to replace the fear response to phobic stimuli with a new response that is incompatible with fear. Clients are initially given relaxation training. Movie images such as a *Safe Place* or an *Inner Guide* can support the relaxation.

Preparing Flooding and Implosion

Flooding and implosion are anxiety-induction therapies for phobias in order to extinguish the phobic response. During flooding the client is exposed to the feared object without chance of escape or avoidance. Implosive therapy requires the client to imagine unrealistic, exaggerated, or unlikely harmful events that are associated with the phobic reaction. Since anxiety is encouraged during these treatments, the clients need to access inner courage and strength. Remembering and identifying with movie characters who model strength in the face of adversity can be very helpful in this work.

Preparing Exposure with Response Prevention
The predominantly and most successfully used treatment modality of OCD is exposure with response prevention. Clients are exposed to a particular feared situation, the triggers of the obsessions or compulsive rituals, such as sources of contamination. As they fully interact with the feared stimuli, like touching a doorknob or the floor, they feel their fear rising. Response prevention means that they must block any rituals used to prevent the harm that they anticipate as a consequence of the exposure, such as hand washing. They agree to tolerate the discomfort associated with not performing the ritual until they are habituated to the stimulus. To help tolerate the fear, accessing inner courage and strength through identification with courageous film characters supports this process.

Preparing Aversion Therapy and Covert Sensitization
The same strength building support through movies applies to these methods. Both aversion therapy and covert sensitization teach clients to associate negative consequences with a stimulus, like smoking or drinking. During covert sensitization, clients only imagine behaviors associated with particular consequences while they experience them directly in aversion therapy.

Parts Work and the Movie Experience
Movie characters with their distinct personalities and behaviors can become placeholders for parts in therapies such as Empty Chair, Gestalt, Ego States Work, Psychosynthesis, Voice Dialog, etc.

Attributing film characters to inner parts helps

- identify and distinguish these parts,
- understand their relationship to each other,
- adopt an attitude of respectful attention to parts,
- accept disowned parts,
- reassign new roles to parts, and
- mediate between parts and resolve conflicts.

Hypnotherapy and the Movie Experience
Hypnotherapy involves going into a state of deep relaxation and creating a mental image of recovery and wellness.

Film Re-entry
In trance, clients enter the story of a movie as a specific character, or in relation to a character who is important to them. With the guidance of the therapist, they subsequently let their own story unfold in their "inner movie." Frequently, unconscious material gets revealed and resolved.

Skill Mastery
In trance, clients are guided to "become" the movie character who modeled desired behaviors and skills and take on these attributes. This is another way to help them acquire the film character's capacities.

Calming Film Scene to Create a Safe Place
As a tool of deepening trance, hypnotherapists often guide clients to a *Safe Place* of their choice. Many peaceful movie scenes can serve well in this process. Clients "step into" their *Safe Place* by "stepping into" the movie screen, on which the calming and safe place appears.

Characters as Inner Parts Like Inner Guide *or* Inner Critic
This method is basically parts work in trance.

EMDR and the Movie Experience
EMDR creates eye movements that mimic those of REM sleep to create the same brain waves present during REM sleep while the individual is awake.

Resource Development and Installation
What was said about the use of movie scenes and characters in hypnotherapy applies in a very similar way for the resource installation during the preparation phase in EMDR. The only difference is that EMDR therapists do not use formal trance induction. With EMDR, clients go through an abreaction in their trauma work which often is emotionally very demanding. Using movie scenes and characters, strengthening resources, such as a *Safe Place*, *Inner Guide*, etc., are first installed. Clients feel safer this way because they know that these resources are available if they start feeling overwhelmed during the EMDR process.

Positive Psychology EMDR
During positive psychology EMDR, such as peak performance EMDR, the installation of the following resources, drawn from movie scenes and characters, have proven useful:

- Calming film scenes serve to create a *Safe Place*.
- Healthy or inspirational film characters are used as *Inner Coaches or Inner Advisors*.
- Favorite movie characters are used as an *Inner Team* of support people.
- Identification with film characters' success helps to reach an aspired goal.

Narrative Therapy and the Movie Experience
Narrative therapy is based on the assumption that, as people make sense of their day-to-day lives, they construct their lives into narrative form – stories. They arrange

their experiences into patterns and sequences that make sense of themselves and their lives, called dominant narrative. This perception can be distorted and dysfunctional, as much of the client's strength remains unrecognized. Through narrative therapy, clients reshape their perception of self, their relationships, and their life by re-constructing their narratives. One main intervention in this work is to help clients find an experience or capacity that they dismissed before, because it did not fit into their dominant view of themselves: A "unique outcome." This exceptional experience reconnects clients to their forgotten resources.

Guided by the therapist, certain film scenes and the strength or courage of characters remind clients of their own forgotten resources, in narrative terms their "unique outcome." This is especially relevant when clients keep dismissing their own inner resources without the "bridge" of a movie intervention.

Couples and Family Therapy and the Movie Experience

Couples and family members sometimes struggle to accurately express the complexity of their issues. A film can serve as a metaphor, and therefore represents feelings and ideas that they had trouble putting into words.

Systems-oriented therapy and communication training in combination with watching films that show couples and family dynamics helps clients

- understand their problem as a function of being part of a larger system,
- identify by comparison with movie characters how they had or had not satisfactorily adjusted in their system,
- retrieve or learn necessary attitudes, perceptions, behaviors, etc.,
- communicate unfamiliar concepts to their partners through films that introduce readily grasped images, and
- meaningfully connect or reconnect through improved communication by learning from watching good communication between characters or by understanding how not to communicate from watching characters who demonstrate a lack of communication skills.

When one family member resists therapy, encouraging them to watch a movie where a character struggles with similar issues often allows the resisting client to open up because they are less intimidated by the therapeutic process and less afraid of getting blamed than before.

Coaching and the Movie Experience

In general, coaches guide their clients through the following process:

1. Identifying specific goals
2. Setting goals high enough to truly challenge client
3. Focusing on the specific steps toward these goals
4. Creating strategies to make goals happen
5. Managing time and resources effectively

6. Constantly reevaluating progress, recognizing and applauding client's achievement, and identifying new goals for which to strive.

Examples of different kind of coaches are

- *Personal* or *life coaches* help to realize and accomplish particular life goals.
- *Business coaches* help to make positive changes in a business such as increase effectiveness, build and sustain momentum, increase profits, etc.,
- *Executive coaches* help people at the top of an organization improve decision-making ability and skills required to lead others.
- *Corporate coaches* provide coaching services to individual employees.
- *Sports coaches* get athletes to perform better.
- *Niche coaches* have a clear identified area or issue such as weight loss, fitness, book publishing, etc.

Watching movies in conjunction with the coaching process can be especially effective if *The Prescriptive Way* is applied. Specific films, in which a character successfully pursues a goal, are prescribed to guide support clients through the above-mentioned coaching process and to help them access and develop their potential.

Many films have such a powerful supportive effect in the coaching process because they follow the pattern of the mythological *Hero's Journey*. The stages of the *Hero's Journey* can be traced in all kinds of stories, not just those that feature heroic physical action and adventure, but also in romance, comedy, and thrillers, etc. "The protagonist of every story is the hero of a journey, even if the path leads only in his own mind or into the realm of relationships" (Volger, 1998, p. 13).

Cathie Glenn Sturdevant describes the typical plot development according to modern rules of screenplay writing similar to the *Hero's Journey*. The main character commits to a quest after a surprising loss of innocence, goes through a phase of inner conflict about taking on a challenge, and reaches a point of no return. Then the film hero acts despite fear, releases old ideas, renews his or her commitment, acts without fear, sometimes revises plans into realistic goals, and concludes the original quest by resolving it from a new perspective (Sturdevant, 1998).

John and Jan Hesley emphasize " . . . in client's choice of movies, we find clues to their working role models . . . ideal self-images, internal resources, potential goals, perceived obstacles, degrees of imagination and creativity, and overall philosophy in life" (Hesley & Hesley, 2001, p. 41).

Cinema Alchemy Groups

In therapy and support groups, members often experience healing and transformation, because others witness their process of sharing with presence and empathy. The impact of films as catalysts for psychological processes dovetails well with the therapeutic effects of group dynamics. Group members' reflections about their emotional response to a movie are an added component that enriches group therapy. By understanding and sharing what moved them about certain movie scenes or characters, participants acquire an effective tool to get to know themselves and others. After leaving the group they are able to continue using what they have learned about self-discovery when watching movies.

The general mood of a film often reappears as a feeling among members in the group. There frequently is a joyful atmosphere during the meeting after a humorous or uplifting movie. A heavier mood is usually felt after darker films with content that addresses problematic lives and interactions. When they become aware of this, members learn how susceptible we all are to outside influences. Since a movie is not even a *real* outside influence but just light projected on a screen, it becomes even more obvious to everyone how their inner experience is shaped by projections on their environment.

Becoming consciously aware of the atmosphere during the subsequent group interactions, which are affected by the general mood of the film, helps members acknowledge their projections. This is usually easier when a lighthearted mood is observed than when tension appears. Group participants often recognize the darker projection in other members first, which can help as a bridge to becoming more aware of their own unconscious responses eventually. As group members apply these insights to their everyday life, they learn to understand themselves better, which helps them become more authentic and real.

When Transformation Works – and Not!

Guidelines and Limitations
Movie examples for cinema therapy work
- *Frida* – grief, courage, illness, disability, creativity, transformation
- *My Big Fat Greek Wedding* – self-esteem, relationships, cultural issues, especially cross-cultural relationships
- *Under the Tuscan Sun* – separation, divorce
- *Groundhog Day* – repetitive patterns; The main character experiences waking up to exactly the same day over and over until he goes through a transformation. Clients can contemplate being stuck in a repetitive pattern and how to get out of it and use their experience to learn from it.
- *Sliding Doors* – movie follows two possible alternative lives of the main character. Clients can contemplate how certain decisions can have significant consequences, even split second decisions. What does this mean for them? The film can make clients see each moment as important and precious. This promotes mindfulness.
- *About Schmidt* – retirement, learning by proxy, aging, depression, retirement
- *Harold and Maude* – finding one's authentic self, meaning of life, follow your heart, authenticity, humor
- *Field of Dreams* – following inner guidance, follow a dream and intuition, relationship

- *The Piano* – getting in touch with passion, willpower, strength in the face of adversity
- *Before Sunset* – intimacy issues
- *The Secret Lives of Dentists* – communication
- *As Good as it Gets*– working with OCD and obsessive compulsive tendencies

Possible Applications of Work with Certain Movies
- Addictions: *28 Days, Postcards from the Edge, Leaving Las Vegas, Clean and Sober*
- Anger and forgiveness: *The Straight Story, Gandhi, An Unfinished Life, Changing Lanes*
- Aspiration: *Gandhi, Billy Elliot, Whale Rider, Pay It Forward*
- Authentic self: *Harold and Maude, Nell, My Life*
- Body image: *Shallow Hal, My Big Fat Greek Wedding, Real Women Have Curves*
- Communication, couples', family issues: *A Walk on the Moon* (communication, adolescents, affair), *The Story of Us* (conflict and negotiation, commitment), *Philadelphia* (nontraditional relationships), *Sally, Two Family House*
- Eating disorders: *What's Eating Gilbert Grape, Fried Green Tomatoes, Eating*
- Following inner guidance and dream, intuition: *Constant Gardner, Field of Dreams, Motorcycle Diaries, The Piano*
- Grief, death, and Transformation: *Frida* (illness, disability)*, In America, Shadowlands* (bereavement), *Mr. Holland's Opus* (aging, disability)
- Inner guidance: *Field of Dreams, Places in the Heart*
- Retirement and aging: *About Schmidt, Dad, Space Cowboys, Something's Gotta Give*
- Self-esteem: *My Big Fat Greek Wedding, Gattaca, The Other Sister, Real Women Have Curves*
- Separation and divorce: *Under the Tuscan Sun, The Story of Us, Kramer vs. Kramer*
- Sexual abuse: *Mystic River, A Thousand Acres, Dolores Clairborne*
- Spirituality and spiritual awareness: *Jonathan Livingston Seagull, It's a Wonderful Life, Powder, City of Angels, Resurrection*
- Vocational issues: *Patch Adams* (fighting for vocation), *Erin Brockovich* (finding true vocation)
- Willpower: *The Piano, The Horse Whisperer, Cast Away*

Many more categorized movie suggestions can be found in the film indices on www.cinematherapy.com and in *E-Motion Picture Magic* (Wolz, 2005).

Guidelines for Cinema Alchemy Work
First the use of film scenes versus using a whole movie needs to be clarified. The length of the therapeutic hour does not allow showing a whole film. Either movie clips are shown in session or clients watch a whole film at home. Showing a movie scene during a session has the advantage of providing an immediate experience, and

therapists have more control over the message they want to convey. Asking a client to watch a whole movie at home has the following advantages:

1. Because of equipment limitations and time constraints during a session, this approach is usually more practical.
2. Conversations about films early in the therapeutic relationship are possible. This allows clients to express feelings that may be too threatening to express directly. "It also helps determine if using movies in therapy will be productive and, if they are, which type will work best" (Hesley & Hesley, 2001, p. 41).
3. The experience of a whole movie allows the viewer to get "pulled" into the experience more and therefore identify with a character.
4. Experiencing a movie character throughout an entire cycle of transition is often helpful. For many clients it is easier to understand how to resolve a movie character's dilemma first before they apply it to their own situation. In most cases, only the whole movie can provide this experience.
5. Watching movies at home in this context serves as a bridge between therapy and life.
6. If a focus on specific scenes is required, the therapist can direct the clients' attention to it before and after they watch the whole film.

General Guidelines for Therapists and Coaches

- Clarify your intent when assigning a film, especially if a client might mistake a role identification.
- Provide written guidelines (for example, guidelines for watching movies with *conscious awareness* as described above).
- Suggest taking notes about responses to scenes during or after the film.
- If appropriate, encourage client to watch the movie with friends or family.
- For *The Prescriptive* and the *Cathartic Way* as well *as Cinema Coaching* to be effective, it is important that the choice center on finding a film that speaks to clients about their specific life situation, not on whether it has artistic merit. A movie that touches clients deeply or demonstrates a character development they are aspiring to help them best with their healing or personal growth.
- Discuss reactions to film. Use client's response according to your theoretical orientation. Some possible evocative questions are

  - How did the movie touch you, positively or negatively?
  - Did the film have a unique message for you? If so, how did this message connect you with health and wholeness, your inner wisdom, or *Higher Self*?
  - What ideas for new behaviors – adding new patterns or letting go of old ones – did the movie introduce?
  - What other films do you remember having seen that might take the discussion a step further?

Limitations of Using Movies in Psychotherapy and Coaching

The limitations of the use of movies in therapy and coaching are well described in *Rent Two Films and Let's Talk in the Morning* (Hesley & Hesley, 2001).

No Film Assignment to Clients with Serious Psychiatric Disorder Seen in Private Practice: When these clients watch films in their own homes, it might be difficult for them to deal with issues that come up during or immediately after viewing. This is especially true for clients that have some kind of psychotic disorder because they might have trouble distinguishing reality from fantasy (Ulus, 2003).

No Film Assignment when Violence in Client's Home: Films sometimes introduce subjects that clients may have avoided in therapy, which can be very productive under many circumstances. When there is violence in the home, the risk of unmonitored film assignment and an unpredictable reaction is too great.

No Film Assignment When Client Recently Had Trauma Similar to a Character in the Movie: When a client recently went through a traumatic experience similar to that of the character in a movie, the film experience can potentially be re-traumatizing. As clinicians we need to make decisions about a client's readiness for a film by using the same criteria as we use with any high-impact homework or other kind of intervention.

Prescribing Films Is Often Not Effective with Small Children Except in Family Therapy: Young children's developmental limitations reduce the effectiveness of prescribing films usually because of the time lapse between their viewing of the film at home and the discussion in session. This is different when a discussion follows immediately after a clip is shown in session or when families watch movies together at home in the context of family therapy.

No Film Assignment, if Client Might Infer Wrong Motives: It is possible that a client might infer the wrong motives into your film assignment when the movie shows a certain unattractive character, which fits the client in ways that could be offensive. This could negatively affect the therapist's or coach's rapport with the client. If such a film has been assigned, a therapist might consider using the client's response for transference work.

The effectiveness of Cinema Alchemy suffers with clients who are incapable of drawing insights from metaphor.

References

Bandura, A. (1973). *Aggression: A social learning analysis*. Englewood Cliffs, NJ: Prentice-Hall.

Bergman, I. (1988). *The magic lantern*. New York: Viking Press.

Burns, D. D. (1999). *The feeling good handbook*. New York: Plume.

Erickson, M. H., & Rossi, E. L. (1980). *Hypnotic investigation of psychodynamic processes*. New York: Irvington Publishers.

Fischoff, S. (2006). *From script to score: How film talents manipulate our emotions*. Unpublished manuscript.

Gardner, H. (1993a). *Frames of mind: The theory of multiple intelligences*. New York: Basic Books.

Gardner, H. (1993b). *Multiple Intelligences: The theory in practice*. New York: Basic Books.

Gendlin, E. T. (1982). *Focusing*. New York: Bantam Books.

Goleman, D., Davidson, R. J., Ekman, P., Greenberg, M., Flanagan, O., Ricard, M., & Tsai J. (2003). *Destructive emotions: How can we overcome them? A scientific collaboration with the dalai lama*. New York: Bantam Dell.

Gordon, D. (1978). *Therapeutic metaphors*. Capitola, CA: Meta Publications.

Hesley, J. W., & Hesley, J. G. (2001). *Rent two films and let's talk in the morning: Using popular movies in psychotherapy* (2nd ed.). New York: John Wiley & Sons.

Horenstein, M. A., Rigby, B., Flory, M., & Gershwin, V. (1994). *Reel Life/Real Life: A Video Guide for Personal Discovery* Kendall Park, NJ: Fourth Write Press.

Hudson, W., & Martin, M. (1992). *Solution oriented hypnosis: An Ericksonian approach.* New York: W.W. Norton and Company.

Jung, C. G. (1927). The structure of the psyche. Coll. Works Vol. 8. In J. Campbell (Ed.), *The portable jung.* New York: Penguin Books.

Jung, C. G. (1964). *Man and his symbols.* New York: Dell.

Kalm, M. A. (2004). *The healing movie book – precious images: The healing use of cinema in psychotherapy.* Lulu Press: Morrisville, NC.

Klein, A. (1988). *The healing power of humor.* New York: Tarcher/Putnam.

Leonard, K., & Robin, D. (2004). *Movies, meaning and metamorphosis: Films as modern vehicle of personal evolution.* Unpublished manuscript.

Levine, A. P., & Frederick, A. (1997). *Waking the Tiger: Healing trauma: The innate capacity to transform overwhelming experiences.* Berkeley, CA: North Atlantic Books.

Mellon, N. (2003). *Storytelling and the art of imagination.* Cambridge, MA: Yellow Moon Press.

Merriam-Webster's (1998). *Merriam-Webster's collegiate dictionary* (10th ed.). Springfield, MA: Merriam-Webster.

Mitry, J. (2000). *The aesthetics and psychology of the cinema* (Christopher, K. trans.). Bloomington, IN: Indiana University Press.

Murnaghan, S. (1951). Sucking the juice without biting the rind: Aristotle and tragic mimesis. *New Literary History, 26*(4), Autumn 1995, 755–773.

Nichols, M., & Zax, M. (1977). *Catharsis in psychotherapy.* New York: Gardner Press, Inc.

Nichols, M. P., & Bierenbaum, H. (1978, July). Success of cathartic therapy as a function of patient variables. *Journal of Clinical Psychology, 34*(3), 726–728.

Ogden, P., & Minton, K. (2000, October). Sensorimotor psychotherapy: One method for processing traumatic memory. *Traumatology, 6*(3), Article 3.

Riordan, R. J., & Wilson, L. S. (1989). Bibliotherapy: Does it work? *Journal of Counseling and Development, 67,* 506–508.

Rosen, S. (1982). *My voice will go with you: The teaching tales of Milton H. Erickson.* New York: W.W. Norton and Company.

Sinetar, M. (1993). *Reel power & spiritual growth through film.* Ligouri, MO: Triumph Books.

Solomon, G. (1995). *The motion picture prescription.* Santa Rosa, CA: Aslan Publishing.

Solomon, G. (2001). *Reel therapy: How movies inspire you to overcome life's problems.* New York: Lebhar-Friedman Books.

Sturdevant, C. G. (1998). *The laugh & cry movie guide: Using movies to help yourself through life's changes.* Larkspur, CA: Lightspheres.

Ulus, F. (2003). *Movie therapy, moving therapy: The healing power of film clips in the therapeutic settings.* Victoria, BC, Canada; Trafford Publishing.

Volger, C. (1998). *The writer's journey: Mythic structure for writers.* Studio City, CA: Michael Wiese Productions.

Voytilla, S. (1999). Myth and the movies: *Discovering the mythic structure of 50 unforgettable films.* Studio City, CA: Michael Wiese Productions.

Wolz, B. (2005). *E-motion picture magic: A movie lover's guide to healing and transformation.* Centennial, Colorado: Glenbridge.

Deconstructing: Perspectives on Perspective-Making

M. Gene Ondrusek

Critic as Artist

Being asked to provide commentary and critique on this compelling collection of perspectives on two powerful and converging disciplines – the media and psychology – proved to be both a compliment and a daunting task. It forced me to collect thoughts that always bounce around in my head, and try and order them in a way that both spoke to the request, but also added something that extends the work overall. To do this, I needed some sort of mental model, something to organize my thoughts and direct them toward a goal. I ended up by deciding to think of myself as an art critic, who has been invited to peruse a new exhibit, made up of various pieces of art, executed by a variety of artists, who were selected by a curator who had their own vision of some theme or unifying construct that drove the individual choices for the exhibit.

The mission of an accomplished critic here is not to really evaluate or judge the show or the individual pieces, but rather to extend the show, by offering perspectives that might emerge from a kind of "the whole is bigger than the sum of the parts" view. Perhaps these perspectives were intended by the curator, but perhaps they were not built in overtly. A good critic adds value by either finding or generating something fresh and not immediately available from just a cursory and passive walk-through. To really come away with a genuine aesthetic experience, the critic/observer is not just a passive recipient and consumer of what is offered. An active process of providing worked-for perspectives means the good critic actually has to "complete" or, more importantly, extend the overall work. This makes the complete art experience not just a visual one, but a cognitive one as well. And that means the observer/critic must be aware of and take into account both unique and sometimes subjective dynamics as well as bring in external, situational factors. The more one knows about the contexts and relational variables that the exhibit operates in and is informed by, the richer and more nuanced the observer's experience will be.

M.G. Ondrusek (✉)
San Diego, CA 92123
e-mail: mgeneo@aol.com

M.B. Gregerson (ed.), *The Cinematic Mirror for Psychology and Life Coaching*,
DOI 10.1007/978-1-4419-1114-8_12, © Springer Science+Business Media, LLC 2010

Ultimately, the critic's ability to articulate and express these ideas lends quality to the ultimate review. A critic's role is not providing or even evaluating answers to the questions posed and responded to by the curator, but rather offering new ways to ask better questions, and perhaps even leave the viewer feeling challenged and unsettled, rather than satisfied that they "got it." If that is to be the outcome experienced by the reader, then perhaps I will have succeeded in adapting this role.

Fresh Eyes for Readers

This role of attempting to provide the consumer with more than just an explanation and interpretation of an art exhibit is one where I do happen to have considerable experience. So the idea of applying such a mental model to extend the impact of this current book appeals to me. For over 25 years, I held the role of docent for the San Diego Museum of Contemporary Art, which brings with it the challenge of helping viewers come away with a true aesthetic experience from what were quite often rather challenging and difficult exhibits to field questions from "why is this art?" to "what does this particular piece of art mean?" meant I had to do more than just describe to people what they were seeing and name the artist and the date the piece was created.

Since many of the exhibits required people to work with their brains as much as with their eyes in order to fully appreciate what was before them, I had to explain that my role was not to tell them what to think and how to interpret what they were viewing. I had to make them aware that often many of their preconceived notions about what was *art* were going to be challenged. That meant I had to make them aware that, whether they realized it or not, they actually *had* preconceived notions. And, in order to gain insight into those notions, they needed fresh eyes.

I reminded them that Cezanne said that in order to have an insight into culture, you need to be an outsider. And, that you don't want your brain to just be applying the prejudices of its time to the art form; want to look at it with clear, fresh eyes. This is best accomplished with the process of deconstruction, and is, I think, the key to understanding the various and complex elements of a postmodern culture, especially all its art forms.

Deconstruction is taking apart what seems to be a nonreducible "entity" and seeing how it exists only in the context of the situation it's in and the relationships that it has. And that in doing so, traditional values of "good" or "bad" or even "right" or "wrong" were no longer applicable; in fact, those judgmental elements existed only in the context of the relational and situational conditions in which those entities were defined. So, western art wasn't "better" than eastern art or aboriginal art and our "culture" was not superior to a different "culture." Often a terrifying or cynical process, as ultimately, that meant there was no such thing as "truth" or even "facts" that were "objective." Everything is up for grabs and there's nothing sacred. But that's what Cezanne meant when he said you had to be an outsider.

In attempting to add value to this current book, I wanted to look at the various elements presented with fresh eyes and try and surface some of the preconceived notions that underlie our understanding about media, about psychology, and about the boundaries that separate them. To do that, I have to suspend the value systems that define both the romanticist and modernist models that are often used to assess and evaluate the impact of media. So I am an outsider.

Critic as Scientist/Engineer

Each of these chapters provides information on various elements of the media, from cinema to television, that may prove relevant toward psychology's leveraging them in service to both therapeutic and life coaching goals. As psychologists, we are always on the lookout for dynamics that aid in our quest to understand the human condition – what determines behavior, both healthy and dysfunctional, and how we can use that knowledge to expand our understanding of and improve the human condition.

In our contemporary society, it is a given that we are saturated by the offerings of the media. And the impact is reciprocal. Society determines the content of media, with market forces driving what we view as we vote for what we want to consume with our pocketbooks. At the same time, it is clear that what we consume from the media, what we see and hear, affects who we are and how we think, feel, and behave. And the boundaries between these factions, far from discrete or robust, continue to disappear. The point where we – or some previously discrete entity – stop and the media takes up is often downright blurry.

Look what has happened in the political sphere, as it has merged with the media. You're not a serious politician with credibility unless you are a guest on a late night talk show, segued between Lindsay Lohan and Robin Williams. The media confers validity for politicians in the same fashion as celebrities. So this can be a pretty scary phenomenon; knowing that these are powerful forces and, if not acknowledged and understood, powerful and dramatic effects can result.

At the same time, as we increase our knowledge of this dynamic, it can provide us with novel and impressive tools and interventions that can be channeled to yield benefits and better control negative outcomes. After all, this has been pretty much the story of mankind, as we discovered and harnessed the power of forces such as fire, electricity, and nuclear energy; all have the simultaneous potential for both great destruction and tremendous benefit. To harness the forces of the media, we are uniquely equipped as psychological professionals to provide the understanding and create the tools much like the engineers and scientists did for the disciplines mentioned above. As psychologists attempting to understand and leverage the forces of the media, however, we have our work cutout for us! And know how to be outsiders.

I remember my first personal brush with the notion of boundaries and their permeability when I was a postdoctoral research fellow in neurochemistry at the University of North Carolina School of Medicine. I was involved in a research project looking at the potential efficacy of low-dose antipsychotic medication as a treatment modality for borderline personality disordered patients. Part of my role was in determining and designing a standard diagnostic assessment battery to identify this often confusing and multifaceted diagnosis. One of the elements we were looking at was the notion that borderlines have "boundary issues," where it is difficult for them to know where they stop and other individuals take up. Those of us in clinical practice are well aware that the emotional brittleness and lability of these clients often stem from their mood and overall sense of mental stability being linked much more to outside forces, such that they are constantly buffeted by their environment and the people around them. For example, many are unable to watch news reports of disasters and traumas, because the intensity of these stimuli can be overwhelming and disorienting to them.

In my quest to try and operationalize this and find a way to quantify it, I found myself looking at the "loss of distance" such clients experience when confronted with various cards from the Rorschach Inkblot test. This was often observed when responses to the ambiguous splatterings of ink yielded reactions like "looking at this card makes me feel hot and I'm beginning to perspire," or "when I look at this image, I can feel my throat constricting and I'm having a difficult time breathing and I'm getting more and more anxious." So, the integrity of the interface between an external stimulus and its ultimate impact on thoughts, emotions, and behavior is a key to an intact and durable sense of self.

Moreover, the fact that this permeability can be both challenged and exploited is also a key to understanding the tremendous impact the media can have on our internal cognitive and emotional workings. The more this boundary can be dissolved, the more dramatic the impact. This capacity to induce internal arousal gives the media its addictive potential. And also its deleterious effects. At the same time, as we can see from Kuriansky's work in this book on the applications of cinematherapy, also great therapeutic potential.

With this incredible bandwidth, leading to outcomes ranging from corruptive to rehabilitative, it behooves us to understand as much as we can about the media, the boundaries, and the human experience that it sculpts. One dramatic example of this is suggested by Kalayjian and Abdolian's chapter on trauma and the media. The capacity of trauma imagery (sensationalized trauma) exposure to extend and exacerbate physical and emotional symptomatology underscores the power of imagery on the brain, implying boundaries may be more porous than we appreciate. As a professional community charged with bringing our insights to society as a whole, this could perhaps lead to more informed "public service announcements" during times of tragedy such as 9/11 or Hurricane Katrina. Psychologists are often trotted out during these large-scale public events as "talking heads" for standard commentary on how to cope, etc., and this type of novel information can be quite helpful to a viewing public that is being continually seduced by often saturating media coverage.

An even more exciting example of leveraging the impact of imagery on the brain is the cutting edge research using virtual reality exposure to treat PTSD victims from combat scenarios. In this case, the power of technology to create a virtual world exactly like that of the original combat scene but without the actual danger allows a more sophisticated approach to the exposure component of PTSD treatment. In exposure therapy, the brain is presented with images of the original traumatizing scenarios to elicit the physiological and psychological responses "learned" by the brain during the original trauma, but without any actual physical consequences. This helps the brain "unlearn" these associations and "relearn" more neutral responses to these stimuli. In a sense, it helps the brain "digest" all these overwhelming stimuli. Typically this is accomplished through helping the client cognitively "imagine" the scene through detailed narratives presented by the therapist. With the aid of a virtual reality world, the brain is introduced to, for all intents and purposes, all the actual sensory experiences of the real world. Here the boundary between the real and the perceived is almost completely obliterated in service to therapeutic goals.

Critic as Dramaturgist

A brief history of drama as a force to kindle human thoughts and emotions starts around 400 BC, with Aeschylus the father of Greek tragedy. He wanted the Greek citizenry to be able to experience, with as much impact as possible, the drama and angst of various battles and political intrigues the public could not experience directly – essentially the beginning of the media as we know it. "Actors" were given "lines" to replicate (with some spin, I'm sure, even at that early date, to underscore the notion that no story is so good that you can't make it better by embellishing it) the events and the players, ultimately telling a story. This allowed the audience a vicarious thrill and the opportunity to identify with the characters and take away an emotional experience. As Wolz shares with us in her chapter, this was a much more intense involvement than we would be familiar with in theatres today.

Essentially, this was the first formal attempt to dissolve the boundaries between actual tragedy and drama and hook the viewers on an opportunity for future vicarious emotionality in the next play. This model, to a large extent, remains essentially unchanged today as the mechanism delivering this type of arousal. If success is measured by durability over time, this format has been wildly successful, although, as we will see, advances in technology have allowed the delivery of a more potent "fix."

It is the nature of mankind, I think, to want to isolate, refine, and increase the potency of any opportunity for arousal. Whether it is taking the concept of a motorized vehicle and making modifications for more speed and more performance or noting the high from coca leaf chewing and isolating and purifying cocaine to make the much more intense euphoria of crack, we are driven by a pursuit to intensify experience. So, perhaps we have Aeschylus to blame for the dilemmas we face in contemporary society. After all, he started it! (hohohohohoho) Perhaps it is fitting, then, to know that he reportedly died when an eagle dropped a tortoise on his head. Too bad there wasn't a *Greece's Funniest Home Videos* program at the time to capture and immortalize that moment!

Critic as Television Consultant

That more potent "fix" came via the recent surge in reality programming, heralded by the still-popular-and-long-running *Survivor* (King & Simon, 2000 to present). This was originally a Swedish creation, there called *Expedition Robinson* (Parson,

1997 to present), and was produced for two seasons there before Mark Burnett purchased the rights to produce it for American audiences. Having been intricately involved in the creation and production of this show as the consulting psychologist, I got to witness – and contribute to – firsthand, the emergence of a new genre of programming that has since taken its place alongside the more traditional television vehicles.

The addictive power of this type of programming arises largely from the fact that this format utilizes real people, as opposed to professional actors, who are put into compelling situations, where a unique "reality" is created for them, and then their interactions are filmed pretty much 24/7. The resulting programming is then a function of clever and creative editing to find and develop (and, of course, sometimes create) story lines. This television format actually goes farther in dissolving what little boundaries remain between the media and the viewing public. And it's more than just the fact that they take advantage of nonprofessional people like you and me, creating the fantasy of "hey that could be me on that show!" What is occurring is the removal of one more layer of that boundary in our minds which knows that, despite the compelling drama unfolding on your television screen from traditional media productions, we know that it is, actually, acting!

We heavily prize and reward with fame and fortune – those professional actors that cause us to suspend disbelief. The more effectively an actor can create a character that we truly believe is real, and is actually experiencing what is happening on that "silver screen" or "small screen," the more intense and compelling will be our identification and arousal. With the advent of information about mirror neurons, the more we understand about how these neurons go about re-creating in our brains what we are watching others do. And, even though we may not always be in touch with the thought, we still *know* that what is happening up there is *not real*. And this seems to be a powerful and inescapable reality.

How powerful? Consider the way society looks at violence in the media versus sex. We often decry that we are fed constant doses of violence, mayhem, and murder in the media, but nonetheless evidence exists that its prevalence and graphic nature continues to grow. And, pretty much every manner of killing and maiming imaginable is available, with minimal censorship, at every hour of the day for the general public. Sex is, however, another matter. Yes, certainly, overt and covert sexual imagery is on the rise in pretty much every genre, as clearly documented by some of the work in this very book. But there remain strict boundaries and taboos about what can be seen where, and pornography is pornography and has its own channels and outlets and much more effort and consensus exists about what the general public will see and when.

So, why the discrepancy? Consider for a moment that there is one significant distinction. No matter how graphic and realistic the cinematic violence is that we are consuming, the fact remains that it is *not real*. It is always the product of increasingly realistic special effects technology, so despite what you think you are seeing, at some level, you know that it is not happening and that all those people that are part of the body count aren't really dead. It's all pretend! That sex you're seeing, however, is *real*! Those people are actually engaged in those acts and it is *real*.

Traditional ways of thinking assume that if it isn't real and it's all just make-believe, then that should mitigate the impact. The real danger lies in the actual depiction of reality, so we distinguish this in our efforts and need to control it. So, with traditional, modernistic ways of thinking, if it's "not real" then it isn't as dangerous or impactful as something that "is real."

Unfortunately, as we will see, these constructs and assumptions are no longer valid, and a higher complexity of thinking is required to fully appreciate what is happening as these notions of boundaries continue to vanish. Is there really a difference in media imagery that is "real" versus "not real?" Or is it a distinction without a difference?

The Real(ity) Effects of the Media

Recall that the engine of the addictive nature of the media is the direct production of arousal in the brain, as we "suspend disbelief" and are swept up in the emotionality of the dramas unfolding before us, vicariously living alongside and in real relationships with those on the screen. Reality television has removed that fragment of an already-dissolving boundary, as we now actually know that not only are those people real – and in fact, like you and me, much more than even celebrities are – but that what they are experiencing is *real*. And, those are *real* feelings; real passion, real joy, and real fear and real anger. Now, that part of the brain that used to whisper "it's just acting" isn't granting us that distinction any longer. We are getting a much more direct jolt of arousal to the brain, unfiltered and unadulterated, and we can actually *care* about what happens to such real persons, because they are certainly caring and it's really happening to them.

This genre of programming became known in the industry as the "crack" of the television networks, for more reasons than simply that these are cheap programs to produce, with revenues matching if not exceeding scripted material. The proliferation of this type of production continues to this day, as networks and production companies seek to find more magic formulas whereby they find compelling people to put into compelling situations to create compelling television for compelling returns on investment. As an aside, it is interesting that no author in this collection of chapters chose to look at reality programming directly with respect to its potential for exploitation. However, I can tell you that one of the outcomes of my long involvement with reality television production was being approached more than once by social psychology colleagues who commented that many of these productions were excellent opportunities for social psychological research, from the standpoint of the interesting scenarios created for people in very controlled environments for often long periods of time. And they all noted and lamented the fact that their university ethics committees would never allow such exploitative and potentially damaging experiments to be performed in an academic setting. It seems that networks have many fewer qualms about how they go about exploiting people and also much larger budgets! So if they are conducting the "experiments" we cannot, then the least we can do is try and learn from what they are already producing!

Fast forward from Aeschylus to the present and it is obvious that media drama, whether television or movies, undoubtedly provide the most emotionally wrenching experiences of the average week for the average person. Face it, most people's lives are not filled with a steady stream of intense arousal, passion, or strong emotion. The "fix" offered by media drama creates the need for more of it, with the need for this stimulation increasing due to the brain's capacity for habituation. Normal relationships simply cannot match the power of artifice.

Celebrity worship is the easiest, most common "social glue." It provides a common frame of reference and a currency of familiarity. Harken back to the death of Princess Diana. When she died, a small part of many individual's daily lives disappeared. In fact, based on my personal schedule and viewing preferences, it is obvious to me that I spend more time with Diane Sawyer's iconic image/persona on Good Morning America than I do with any other single individual in my life. Pathetic, you say? Or, simply one version of my socio-technical reality? Perhaps yours as well? Or are you more a Katie Couric-type?

Distal Does Not Mean Distant

With no give-and-take or any face-to-face interaction, is this type of relationship even valid? It is of course not without precedent, as some of the most intense affairs of the heart (Heloise and Abelard, Elizabeth Barrett and Robert Browning) were carried on without actually meeting. Is reciprocal interchange essential? Well, we are encouraged to have a "personal" relationship with God/Jesus in religious contexts and to view this as a guiding force in decisions that we make. And with the advent of the internet, a plethora of possibilities, both positive and negative are now available to anyone with basic computer access. Marriages have broken up as a result of internet affairs where no actual physical contact has even occurred. And many successful marriages have resulted from American men hooking up with Russian women, with the entire courtship and proposal process conducted solely through email and instant messaging.

Anecdotal scenarios of the power of these constructed relationships continue to proliferate. As I write this piece, I am following the tragic story of a young woman, ironically named Paula, who was an avid fan of Paula Abdul, of Laker Girl and *American Idol* (Gowers, Pritchett, Warwick, & Drake, 2002 to present) fame. This fan had idolized Ms. Abdul and apparently her audition tape for the fifth season of the show was included in a 2006 airing as one of the auditions selected for its ineptitude and thus the expected on-air ridiculing by not only Simon Cowell, but also by Ms. Abdul herself. This public humiliation was further augmented by scores of bloggers trashing her appearance, along with similar commentary on her MySpace posting. Likely as a result of this extreme and personal rejection, this fan was found dead in her car outside the Los Angeles home of Ms. Abdul, the victim of an apparent suicide. Ms Abdul's publicist, of course, released the perfunctory statement, "My heart and prayers go out to her family." An "arm chair" diagnostic appraisal by one of the talking head psychologists on a morning talk show implied that the victim was the one failing to appreciate the inherent vulnerability that led to this tragedy. In fact, one of the roles I performed for many of the early reality shows was that of risk management, where I conducted brief psychological evaluations, including psychological testing, to help networks identify and screen out participants with potentially problematic psychopathology.

We are all aware of the power of the media to impact people, and the seductive lure of "being on TV" draws a multitude of people, with varying degrees of mental health. However, as we have seen in countless experiments, ranging from Milgram's work on authoritarian compliance behavior to Zimbardo's famous Stanford Prison Experiment, the power of the environment can pretty much trump anyone's internal psychological makeup. In fact, it may well be, in this new, socio-technical world, many of the assumptions arising from the constructs of a core "personality" and durable "self" are no longer applicable. As Zimbardo (2007) points out in his recent work, *The Lucifer Effect: How Good People Turn Evil,* everyone has inside them the potential for being an angel or a devil, committing good deeds or bad deeds, depending on the situations in which we find ourselves. According to Zimbardo, these were not "bad apples" at Abu Ghraib, but there was a "bad basket" (referred to in Gregerson's writings in this edited volume as the "holding environment"). Enron did not hire hordes of antisocial, exploitative workers to commit those enormous acts of fraud and deceit. But as the culture grew stronger and more potent, it shaped the people that worked there. And what they ended up doing without any dissonance, on a daily basis, would never have been imaginable when they first signed on.

Thus, the interface with the media that previously separated two seemingly discrete entities – it and us – is constantly eroding, and the power and saturability of this virtual environment far surpass a faux prison cell at Stanford University or a corporate culture gone rogue. And, like nuclear energy, this "fission" implies both great destructive and beneficial potential. As the contextual dynamics of this environment then determine not only what we do (to an extent often greater than any dispositional factors), it even defines who we are. And, as the media grows more potent, not only in its technological impact, but in its inherent drive to dissolve the boundaries separating "it" from "us," we have to appreciate the need to understand what's happening. And we have to remain outsiders. And not just look with "the prejudices of our time."

Values as Mental Models

In this increasingly postmodern society, the use of either romanticist or modernist value systems as mental models for evaluation stretches their utility, causing us to get sidetracked into making value judgments. This dilutes our ability to keep the viewpoints of outsider and may hold up inquiry. It may also lead to "lazy" thinking, where we look for simple answers to complex questions, or fail to see the entire arc of change. For example, not so long ago, the feeling that dissecting the human body was degrading and irreligious held up our understanding of anatomy and human physiology. This type of clash between scientific and traditional values still goes on, which is frustrating enough. Add to this the clash between deconstructionist dynamics and pretty much every other value system and a higher complexity of mind is needed to continue and to advance this dialog. Robert Gergen's developmental theories on the complexity of mind would suggest that this requires a fifth order level of complexity of mind. This order implies the cognitive ability to see that entities only exist in a relational context. Gergen essentially defines what sort of thinking capacity is required to successfully navigate the treacherous waters of postmodernism. Particularly, grasping the impact of the media requires using deconstructive dynamics to gain a richer appreciation of what's happening "out there."

Much of the material in this book deals with the media's depiction of constructs that particularly appeal to psychology – relationships, the family, love, children, sexuality, etc. And seeing words like "degraded" and "undermined" suggests that value systems arising from both romanticist and modernist value systems are being applied with regard to describing what is happening. And, with this type of mental model, conclusions are reached (or at least implied) about mitigating these dangers.

But doesn't this smack of the age-old tradition of decrying change? Isn't this just the current version of voices raising alarm about the current state of a decaying society and the corruptive effects seen in the youth of today? Didn't Socrates point out the very same thing in his time? Isn't it inherent to every society to see the onslaught of whatever particular flavor of corruption they are seeing to be uniquely grave and that *this time* things have finally gone *too far*?

But as change is absorbed and assimilated into the culture, the outcries subside and the once brazen becomes mundane. Glance backward and some of the solutions to moral decay can even appear quaint. Remember when television of the 1950s required that even a married couple's bedroom have two twin beds, as Kuriansky notes, to prevent a naïve and impressionable youthful viewing audience from contemplating that these people actually slept [had sex] together? I do recall my own period of confusion as I noted that my parents, and all of my friends' parents, had only a single bed in the master bedroom, contrary to Rob and Laura Petrie, Lucy and Ricky, etc. What was up with that? Let's not forget that these were the images that escorted us into the free love 1960s!

Literally Save the Children

That of course, doesn't mean that there isn't a role for caution and restraint. There are always forces constantly vetting the process and trying to slow or blunt the arrow of time; after all, society has to catch up and prevent assimilation from overwhelming people's capacity to cope. Remember not too long ago when there were uniformed, professional "operators" in every bank of elevators, supervising the journeys of passengers to their various floors? Looks quaint in all those movies from the

1930s, doesn't it? Well, this mode of vertically transporting people to great heights via some new-fangled invisible apparatus was not something to be handled back then without professional technical contribution, thus making the job of the operator necessary for people to actually participate. Fear of the unknown was bound up by authority figures until everyone could catch up and feel confident in pushing the buttons themselves. Now the riding of an elevator is a mindless activity. Fear of the unknown is such a cliché, but no one is a priori exempt from it; in fact, if it isn't unsettling and doubt- and uncertainty-generating, it probably isn't significant change. Everyone, liberal or conservative, finds something to fear as they try and deal with and determine "what's this world coming to, how did this happen, and what can we do about it?" Social psychologist Dan MacAdams' recent research suggests that conservatives fear societal collapse, while liberals fear a world without deep feelings and intense experiences. With contributions from evolutionary psychologists, we know these alarmist sounds to activate fear go out for the usual suspects on which our species depends – the decay of the nuclear family, the deterioration of healthy environments for children to grow up in, the dangers of excess and indulgence with sex, drugs, and rock and roll, etc. Without protecting the children, there will be no future, so we must defend the institutions charged with their safe development (referred to in Gregerson's writings in this edited volume as the "holding environment").

But let's look at the vast arc of change in the ability and even definition to "protect children" that has occurred just in the last few decades. At the beginning of the twentieth century, children were almost completely insulated from information about the private lives of adults. Family and social institutions shielded children from practically all adult proceedings, simply by having them in private places, not accessible to children. Any material dealing with the misgivings, flaws, and conflicts of the adult world were essentially unavailable.

So, children were children, totally distinct from adults, and were true children for longer. In a sense, this was the true "innocence" of childhood. Moreover, without modern transportation opportunities, most children grew up, lived, and died within the geographical and relational confines of the extended family. The first destructive force that "degraded" the family was the advent of the ability to pack up and move across the country, leaving their roots behind, re-planting somewhere else. I am reminded of a scene in *How the West Was Won* (Ford, Hathaway, & Marshall, 1962), an epic film chronicling the movement to settle the west, where a settler was grieving over the deaths resulting from a vicious Indian attack, asking if it were all worth it, and were the screams of these just-orphaned children not reason enough to turn back. The response from a fellow settler was "Those aren't screams, that's the sound of life happening!"

Looking at the entire arc of the arrow of change, it is clear that forces are constantly at work driving this arrow and it is hubris to think that we have the answer as to what's ultimately good or bad. Or progress or regress. As Wolz in this volume reminds us, change is violent. The emergence of the media in all its varieties and relentlessness has pretty much obliterated the insulations that defined the "innocence" of childhood and its protection from the proceedings of adults. And it's only one of a number of forces that impinge on the "holding environment." Without question, this evolution has been going on forever and will certainly continue. In fact, our current notion of the primacy of children and their inherent fragility is pretty much a blip on the historical screen; it wasn't that long ago, in Western Europe, when children were seen as inconvenient commodities that were pretty much expendable. This notion of having their "protection" as a primary and irreducible fact with no sustainable counterargument is just one snapshot of a perspective that is constantly morphing. And technology is brokering the process.

In fact, in many cases the availability of this information about the adult world and the greater ease with which most children can access it through their greater degree of sophistication in using new technologies often means the kids now know more about adult proceedings than many adults do. Children don't stay "children" nearly as long, with even biological evidence validating this with research suggesting that the average age of puberty is decreasing. It behooves us to retain that "outsider" viewpoint to see what we can learn about the "biodiversity" that arises whenever ecosystems interface, entities are deconstructed, and the boundaries that separate them lose their integrity. Certainly one of the effects is the constant redefinition of the entity of "children" and "parents" and "family," all of which become fodder for entertainment vehicles wishing to exploit this heterogeneity.

The media's work in deconstructing the "entity" of the family and the way in which intimate, parent/child, and related social relationships can be conducted has provided a seemingly endless array of fascinating and multifaceted permutations. After all, when something is deconstructed, it is a deliberate and overt act to reconstruct in new ways what you have just taken apart. So we have observed a vast array of role re-definitions within scripted programming. The "father" role from Jim Anderson's *Father Knows Best* (Russell & Tewksbury, 1954–1960) to Homer Simpson (*The Simpsons*; Kirkland, Moore, Reardon, Anderson, Archer, Anderson, Silverman, Nastuk, Kruse, Moore, Polcino, Lynch, Dietter, Michels, Kramer, Baeza, Polcino, Sheetz, Persi, Scott III, Affleck, Marcantel, MacMullan, Ervin, Kamerman, Clements, Gray, Bird, Butterworth, Sosa, Faughnan, & Oliver, 1989 – present). Wives smarter than, or dumber than, husbands. Children's roles from dependent and compliant to running the entire show. Single parent models to same-sex parents. With the ability, technology, and sophistication to "frame" a particular perspective and create a social reality, it is abundantly clear that there are many ways to conduct and even define a "family." And to conduct a life. Every version contains upsides and downsides, and with all the relational and contextual variables controlled for and constructed through media manipulation, it is practically impossible to mount any coherent attack from those with opposing views. It isn't my "right" versus your "wrong." And it's not as simple as saying that the downsides of some particular perspective were not presented. They are just different ways to create reality. And when the boundaries dissolve, well, as they say, life imitates art, and vice versa. Contrary to Cashill's provocative title, Hollywood is always getting the family right! Consider some of the following observations:

– In London, Amy Taylor is ending a real-life ("rl") marriage because she discovered her husband cheating with his avatar in *Second Life* (http://secondlife.com/), an online community where players adopt personas (avatars), mingle with others, and teleport themselves into a series of artificial worlds. "I caught him cuddling a woman on a sofa in the game. It looked really affectionate. He confessed he'd been talking to this woman player in America for 1 or 2 weeks; I told him our marriage was over and that he didn't love me anymore." Their marriage started to fall apart after Taylor caught her husband's avatar having cybersex with a virtual prostitute last year. This was his second chance! Taylor has reportedly found a new man in an alternative cyber-universe and can't wait to marry her new fiancée "in rl" (real life??)

– There is an argument put forth by writer Alisa Valdes-Rodriguez that *The Cosby Show* (Sandrich, Singletary, Lauten, Bowab, Vinson, Life, Barnette, Warner, Falcon, & Scott, 1984–1992) laid the groundwork for President-Elect Obama by presenting an appealing black family, the Huxtables, to young TV viewers who grew up equipped to thwart stereotypes and barriers, as Cashill notes in this edited volume. This "Huxtable Effect" suggests that viewers embraced the family created by Bill Cosby as "America's family" rather than a black one, setting the stage for commentary that Obama is actually a product of "postracial" thinking. Ironically, Cosby launched the idea for this sitcom out of dismay at the sitcoms of the day that portrayed households where the children had taken over the house from the bumbling adults. He wanted a more "dignified" show where he and his wife kept a loving, firm hand on their five children. In fact, this was not an overt attack on racial stereotypes as much as it was a shot at the dominant themes at the time where sitcoms depicted weak parents who were losing to their kids (think *Married with Children* [Cohen, Day, Bearse, Orender, Singletary, Samuels, Cottrell, & Smith, 1987–1997]). Further, the portrayal was not at all couched in identifiable African-American ethnic constructs, leading to many white fans saying Cliff Huxtable reminded them of their dad. It is a compelling argument that the immense popularity of this show, running for over 8 years, saturated the culture with a perspective of an affluent, professional black family and paved the way for a successful presidential run by a black candidate, where racial themes were basically nonissues. The media no longer simply reflects culture; it can obviously drive it as well, in this case creating a construct that was later filled in "rl."

– Some years ago, the case of Thomas Beatie and his wife was making the rounds of television's talk shows, as the first case of the husband giving birth to their first child. It seems that Mr. Beatie was previously Ms. Beatie, a transgendered individual who underwent female-to-male sex reassignment surgery. However, leaving her reproductive organs and her fertility intact and his/her wife being unable to conceive, the now-Mr. Beatie, sporting a nice Edwardian beard and otherwise masculine appearance, was splashed first through the tabloids and then the mainstream media, clearly "showing" in his last trimester of pregnancy. They became the first couple to bear a child with the husband actually carrying the child to term. As of this writing, Mr. Beatie is again pregnant, and the ubiquitous Barbara Walters assured us that for all intents and purposes, life in the Beatie household is "completely normal." Apparently, we as psychological professionals now share the role with various media icons and talking heads for making judgments and decisions about what is "normal." Coupled to the political furor that surrounds the movement by the gay community to acknowledge same-sex marriage as equally valid to heterosexual marriage, it is clear that deconstruction of the entities that comprise the nuclear family and the culturally defined roles within it continue to be re-constructed in increasingly novel ways. This makes for quite a diverse range of possible "normals."

Morality Tales for Teens

Let's follow yet another iconographic image in its journey from being defined by revision, firmly embedded in a postmodern society, defined by multiple perspectives arising out of the contextual and relational variables that impinge on it. Countless images in literature and the media exist for the construct of the unwed, teenage mother and the adolescent sexuality that led to it.

Consider the application of romanticist value systems, where it is a morality play about the tragic consequences of unbridled, youthful passion sweeping away fragile and poorly installed traditionalist/religious moral structures. What followed was always a tragedy of some emphasis, as moral failings must have consequences. Either an abortion, or worse, a botched one, where either the mother or the child – or both – die, is a common plot in literature, movies, plays, and other story-telling vehicles too numerous to mention. In this scenario, no one lived happily ever after. There was often abandonment by the youthful and immature father, or perhaps banishment with the scarlet letter of a short residency in a far-away "home for unwed mothers," to minimize the shame heaped upon the family by keeping it hidden and not available for all to judge.

Alternately, in the spirit of "doing the right thing by the woman and stepping up to the plate as a man" according to traditionalist values, the young couple went ahead and tied the knot. Thus was launched a doomed-from-the-start loveless and tainted marriage that likely set the stage to repeat this drama when the "unwanted child" reached puberty and became aware of how they came into this world. Truly, it would be hard to find any scenario in a version informed by romanticist values, where anyone lived happily ever after or that generated an outcome where mistakes weren't punished.

Morality tales have to teach a lesson and this makes premarital sexual activity a taboo that must be met only with abstinence as a remedy. In other words, there are never acceptable rationales for such behavior, so to avoid the inevitable consequences, one must avoid all situations that make such expressions of immature sexuality likely to occur. Just say "No!"

With modernist values sharing the stage, a diminishing of the traditionalist value judgments that erected strong, clear boundaries began to make teen unwed pregnancy and the youthful, hormone-fueled sexuality that drove it something that was tempered with realism. After all, wasn't it futile to actually think any interventions could be effective in eliminating teen sexuality, particularly with the onslaught of the media-crafted sexual messages saturating adolescents from every vantage point? It was something to avoid simply because of the negative impact on the lives of all concerned, so it must be dealt with rationally, as a problem to solve.

Since every situation was unique to the players involved, all the options needed to be considered, and the "right" or "best" solution to deal with the dilemma emerged from weighing all the options equally. It was making the best out of a bad situation. Applying logic usually meant having to downplay, or at least equalize, moral considerations, as they only muddied the waters and prevented people from entertaining the entire gamut of possibilities and thus acting to "create the greater good for the greater number."

For some, it was highly relevant, for others, not so much. And solutions that worked in one situation might not work for someone else. So no one should be unfairly prevented from exercising whatever option they chose to pursue. And to judge one solution as superior to another simply by citing morality was, well, not logical!

Once the gates were opened to variability in how one looks at the whole issue of teen pregnancy and teen sexuality, the road was paved toward the possibilities of actually glamorizing it, since there were already such obvious examples showing up in celebrity land. And this celebrity role modeling came with full disclosure of all the details, making it all the much easier to identify with and bond with the various role models offered. You could even shop at the very boutiques the stars chose to accessorize their maternity wardrobes. That's what glamorous and famous people do and how they handle this sort of thing. Just another "it" factor in the celebrity market.

This perspectivist or pluralistic approach underscores the notion that every conceivable framing of adolescent sexuality and unwed teen pregnancy is an "entity" in its own right, and with the sophistication of media technology and its capacity to coherently present any particular perspective, all are real because all are possible. Every conceivable route into, through, and out of teen pregnancy gets a thorough airing. And, depending on the viewpoint taken, the various social contexts, and of course the type and quality of the relationships involved, all viewpoints carry equal weight.

Is teen sexuality and pregnancy then a good thing? Can it ever be a good thing? Is it a bad thing? Is it always a bad thing? Does it, as suggested by work in this book, suck the "vitality" out of the identified teen? Or would that particular outcome depend completely on the particular perspective that this or that example was embracing as their "reality?" And, if so, shouldn't it follow that in order to preserve the construct of "vitality," – or accomplish some similar, desirable outcome – that overtly changing one's perspective would do the trick? And, isn't it apparent that the only way this particular outcome is even possible is due to forces convincing the teen that this is the inevitable way such a thing affects you, so if you buy into that reality, this loss of vitality is part of the package. And, if you chose to shift your awareness – in fact, be more mindful of how you are choosing to look at this scenario, then you can change how you perceive it, and have a lot more say in your vitality.

You are not the passive receiver of this reality station. You have control over how you think and, thus, the entire process of meaning making in your life. That's the essence of mindfulness. In fact, it should be obvious that the more we understand about how media harnesses and crafts the relevant relational and contextual variables and weaves them into a compelling perspective, the more we can deliberately create specific social realities. And, the more we understand about how the human brain absorbs and is changed by these sources of information and meaning, the more effectively we can control the process.

I remember a conversation I had with Albert Bandura some years ago about his plans to work with writers and directors to insert personal health and sexual hygiene messages into the scripts of famous soap opera stars in parts of Africa where these daily televised "stories" enjoy significant cultural participation. These stars were hugely popular role models and skillfully weaving public health messages into their personalities and life stories via scripting would likely be more impactful than having them simply read them as PSAs as we do in this culture – social learning theory in a socio-technical society in a third world country.

In perhaps one of the most dramatic examples of the power of this type of reality construction, we need only look to the most recent public scenario involving teen pregnancy and unwed motherhood status. That would, of course, be the unwed-teen-preggers situation of one of the daughters of the recent Republican Vice Presidential candidate, Sara Palin, as Gregerson notes in this edited volume. Despite coming from an ultra-conservative and evangelical background with strict and traditional moral values, it became known that the Vice Presidential candidate's teen daughter had been knocked up by a local boy hockey player.

The surprising element here was actually that this potential blockbuster story was a relative nonevent. No one really made a big deal out of it and it was a relative nonissue in the campaign, primarily by being spun and packaged with the media's created social reality of Palin's family as "just like yours and mine." Hers was a Real American Family and in Real American Families these things happen and it's dealt with as a family issue. Tragic, but that's life. In this relational context, a perspective was created that prevented any evaluative appraisals that included hypocrisy or disingenuousness with respect to the family's overall value system. Just as Obama's ethnic status was really a nonissue, because he was seen as "postracial," Palin's family dysfunction was, well, postdysfunction! From moral depravity to family problem to glamorous accessory, finally to just one of those things that can happen to any family, the various social realties of teen pregnancy all have objective validity. And, with the extreme bandwidth and diversity of perspective that distinguishes among all these social realities, it is simplistic if not impossible to apply a blanket label, judgment or even remedy that would apply across all of them.

Portrayals Deconstruct Real Values

As many of the authors in this book demonstrate, this deconstructionism is apparent in a diverse variety of constructs. For example, in reviewing Balter's article in this edited volume on media framing of disability, characters with various physical challenges have historically been portrayed as heroic and inspirational, rising above their "handicaps" as role models for others. But, increasingly, these character portrayals have become more mundane and "normal," not wholly defined by their physical shortcomings; their disability is simply one of the factors that contribute to their self-image. Perhaps we are moving also toward a "postdisability" reality as well.

Conclusion

To begin to tie up all the loose ends arising from this deconstruction of the material and the concepts addressed in these chapters, I think it will be crucial to operationalize some of the constructs introduced in order to suggest some concrete ways to navigate in this postmodern world. As Cezanne recommended, I have tried to maintain the position of outsider here, so that I can look at these constructs with the fresh eyes required to keep from applying the prejudices of this culture.

This insider-to-outsider shift is defined by Robert Kegan in his developmental theories concerning the Orders of Mind as the movement from Subject to Object. In his theoretical framework, he posits five qualitatively different ways of constructing reality, which develop from less to more complexity. Briefly, these ways range from how a 2-year-old constructs reality to that of a person well into the second half of life. A move from Subject to Object is when the entire meaning-making system moves from that which unquestioningly runs the person to that which the person can actively control. As it is a developmental theory, each Order represents a qualitative shift in meaning making and complexity from the Order preceding it. These Orders become more complex with time, but no Order is inherently better than any other. What is important is the fit between the Order of Mind and the task required. According to Kegan, societal demands made at different points in human history are also helpful for understanding the different Orders of mind and grasping why so many of us are now in over our heads – not yet developmentally ready to meet the demands placed on us. He goes on to explore three historical eras – traditionalism, modernism, and postmodernism – and relates them to Third, Fourth and Fifth Orders, respectively. Postmodernists no longer seek to perfect a philosophy, idea, or ideology; instead, postmodernists look at the ways in which dichotomous philosophies create one another and focus on the systems that underlie the dichotomies. This dynamic can be applied to dissecting the relational and contextual factors that create the social realities engineered by the media, and, of course, how the social realities define the media. This Fifth Order of complexity is well suited to the demands of the media-driven postmodern age. And, here, almost all of us are in over our heads!

But it is where we must function to glean insight into shifting control in the meaning-making process. As we understand the mental model of different Orders of Mind and gain an appreciation for the "fit" between where our client is functioning and the requirements of the role they are in, we have a model for development. For example, for those of us working as executive coaches, this model is particularly helpful for working with executive clients whose complexity is less than (or, in some cases, more than) that required by his or her role or environment. And a key to fully leveraging this model is making full use of the concepts and techniques offered by mindfulness theory.

Mindful Media

From the point of view of mindfulness theory, personal control of perception takes center stage. Essentially, mindfulness asks the question "Is my way of perceiving the relationships and contexts among the pieces of my experience so automatic that it is beyond my control?" Ellen Langer reminds us that mindfulness makes us sensitive to context and perspective. When we are mindless, our behavior is governed by rules and routines – the prejudices of our culture. In contrast, when we are mindful, our behavior may be guided by rules and routines, but we stay sensitive to the ways our situation changes. When we are mindful, we are actively aware of different perspectives and in control of our meaning-making process. Many of the authors in this book, along with a wide array of proponents of positive psychology, recognize and cite the utility of mindfulness as a coping strategy. Exploring how it can equip us to aid us in our quest to get our collective heads around the powerful meaning-making forces of the media is the first step toward being in control of it.

Several authors in this book offer some intriguing observations about how this process occurs at the boundaries of the interface with the media. Gregerson, for example, points out that teens cite peers as a more powerful influence over their values and behavior than the media. She goes on to emphasize that individuals, however, feel that their peers are more influenced by the media than they are. In effect, they see themselves as different in their capacity to be affected by media imagery and messages, whereas their peers are much more vulnerable. Is this simply evidence for denial? Or is it part of a coping strategy that suggests an ability to distance themselves, a move from Subject to Object? One of the features of the *Up* series noted by Lanning is the fact that viewers of this film are compelled to go through a self-examination process, asking the questions "Why am I me and why not you? Why am I here and not there?" This suggests an active process of deliberate meaning-making, right at the boundary between real life and media creations. Likely it was not an intended agenda, installed by the filmmakers, but arose out of the interface between the viewers and the subject of this developmentally oriented documentary.

Many of us reading this book probably remember before television, and certainly before it evolved as part of a media dominated, culture-saturating and culture-defining force. Therefore our social milieu didn't include the need to develop strategies to cope with the complex technological forces with which our youthful population contends. Likely their ability to see through or deconstruct messages traveling over the airwaves exceeds ours. And the Subject–Object movement separating "rl" from that created by the media may even be postmodern. That is, the various social realities presented by the media and the way in which they can be spun to construct an intact, coherent, and valid perspective can be "seen through" by the average savvy viewer.

We are worried about the ability of the media to glamorize prostitution or make teen pregnancy acceptable and desirable. And we *Fear Factor*'s (Einhorn, Perez, & Thompson, 2001–2006) worry about the "impressionable youth" that will be corrupted by such messages. Meanwhile, techno-savvy consumers merely say "Well, that's what television does," and just add it to the list of societal influences that contemporary young citizens access to create an identity. I recall being on the set as "resident shrink," particularly during the episode of *Family Fear Factor* (Thompson, 2006), which involved contestants comprised of a parent and their 10–12 year old.

It may come as a surprise to you that this long-running "T & A" fueled reality show featuring outrageous stunts and the consumption of some truly vile substances was most popular among the 10–12 year old demographic. Since this was their audience, several episodes were filmed involving parents and children. In my risk-management capacity, I was asked to be on set during the filming of these stunts, in case problems occurred from participation (or, in some cases, hesitation to partici-pate) in some often truly scary – or gross – stunts. Even though the overt agenda was to "protect the children," more often than not in these productions, I found the chil-dren to be more supportive and encouraging to the parents, who often got wrapped up in the stunts and competition. So, instead of the parent comforting the child, it was more the children reminding their parent that is was "just a game," and "its just television," and "we're here to have fun and maybe win some money, so loosen up!" Clearly the children understood the construction and intent of the show and their role in it way more than the parents did!

Media Mythmaking

Advocates of cinematherapy point out that our vast array of media-brokered enter-tainment products constitutes our culture's way of providing story-telling and myth-making opportunities to pass on cultural values and lessons learned. All soci-eties leverage such vehicles for the purpose of educating its members on how to survive and thrive and play well with others, and this socio-technical system is ours. They go on to suggest that a careful and mindful utilization of these offerings select-ing the right material for the right client along with the appropriate techniques to generate meaningful dialog and discussion expands our therapeutic tool kit in are-nas ranging from mental health treatment to life coaching. Much due diligence is expended to provide an admirable and diverse listing of cinematic vehicles offering psychologically relevant constructs. And, as Niemiec's contribution points out, there is even an abundance of material from international cinema that increases the band-width of these resources to truly magnify the potential benefit through addressing unique cultural issues.

But one facet is not really addressed. What is the origin of these metaphors and how did they get there? Is this symbolism and metaphor actually a result of a delib-erate and overt agenda by the writers and directors? Were they the architects and authors of stories that identified and conveyed these particular cultural norms? If so, what were their selection criteria? Who appointed them the purveyors of cultural, social, and personal values? Who provides checks and balances to vet their method-ologies and messages? So are these "lessons" embedded in the material from the outset, and left there to be discovered by the astute therapist and his or her client?

Most of the work in this book that deals with applied issues, relevant to therapy or coaching, assumes that these symbolisms and messages are already installed and psychological benefit accrues from extracting them in personally relevant ways. In a true mindfulness orientation, though, aren't we also charged with looking with a deconstructive eye at the various messages and metaphors, challenging their "entity" status? Moreover, we can focus on what we think of as core, irreducible values and appreciate their contextual relationships as well. And don't we also have the added advantage (or dilemma?) of superimposing and even creating such metaphor? As with postmodern artwork, we can be called upon to complete or extend the work itself by being aware of the contextual and relational factors that actually define the metaphor. For ourselves and our clients, we should always be attentive to taking control of the meaning-making process and remain alert to multiple perspectives, regardless even of the intentions put forth by the artist. Mark Twain, ever the prescient chronicler of his time, admonished us in *The Adventures of Huckleberry Finn*:

> *Persons attempting to find a motive in this narrative will*
> *be prosecuted; persons attempting to find a moral in it will*
> *be banished; persons attempting to find a plot in it will be shot.*
> By Order of the Author

Although great value can result from this model of extracting embedded meaning, it also implies a passive process, with restrictions on the freedom to learn. Here are the facts, here is the lesson, and here is what you should take away in order to experience the benefits of this modality of growth and learning.

In a sense, this can be contrary to the tenets of mindfulness, which urge us to be aware of novel distinctions and pay attention to contexts and categories. It makes this learning a passive process, focused on extracting the "right" meaning. Its agenda is to reduce doubt and minimize uncertainty. Mindfulness, on the other hand, emphasizes that uncertainty creates the freedom to both discover and create meaning.

Rather than trying to overcome uncertainty, embracing it expands our sense of personal control. For example, we may be uncomfortable when confronted with the various constructs the media presents with respect to sexuality, the family, etc., but if we are aware that this compels us to make our own meaning, then we are motivated to continue to generate perspectives and discover new ways of categorizing the world. And in the sweeping arc of history, there always have been perspectives and changes that cause discomfort and uncertainty about these constructs. And yet the world continues on . . .

Cashill's work pointed out the cynicism involved in one of the more overtly postmodern films, *Pleasantville* (Ross, 1998), when, in the closing scene, one of the characters complains that "It's not supposed to be like this." The response to this lamentation, with a reassuring intention, was "It's not supposed to be about anything." Cashill's perspective on this is to categorize it as "Hollywood sophistry." From a mindfulness perspective, however, this is the inevitable starting point. It challenges us – and our clients – to then determine what it *is* about and to embrace the meaning-making challenge that defines personal control. And it's as much about making the right choice as it is about making the choice right.

The Final Curtain: Movies as Models

Danny Wedding

Albert Bandura (1977) as noted the power of modeling, stating:

> "Learning would be exceedingly laborious, not to mention hazardous, if people had to rely solely on the effects of their own actions to inform them what to do. Fortunately, most human behavior is learned observationally through modeling: from observing others one forms an idea of how new behaviors are performed, and on later occasions this coded information serves as a guide for action" (p. 22).

Unfortunately, models displaying exemplary behavior are often not readily available in daily life. We are just as likely to see someone behaving in a negative, hateful, and mean spirited way as to see someone behaving with honor, dignity, and decorum. We live in a world where people routinely say unkind things, behave rudely, and model behaviors that we find deplorable. However, anyone interested in cultivating personal growth will want to seek out role models who exhibit positive personality traits and who are what Carl Rogers called "fully functioning people" (Rogers, 1963):

> [A] person functioning freely in all the fullness of his organismic potentialities; a person who is dependable in being realistic, self-enhancing, socialized and appropriate in his behavior; a creative person, whose specific [behaviors] are not easily predictable; a person who is ever changing, ever developing, always discovering himself and the newness in himself in each succeeding moment of time. (p. 26)

The work of Carl Rogers and Abraham Maslow (1968), two past American Psychological Association (APA) presidents, laid the foundation for the development of the positive psychology movement. As Martin Seligman, another APA president and the father of positive psychology, noted, "psychology is not just the study of pathology, weakness, and damage; it is also the study of strength and virtue. Treatment is not just fixing what is broken; it is nurturing what is best" (Seligman & Csikszentmihalyi, 2000, p. 7).

I believe systematic exposure to positive role models through films can help us "nurture what is best." However, most viewers need assistance in identifying

D. Wedding (✉)
Missouri Institute of Mental Health, St. Louis, MO 63139, USA
e-mail: danny.wedding@mimh.edu

M.B. Gregerson (ed.), *The Cinematic Mirror for Psychology and Life Coaching*,
DOI 10.1007/978-1-4419-1114-8_13, © Springer Science+Business Media, LLC 2010

those films that are the most likely to be personally rewarding and psychologically beneficial; reading this book is a good beginning.

I have devoted much of my professional life to viewing, cataloging, and writing about films that illustrate that which is best in human beings. In addition, as editor of the American Psychological Association journal *PsycCRITIQUES: Contemporary Psychology – APA Review of Books*, I reinstated film reviews, a practice introduced by *Contemporary Psychology's* first editor, E. G. Boring. Psychologists and other readers interested in identify psychologically significant and uplifting films can use the journal (and its companion web site, psyccritiquesblog.apa.org) to identify those movies most likely to facilitate personal growth.

Chris Peterson and Martin Seligman (2004), two of the senior figures in positive psychology, developed a taxonomy for character strengths and virtues; their model includes six overarching core virtues (wisdom and knowledge; courage; humanity; transcendence; temperance; justice); each virtue is built on three to five specific character strengths (e.g., the virtue of humanity is comprised of the character strengths of love, kindness, and social intelligence). These virtues and character strengths are shown in Fig. 1, along with representative films that illustrate each of the 24 character strengths. The film examples are meant to be heuristic illustrations; a few moments of reflection will allow most readers to come up with dozens of similar examples of films that illustrate each of the virtues and character strengths being discussed.

Wedding and Niemiec (2003) have discussed the ways in which films can be incorporated into therapy, much in the way that bibliotherapy has historically been used in therapy (Campbell & Smith, 2003). Films are one possible way of facilitating "positive psychotherapy." "Positive psychotherapy (PPT) contrasts with standard interventions for depression by increasing positive emotion, engagement, and meaning rather than directly targeting depressive symptoms" (Seligman, Rashid, & Parks, 2006, p. 774).

John Norcross (2006) has discussed self-help initiatives in therapy, and this is what he has to say about movies and therapy:

> Films are a powerful and pervasive part of our culture. Gallup polls indicate that watching movies at home and in theaters is amongst adults' favorite pastimes. Watching movies toward therapeutic ends—call it "videotherapy" or "cinema therapy"—is like self-help books and autobiographies. But movies possess a number of advantages: They are fun to watch, require only a small investment of time, are widely available, appeal to more people than reading, and are already part of many clients' usual routines. As a result, clients may be more accepting of recommendations for movies (p. 685).

Niemiec and Wedding (2008) expanded on the idea that watching films could facilitate personal growth and wrote a book, *Positive Psychology at the Movies: Using Films to Build Virtues and Character Strengths*, that describes hundreds of films that illustrate character strengths and virtues. An appendix from this book listing "positive psychology movies" can be downloaded at no charge at the Hogrefe web site. Almost all of these movies are "positive psychology films," defined by Niemiec (2007) as movies that offer (a) a balanced portrayal of a character displaying at least one of the 24 strengths; (b) depiction of obstacles and/or the struggle or

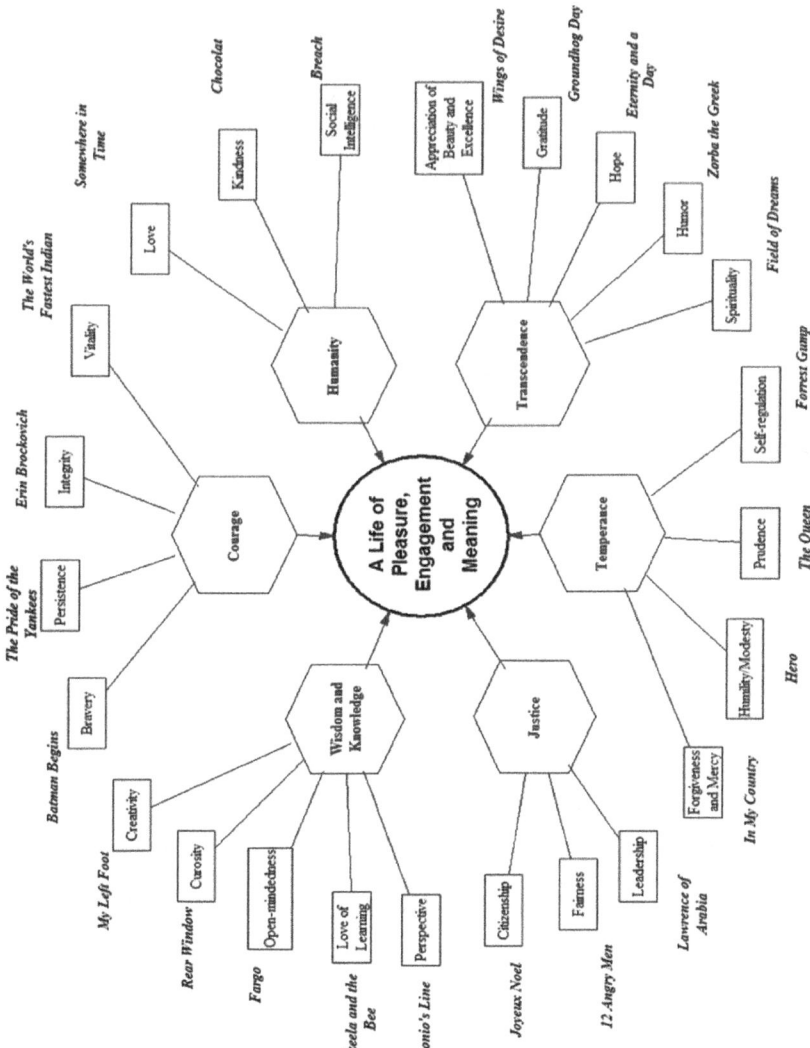

Fig. 1 Character Strengths and Virtues: A Life of Pleasure, Engagement and Meaning

conflict the character faces in reaching or maximizing the strength; (c) a character portrayal that illustrates how to overcome obstacles and/or build and maintain the strength; and (d) a tone or mood that is inspiring or uplifting.

These are movies that produce "cinematic elevation." Jonathan Haidt is the scholar who has written most eloquently about the emotion of "elevation"; he notes, "Elevation is elicited by acts of virtue or moral beauty; it causes warm, open feelings ('dilation') in the chest; and it motivates people to behave more virtuously themselves" (2003, p. 276).

I'm convinced that films offer an unparalleled way of experiencing cinematic elevation and exposing oneself to characters who can serve as powerful role models, illustrating virtues and character strengths and helping us all become more fully functioning people.

References

Bandura, A. (1977). *Social learning theory*. New York: General Learning Press.

Campbell, L. F., & Smith, T. P. (2003). Integrating self-help books into psychotherapy. *Journal of Clinical Psychology, 59*, 177–186.

Haidt, J. (2003). Elevation and the positive psychology of morality. In C. L M. Keyes & J. Haidt (Eds.), *Flourishing: Positive psychology and the life well-lived* (pp. 275–289). Washington, DC: American Psychological Association.

Maslow, A. H. (1968). *Toward a psychology of being* (2nd ed.). Oxford, England: Van Nostrand.

Niemiec, R. M. (2007). What is a positive psychology film? *PsycCRITIQUES, 52*, No Pagination Specified.

Niemiec, R. M., & Wedding, D. (2008). *Positive psychology at the movies: Using films to build virtues and character strengths*. Ashland, OH: Hogrefe.

Norcross, J. C. (2006). Integrating self-help into psychotherapy: 16 practical suggestions. *Professional Psychology: Research and Practice, 37*, 683–693.

Peterson, C., & Seligman, M. E. P. (2004). *Character strengths and virtues: A handbook and classification*. New York: Oxford University Press.

Rogers, C. R. (1963). The concept of the fully functioning person. *Psychotherapy: Theory, Research & Practice, 1*, 17–26.

Seligman, M. E. P., & Csikszentmihalyi, M. (2000). Positive psychology: An introduction. *American Psychologist, 55*, 5–14.

Seligman, M. E. P., Rashid, T., & Parks, A. C. (2006). Positive psychotherapy. *American Psychologist, 61*, 774–788.

Wedding, D., & Niemiec, R. M. (2003). The clinical use of films in psychotherapy. *Journal of Clinical Psychology, 59*, 207–215.

Film Reference List – Compiled by Mary Banks Gregerson

Abed II, R. (Director; Producers, J, D., Abed II, R., & Staggs, A.; 2007). *Black dahlia* [Film]. Los Angeles, CA: Universal Pictures.

Abu-Assad, H. (Director & Writer; Producer & Writer, Beyer, B.; Producers, Harel, A., Meixner, G., Panahi, H., & Paul, R.; 2005). *Paradise now* [Film]. Burbank, CA: Augustus Film.

Ackerman, A., Cherones, T., Steinberg, D., & Trainer, D. O. (Directors; Producers, Kaiser, T., Shapiro, G., West, H., Seinfeld, J., Mamann-Greenberg, S., David, L., Mehlman, P., Gammill, T., Pross, M., Cherones, T., Charles, L., Scheinman, A., Berg, A., Schaffer, J., Ackerman, A., Gross, M., Barron, F., Kass, S. H., & Stott, J.; 1990-1998). *Seinfeld* [TV series]. Beverly Hills, CA: Castle Rock Entertainment.

Adamson, A., & Jenson, V. (Directors; Producers, Katzenberg, J., Warner, A., Williams, J. H.; 2001). *Shrek* [Film]. Glendale, CA: DreamWorks Animation.

Adamson, A., Asbury, K., & Vernon, C. (Director & Writer; Directors; Producers, Lipman, D., Warner, A., & Williams, J. H.; 2004). *Shrek 2*. Glendale, CA: DreamWorks Animation.

Alda, A. (Director & Writer; Producer, Bregman, M;1981). *Four seasons* [Film]. Universal City, CA: Universal Pictures.

Alea, T. G., & Tabío, J. C. (Directors; Producers, Balzeretti, G., & Cabrera, F.; 1994). *Strawberry and chocolate. Fresa y chocolate* [Film]. West Hollywood, CA: Miramax Films.

Alexandrowicz, R. (Director/Writer; Producer, Harel, A.; 2003). *James' journey to Jerusalem* [Film]. Tel Aviv, Israel: Lama Productions.

Allen, C. (Director; Producers, Freeman, L.; 1974). *Cry rape* [Film]. Norwalk, CT: Leonard Freeman Productions.

Allen, W. (Director & Writer; Producers, Joffe, C. H., & Rollins, J.; 1997). *Annie Hall* [Film]. Los Angeles, CA: Rollins-Joffe Productions.

Allen, W. (Director & Writer; Producer, Greenhut, R.; 1989). *Crimes and misdemeanors* [Film]. New York, NY: Orion Pictures Corporation.

Allen, W. (Director & Writer; Producers, Aronson, L., Darwin, L., & Wiley, G.; 2005). *Match point* [Film]. London, England: BBC Films.

Allen, W. (Director & Writer; Producers, Aronson, L., Tenebaum, S., & Wiley, G.; 2008). *Vicky Cristina Barcelona* [Film]. New York, NY: Gravier Productions.

Almond, P.. (Director; Producer; Hewatt, T.; 1964). *Seven Up!* [TV documentary]. NY: First Run Features.

Altman, R. (Director & Writer; Producer, Brokaw, S.; 1993). *Short cuts* [Film]. Culver City, CA: Avenue Picture Productions.

Altman, R. (Director; Producers, Boeken, L., & Heyter, E.; 1990). *Vincent and Theo*. Century City, CA: Arena Films.

Amenábar, A. (Producer, Director, Writer, Composer, & Editor; Producer, Bovaira, F.; 2004). *The sea inside* [Film]. Madrid, Spain: Sogepaq.

Anderson, W. (Producer, Director, & Writer; Producers, Mendel, B., & Rudin, S.; 2001). *The royal tennenbaums* [Film]. New York, NY: American Empirical Pictures.

Anderson, S. M., & Anderson, S. (Directors; Producers, Stone, O., Spielberg, M., Gilbert, B. M.; 1992). *Crips, South Central* [Film]. Los Angeles, CA: Enchantment Films.

András, F. (Director; Producer Managers, Csernai, J., & Elek, A.; 1985). *The greatest generation. A nagy generáció* [Film]. Budapest, Hungary: Mokép.

Antonijevic, P. (Director; Producers, Stone, O., & Wilson, I.; 2003) *Savior* [Film]. Santa Monica, CA: Initial Entertainment Group.

Antonioni, M., Soderbergh, S., & Wong, K. W. (Directors & Writers; Producers, Guerra, T., Bar, J., Berdugo, Jacobs, G., Procacci, D., Gadjieff, S. T., & Wah, J. P. Y.; 2004). *Eros: The dangerous thread of things/Equilibrium/The hand* [Film]. Paris, France: Roissy Films.

Apted, M. (Director; Producer, Foster, J. & Missel, R; 1994). *Nell* [Film]. Torrance, CA; Egg Productions.

Apted, M. / Apted, M. / Apted, M., / Apted, M. / Apted, M. / Apted, M. (Producer & Director/Producer & Director / Producer & Director / Producer & Director / Producer & Director / Producer & Director; 1970 / 1977 / 1984 / 1991 / 1998 / 2005). *Seven + seven UP/21 UP/ 28 UP/ 42 UP! / 49 UP!* [TV documentary]. NY: First Run Features.

Aranda, V. (Director & Writer; Producer, Cerezo, E.; 2001). *Mad love* [Film]. Madrid, Spain: Canal + Espana.

Arau, A. (Producer & Director; 1992). *Like water for chocolate* [Film]. West Hollywood, CA: Arau Films Internacional.

Arcand, D. (Director & Writer; Producers, Louis, D., & Robert, D.; 2003). *The barbarian invasions* [Film]. Marina del Ray, CA: Astral Films.

Ardolino, E. (Director; Producers, Cannold, M., Reuther, S., Gottlieb, L.; 1987). *Dirty dancing* [Film]. Los Angeles, CA: Great American Limited Partnership.

Arkush, A. (Director; Producer, Rosen, A.; 1997). *Elvis meets Nixon* [Film]. Los Angeles, CA: Showtime Networks.

Armendáriz, M. (Directer & Writer; Producer, Santana, A.; 1997). *Secrets of the heart* [Film]. Madrid, Spain: Aiete Films S.A.

Aro, H., Eriksson, A., Glansén, K., Hylin, M., Jankert, J., Leinstedt, C., Lindberg, A., & Olsson, M. (Producers; 1997 to present). *Expedition Robinson* [TV reality series]. Stockholm, Sweden: Strix Television AB.

Ashby, H. (Director; Producer, Higgins, C., & Mulvehill, C. B.; 1971). *Harold and Maude* [Film]. Los Angeles, CA: Paramount Pictures.

Ashby, J. (Director; Producers, Hellman, J., & Gilbert, T.; 1978). *Coming home* [Film'. Beverly Hills, CA: Jerome Hellman Productions.

Attenborough, R. (Producer & Director; 1982). *Gandhi* [Film]. Culver City, CA: Carolina Bank.

Attenborough, R. (Director & Producer; & Producer, Eastman, B.; 1993). *Shadowlands* [Film]. Los Angeles, CA: Price Entertainment.

August, B. (Director; Producer, Holst, P.; 1987). *Pelle the conqueror. Pelle erobreren* [Film]. New York, NY: Per Holst Filmproduktion.

Avidsen, J. G. (Director; Producers, Chartoff, R., & Crabe, J.; 1976). *Rocky* [Film]. Los Angeles, CA: Chartoff Winkler Productions.

Avnet, J. (Director; Producer, Kerner, J.; 1991). *Fried green tomatoes* [Film]. Burbank, CA: Act III Communications.

Axel, G. (Director; Producers, Betzer, J., Christensen, B., & Kastholm Hansen, C.; 1997). *Babette's feast. Babet's gastebud* [Film]. New York, NY: New Yorker Films.

Ayers, T. (Director; Producer, Watts, L; 2002). *Walking on water* [Film]. Darlinghurst, Australia: Porchlight Films.

Ayouch, N. (Director; Producer, Cotton, J.; 2000). *Ali Zora: Prince of street [Ali Zaoua, prince de la rue;* Film]. Los Angeles, CA: 2 M Productions.

Babenco, H. (Director & Writer; Producer, Naves, S.; 1981). *Pixote* [Film]. Sao Paolo, Brazil: Embrafilme.

Bailly, P. (Director; Producer, Sarde, A., 2001). *God is great and I'm not* [Film]. Paris, France: Canal.

Bailey, R., Moore, C., Scott, O., von Ancken, D., Barba, N., Hemingway, A., Sarafian, D., Glassner, J., Clark, D., DePaul, St., Zakrzewski, A., Lautanen, S., Adamns, M., Hunt, j. G., Grossman, D., Estevez, E., Thomas, J. T., & Jackson, D. (Directors; Producers, Bruckheimer, J., Littman, J., Zuiker, A. E., Veasey, p., Cannon, D., Lenkov, P. M., Donahue, A., Mendelsohn, C., Sinise, G., Williams, V., Lipsitz, A., Talbert, E., Callaway, T., Bailey, R., Hemwall, G., Barkley, S. A., Kligman, B., Sarafian, D., Reiter, Z., Simon, R. D., Golin, B., & Smith, E.; 2004 to present). *Crime scene investigation: New York* [TV series]. Toronto, ON, Canada: Alliance Atlantis Communications.

Balsmeyer, J. (Director; Producers, Hughes, C., Baldwin, H., & Baldwin, N.; 2003). *Danny Deckchair* [Film}. Queensland, Australia: Crusader Entertainment.

Bamford, M. & Bamford, S. K. (Directors; Producers, Kay II, S., Hofmeyr, G., & Bamford, S. K.; 2004). *Cape of Good Hope* [Film]. Los Angeles, CA: Wonder View Films.

Barratier, C. (Director & Writer; Producers, Cohn, A., Mauvernay, N., & Perrin, J.; 2004). *The chorus. Les choristes.* Zurich, Switzerland: Vega Film.

Bartlett, H. (Producer, Director, & Writer; 1973). *Jonathan Livingston Seagull* [Film]. Los Angeles, CA: Paramount Pictures.

Bay, M. (Director; Producers, Bryce, I., DeSanto, T., di Bonaventure, L., & Murphy, D., 2007). *Transformers* [Film]. Universal City, CA: DreamWorks SKG.

Beineix, J. (Director; Producers, Ossard, C., Beineix. J., & Beineix, J.; 1986). *Betty blue. 37° 2 le matin* [Film]. Los Angeles, CA: Sony Pictures.

Beineix, J. (Director & Writer; Producer, Klooss, R.; 2001). *Mortal transfer* [Film]. Paris, France: Canal+.

Benigni, R. (Director & Writer; Producers, Braschi, G., Davis, J. M., & Ferri, E.; 1997). *Life is beautiful* [Film]. West Hollywood, CA: Cecchi Gori Group Tiger Cinemagrafica.

Benton, R. (Director & Writer; Producer, Jaffe, S. R.; 1979). *Kramer vs. Kramer* [Film]. Culver City, CA: Columbia Pictures Corporation.

Benton, R. (Director & Writer; Producer, Donovan, A.; 1984). *Places in the heart* [Film]. Culver City, CA: Delphi II Productions.

Bergman, I. (Director & Writer; Producer, Donner, J.; 1982). *Fanny and Alexander* [Film]. Stockholm, Sweden: Cinematograph AB.

Bergman, I. (Producer, Director, & Writer; 1966). *Persona* [Film]. Stockholm, Sweden: Svensk Filmindustri.

Bergman, I. (Director & Writer; Producer, Carlsberg, L.; 1973). *Scenes from a marriage* [Film]. New York, NY: Criterion Collection.

Bergman, I. (Director & Writer; Producer, Ekelund, A.;1957). *Wild strawberries* [Film]. S Stockholm,Sweden: Svensk Filmindustri (SF).

Bertolucci, B. (Director & Writer; Producer, Grimaldi, A.; 1972). *Last tango in Paris* [Film]. New York, NY: Produzioni Europee Associati.

Bertolucci, B. (Director & Writer; Producer, Thomas, J.; 1993). *Little Buddha* [Film]. West Hollywood, CA: CiBy2000.

Bertolucci, B. (Director & Writer; Producer, Bertolucci, G.; 1979). *Luna* [Film]. Los Angeles, CA: Fiction Cinematografica S. P. A.

Bertolucci, B. (Director & Writer; Producer, Thomas, J.; 1987). *The last emperor* [Film]. Culver City, CA: Yanco Films Limited.

Besson, L. (Director & Writer; 1990). *La femme Nikita* [Film]. Neuilly-sur-Seine, France: Gaumont.

Bezucha, T. (Director & Writer; Producer, London, M.; 2005). *The family Stone* [Film]. Los Angeles, CA: Family Stone.

Bird, A. (Director; Producers, Faber, G., & Ward, J.; 1994). *Priest* [Film]. West Hollywood, CA: Miramax Films.

Boe, C. (Director & Writer; Producer, Pfeiffer, T. G.; 2003). *Reconstruction* [Film]. New York, NY: Director's Cut.

Bogdanovich, P. (Director & Writer; Producer, Friedman, S. J.; 1971). The *last picture show* [Film]. Culver City, CA: Columbia Pictures.

Bogdanovich, P. (Producer & Director; Producer, Marshall, F. ; 1973). *Paper moon* [Film]. Los Angeles, CA: The Director's Company.

Bollain, I. (Director & Writer; Producer, de Leániz, S. G.; 2003). *Take my eyes* [Film]. New York, NY: Alta Produción.

Boorman, J. (Producer, Director, & Writer; Producers, Eberts, J., & Gross, E. F.; 1987). *Hope and glory* [Film]. Culver City, CA: Columbia Pictures Corporation.

Boorman, J. (Producer & Director; Producer, Chartoff, A., Corrigan, K., Hendee, L., Medavoy, M., & Deasy, S.; 2004). *In My Country* [Film]. Santa Monica, CA: Chartoff Productions.

Boyle, D. (Director; Producer, MacDonald, A.;1996). *Trainspotting* [Film]. London, UK: Channel Four Films

Bresson, R. (Director; Producer, Nouvelles Éditions de Films; 1956). *A man escaped. Un condamné à mort s'est échappé ou Le vent souffle où il veut* [Film]. Paris, France: Nouvelles Éditions de Films.

Bretherton, H. (Director; Producer, Sherman, H.; 1935). *Hopalong Cassidy* [Film]. Los Angeles, CA: Harry Sherman Productions.

Brickman, P. (Director & Writer; Producers, Avnet, J., & Tisch, S.; 1983). *Risky business* [Film]. Burbank, CA: Geffen Productions.

Brooks, A. (Director & Writer; Producers, Bing, S., & Nanas, H.; 2005). *Looking for comedy in a Muslim world* [Film]. Burbank, CA: Seventh Picture Productions LLC.

Brooks, J. (Producer & Director; 1997). *As good as it gets* [Film]. Los Angeles, CA: Sony Pictures.

Brooks, S. (Director; Producer, Maslin, S.; 2003). *Japanese story* [Film]. Amsterdam, The Netherlands: Fortissimo Films.

Brunel, L. (Director; Producer, Silberman, S.; 2001). *That obscure object of desire. Cet obscur objet du désir* [Film]. New York, NY: Greenwich Film Productions.

Butler, G. (Producer & Director; 2000). *The endurance* [Documentary]. Silver Springs, MD: Discovery Channel Pictures.

Butterworth, J., Lubarsky, A., Sleeth, L., (Director & Cinematographer; Director & Editor; Director & Cinematographer; 2004). *Seoul train* [Documentary]. Denver, CO: Incite Films.

Cameron, J. (Producer, Director, Writer, & Editor; Producer, Landau, J.; 1997). *Titanic* [Film]. Los Angeles, CA: Twentieth Century-Fox Film Corporation.

Campanella, J. J. (Director & Writer; Producers, Besuievski, M., Blanco, F., Bossi, F., Herreo, G., & Mora, J.E.; 2001). *Son of bride* [Film]. Culver City, CA: Columbia TriStar Pictures.

Campion, J. (Director; Malick, T., 1990). *An angel at my table* [Film]. Sydney, Australia: Australian Broadcasting Corporation.

Campion, J. (Director & Writer; Producer, Maynard, J.; 1989). *Sweetie* [Film]. Culver City, CA: Arenafilm.

Campion, J. (Director & Writer; Producer, Chapman, J.; 1993). *The piano* [Film]. Woolloomooloo, Australia: Australian Film Commission.

Capra, F. (Producer & Director; 1946). *It's a wonderful life* [Film]. Los Angeles, CA: Liberty Films.

Cardoso, P. (Director; Producer & Writer, LaVoo, G.; & Producer, Brown, E; 2002). *Real women have curves* [Film]. Los Angeles, CA: HBO Independent Productions.

Caro, M. (Production Designer, Director, & Writer; Producers, Dutertre, F., Hebrero, M. V., Lopez, J. L., Mas, A., Novak, S., Ossard, C., & Rabes, F.; 1995). *The City of Lost Children* [Film]. New York, NY: Club d'Investissement Média.

Caro, N. (Director & Writer; Producers, Gavin, B., & Knowlton, L. G.; 2002). *Whale rider* [Film}. Neubiberg, Germany: ApolloMedia.

Carrera, C. (Director; Producer, Ripstein, D. R., & Ripstein, A.; 2002). *The crime of Father Amaro* [Film]. Mexico City, Mexico: Alameda Films.

Carter, T. (Director; Producers, Cort, R. W., & Madden, D.; 2001). *Save the last dance* [Film]. Los Angeles, CA; MTV Films.

Cates, G. (Producer & Director; 1970). *I never sang for my father* [Film]. Culver City, CA: Columbia Pictures Corporation.

Chachine, Y., Gitaï, A., Iñárritu, A. G., Imamura, S., Lelouch, C., Loach, K., Makhmalbaf, M., Nair, M., Ouedraogo, I., Penn, S., & Tanovic, D., (Director & Writer; Director; Director, Producer, & Writer; Director; Director & Writer; Director & Writer; Director & Writer; Director; Director & Writer; Director & Writer; & Director & Writer; 2002). *September 11* [Film]. New York, NY: CIH Shorts.

Chappelle, J., Lautanen, S., Gaviola, K., Hill, S., Sarafian, D., Egilsson, E., Clark, D., Beesley, M. E., Lamar, G., Grossman, D., Glassner, J., Yaitanes, G., Correll, C., Keller, F. K., Barba, N., Meyer, C., & Cannon, D. (Directors; Producers, Bruckheimer, J., Devine, E., Donahue, A., Lamar, G., Littman, J., Mendelsohn, C., Zuiker, A. E., Nayar, S., Tardino, D., Hill, S., Cannon, D., Maeda, S., Chappelle, J., Egilsson, E., Dube, M., Miller, C. D., Modrovich, I., Shiffman, S., Black, M., Miller, N., Stangis, S., Black, D., & Zito, S.; 2002 to present). *Crime scene investigation: Miami* [TV series]. Los Angeles, CA: CBS Productions.

Ciminio, M. (Producer, Director, & Writer; Producers, Deeley, M., Peveral, J., & Spikings, B.; 1978). *The deer hunter* [Film]. Universal City, CA: Universal Pictures.

Christiansen, R., Kendall, D., Correll, R., Margolin, J., Flynn, S., Savage, F., Chemel, L. S. , & Cendrowski, M. (Directors; Producers, Peterman, S., Poryes, M., & King, R. G.; 2006 to present). *Hannah Montana* [TV series]. Burbank, CA: Disney Channel.

Clark, B. (Producer, Director & Writer; Producer, Dupont, R; 1983). *A Christmas story* [Film]. Los Angeles, CA: Metro-Goldwyn-Mayer (MGM).

Claxton, W. F., Allen, L., Benson, L., McDougall, D., Witney, W., Nyby, C., Landon, M., Florea, J., Penn, L., Daugherty, H., Oswald, G., Richardson, D., Altman, R., Wjard, W., Garnett, T., Golden, M., Springsteen, R.G., Daves, D., Pevney, J., Black, R. E., Neilson, J., Rich, J., Vogel, V. W., Kane, J., Landres, P., Haas, C. F., Lubin, A., Moder, D., Friend, R. L., Daniels, M., Leacock, P., Yarbrough, J. P., Carr, T., Faralla, W. D., Nadel, A. H., McEveety, B., Totten, R., Mayer, G., Webster, N., Colasnto, N., & Kjellin, A. (Directors; Producers, Dortort, D., Lane, J. W., Thompson, T., Collins, R., Blees, R., Hawkins, J., & Stillman, R., 1959-1973). *Bonanza* [TV series]. Burbank, CA: National Broadcasting Corporation.

Clayton, J. (Director; Producer, Merrick, D., 1974). *The great Gatsby* [Film]. Los Angeles, CA: Paramount Pictures.

Cohen, G., Day, L., Bearse, A., Orender, S. W., Singletary, T., Samuels, M K., Cottrell, R., & Smith, A. (Directors; Producers, Move, M. G., Green, K., Leavitt, R., Anderson, J. M., Lipp, S., Gurman, R., Fogle, E. L., Weiskopf, K., Curran, K., Sprung, S., Vosburgh, M., Eells, P., & Gordon, M. Z.; 1987-1997). *Married with children* [TV series]. Beverly Hills, CA: Fox Network.

Colombani, L. (Director; Producer, Gassot, C.; 2002). *He loves me, he loves me not* [Film]. New York, NY: Cofimage.

Columbus, C. (Director; Producer, Heyman, D.; 2002). *Harry Potter and the Chamber of secrets* [Film]. Burbank, CA: 1492 Pictures

Columbus, C. (Director; Producer, Heyman, D.; 2001). *Harry Potter and the sorcerer's stone* [Film]. Burbank, CA: 1492 Pictures.

Columbus, C. (Director; Producer, Hughes, J.; 1990). *Home alone* [Film]. Los Angeles, CA: Twentieth Century-Fox Film Corporation.

Columbus, C. (Director; Producer & Writer, Hughes, J.; 1992). *Home alone 2: Lost in New York* [Film]. Los Angeles, CA: Twentieth Century-Fox Film Corporation.

Columbus, C. (Producer & Director; Producers, Barnathan, M., De Niro, R., Radcliffe, M., & Rosenthal, J.; 2005). *Rent* [Film]. Culver City, CA: Rent Productions LLC.

Columbus, C. (Producer & Director; Producers, Barnathan, M., Bass, R., Finerman, W., Isaac, M. F., McCormick, P, Porter, P., Radcliffe, M., Roberts, J., & Saradon, S.; 1998). *StepMom* [Film]. Burbank, CA: 1492 Pictures.

Cooper, H., Senensky, R., Bixby, B., Komack, J., Falk, H., Nelson, G., Weis, D., & Sweeney, B. (Directors; Producers, Komack, J. & Riskin, R.; 1969-1972). *The courtship of Eddie's father* [TV series]. Los Angeles, CA: MGM Television.

Coppolla, S. (Producer, Director, & Writer; 2006). *Marie Antoinette* [Film]. Culver City, CA: Columbia Pictures Corporation.

Corbijn, A. (Director; Producers, Canning, I., Ishii, A., & Marshall, K.; 2003). *Control* [Film]. New Castle, New Zealand: 3 Dogs and a Pony.

Costas-Gravas. (Director; Producers, d'Argila, P., & Schlumberger, E.; 1969). *Z* [Film]. Paris, France: Office National pour le Commerce et l'Industrie Cinématographique.

Costner, K., Huneck, J., & Pfeiffer, P. C. (Directors; Producers, Eberts, J., Wilson, J., & Costner, K.; 1990). *Dances With Wolves* [Film]. Burbank, CA: Tig Productions.

Costner, K. (Producer & Director; Producers, Tisch, S., & Wilson, J.; 1997). *The postman* [Film]. Burbank, CA: Tig Productions.

Cox, P. (Producer, Director, & Writer; Producer, Ballantyne, J.; 1984). *My first wife* [Film]. Queensland, Australia: Dofine Productions.

Cox, P. (Director, Writer, Cintematographer, & Editor; Producer, Llewellyn-Jones, T.; 1987). *Vincent* [Film]. San Francisco, CA: Daska.

Craven, W. (Director; Producers, Konrad, C., & Woods, C.;1996). *Scream* [Film]. New York, NY: Dimension Films.

Cronenberg, D. (Producer & Writer; Producers, Bailey, C. & Hadida, S.; 2002). *Spider* [Film]. London, UK: Capitol Films.

Crowe, C. (Producer & Director; 2000). *Almost famous* [Film]. Los Angeles, CA: DreamWorks.

Crowe, C. (Director & WRiter; Producer, Platt, P.; 1989). *Say anything* [Film]. Culver City, CA: Gracie Films.

Crystal, B. (Producer, Director, & Writer; Producer, Schlinder, P.; 1995). *Forget Paris* [Film]. Beverly Hills, CA: Castle Rock Entertainment.

Cuarón, A. (Director; Producers, Aguero, S., Linde, D., Kaufman, A., & Vergara, J.,). (2001). *And,your mother, too [Y tu Mama Tambien*; Film]. Los Angeles, CA: Icon Film Distribution.

Cuarón, A. (Director; Producers, Bliss, T., Bernstein, A., & Shor, H.; 2006). *Children of men* [Film]. Los Angeles, CA: Universal Pictures.

Cuarón, A. (Director; Producers, Columbus, C., Heyman, D., Orleans, L., & Radcliffe, M.; 2004). *Harry Potter and the prisoner of Azkaban* [Film]. Burbank, CA: Warner Bros. Pictures.

Cukor, G./ Castellanni, R./Zeferelli, F./ Luhrmann, B. (Director; Producer, Thalberg, I; 1936/ Director & Writer; Producer, Ghenzi, S., & Janni, J.; 1954/ Director & Writer; Producers, Brabourne, J., Havelock-Allen, A., 1968/ Producer, Director & Writer; Producer, Martinelli, G.; 1996). *Romeo and Juliet* [Film]. Los Angeles, CA: The Rank Organisation/ Los Angeles, CA: Metro-Goldwyn-Mayer (MGM)/ Los Angeles, CA: BHE Films/ Los Angeles, CA: Bazmark Films.

Curran, J. (Director; Producers, Colleton, J., Fonlupt, F., Norton, E., Watts, N., & Yari, B.; 2006). *The painted veil* [Film]. Burbank, CA: Warner Independent Pictures.

Curtiz, M. (Director; Producer, Wallis, H. B.; 1942). *Casablanca* [Film]. Burbank, CA: Warner Bros. Pictures.

Daldry, S. (Director; Producer,s Wharton, N., Brand, C., & Ross, T.; 2000). *Billy Elliot* [Film]. Los Angeles, CA: Universal Pictures.

Daldry, S. (Director; Producers, Fox, R., & Rudin, S.; 2002). *The hours* [Film]. Los Angeles, CA: Paramount Pictures.

Dardenne, J. & Dardenne, L. (Producers, Directors, & Writes; Producer, Freyd, D.; 2005). *The Child* [Film]. New York, NY: Les Filmes de Fleuve.

Davaa, B. (Director & Writer; Director, Writer, & Cinematographer, Falomi, L. ;& Siebert, T.; 2003). *The story of the weeping camel* [Documentary]. Munich, Germany: Hochschule für Fernsehen und Film München (HFF).

Davis, T. (Director; Producers, Toffler, V., Gale, D., & Calder, C.; 2002). *Crossroads* [Film]. Los Angeles, CA: Paramount Pictures.

Debrauwer, L. (Director & Writer; Producer, Janne, D.; 2001). *Pauline and Paulette* [Film]. New York, NY: Canal.

de Felitta, R. (Director & Writer; Producers, Harrision, A., & Klingenstein, A.; 2000). *Two family house* [Film]. New York, NY: Filbert Steps Productions.

del Toro, G. (Producer, Director, & Writer; Producers, Augustin, Á., Cuarón, A., Navarro, B., & Torresblanco, F.; 2006). *Pan's labyrinth* [Film]. New York, NY: Esperanto Filmoj.

Demme, J. (Producer & Director; Producer, Saxon, E.; 1993). *Philadelphia* [Film]. Culver City, CA: Clinica Estetito.

Demme, J. (Director; Producers, Goetzman, G., Saxon, E., & Utt, K.; 1991). *Silence of the lambs.* New York, NY: Orion Pictures.

de Palma, B. (Producer, Director, & Writer; Producer, Gottfried, H.; 1984). *Body double* [Film]. Culver City, CA: Columbia Pictures Corporation.

Derrington, R. (Director; Producer, Silver, J.; 1999). *Road house* [Film]. Los Angeles, CA: ilver Pictures.

De Sica, V. (Director & Writer; Producer, Arnato, G.; 1948). *The bicycle thief. Ladri de biciclette* [Film]. Rome, Italy: Produzioni De Sica

deVito, D. (Director; Producers, Brooks, J. L., & Milchan, A.; 1989). *War of the Roses* [Film]. Culver City, CA: Gracie Films.

Dey, T. (Director; Producers, Aversano, S., & Rudin, S; 2006). *Failure to launch* [Film]. Los Angeles, CA: Paramount Pictures.

DiNapoli, V., Simon, L., squires, E., Clash, K., Diego, K., May, T., Martin, J., Gordon, D., Guadarrama, T., Mazzarino, J., Feldman, S., Zylstra, N., Dilworth, J., Stone, J., Henson, J., Broder, T., Saks, E., Balsmeyer, R., DeSeve, M., Lathan, S., & Schwarz, B. (Directors; Producers, Clash, K., Carter, T., Dino, M., Parente, C., Rosa, R., Lehmann, B., Bernstein, L., de Sena, D., Jalacoi, K., Chadderdon, A., James, T. E., Whaley, C., Cunniff, R., Miller, C., Stone, J., Singer, D., Mayes, C., Broder, T., Saks, E., Burgund, A., Connell, D. D. , Cooney, J. G., Dallard, S. , Elias-Bamberger, N., Garfinkel, S., Kirbyson, R., Klugman, l., Lee, H., B., Murphy, M., Rogoff, L., & Zornow, E.;1969 to present). *Sesame Street* [TV series]. New York, NY: Children's Television Workshop (CTW).

Doillon, J. (Director & Writer; Producer, Sarde, A.; 1996). *Ponette* [Film]. Issys Mollineaux, France: Les Films Alain Sarde.

Donaldson, R. (Producer, Director, & Writer; Producer, Hannam, G.; 2005). *World's fastest Indian* [Film]. Wellington, New Zealand: New Zealand Film Commission.

Donner, R. (Director; Producer, Bernard, H.; 1976). The *omen* [Film]. Los Angeles, CA; Twentieth Century-Fox Productions.

Dupeyron, F. (Director; Producers, Pétin, L. & Pétin, R.; 2003). *Monsieur Ibrahim* [Film]. Paris, France: ARP Sélection.

Eastwood, C. (Producer & Director; Producer, Kennedy, K.; 1995). *Bridges of Madison County* [Film]. Universal City, CA: Amblin Entertainment.

Eastwood, C. (Producer & Director; Producer, Lazar, A.; 2000). *Space* cowboys [Film]. Burbank, CA: Mad Chance.

Eaton, I. (Director; Producers, Oppenheimer, P., VanZandt, J., & Eastwood, A.; 2005). *Don't tell. La bestia nel cuore.* Rome, Italy: Cattleya.

Edel, U. (Director; Kaden, H.H., Eichinger, B., & Weth, H.; 1981). *Christiane F. wir kinder vom Bahnhof Zoo.* Indianapolis, IN: Solaris Film.

Edwards, B. (Director; Producer, Manulis, M.; 1962). *Days of wine and roses* [Film]. Burbank, CA: Warner Bros. Pictures.

Einhorn, R., Perez, M., & Thomspon, R. T. (Directors; Producers, Sutherland, S., Glazer, M. J., Hurwitz, D. A., Barndt, P., Brown, R., de Mol, J., Herschko, T., Larsen, S., & Shumsky, R.; 2001-2006). *Fear factor* [TV series]. Los Angeles, CA: Endemol Entertainment.

Ephron, N. (Director & Writer; Producer, Foster, G.; 1993). *Sleepless in Seattle* [Film]. Culver City, CA: TriStar Pictures.

Eyre, R. (Director & Writer; Producers, Fox, R., & Rudin, S.;2001/I). *Iris* [Film]. West Hollywood, CA: Miramax Films.

Fairman, D. (Producer & Director; Producer, Skeggs, H.; 2004). *Lighthouse hill* [Film]. London, UK: Carnaby International.

Fall, J. (Director; Producer, Rogow, S.; 2003). *The Lizzie McGuire movie* [Film]. Burbank, CA: Walt Disney Pictures.

Farrelly, B., & Farrelly, P. (Producers, Directors, & Writers; Producer, Thomas, B.; 2000). *Me, myself, and Irene* [Film]. Santa Monica, CA: Conundrum Entertainment.

Farrelly, P, Farrelly, B., & Klausner II, J. (Directors, Producers, Thomas, B., Wessler, C. B., & Farrelly, B.; 2001). *Shallow Hal* [Film]. Los Angeles, CA: Twentieth Century-Fox Film Corporation.

Farrelly, B., & Farrelly, P. (Directors & Writers; Producers, Steinberg, M., Thomas, B., & Wessler, C. B.; 1998). *There's Something About Mary* [Film]. Los Angeles, CA: Twentieth Century-Fox Film Corporation.

Fassbinder, R. W. (Director & Writer; Producer, Schüly, T.; 982). *Veronika Voss* [Film]. Berlin, Germany: Laura Films.

Figgis, M. (Director & Writer; Producer, Cazès, L.; 1995). *Leaving Las Vegas* [Film]. Century City, CA: MGM Home Entertainment.

Filoni, D. (Director; Producer & Writer, Lucas, G., Producer, Winder, K.; 2008). *Star Wars: The clone wars* [Film]. Nicasio, CA: Lucasfilm.

Fink, K., Lewis, R. J., Cannon, D., Hunt, J. G., Smight, A., Grossman, D., Clark, D., Eagles, B., O'Hara, T., Antonio, L., Wright, T. J., Correll, C., Markle, P., Sarafian, D., Slovis, M., Tanenbaum, B., Beesley, M. E., Bailey, R., Tarantino, Q., Coolidge, M., Leitch, C., & Barclay, P. (Directors; Producers, Bruckheimer, J., Littman, J., Mendelsohn, C., Chvatal, C., Petersen, W., Donahue, A., Zuiker, A. E., Fink, K., Shankar, N., Milito, L. S., Cannon, D., Felder, S., Berman, J., Lipsitz, A., Goldfinger, S., Golin, B., Abraham, D., Rambo, D., Myers, H. A., Laramie, B., Catalani, R., Mitchell, R., & Dunne, P.; 2000 to present). *Crime scene investigation* [TV series]. Santa Monica, CA: Jerry Bruckheimer Television.

Fleming, V. (Director; Producer, Lighton, L. R.; 1937). *Captains courageous* [Film]. Los Angeles, CA: Metro-Goldwyn-Mayer.

Fleming, V. (Director; Producer, Selznick, D. O.; 1939). *Gone with the wind* [Film]. Burbank, CA: Selznick International Pictures.

Fleming, V. (Director; Producer, LeRoy, M.; 1939). *The wizard of Oz* [Film]. Los Angeles, CA: Metro-Goldwyn-Mayer (MGM).

Fleury, P. (Director; 2004). *North Korea: A day in the life* [Documentary]. Los Angeles, CA: Golden Monkey Enterprises.

Ford, J. (Director; Producer, Zanuck, D. F.; 1940). *Grapes of wrath* [Film]. Los Angeles, CA: Twentieth Century-Fox Film.

Ford, J., Hathaway, H., & Marshall, G. (Directors; Producer, Smith, B.; 1962). *How the west was won* [Film]. Los Angeles, CA: Metro-Goldwyn-Mayer (MGM).

Forman, M. (Director; Producers, Douglas, M., & Zaentz, S.; 1975). *One flew over the cuckoo's nest* [Film]. Los Angeles, CA: Fantasy Films.

Fricke, R. (Director, Editor, & Cinematographer; Producer & Editor, Magidson, M.; 1992). *Baraka* [Documentary]. Culver City, CA: Magidson Films.

Frears, S. (Director; Producers, Harries, A., Langan, H., & Seward, T.; 2006). *The queen* [Film]. Burbank, CA: Scott Rudin Productions.

Friedkin, W. (Director; Producer & Writer, Blatty, W. R.; 1973). *The exorcist* [Film]. Burbank, CA: Hoya Productions.

Gandhi, A. (Producer, Director, Writer, Editor, Cinematographer; 2003 short). *Right here, right now* [Film]. Mumbai, India: Cyclewala Productions.

George, T. (Producer & Director; Producer, Ho, A. K.; 2004). *Hotel Rwanda* [Film]. Los Angeles, CA: United Artists.

Geronimi, C., Jackson, W., & Luske, H. / Hogan, P. J. (Directors / Director; Producers, Fisher, L., McCormick, P., Wick, D., & McAlpine, D.; 1953/2003). *Peter Pan* [Film]. Burbank, CA: Walt Disney Productions/ Universal City, CA: Universal Pictures.

Gibson, M., Rodgers, M., & Beesley, M.E. (Directors; Producers, McEveety, S., Gibson, M., & Ladd Jr., A. *Braveheart* [Film]. Los Angeles, CA: Icon Productions.

Gilbert, L. (Producer & Director; Producer, Andrews, A.; 1995). *Haunted* [Film]. New York, NY: October Films.

Gilbert, L. / Shyer, C. (Producer & Director / Producer, Director, & Writer; 1966 / Producer & Writer, Pope; 1966 / 2004). *Alfie* [Film]. Los Angeles, CA: Lewis Gilbert / Los Angeles, CA: Paramount Pictures.

Gilley, J. (Director & Writer; 2004). *Peace one day* [Documentary]. London, UK: Peace One Day, BBC.

Goldberg, G. D. (Director; Producers, Spielberg, S., Marshall, F., & Kennedy, K; 1989). *Dad* [Film]. Universal City, CA: Amblin Entertainment.

Goldsmith, D. (Director & Writer; Producers, Collins, T. & Thomas, K; 2000). *Sally* [Film]. Beverly Hills, CA: Creative Light Worldwide.

Goldwyn T. (Director; Producer, Burke, G., Coote, G., Koenigsberg, N.; 1999). *A walk on the moon* [Film]. New York, NY: Miramax Films.

Gorris, M. (Producer & Director; de Weers, H.; 1995). *Antonia's line* [Film]. Bergen, Norway: Bergen Films Production Company.

Gosnell, R. (Director; Producer & Writer, Huges, J., & Green, H.; 1997). *Home alone 3* [Film]. Los Angeles, CA: Twentieth Century-Fox Film Corporation.

Gosnell, R. (Director; Producers, Nathanson, M., & Simonds, R. ; 2005). *Yours, Mine, and Ours* [Film]. Los Angeles, CA: Time Productions Inc.

Gowers, B., Pritchett, J., Warwick, K., & Drake, S. C. (Directors; Producers, Fuller, S., Frot-Coutaz, C., Balachandran, P., Lythgoe, N., Warwick, K., Lynn, P., Michaels, M., Manulis, J. B., Bresnan, J., Cooper, B., Entz, J., Gaha, N., Jones, S., Jones, T., Lythgoe, S., McNamara, B., & Meyer, A.; 2002 to present). *American idol* [TV reality series]. Burbank, CA: Fremantle Media North.America.

Greenaway, P. (Director & Writer; Producer, Kasander, K; 1989). *The cook, the thief, his wife, and her lover* [Film]. West Hollywood, CA: Allarts Productions.

Greenwald, R. (Director; Producer, Schreder, C.; 1984). *The burning bed* [TV film]. Burbank, CA: Tisch/Avnet Productions.

Guest, V. (Director; Producer, Smith, G.; 1980). *And the band played on* [Film]. Arlington, VA: Public Broadcasting Corporation.

Guit, G. (Director; Producer, Goldman, A.; 2003). *The pact of silence* [Film]. Paris, France: Canal+.

Guttenberg, S. (Producer, Director, & Writer; Producer, Clark, K.A.; 2002). *P.S. Your cat is dead!* [Film]. Philadelphia, PA: Mr. Kirby Productions.

Hackford, T. (Producer & Director; Producers, Mulvehill, C., & Yale, J.; 1995). *Dolores Claiborne* [Film]. Beverly Hills, CA: Castle Rock Entertainment.

Haines, R. (Director; Producer, Ziskin, L.; 1991). *The doctor*. Burbank, CA: Silver Screen Partners IV.

Hallström, L. (Director; Producer, Roth, J., Weinstein, H., & Rhodes, M.; 2005). *An unfinished life* [Film]. New York, NY: Miramax Films.

Hallström, L. (Director; Producers, Brown, D., Golden, K., & Holleran, L.; 2000). *Chocolat* [Film]. West Hollywood, CA: David Brown Productions.

Hallström, L. (Director & Writer; Producer, Bergendahl, W.; 1985). *My life as a dog* [Film]. New York, NY: Film Teknik.

Hallström, L. (Director; Producers, Sylbert, A., & Weinstein, P.; 1995). *Something to talk about* [Film]. Burbank, CA: Hawn/Sylbert Movie Company.

Hallström, L. (Director; Producers, Matalon, D., Ohlsson, B., & Teper, M.; 1993). *What's eating Gilbert Grape* [Film]. Los Angeles, CA: J&M Entertainment.

Halvorson, G., Bright, K., Lembeck, M., Burrows, J., Mancuso, G., Bonerz, P., Schwimmer, D., Weiss, B., Benson, R., Jensen, S., Hughes, T., de Vally Piazza, D., Epps, S., Fryman, P., Myerson, A., Schlamme, T., Zuckerman, S., Christiansen, R. (Directors; Producers, Bright, K., Crane, D., Kauffman, M., Stevens, T., Knoller, W., Goldberg-Meehan, S., Silveri, S., Cohen, T., Reich, A., Malins, G., Chase, A., Bilsing, S., Plummer, E., Buckner, B., Jones, S., Borkow, M., Curtis, M., Calhoun, W., Junge, A., Klein, D., Kunerth, M. J., Carlock, R., Ungerleider, I., & Borns, B.; 1994-2004). *Friends* [TV series]. Burbank, CA: Warner Bros. Television.

Hand, D. (Director; Producer, Walt Disney Productions; 1937). *Snow White and the seven dwarves* [Film]. Burbank, CA: Walt Disney Productions.

Hanes, R., & Palmer, P. (Directors; Producers, Sugarman, B., Palmer, P., & Koethe, C.; 1986). *Children of a lesser God* [Film]. Los Angeles, CA: Paramount Pictures.

Hanson, C. (Producer, Director, & Writer; Producers, Milchan, A., Nathanson, A., & Spinotti, D.; 1997). *L.A. confidential* [Film]. Los Angeles, CA: Regency Enterprises.

Hardwicke, C. (Producer & Director; Producers, Rich, M., van Hellim, T.; 2006). *The Nativity Story* [Film]. Los Angeles, CA: New Line Cinema.

Hardwicke, C. (Director & Writer; Producers, Levy-Hinte, J., & London, M.; 2003). *Thirteen* [Film]. Beverly Hill, CA: Michael London Productions.

Hatland, L. (Director; Producer, Myren, H.; 2005). *How happy can you be?* [Documentary]. Oslo, Norway: Medieoperatrene.

Hawks, H. & Rosson, A. (Producer & Director; Co-Director; Producer, Feldman, C.; 1948). *Red River* [Film]. Beverly Hills, CA: Charles K. Feldman Group.

Heckerling, A. (Director; Producers, Rudin, S., Lawrence, R., & Berg, B.; 1995). *Clueless* [Film]. Los Angeles, CA: Paramount Pictures.

Heckerling, A. (Director; Producer, Simmons, M.; 1985). *National Lampoon's European vacation* [Film]. Burbank, CA: Warner Bros. Pictures.

Hedges, P. (Director & Writer; Producers, Epstein, B., & Shestack, J.; 2007). *Dan in real life* Film]. Burbank, CA: Touchstone Pictures.

Hernández, A. (Director & Writer; Producers, Nolla, J., & Saura, A.; 2002). *The city of no limits En la Ciudad Sin Limites* [Film]. Madrid, Spain: Icónica S. A.

Herschbiegel, O. (Director; Producers, Rothe, C., & Eichinger, B.; 2004). *Downfall. Der Untergang*. München, Germany: Constantin Film Production.

Herzog, W. (Director; Producer, Katz, P. 1972). *Aguirre: The wrath of God [Aguirre: Der Zorn Gottes* Film]. Boston, MA: Starz.

Hess, J. (Director & Writer; Producer & Editor, Coon, J.; Producers, Covel, S. & Wyatt; 2004). *Napoleon Dynamite* [Film]. Santa Monica, CA: Access Films.

Hicks, S. (Director & Writer; Producer, Scott, J.; 1996). *Shine* New York, NY: First Line Features.

Hirschbiegel, O. (Director; Producer, Conrad, M., Preuss, N., & Wildfeuer, F.; 2001). *The experiment* [Film]. Munich, Germany: Fanes Film.

Hoblit, G. (Director; Producer, Luchessi, G.; 1996). *Primal fear* [Film]. Los Angeles, CA: Paramount Pictures.

Hoefer, S., Weissman, A., Grossman, M., Kendall, D., Holland, S. S., Christiansen, R., & Savage, F. (Directors; Producers, O'Dowd, B., Schneider, D., Catania, J., Westerkamp, J., Moore, L., Doty IV, G., Körbelin, J., & Spidell, D.; 2005 to present). *Zoey 101*. Bavaria, Germany: ApolloProScreen Filmproduktion.

Hogan, P. J. (Director; Producer & Writer, Bass, R.; Producer, Zucker, J.; 1997). *My best friend's wedding* [Film]. Culver City, CA: TriStar Productions.

Hogan, P. J. (Directo & Writer; Producer, Fisher, L., McCormick, P., & Wick, D.; 2003). *Peter Pan* [Film]. Universal City, CA: Universal Pictures.

Holland, S. S., de Jarnatt, S., Rosman, M., Williams, A., Montgomery, P., Roberts, B. K., Israel, N., & Carradine, D. (Directors; Producers, Jansen, S. E., Rogow, S., & Danton, J. L.; 2001-2004). *Lizzie McGuire* [TV series]. Los Angeles, CA: Stan Rogow Productions.

Hood, G. (Director & Writer; Producer, Fudakowski, P.; 2005). *Tsotsi* [Film]. London, UK: The UK Film & TV Production Company PLC.

Horsten, M. W. (Director & Writer; Producer, Lense-Mller, L.; 2005 short). *Little daddy* [Film]. Copenhagen, Denmark: Magic Hour Films APS.

Howard, C. (Director; Producer, Susskind, D.; 1970). *Lovers and other strangers* [Film]. Burbank, CA; American Broadcasting Corporation.

Howard, R. (Director; Grazer, B., Producer; 2001). *A beautiful mind* [Film]. Los Angeles, CA: Universal Pictures.

Howitt, P. (Director; Producers, Braithwaite, P., Horberg, W., & Pollack, S.; 1998). *Sliding doors* [Film]. West Hollywood, CA: Miramax Films.

Hudson, H. (Director; Producers, Fayed, D., Puttnam, D., & Crawford, J.; 1981). *Chariots of fire* [Film]. Coral Springs, FL: Engima Productions.

The Hughes Brothers. (Directors; Producer, Scott, D.; 1993). *Menace II society* [Film]. Los Angeles, CA: New Line Cinema.

Hughes, J. (Producer, Director, & Writer; Producer, Colby, R.; 1988). *She's having a baby* [Film]. Los Angeles, CA: Paramount Pictures.

Hughes, J. (Producer, Director, & Writer; Producer, Tannen, N; 1985). *The Breakfast Club* Film]. Universal City, CA: A&M Films.

Huston, J. (Director; Producer & Writer, Fitzgerald, M.; Producer, Fitzgerald, K.; 1979). *Wiseblood* [Film]. Los Angeles, CA: New Line Cinema.

Imamura, S. (Director & Writer; Producer, Nakamura, M.; 2001). *Warm water under the red bridge* [Film]. New York, NY: BAP Inc.

Iñárritu, A. G. (Producer, Director & Writer; Producer, Kilik, J.; 2006). *Babel* [Film]. Los Angeles, CA: Paramount Pictures.

Jackson, P. (Director; Producer, Booth, J.; 1994). *Heavenly Creatures* [Film]. Burbank, CA: Fontana Productions.

Jackson, P. (Producer, Director, & Writer; Producers, Walsh, F., Osborne, B. M., & Sanders, T.; 2001 / Producer, Director, & Writer; Producers, Walsh, F., & Osborne, B. M.; 2002 / Producer, Director, & Writer; Producers, Walsh, F., & Osborne, B. M.; 2002). *The lord of rings: The fellowship of the ring / The lord of rings: The two towers / The lord of the rings: The return of the king* [Film]. Los Angeles, CA: New Line Cinema.

Jacquet, L. (Director & Writer; Producers, Darondeau, Y., Liode, C., & Priou, E.; 2005). *March of the penguins* [Documentary]. Paris, France: Bonne Pioche.

Jacquot, B. (Director & Writer; Producers, Benayoun, G., & Saada, R.; 2004). *Right now* [Film]. New York, NY: Natan Productions.

Jaeckin, J. (Director; Producer, Rousset-Rouard, Y; 1974). *Emmanuele* [Film]. Boulogne-Billancourt, France: Trinacra Films.

Jaeckin, J. (Director ; Producers, Lorin, G., & Rochat, E. ; 1975). *The story of 'O'. Histoire d'O* [Film]. San Dimas, CA : A. D. Creation.

Janglom, H. (Director; Producer Wolinsky, J.; 1990). *Eating* [Film]. Santa Cruz, CA: Jagfilms.

Jaoui, L. (Director; Producer M6 Métropole Télévision; 2002). *The accidental hero* [Film]. Neuilly-sur-Seine, France: M6 Métropole Télévision.

Jarrold, J. (Director; Producers, Bernstein, R., Loader, K., & Rae, D.; 2008). *Brideshead revisited* [Film]. West Hollywood, CA: Miramax Films.

Jeffs, C. (Director & Writer; Campbell, P; 2001). *Rain* [Film]. Edinburgh, Scotland: Communicado Productions.

Jeffs, C. (Director; Producer, Owen, A.; 2003). *Sylvia* [Film]. Universal City, CA: Focus Features.

Jensen, A. T. (Director; Producers, Frederiksen, J., Windelv, V.; 2002). *Open Hearts* [Film]. Copenhagen, Denmark: Det Danske Filminstitut. Jensen, S., Melman, J., Falcon, E., Rogers, R., Vinson, R., Virgil, M. C., Cripe, M., Allen, D., Kraus, R., Walian, W. (Directors; Producers, Walian, W., Jones, Q., Pollack, J., Medina, B., Williams, S., Gard, C., Hervey, W., Borowitz, A., Ray, L., Simon, D. S., Rosenthal, L., Wendle, K., Gurstein, B., Pitlik, D., Williams, M.,

Borowitz, S., Miller, G. H., Boulware, B., Smith, W., & Richburg Jrs., B. R.; 1990-1996). *The fresh prince of Bel-Air* {T series]. Burbank, CA: National Broadcasting Corporation.

Jeunet, J. (Director; Producer, Simkine, A.; 2002/2001). *Amelie* [Film]. Los Angeles, CA: Fox.

Jeunet, J. (Director; Producer, Gerber, B., Finney, A., Puttnam, D.; 2004). *A very long engagement. Un long dimache de fiançailles* [Film]. Los Angeles, CA: Warner Bros.

Joanou, P. (Director; Producers, Witt, P. J., Roven, C., & Thomas, T.; 1992). *Final analysis* [Film]. Burbank, CA: Warner Bros. Pictures.

Jobson, R. (Producer, Director, & Writer; Producer, Burton, M.; 2003). *15 years of alcohol* [Film]. Los Angeles, CA: Tartan Works Ltd.

Jordan, N. (Director; Producers, Invernel, P., McCraken, C., McCarthy, B.; 2005). *Breakfast on Pluto* [Film]. London, England: Pathé Pictures International.

Jordan, N. (Director & Writer; Producers, Morris, R., & Wooley, S.; 1997). *The butcher boy [Film].* Los Angeles, CA: Geffen Productions.

Kalvert, S. (Director; Producers, Blackwell, C., Genetti, D., & Heller, L.; 1995). *Basketball diaries* [Film]. New York, NY: New Line Cinema.

Kalin, T. (Director; Producers, D'Amico, K., & Vachon, C; 2001). *My dark places* [Film]. Santa Monica, CA: Myriad Pictures.

Kanievska, M. (Director; Producers, Avnet, J., & Kerner, J.; 1987). *Less than zero* [Film]. Los Angeles, CA: Twentieth Century-Fox Film Corporation.

Kapadia, A. (Director & Writer; Producer, Faivre, B.; 2001). *The warrior* [Film]. London, UK: The Bureau.

Kaplan, S. (Producer & Director; Producer, Horowitz, S.; 2004). *Three of hearts: A postmodern family* [Documentary]. New York, NY: Hibiscus Films.

Kári, D. (Director, Writer, & Composer; Producers, Bober, P., Ingemann, L., Magnusson, K., Malmquist, S. F., & Sirgurjónsson, . S.; 2003). *Noi the albino* [Film]. Reykjavik, Iceland: Zik Zak Kuvkmyndir.

Kasdan, L. (Producer & Director; Producer, Okun, C. & Roizman, O; 1991). *Grand canyon* [Film]. Los Angeles, CA; Twentieth Century-Fox Film Corporation.

Kasdin, L. (Director & Writer; Producers, Lucas, G., & Gallo, F. T.; 1981). *Body heat* [Film]. Beverly Hills, CA: The Ladd Company.

Kassovitz, M. (Director; Producers, Levin, S., Levin, L., Silver, J., & Zemeckis, R.; 2003). *Gothika* [Film]. Culver City, CA: Columbia Pictures Corporation.

Kastelas, M. (Director; Producers, Frankovich, M., & Whitelaw, A.; 1972). *Butterflies are free* [Film]. Los Angeles, CA: Columbia Pictures.

Kauffman, R., & Briski, Z. (Producers & Directors; Producer, & White Dreyfous, J.; 2004). *Born into brothels: Calcutta's red light kids* [Film]. Red Light Films.

Kaurismäki, A. (Producer, Director, & Writer; 2002). *The man without a past* [Film]. Bavaria, Germany: Bavaria Film.

Kazan, E. (Producer & Director; 1961). *Splendor in the grass* [Film]. Burbank, CA: NBI Productions.

Kellett, B. (Director; Producers, Granger, D., Macdonald, W., & Wilson, S.; 2005-present). *Swinging* [TV reality series]. Los Angeles, CA: Monkey Kingdom Productions.

Kershner, I. (Director; Producers, Kurtz, G., & McCallum, R.; 1980). *Star Wars. Episode V: The Empire strikes back* [Film]. Nicasio, CA: Lucasfilm.

Kiarostami, A. (Producer & Director; 1997). *Taste of cherry. Ta'm e guilass* [Film]. New York, NY: Abbas Kiarostami Productions.

Kiewslowski, K. (Director & Writer; Producer, Karmitz, M.; 1993). *Three colors: Blue* [Film]. Paris, France: Canal+.

Kim, K. (Producer, Director, Writer, & Editor; 2004). *3-iron* [Film]. Seoul, Korea: Kim Ki-Duk Films.

Kim, K. (Director, Writer, & Editer; Producers, Baumgartner, K., & Lee, S.; 2003). *Spring, summer, fall, winter, & spring* [Film]. Seoul, Korea: Korea Pictures.

King, D. R., & Simon, M. (Directors; Producers, Cacciatore, V., Dryden, D., Pekich, L., Wofford, H., Kennedy, T., Fisher, M., Pritikin, D., Nosser, R., Armstrong, C., Baltazzia, M., Beresford-Redman, B., Bienstock, J., Bishop, A., Briles, A., Connell, B., Feist, J., Goldberg, ., Keller, ., Kirhoffer, J., Lofgren, D., Mills, F., Nilsen, ., Piligian, C., & Schutz, J.; 2000 to present). *Survivor* [TV reality series]. Beverly Hills, CA: Mark Burnett Productions.

King, M. P. (Producer, Director, & Writer; Producer & Writer, Star, D.; Producers, Cyphers, E. M., Melfi, P. J., & Parker, S. J.; 2008). *Sex and the city* [Film]. Burbank, CA: Darren Star Productions.

Kirkland, M., Moore, S. D., Reardon, J., Anderson, B., Archer, W., Anderson, M. B., Silverman, D., Kruse, N., Nastuk, M., Moore, r., Polcino, M., Lynch, J., Dietter, S., Michels, P., Kramer, L., Baeza, C., Polcino, D., Sheetz, C., Persi, R. S., Scott III, S. O., Affleck, N., Marcantel, M., MacMullan, L., Ervin, M., Kamerman, J., Clements, C., Faughnan, M., Gray, M., Bird, B., Butterworth, K., Sosa, R., & Oliver, R. (Directors; Producers, Brooks, J. L., Groening, M., Simon, S., Jean, A., Sakai, R., Reiss, M., Silverman, D., Meyer, G., Mendel, J. M., Mirkin, D., Raynis, R., Scully, M., Oakley, B., Weinstein, J., Collier, J., Daniels, G., Maxtone-Graham, I., Wolf, M., Swartzwelder, J., Duke, A., Boucher, J.A., Cohen, D. X., Richdale, J., Adamson, L., Roman, P., Schultz, B., Kogen, J., Wolodarsky, W., Keeler, K., Tompkins, S., O'Brien, C., Csupo, G., Gunther, S., Vitti, J., Sacks, D., Odenkirk, B., Mula, F., Appel, R., Lewis, C. A. B. V., Tsumura, K., Hauge, R., Long, T., Greaney, D., McGrath, D., Forrester, B., Martin, J., Kimmel, H., Omine, C., Selman, M., Frink, J., Payne, D., Curran, K., Gammill, T., Pross, M., Biernacki, L., Price, M., Burns, J. S., Cohen, J. H., Wilmore, M., Pietila, B., Sirkot, D., Thacker, J., Braud, D., Chung, R., Nalivansky, F., Polizzi, R., Stern, D. M., Hyde, J. W., Gould, D., Warburton, M., Westbrook, J., Richardson, D., Cary, D., Scully, B., Chun, D., Greenberg, S. D., Goldstein, J. L., Richardson, G., LaZebnik, R., Knizek, C., Doyle, L., Martin, T., Kelley, B., Bikowski, J., Kelley, B., Argaman, S., Pipkin, M., Hyde, J., Germain, P., Brady, T., Verrone, P., Kuwahara, J., Lieb, J., & Vein, J. F.; 1989 to present). *The Simpsons* [TV series]. Los Angeles, CA: 20th Century Fox Television.

Kirostami, A. (Producer, Director, Writer, & Editor; Producer, Karmitz, M.; 1999). *The wind will carry us* [Film]. Paris, France: MK2 Productions.

Kleiser, R. (Director; Producers, Kleiser, R., & Franklin, R.; 1980). *Blue lagoon* [Film]. Los Angeles, CA: Columbia Pictures Corporation.

Konchalovsky, A. (Producer & Director; Producer, Kleiman, F.; 2002). *House of fools* [Film]. Paris, France: Bac Films.

Koreeda, H. (Director; Producer, (1998). *After life [Wandâfuru raifu*; Film]. Boston, MA: Engine Film.

Koreeda, H. (Producer, Director, Writer, & Editor; *Nobody knows* [Film]. Tokoyo, Japan: Bandai Visual Company.

Kragh-Jacobsen, S. (Director; Producers, Cohen, R., & Magnusson, T.; 1997). *The Island on Bird St.* [Film]. Burbank, CA: April Productions.

Kramer, S. (Producer & Director; 1967). *Guess who's coming to dinner?* [Film]. Culver City, CA: Columbia Pictures Coporation.

Kubrick, S. (Producer & Director). (1991). *A clockwork orange* [Film]. Los Angeles, CA: Warner Brothers. Burbank, CA: Warner Bros. Pictures.

Kubrick, L. (Director; Producer, Harris, J. B.; 1962). *Lolita* [Film]. Los Angeles, CA: A.A. roductions, Ltd.

Kubrick, S. (Producer, Director, & Writer; Producer, Harlan, J.; 1980). *The shining* [Film]. Beverly Hills: Producers Circle.

Kumble, R. (Director; Producers, Fottrell, M., Tyrer, W., & Mellon, B.; 1999). *Cruel intentions* [Film]. Los Angeles, CA: Columbia Pictures Corporation.

Kurosawa, K. (Director; Producers, Nakamura, M., Ikeguchi, N., & Kanno, S.; 1999). *Charisma* [Film]. Tel Aviv, Israel: Institute of Israeli Films.

Kurosawa, A. & Hônda, I. (Directors; Producers, Ilizumi, S., Kurosawa, H., & Inoue, M. Y.; 1990). *Dreams* [Film]. Los Angeles, CA: Warner Bros. Pictures.

Kuzui, F.R. (Director; Producers, Baum, C., Gallin, S., & Kuzui, F. R.; 1992). *Buffy the vampire slayer*. [Film}. Los Angeles, CA: Twentieth Century Fox Film Corporation.

LaBute, N. (Director; Producers, Archer, M., Pevner, S., & Hettinger, T.; 1997). *In the company of men* [Film]. New York, NY: Fair and Square Productions.

Landis, J. (Director; Producer, Simmons, M.; 1978). *Animal house* [Film]. Los Angeles, CA: Universal Studios.

Lathan, S., Barnette, N., Martin, D., & Singletary, T. (Directors; 1986). *The Redd Foxx show* [TV series]. Burbank, CA: American Broadcasting Corporation.

Lawrence, R. (Director & Writer; Producer, Buckley, A.; 1985). *Bliss* [Film]. Irving, TX: New South Wales Film Corp.

Lawrence, R. (Director; Producer, Chapman, J.; 2001). *Lantana* [Film]. Sydney, Australia: Australian Film Finance Corporation.

Lax, L. (Director; Producer, Stern, N.; 2005). *Emmanuelle's gift* [Film]. New York, NY: Lookalike Productions.

Leconte, P. (Director; Producer, Sarde, A.; 2004). *Intimate strangers* [Film]. Issys Moullineaux, France: Les Films Alain Sarde. Leconte, P. (Director; Producers, Brillion, F., Carcassonne, P., & Legrand, G.; 1996). *Ridicule* [Film]. West Hollywood, CA: Epithète Films.

Leder, M. (Director; Producers, Abrams, P., Levy, R. L., & Reuther, S.; 2000). *Pay it forward* [Film]. Burbank, CA: Warner Bros. Pictures.

Lee, A. (Director; Producer & Writer, Ossana, D., & Schamus, J.; 2005). *Brokeback Mountain* [Film]. Universal City, CA: Focus Features.

Lee, A. (Director; Producers, Schamus, V., Linde, D., & Kong, B.; 2000). *Crouching tiger, hidden dragon [Wo hu cang long; 2000).* Hong Kong: Asia Union Film & Entertainment Ltd.

Lee, S. (Producer, Director, & Writer; Producer, Kilik, T.; 1999). *The son of Sam killer,* a.k.a., *Summer of Sam* [Film]. Brooklyn, NY: 40 Acres and a Mule Filmworks.

Leigh, M. (Director; Producer, Channing, S. C.; 1993). *Mike Leigh's naked [Film].* New York, NY: Thin Man Films.

Leigh, M. (Director & Writer; Producers, Williams, S. C., & Sarde, A.; 2004). *Vera Drake* [Film]. Isyss Moullineaux, France: Les Films Alain Sarde.

Levy, S. (Director; Producers, Barnathan, M., Myron, B., & Simonds, R.; 2003). *Cheaper by the dozen* [Film]. Los Angeles, CA: Twentieth Century-Fox Film Corporation.

Lewis, J. H., Laven, A., Nadel, A. H., Nelson, G., Medford, D., Donner, R., Allen, L., Dobkin, L., Hiller, A., Hopper, J., Peckinpah, S., Landres, P., Taylor, D., Post, T., Claxton, W. F., Johnson, L., Neilson, J., Slavell, J., Moder, D., Rich, J., & Wendkos, P. (Directors; Producers, Gardner, A., Levy, J. V., & Laven, A.; 1958-1963). *The rifleman* [TV series]. Burbank, CA: Four Star Productions.

Liman, D. (Director; Producers, Foster, L., Goldsman, A., McLeod, E., Milchan, A., & Wachsberger, P.; 2005). *Mr. and Mrs. Smith* [Film]. Los Angeles, CA: Regency Enterprises.

Lindsay-Hogg, M. (Director; Producer, D'Onofrio, V. & Missell, R.; 1997). *Guy* [Film]. New York, NY: Polygram Filmed Entertainment.

Lucas, G. (Director; Producers Lucas Film; The Coppola Company, Universal Pictures; 1973). *American graffiti* [Film]. Los Angeles, CA: .Universal Pictures.

Lucas, G. (Director; Producers, Kurtz, G. & McCallum, R.; 1977). *Star wars, episode IV: A new hope.* Nicasio, CA: Lucasfilm.

Lucas, G. (Director & Writer; Producer, McCallum, R.; 1999). *Star wars, Episode I: The phantom menace* [Film]. Nicasio, CA: Lucasfilm.

Lucas, G. (Director & Writer; Producers, McCallum, R. & Orleans, L.; 2002). *Star wars, episode II: Attack of the clones* [Film]. Nicasio, CA: Lucasfilm.

Lucas, G. (Director & Writer; Producer, McCallum, R.; 2005). *Star wars, episode III: Revenge of the sith* [Film]. Nicasio, CA: Lucasfilm.

Lumet, S. (Director; Kastner, E., Persky, L., & Holt, D.; 1997). *Equus* [Film]. New York, NY: Persky-Bright Productions.

Lürsen, J. (Durector; Producers, Beker, J., Maltha, D. F., & van Gestel, F.; 2004). *In Orange* [Film]. Amsterdam, The Netherlands: Motel Films.

Lyn, T. (Director; Producer, Eames, B.; 2002). *Eldra* [Film]. Wales, England: Sianel 4 Cymru (S4C).

Lynch, D. (Director; Producer, Writer, & Editor, Sweeney, M.; Producer, Edelstein, N.; 1999). *The Straight Story* [Film]. Burbank, CA: Walt Disney Pictures.

Lyne, A. (Director; Producers, Jaffe, S. R., & Lansing, S.; 1987). *Fatal attraction* [Film]. Los Angeles, CA: Paramount Pictures.

MacKenzie, D. (Director; Producers Kaslow, H. M., Davis, B., & Barlow, M.; 2005). *Asylum* [Film]. Los Angeles, CA: Paramount Vantage.

Macdonald, K. (Director; Producers, Bryer, L., Calderwood, A., & Steel, C.; 2006). *The last king of Scotland* [Film]. London, UK: DNA Films.

Macdonald, K. (Director; Producer, Smithson, J.; 2003). *Touching the void* [Film]. London, UK: Darlow Smithson Productions.

Majidi, M. (Director & Writer; Producers, Esfandiari, A., & Esfandiari, M.; 1997). *Children of heaven* [Film]. Burbank, CA: Buena Vista Television.

Majidi, M. (Director; Producers, Sayad-zadeh, S. S., Esfandiari, A., & Esfandiari, M.; 1999). *The Children of heaven.* [*Bacheha-Yeaseman*; Film]. Tehran, Iran: The Institute for Intellectual Development of Children and Young Adults.

Makris, C., Alexander, J., Dobbs, R., Sherin, E., Platt, D., Penn, M., Scardino, D., Mitchell, M., Misiano, Ch., Quinn, J., Forney, A. W., Gould, L., de Segonzac, J., Swackhamer, E. W., Sackhelm, D., Pressman, M., Gerber, F., Muzio, G., Frawley, J., Misiano, V., Gillum, V., Wertimer, S., Watkins, M. W., Whitesell, J., Robman, S., Florek, D., Mertes, B., Correll, S., Arner, G., Hayman, J., Shilton, G. M., Ellis, J., Shill, S., Martin, D., Chapples, A., Hunter, T., & McKay, J. (Directors; Producers, Wolf, D., Forney, A. W., Hayes, J. L., Ellis, J., Sweren, R., Sherin, E., Balcer, R., Fordes, W. N., Gould, L., Karr, G., Jankowski, P., Johnston, K., Chernuchin, M. A., Battles, W., Penn, M., Overmyer, E., Weinman, R., Fox, B., O'Connell, K., Green, W., Stern, J., Zuckerman, E., Schindel, B., Palm, R., Sakheim, D., Wootton, N., Giuliano, P., Guggenheim, M., Wertimer, S., Guiliano, P., Kopp, T., Goldsmith, J., Mamet, L., Santora, N., Carcaterra, L., Zelman, A., Shore, D., Johnson, L., Berner, F., Gionfriddo, G., Senqupta, S., Finkelstein, W. M., Penn, A., & Plageman, G.; 1990 to present). *Law and order* [TV series]. New York, NY: Studios USA Television.

Malle, L. (Producer, Director, & Writer; 1987). *Au revoir les Enfants Goodbye, children.* [Film]. New York, NY: Stella Films.

Malle, L. (Director & Writer; Producer, Quefféléan, A.; 1963). *The fire within* [Film]. New York, NY: Nouvelles Éditions de Films.

Malle, L. (Director; Producer, Berner, F.; 1994). *Vanya on 42nd street* [Film]. London, UK: Channel Four Films.

Mandoki, L. (Director; Producers, Avnet, J., Kerner, J.; 1994). *When a man loves a woman* [Film]. Burbank, CA: Touchstone Pictures.

Mangold, J. (Director; Producers, Konrad, C., Wick, R., & Green, J.; 1999). *Girl interrupted* [Film]. Beverly Hills, CA: 3 Art Entertainment.

Mangold, J. (Director & Writer; Producer, Konrad, C.; 2001). *Kate and Leopold* [Film]. Culver City, CA: Konrad Pictures.

Mann, D. (Director; Producer, Hecht, H.; 1955). *Marty* [Film]. Los Angeles, CA: Hill-Hecht-Lancaster Productions.

Marquand, R. (Director; Producers, Kazanjian, H., & McCallum, R.; 1984). *Star wars, episode VI: The return of the jedi* [Film]. Nicasio, CA: Lucasfilm.

Marshall, P. (Director; Producers, Lasker, L. & Parkes, W. F.; 1990). *Awakenings* [Film]. Culver City, CA: Columbia Pictures Corporation.

Marshall, G. [Director; Producers, Milchan, A., & Reuther, S.; 1990]. *Pretty woman* [Film]. Burbank, CA: Silver Screen Partners IV.

Marshall, G. (Director; Producers, Cort, R.W., Field, T., Kroopf, S., & Rosenberg, T.; (1999). *Runaway bride* [Film]. Los Angeles, CA: Paramount Pictures.

Marshall, P. (Director; Producers, Ansell, J., Brooks, J. L., Colleton, S., Mark, L., & Sakai, R.; 2001). *Riding in cars with boys* [Film]. Culver City, CA: Gracie Films.

Marshall, G. (Director & Writer; Producer & Writer, Rose, A.; & Producer, Iscovich, M; 1999). *The other sister* [Film]. Burbank, CA: Mandeville Films.

Marston, J. (Director & Writer; Producer, Mezey, P.; 2004). *Maria, full of grace* [Film]. Los Angeles, CA: HBO Films.

Mazursky, P. (Director & Writer; Producer & Writer, Tucker, L.; 1969). *Bob & Carol & Ted & Alice* [Film]. Culver City, CA: Columbia Pictures Corporation.

McCulloch, B. (Director; Producer, Michaels, L.). *Superstar* [Film]. Los Angeles, CA: SNL Studios.

McKay, J. (Director & Writer; Producer, Thomas, L.; 2001/I). *Crush* [Film]. Los Angeles, CA: Industry Entertainment.

McLaglen, A. V. (Director; Producer, Arthur, R. ; 1965). *Shenandoah* [Film]. Universal City, CA: Universal Pictures.

McNamara, S. (Director; Producers, Carver, B., Arad, A., & Paul, St.; 2007). *Bratz: The movie*[Film]. Westport, CT: Avi Arad Associates.

McTeigue, J. (Director; Producers, Hill, G., Orleans, L., Silver, J., Wachowski, A., & Wachowski, L.; 2005). *V for vendetta* [Film]. Los Angeles, CA: Silver Pictures.

Mehta, D. (Director & Writer; Producer,Hamilton, D.; 2006). *Water* [Film]. Toronto, ON, Canada: Deepa Mehta Films.

Meirelles, V. (Director; Producer, Channing, S. W.; 2005). *The constant gardener* [Film]. London, UK: Potboiler Productions.

Meirelles, F., & Lund, K. (Directors; Producers, Ribeiro, A.B., Famos, A. M., & Salles, W.; 2002). *City of God. [Cidade de Deus; Film]*. Redondo Beach, CA: 02 Films

Mendes, S. (Director; Producers, Cohen, S., & Jinks, D.; 1999). *American beauty* [Film]. Universal City, CA: DreamWorks SKG.

Metter, A. (Director; Producers, Ring, M., & Steinberg, N.; 1999). *Passport to Paris* [Video]. Burbank, CA: Hollyridge Productions.

Meyers, N. (Director & Writer; Producer, Block, B.A., 2003). *Something's gotta give* [Film]. Culver City, CA: Columbia Pictures Corporation.

Michell, R. (Director; Producer, Coulter, M.; 1999). *Notting Hill* [Film]. Universal City, CA: Polygam Filmed Entertainment.

Miller, C., & Hui, R. (Directors; Producer & Writer, Warner, A.; 2007). *Shrek 3* [Film]. Glendale, CA: DreamWorks Animation.

Miller, G. & Paris, D. (Directors; Producers, Gibbs, B., Taekuchi, P., & Shenfield, R.; 1998). *Babe 2: Pig in the City* [Film]. Sydney, Australia: Kennedy Miller Productions.

Miller, P., McCoy, T., Wayans, K. I., & Wickline, M. (Directors; Producers, Wayans, K. I., Fields, G., Petok, M., Berg, K., & Jason, R.; 1990-1994). *In living color* [TV series]. Los Angeles, CA: Twentieth Century-Fox Television.

Minghella, A. (Director & Writer; Producers, Berger, A., Horberg, W., Pollack, S., & Yerxa, R.; 2003). *Cold mountain* [Film]. West Hollywood, CA: Miramax Films.

Minghella, A. (Director & Writer; Producer, Cooper, R; 1990). *Truly, madly, deeply* [Film]. London, UK: British Broadcasting Corporation.

Minnelli, V. (Director; Producer Pasternak, V.; 1965). *The courtship of Eddie's father* [Film]. Los Angeles, CA: Metro-Goldwyn-Mayer.

Misiano, C., Graves, A., Schlamme, T., Glatter, L. L., Innes, L., Misiano, V., D'Elia, B., Barclary, P., Olin, K., Yu, J., Hébert, J., Bernstein, A., Taylor, A., Kagan, J., Berlinger, R., Coles, J. D., Schiff, R., McCormick, N. (Directors; Producers, Harms, K., Wells, J., Misiano, C., Ward, P., Wells, L., Hissrich, M., Graves, A., Schlamme, T., Sorkin, A., Redford, P., O'Donnell, L., Attie, E., Stearn, A., Noah, P., Massin, D. K., Ahern Jr., N., Flint, C., Young, J. S., Cahn, D., Antosca, S., & Fountain, M.; 1999-2006). *The west wing* [Film]. Los Angeles, CA: John Wells Productions.

Mitchell, A. J., & Mitchell, J. L. (Producers & Directors; 1972). *Behind the green door* [Film]. Paris, France, Jartech.

Mitchell, M. (Director; Producer, Gunn, A; 2005). *Sky high* [Film]. Burbank, CA: Buena Vista Pictures.

Mitchell, R. (Director; Producers, Bozman, R., Schroeder, A., & Rudin, S.; 2002). *Changing lanes* [Film]. Los Angeles, CA: Paramount Pictures.

Molinara, E. (Director & Writer; Producer & Writer, Danon, M.; *The bird cage. La cage aux folles* [Film]. Paris, France: da Ma Produzione.

Moodysson, L. (Director & Writer; Producer, Jönsson, L.; 2002). *Lilya 4-ever* [Film]. Stockholm, Sweden: Memfis Films.

Moore, M. (Director; Producers, Young, R., Tichy, W., & Moore, M.; 2002). *Bowling for Columbine* [Film]. Montreal, Canada: Alliance Atlantis Communications.

Moorhouse, J. (Director; Producers, Bernstein, A., Bliss, T., & Abraham, M.; 1997). *A 1000 acres* [Film]. Burbank, CA: Buena Vista Pictures Distribution. Moorhouse, J. (Director; Producers, Sanford, M.; 1995). *How to make an American quilt* [Film]. Universal City, CA: Amblin Entertainment

Moreau, D., & Palud, X. (Directors; Producers, Granger, D., Manning, M., & Wagner, P.; 2002). *The eye* [Film]. Santa Monica, CA: Lionsgate.

Moretti, N. (Producer, Director, & Writer; Producers, Barbagallo, L., Fabrizio, F., Galluzzo, V., & Luccarrini, L.; 2001). *The son's room* [Film]. Paris, France: Canal+.

Muccino, Q. (Director; Producers, Black, T., Blumenthal, J., Lassiter, J., Smith, W., & Tisch. S.; 2006). *Pursuit of happiness* [Film]. Colver City, CA: Columbia Pictures Corporation.

Mulcahy, R. (Director; Producer & Writer, Lambert, C.; Producers, Baldwin, H., Choi, P. D., & Niami, N.; 1999). *Resurrection* [Film]. Los Angeles, CA: Interlight.

Mulligan, W. (Director; Producer, Roth, R. A.; 1979). *Summer of '42* [Film]. Burbank, CA: Warner Bros. Pictures.

Mulligan, R. (Director; Producer, Pakula, A. J.; 1962). *To kill a mockingbird* [Film]. Universal City, CA: Brentwood Productions.

Murphy, R. (Producer, Director, & Writer; Producers, Garden, D., Grey, B., & Pitt, B.; 2006). *Running with scissors* [Film]. Beverly Hills, CA: Plan B Entertainment.

Murray, R. (Director & Editor; Producer, Finzi, B.; 2005). *Unknown white male* [Documentary]. New York, NY: Court TV.

Naess, P. (Director; Producer, Alveberg, D.; 2001). *Elling* [Flm]. Jarlsberg, Sweden: Maipo Film -og TV- Produksjon.

Nari, M. (Director; Producers, Tejani, A.; Nozik, M.; & Aeur, G.; 1988). *Salaam Bombay* [Film]. New York, NY: Mirabai Films.

Natali, V. (Director; Producers, Federbush, P., Grean, W., LaScala, C., & Lowry, H.; 2002). *Brainstorm* [Film].

Natali, V. (Director & Writer; Producer, Hoban, D., 2003). *Nothing* [Film]. Edmonton, Alberta, Canada: 49th Parallel Productions.

Naughton, G., Cyphers, E. M., Rottenberg, J., Zuritsky, E., Heinberg, A., Jossen, B., Kent, D., Carpenter, B., Leonhardt, U., & Junge, A.; 1998-2004). *Sex and the city* [TV Series]. Santa Monica, CA: Darren Star Productions.

Neill, R. W./de Palma, B. (Director & Producer; Producer, Benedict, H.; 1940/Director & Writer; Producer, Litto, G; 1980). *Dressed to kill* [Film]. Universal City, CA: Universal Pictures/New York, NY: Filmways Pictures [later Orion Pictures].

Nelson, O., & Nelson, D. (Directors; Producers, Nelson, O., Pepin, L., Bank, J., Angus, R., Barker, C., Lewis, B., & Penn, L.; 1952-1966). *The Adventures of Ozzie and Harriet* [TV series]. Burbank, CA: Stage Five Productions.

Newell, M. (Director; Producer, Coulter, M.; 1994). *Four weddings and a funeral* [Film]. ondon, UK: Channel Four Films.

Newell, M. (Director; Producers, Heyman, D., & Orleans, L.; 2005). *Harry Potter and the goblet of fire* [Film]. Burbank, CA: Warner Bros. Pictures.

Niccol, A. (Director; Producers, Shamberg, M., Sher, S., & Idziak, S., 1997). *Gattaca* [Film]. Culver City, CA: Columbia Pictures Corporation.

Nichols, M. (Producer & Director; Producers, Brokaw, C., & Calley, J.; 2003/1). *Closer* [Film}. New York, NY: Icarus Films.

Nichols, M. (Producer & Director; Producer, Calley, 1990). *Postcards From the Edge* [Film]. Culver City, CA: Columbia Pictures Corporation.

Nichols, M. (Director; Producer, Lehman, E.; 1966). *Who's afraid of Virginia Wolff?* [Film]. Burbank, CA: Warner Bros. Pictures.

Ning, H. (Director; Producers, He, B. & Bin, L.; 2005; China). *Mongolian Ping Pong. Lü cao di* [Film]. New York, NY: First Run Features.

Nolan, C. (Director & Writer; Producers, Franco, L., Orleans, L., Roven, C., & Thomas, E.; 2005). *Batman begins* [Film]. Burbank, CA: Warner Bros. Pictures.

Noonan, C. (Director & Writer; Producer & Writer, Miller, G.; Producer, Mitchell, A.; 1995). *Babe* [Film]. Universal City, CA: Universal Pictures.

Norbu, K. (Director & Writer; Producer & Production Designer, Steiner, R; Producer, Watson, M.; 2003). *Travelers and magicians* [Film]. New York, NY: Prayer Flag Films.

Nowoseleski, R. (Director & Writer; Producer & Writer, Hence, K.; Producer & Cinematographer, Duffy, J.; 2006). *9/11 press for truth* [Documentary]. Culver City, CA: Banded Artists.

Noyce, P. (Director; Producers, Neufeld, M., Rehme, R., Singleton, R.; 1994). *Clear and present danger* [Film]. Beverly Hills, CA:

Noyce, P. (Producer & Director; Producer & Writer, Olsen, C.; Producer, Winter, J.; 2002). *Rabbit proof fence* [Film]. Woolloomooloo, Australia: The Australian Film Commission.

Nuridsany, C. (Director; 2004). *Genesis* [Documentary]. Issys Mollineaux, France: Les Films Alain Sarde.

Nuridsany, C. & Pérenou, M. (Directors & Writers; Producers, Barratier, C., Mallet, Y., & Perrin, J.; 1996). *Microcosmos* [Documentary]. West Hollywood, CA: Galatée Films.

Nutley, C. (Producer, Director, & Writer; Producers, Beime, J., & Nilemar, M.; 1998). *Under the sun. Under solen* [Film]. Waterville, MN: Film i Vast.

O'Donnell, D. (Director; Producers, Flynn, J., & Wilson, J.; 2004). *Rory O'Shea was here* ilm]. Universal City, CA: WT2 Productions.

Ozon, F. (Director & Writer; Producer, Delbosc, O., & Missonier, M.; 2003). *Swimming pool* [Film]. Paris, France: Fidélité Productions.

Page, A. (Director; Badalato, B., Producer; 2002). *About Schmidt* [Film]. New York, NY: New Line Cinema.

Paltrow, B. (Producer & Director; Director & Writer, Byrum, J., & Producer, Byrum, J., Canton, N., Jones, K., Ludwig, T., Mayes, L. R., & Riche, A.; 2000). *Duets* [Film]. Burbank, CA: Hollywood Pictures.

Pang Brothers. (Directors, Writers, & Editors; Producers, Chan, P. H., & Cheng, L.; 2002). *The eye* [Film]. Hong Kong, China: Applause Pictures.

Parisol, D. (Director; Producers, Johnson, M., Kasdan, A., Levinson, B. & Newirth, C.; 1998). *Home fries* [Film]. Burbank, CA: Kasdan Pictures.

Parker J. (Producer, Director, Writer, & Composer; 2001). *Bartleby* [Film]. San Raefel, CA: Parker Film Company.

Parson, C. (Concept Creator; Producers, Aro, H., Eriksson, A., Glansén, K., Hylin, M., Jankert, J., Leinstedt, C., Lindberg, A., & Olsson, M.; 1997 to present). *Expedition Robinson* [Swedish TV reality series]. Stockholm, Sweden: Strix Television AB.

Pasolini, P. P. (Director & Writer, Producer, Bini, A.; 1964). *The gospel according to St. Matthew* [Film]. Milano, Italy: Arco Film.

Payne, A., & Parra, G. (Directors; Producers, Toffler, V., Berger, A., & Yerxa, R.; 1999). *Election* [Film]. Los Angeles, CA: Bona Fide Productions.

Peerce, L. (Director; Producer, Felman, E. S.; 1975). *The other side of the mountain* [Film]. Universal City, CA: Filmways

Peirce, K. (Director & Writer; Producers, Hart, J., Kolodner, E., Sharp, J., & Vachon, C.; 1999). *Boys don't cry* [Film]. Los Angeles, CA: Hart-Sharp Entertainment.

Penn, A. (Director; Producer, Coe, F.; 1962). *The miracle worker* [Film]. Los Angeles, CA: Playfilm Productions.

Perrin, J. (Producer, Director, & Writer; Co-Directors, Cluzaud, J. & Debats, M.; Producer, de Trégomain, J., Producers, Barratier, C., & Perrin, J.; 2001). *Winged migration* [Documentary]. Paris, France: Bac Films.

Perry, F. (Director; Producer & Writer, Yablans, F.; 1981). *Mommie dearest* [Film]. Los Angeles, CA: Paramount Pictures.

Perry, T. (Producer, Director & Writer; Producer, Cannon, R.; 2007). *Why did I get married?* [Film]. Santa Monica, CA: Lions Gate Films

Petrie, D. (Director; Producers, Rose, P. & Susskind, D.; 1961). *Raisin in the sun* [Film]. Culver City, CA: Columbia Pictures Corporation.

Petrie, D. (Director; Producer, Babbin, J.; 1976). *Sybil* [TV Film]. Los Angeles, CA: LoriMar Productions.

Philibert, N. (Director, Cinematographer, & Editor; Producer, Sandoz, G.; 2002). *To be and to have* [Documentary]. Paris, France: Canal+.

Platt, D., Makris, C., Leto, P., Campanella, J. J., de Segonzac, J., Forney, A. W., Shill, S., Zakrzewski, A., Kotcheff, T., Dobbs, R., Taylor, J., Fields, M., Wallace, R., Kapalan, J., Lipstadt, A., Glatter, L. L., Rosenthal, R., Wertimer, S., Quinn, J., Beesley, M. E., Pattison, G., & Woods, K. (Directors; Producers, Declerque, D., Kotcheff, T., Wolf, D., Baer, N., Greene, J., Barringer, G., Jankowski, P., DeNoon, D., Leto, P., Molina, J., Palm, R., Singer, J., Burke, D. J., Platt, D., Lazaroy, J., Perry, M. R., Petersen, L. M., Weinman, R., Campbell, R., & Eckerle, J.; 1999 to present). *Law and order: Special victims unit* [TV series]. New York, NY: NBC Universal Television.

Polanski, R. (Director & Writer; Producer, Castle, W.; 1968). *Rosemary's baby* [Film]. Los Angeles, CA: William Castle Productions.

Polanski, R. (Producer & Director; Produers, Benmussa, R., & Sarde, A.; 2002). *The Pianist. Le pianste* [Film]. Paris, France: R. P. Productions.

Pollack, S. (Producer & Director; Producer, Richards, D.; 1982). *Tootsie* [Film]. Culver City, CA: Columbia Pictures Corporation.

Pool, L. (Director; Producers, Allaire, F., Gelbart, A., & Haggiag, M.; 2004). *Blue butterfly* [Film]. Monterey, CA: Monterey Video.

Potter, S. (Director & Writer; Producer, Sheppard, C.; 2000). *The man who cried, Les larmes d'un homme* [Film]. Paris, France: Canal+.

Prinzi, F., de Segonzac, J., Shill, S., Makris, C., Martin, D., Zakrzewski, A., Chapple, A., Barba, N., Swartout, C., DiCillo, T., Muzio, G., Platt, D., Scardino, D., Norton, B. L., Wallace, R., Smith, M., Girotti, K., Coles, J. D., Fields, M., Campanella, J. J., Chopra, J., Torres, M., McKay, J., Treviño, J. S., & Bray, K. (Directors; Producers, Balcer, R., Roman, J. L., Wolf, D., Jankowski, P., Thewlis, M. R., Leight, W., Deluca, T., Kewley, M. R., Berner, F., Sengupta, S., Son, D., Barba, N., Weinman, R.; 2001 to present). *Law and order: Criminal intent* [TV series]. Los Angeles, CA: NBC Universal Television.

Ramis, H. (Director; Producer, Levinson, B.; 2002). *Analyze that* [Film]. Los Angeles, CA: Warner Bros.

Ramis, H. (Director; Producer, Weinstein, P.; 1999). *Analyze this* [Film]. Los Angeles, CA: Warner Bros.

Ramis, H. (Producer & Director; Producer, Albert, T.; 1993). *Groundhog day* [Film]. Culver City, CA: Columbia Pictures Corporation.

Ramsay, L. (Director & Writer; Producer, Emerson, G.; 1999). *Ratcatcher* [Film]. London, England: Arts Council of England.

Rapper, I. (Director; Producer, Wallis, H. B.; 1946). *Now, voyager* [Film]. Burbank, CA: Warner Bros. Pictures.W

Ray, N. (Director & Writer; Producer, Weisbart, D.; 1955). *Rebel without a cause* [Film]. Burbank, CA: Warner Bros. Pictures

Redford, R. (Director; Producer, Schwary, R. L.; 1980). *Ordinary people* [Film]. Los Angeles, CA: Paramount Pictures.

Redford, R. (Producer & Director; Producer, Markey, P.; 1998). *The horse whisperer* [Film]. Burbank, CA: Touchstone Pictures.

Reichle, F. (Director, Writer, Editor, & Cinmetagrapher; Producer, Hoehn, M.; 2004). *Monte grande: What is life?* [Documentary]. Zurich, Switzerland: Schweizer Fernsehen DRS.

Reiner, R. (Director; Producers, Cosgrove, B., & Weinstein, P.; 2005). *Rumor has it* [Film]. Burbank, CA: Warner Bros. Pictures.

Reiner, R. (Producer & Director; Producer & Writer, Zweibel, A.; & Producer & Writer, Nelson, J.; 1999). *The story of us* [Film]. Beverly Hills, CA: Castle Rock Entertainment.

Reiner, R. (Producer & Director; Producer, Sheinman, A.; 1989). *When Harry met Sally* [Film]. Beverly Hill, CA: Castle Rock Entertainment.

Reitman, J. (Director; Producer, Halfon, L.; 2007). *Juno* [Film]. Los Angeles, CA: Fox Searchlight Pictures.

Robbins, J. (Director & Writer; Producer & Writer, Price, R.; 1961). *West side story* [Film]. Universal City: Mirisch.

Robinson, P. A. (Director; Producers, Gordon, C., Gordon, L., & Lindley, J.; 1989). *Field of dreams* [Film]. Beverly Hills, CA: Gordon Company.

Rodgers, J. B. (Director; Producers, Moore, C., Perry, C., & Zide, W.; 2001). *American pie 2* [Film]. Los Angeles, CA: LivePlanet.

Roodt, D. (Director & Writer; Producer, Singh, A. & Spring. H.; 2004). *Yesterday* [Film]. Los Angeles, CA: HBO Films.

Ross, G. (Producer, Director, & Writer; Producer, Degus, B. J., Kilik, J., & Soderbergh, S.; 1998). *Pleasantville* [Film]. Los Angeles, CA: New Line Cinema.

Ross, H. (Director; Producer, Stark, R.; 1989). *Steel magnolias* [Film]. Los Angeles, CA: Rastar Films.

Rozema, P. (Producer & Director; Producer, Raffe, A.; 1987). *I've heard the mermaids singing* [Film]. Burbank, CA: The Canada Council.

Rudolph, A. (Director; Producer, Scott, C.; 2002). *The secret lives of dentists* [Film]. New York, NY: Holedigger Films.

Ruskin, C., Sandrich, J., Senensky, R., Hart, H., Cosby, B., & James, L. (Directors; Producers, Cosby, B., & Miller, M.; 1969-1971). *The Bill Cosby show* [TV series]. Burbank, CA: Bill Cosby.

Russell, W. D., & Tewksbury, P. (Directors; Producers, Rodney, E. B., & Briskin, F.; 1954-1960). *Father knows best. [I told you so;* TV Series]. Burbank, CA: American Broadcasting Company.

Rydell, M. (Director; Producer, Gilbert, B.; 1981). *On golden pond* [Film]. Universal City, CA: Universal Pictures.

Saleem, H. (Director & Writer; Producer, Guez, F.; 2003). *Vodka lemon* [Film]. New York, NY: Dulciné Films.

Salles, W. (Director; Producers, Nozik, M., Tennenbaum, E., & Tenkhoff, K.; 2004). *The motorcycle diaries* [Film]. London, UK: FilmFour.

Salva, V. (Director & Writer; Producers, Birnbaum, R., & Grodnik, D.; 1995). *Powder* [Film]. Burbank, CA: Caravan Pictures.

Sandrich, J., Singletary, T., Lauten, C., Bowab, J., Vinson, C., Life, R., Barnette, N., Warner, M., Falcon, E., & Scott, O. (Directors; Producers, Carsey, M., Werner, T., Guarnieri, T., Leahy, J., Finestra, Ca., Kott, G., Kukoff, B., Kline, S., Williams, M., Gartrelle, G., Trigiani, A., & Mandabach, C.; 1984-1992). *The Cosby show* [TV series]. Burbank, CA: National Broadcasting Company (NBC).

Saville, P. (Director; Producers, Chrisafis, C., & Drabinsky, G. H.; 2003). *The visual Bible: The Gospel of John* [Film]. Burbank, CA: Gospel of John Ltd.

Sayles, J. (Director, Writer, & Editor; Producers, Miller, R. P., & Renzi, M.; 1996). *Lone star* [Film]. Culver City, CA: Columbia Pictures Corporation.

Scardino, D., Whitesell, J., & Ryder, T. (Directors; Producers, Straw, T., Rogers, J., Klein, D., Steinberg, N., Carsey, M., Cosby, B., Curley-Kerner, J., Mandabach, C., Mula, F., Tortorjoi, P., & Werner, T.; 1996-2000). *Cosby* [TV series]. Studio City, CA: Bill Cosby.

Scherfig, L. (Writer; Producer, Tardini, I; 2000). *Italian for beginners: Italianesk for begyndere.* [Film]. Copenhagen, Denmark: Danmarks Radio.

Schindler, M., Fogel, I., Basley, B. F., Funk, D., McKinnon, B., & Monemvassitis, K. (Directors; Producers, Kazdin, C., Orso, A., Ponticiello, G., Alumkal, N., Becker, C., Bermon, J., Bruen, R. J., Lewitinn, A., Ross, S., Seaman, L., Sherwood, B., & Stein, G.; 1975 to present). *Good morning America* [TV morning news program]. Burbank, CA: American Broadcasting Corporation.

Schreiber, L. (Director; Producers, Stillman, M., Turtletaub, M., & Saraf, P.; 2005). *Everything is illuminated* [Film]. Burbank, CA: Warner Independent Pictures.

Schumacher, J. (Director; Producers, Kopelson, A., Weingrod, H., Bartkowiak, A.; 1993). *Falling down* [Film]. Burbank, CA: Alcor Films

Scorsese, M. (Director; Producers, Maas, A., & Susskind, D.; 1974). *Alice doesn't live here anymore* [Film]. Burbank, CA: Warner Bros. Pictures.

Scorsese, M. (Director; Producers, Phillips, M., Phillips, J., & Goldfarb, P. M.; 1976). *Taxi driver* [Film]. Culver City, CA: Columbia Pictures Corporation.

Scott, R. (Producer & Director; Producers, De Laurentis, D., & De Laurentis, M.; 2001). *Hannibal* [Film]. Universal City, CA: Dino De Laurentis Company.

Segal, P. (Director; Producer, Bernardi, B.; 2003). *Anger management* [Film]. Santa Monica, CA; Revolution Studios.

Shadyac, T. (Producer & Director; Producers & Writers, Koren, S., &O'Keefe, M.; 2003). *Bruce almighty* [Film]. Universal City, CA: Universal Pictures.

Shadyac, T. (Director; Producer, Grazer, B.; 1997. *Liar, liar* [Film]. Los Angeles, CA: Imagine Entertainment.

Shadyac, T. (Director; Producers, Farrell, M., Kemp, B., Minoff, M., Newirth, C.; 1998). *Patch Adams* [Film]. Burbank, CA: Bungalow 78 Productions.

Shainberg, S. (Producer, Director, & Writer; Producers, Fierberg, A, & Hobby, A; 2002). *Secretary* [Film]. Santa Monica, CA: Slough Pond.

Shankman, A. (Director; Producers, Shankman, A., Gibgot, J., & Grant, G.; 2005). *Cheaper by the dozen 2* [Film]. Los Angeles, CA: Twentieth Century Fox.

Shea, J., Lally, B., Scott, O., Singletary, T., & Smith, A. (Directors; Producers, Dudon, D. W., Leavitt, A., Milligan, M., Moriarty, J., Moye, M. G., Nicholl, D., Perzigian, J., Rosen, S., Ross, M., Shea, J., Sunga, G., & West, B.; 1975-1985). *The Jeffersons* [TV series]. Los Angeles, CA: CBS Television.

Sherfig, L. (Director & Writer; Producer, Olsen, S. G.; 2002). *Wilbur wants to kill himself* [Film]. Hvidovre, Denmark: Zentropa Entertainment.

Shergold, A. (Director; Producer, Langan, C.; 2004). *Dirty, filthy love* [Film]. Manchester, UK: Granada Television.

Sheridan, J. (Producer & Director; Producer, Lappin, A.; 2002). *In America* [Film]. Los Angeles, CA: Fox Searchlight Pictures.

Sheridan, J. (Director & Writer; Producer, Pearson, N.; 1989). *My left foot: The story of Christy Brown* [Film]. Dublin, Ireland: Ferndale Films.

Shinohara, T. (Director; Producer, Enoki, N; 2005). *Heaven's bookstore* [Film]. Tengoku no Hon'ya: Koibi Film Partners.

Shum, M. (Director & Writer; Producers, Garvier, S., Jennings, C., & Massey, R.; 2002). *Long life, happiness, prosperity* [Film]. Toronto, Ontario, Canada: Chum Television.

Shyer, C. (Producer, Director, & Writer; Producer & Writer, Pope, E.; 2004). *Alfie* [Film]. Los Angeles, CA: Paramount Pictures.

Silbering, B. (Director; Producers, Milchan, A., Newirth, C. J., & Cavallo, R.; 1998). *City of angels* [Film]. Los Angeles, CA: Atlas Entertainment.

Silver, J. M. (Director; Producer, Nozik, M.; 1988). *Crossing Delancey* [Film]. Burbank, CA: Warner Bros. Pictures.

Simon, M., & Burnett, M. (Directors; Producers, Petillo, J., Dryden, D., Goetz, P., Fisher, M., Nosser, R., Baltazzia, M., Beresford-Redman, B., Bienstock, J., Bishop, A., Briles, A., Connell,

B., Feist, J., Keller, C., Kirhoffer, J., Lofgren, D., Mills, F., & Nilsen, C.; 2000 to present). *Survivor* [TV reality series]. Beverly Hills, CA: Mark Burnett Productions.

Singer, R. (Executive Producer; 1991-1993). *Reasonable doubts* [TV Series]. Burbank, CA: National Broadcasting Corporation.

Singleton, J. (Director; Producer, Nicolaides, S.; 1991). *Boyz 'n the hood* [Film]. Los Angeles, CA: Columbia Pictures Corporation.

Skjoldbjærg, E. (Director; Producers, Niederhoffer, G., Miller, M. P., & Weston, B.; 2001). *Prozac nation* [Film]. West Hollywood, CA: Giv'en Films.

Smith, D., Wright, T. J., O'Hara, T., Whitmore Jr., J., Bucksey, C., Levi, A. J., Woolnough, J., Wharmby, T., Ellis, P., Libman, L., Mitchell, M., Webb, B., Cragg, S., & Brown, A. (Directors; Producers, Bellisario, D., Bellisario, D. P., Johnson, C. F., Schilz, M. R., Drewe, A. C., Kelley, J. C., Brennan, S., Stern, J., Binder, S. D., Scovell, N., Military, F., Moreno, A. H., Moran, T. L., Vlaming, J., Harmon, M., North, D., Antosca, S., & Fountain, M.; 2003 to present). *Naval crime scene investigation (NCIS).* [TV series]. Hollywood, CA: Parmount Network Television.

Smith, K. (Director, Writer, & Editor; Producer & Writer, Mosier, S.; 2004). *Jersey girl* [Film]. West Hollywood, CA: Miramax Films.

Smith, W. T. (Director & Writer; Producers, Levy, M. S., Mazzola, J., & Scaccia, J.; 2006). *Kiss me again* [Film]. LaVergne, TN: Foundation Entertainment.

Soderbergh, S. (Director; Producers, Hardy, J., Shamberg, C. S., & DeVito, D.; 2000). *Erin Brockovich* [Film]. Los Angeles, CA: Jersey Films.

Soderbergh, S. (Director; Producer, Weintraub, J.; 2001 / 2004 / 2007). *Ocean's 11 / 12 /13* [Film]. Burbank, CA: Warner Bros. Pictures.

Softley, I. (Director; Producers, Colesberry, R. F., Gordon, L., & Levin, L.; 2001). *K-Pax* [Film]. Santa Monica, CA: Lawrence Gordon Productions.

Sombogaart, B. (Director; Producers, Niens, H., & Smit, A.; 2002). *Twin sisters. De tweeling* [Film]. The Netherlands: IdtV Film and Video Productions.

Sono, S. (Director & Writer; Producers, Kamamata, M., Tanaka, J., Tomida, T., Yoshida, S., & Sato, K.; 2002). *Suicide club* [Film]. Philadelphia, PA: For Peace Co., Ltd.

Spielberg, S. (Director; Producer, Watts, R.; 1989). *Indiana Jones and the last crusade* [Film]. Nicasio, CA: Lucasfilm.

Spielberg, S. (Director; Producer, Watts, R.; 1984). *Indiana Jones and the temple of doom* [Film]. Los Angeles, CA: Paramount Pictures.

Spielberg, S. (Director; Producer, Marshall, F.; 2008). *Indiana Jones and the kingdom of the crystal skull.* Los Angeles, CA: Paramount Pictures.

Spielberg, S. (Director; Producer, Marshall, F.; 1981). *Raiders of the lost ark* [Film]. Nicasio, CA: Lucasfilm.

Spielberg, S. (Director & Producer; Producers, Bryce, I., Gordon, M., & Levinsohn, B.; 1994). *Saving Private Ryan* [Film]. Universal City, CA: Amblin Entertainment.

Stone, O. (Producer, Director & Writer; Producer, Ho, A. K.; 1989). *Born on the 4th of July* [Film]. Los Angeles, CA: Ixtlan Productions.

Stone, O. (Director & Writer; Producers, Hamsher, J., Murphy, D., & Townsend, C.; 1994). *Natural born killers* [Film]. Burbank, CA: Warner Bros. Pictures.

Streisand, B. (Producer & Director; Producer, Karsch, A.; 1991). *The prince of tides* [Film]. Culver City, CA: Columbia Pictures Corporation.

Svjagintsev, A. (Director; Producer, Lesnevsky, D.; 2003). *The return* [Film]. Moscow, Russia: REN Film.

Sweeney, B., Philips, L., Rafkin, A., Ruskin, C., Weis, D., Crenna, R., Hayden, J., Morris, H., Bellamy, E., Baldwin, P., Reynolds, G., Flicker, T. J., Leonard, S., Irving, C., Nelson, G., Ruben, A., & Dobkin, L. (Directors; Producers, Leonard, S., Ruben, A., Linke, R. O., Ross, B., Jameson, J., Sandrich, J., & Thomas, D.; 1960-1968). *The Andy Griffith show* [TV series]. Los Angeles, CA: CBS Television.

Swift, D. / Meyers, N. (Director & Writer / Director & Writer; Producer, Golitzen, G. / Producer & Writer, Shyer, C.; 1961 / 1998). *Parent trap* [Film]. Burbank, CA: Walt Disney Pictures.

Tanovic, D. (Director, Writer, Composer; Producers, Baschet, M., Dumas-Zajdela, F., & Kolar, C.; 2001). *No man's land* [Film]. Paris, France: Noé Productions.

Taurog, N. (Director; Producer, Considine, Jr., J. W; 938). *Boys town* [Film]. Los Angeles, CA: Metro-Goldwyn-Mayer (MGM).

Taymor, J. (Director; Producers, Flickinger, L., Green, S., Hardin, N., Hayek, S., Polstein, J., Sneider, R., Speed, L., & Prieto, R.; 2002). *Frida*[Film]. Los Angeles, CA: Handprint Entertainment.

Thomas, B. (Director; Producer, Topping, J; 2000). *28 days* [Film]. Culver City, CA: Columbia Pictures Corporation.

Tokar, N., Butler, D., Abbott, N., Beaumont, H., Bellamy, E., Reynolds, G., Haas, C. F., Leader, A., Barton, C., & de Cordova, F. (Directors; Producers, Connelly, J., Mosher, B., Nathan, D. & Ackerman, H.; 1957-1963). *Leave it to Beaver* [TV Series]. Los Angeles, CA: Gomalco Productions.

Tornatore, G. (Director, Writer, & Editor; Producers, Gori, M. C., & Gori, V. C.; 1994). *A Pure Formality* [Film]. Rome, Italy: Cecchi Gori Group Tiger Cinematografica.

Tornatore, G. (Director; Producers, Carosio, G., Cristaldi, F., & Caneva, R.; 1988). *Nuova Cinema Paradiso* [Film]. Rome, Italy: Cristaldi Films.

Truffant, F. (Producer, Director & Writer; *The 400 blows. Les quatre cents coups.* [Film]. Paris, France: Les Films du Carrosse.

Tucker, D. (Director & Writer; Producers, Bastian, R., Dungan, S., & Moran, L; 2005). *Transamerica* [Film]. New York, NY: Belladonna Productions.

Tykwer, T. (Director & Writer; Producers, Arndt, S., Bock, K. D., Henke, G., & Köpf, M.; 2000). *Princess and the warrior* [Film]. Berlin, Germany: X-Filme Creative Pool.

Tywker, T. (Director & Writer; Producer, Arndt, S.; 1998). *Run Lola run* [Film]. Berlin, ermany: X-Filme Creative Pool.

Tykwer, T. (Director & Writer; Producers, Arndt, S., Bock, K. D., Henke, G., & Köpf, M.; 2000). *Princess and the warrior* [Film]. Berlin, Germany: X-Filme Creative Pool.

van Patten, T., Patterson, J., Coulter, A., Taylor, A., Bronchtein, H., Bender, J., Buscemi, S., Attias, D., & Chase, D. (Directors; Producers, Chase, D., Bruestle, M., Grey, B., Landress, I. S., Bronchtein, H., Winter, T., Burgess, M., Green, R., Smart, G. M., Weinter, M., Coulter, A., Kessler, T. A., Pugini, M. V., Green, L., & Kaplow, D.; 1999-2007). *The Sopranos* [TV series]. Santa Monica, CA: Home Box Office (HBO).

van Sant, G. (Director; Producer, Escoffier, J. Y.; 1997). *Good Will Hunting* [Film]. Los Angeles, CA: Lawrence Bender Productions.

Vergés, R. (Director & Writer; Producer, Camin, Q.; 2004). *Iris. Aida Vvelidas* [Film]. Spain: Solida.

Vichialak, I. (Producer, Director, Writer, & Editor; Producers, Laodara, P., & Yukol, C.; 2004). *The overture* [Film]. Bangkok, Thailand: Sahamongkolfilm Co.

Vidor, K. (Director; Producer, Selznick, D. O.; 1946). *Duel in the sun* [Film]. Los Angeles, CA: Vanguard Films

Villanseñor, J. P. (Director & Writer; Producers, Gentile, A., & Pagés, G. M.; 1997). *If I never see you again. Por si no te vuelvo a ver* [Film]. Mexico City, Mexico: Centro de Capacitación Cinematográfica.

Vinterberg, T. (Writer; Producer, Hald, B.; 1998). *The celebration. Festen.* [Film]. Copenhagen, Denmark: Danmarks Radio.

von Trier, S. (Director & Writer; Producer, Windelv; 2005). *Manderlay* [Film]. Hvidovre, Denmark: Zentropa Entertainments.

The Wachowski Brothers. (Directors; Producer, Silver, J.; 1999). *The matrix* [Film]. Los Angeles, CA: Silver Pictures.

Wargnier, R. (Director; Producer, Heumann, & E., Labadie, J.; 1992). *Indochine* [Film]. New York, NY: Sony Pictures.

Washington, D. (Producer & Director; Producers, Black, T., & Haines, R.; 2002). *Antwone Fisher* [Film]. Los Angeles, CA: Fox Searchlight Pictures.

Waters, M. (Director; Producers, Michaels, L. & Shimkin, T.; 2004). *Mean girls* [Film]. Los Angeles, CA: Paramount Pictures.

Weir, P. (Director & Writer; Producers, McElroy, H., & McElroy, J.; 1977). *Black rain [The last wave*; Film]. Woolloomoolo, Australia: Australian Film Commission.

Weisman, S. (Producer & Director; Producers & Writers, Goldberg, G. D. , & Hall, B.; 1995). *Bye, Bye love* [Film]. Los Angeles, CA: Twentieth Century-Fox Film Corporation.

Wells, A. (Producer, Director & Writer; Producer, Sternberg, T.; 2003). *Under the Tuscan sun* [Film]. Burbank, CA: Touchstone Pictures.

Wenders, W. (Director; Producers, Felsberg, U., & Wenders, W.; 2005). *Don't come knocking* [Film]. Berlin, Germany: EuroArts Medien AG.

Wenders, W. (Producer & Director; Producer, Jûrges, J.; 1993). *Faraway, so close* [Film]. New York, NY: Bioskop Film.

Wenders, W. (Director; Producers, Dauman, A., & Guest, D.; 1984). *Paris, Texas* [Film]. Burbank, CA: Road Movies Filmproduktion.

Wenders, W. (Producer, Director, & Writer; Producer, Dauman, A.; 1987). *Wings of desire* Film]. Berlin, Germany: Road Movies Filmproduktion.

Whorf, R., Bellamy, E., Tewksbury, P., Kern, J. V. , de Cordova, F., Considine, D., Reynolds, G., & Sheldon, J. (Directors; Producers, Fedderson, D., Henry, F., Tewksbury, P., & Tibbles, G.; 1960-1972). *My three sons [I told you so;* TV Series]. Burbank, CA: American Broadcasting Company.

Wilson, H. (Director; Producer, Rudin, S.; 1996). *First wives club* [Film]. Los Angeles, CA: Paramount Pictures.

Wilson, D., McCarthy-Miller, B., Miller, P., Schaffer, A., King, D. R., Weis, G., Signorelli, J., Wachtenheim, D., Williams, W., Marianetti, R., Schiller, T., Sedelmaier, J J., Brooks, A., McKay, A., Shannon, T. S., Steinmacher, G., Taccone, J., McGrath, D., Lipson, D., Zander, J., Judge, M., White, C., Hader, B., Samberg, A., Idle, E., Wegman, W., Ichaso, L., Dear, W., Kelly, M. P., Guest, C., Corbett, P., McCulloch, B., Gianas, T., Warburton, T., Wetterhahn, M., Alt, M., Lovelace, D., Brooks, D. H., Lennert, D., Miles, A. D., Smigel, R., DeSeve, M., Kerven, C., & Slesin, A. (Directors; Producers, Michaels, L., Higgins, S., Shoemaker, M., Klein, M., Downey, J., Franken, A., Davis, T., Doumanian, J., Ebersol, D., Tischler, B., Herlihy, T., Scharff, S., Smigel, R., Grandy, C., Weis, G., Signorelli, J., Kellem, C., Lipson, D., Spheeris, P., Sedelmaier, J. J., Marianetti, R., Wachtenheim, D., Marshad, N., Kelley, L. C., Issen, R., Christensen, A., Tecson, D., Bianca, K., Winkler, R., Feder, M., Bixler, K., Lieberman, B., & Thomas, P.; 1975 to present). *Saturday night live* [TV series]. Burbank, CA: NBC Studios.

Winkler, I. (Producer & Director; Producer, Cowan, R.; 2001). *Life as a house* [Film]. Beverly Hills, CA: Winkler Films.

Wise, R. (Producer & Director; Levathes, P., & Zanuck, R. D.; 1965). *The sound of music* [Film]. Los Angeles, CA: Robert Wise Productions.

Wong, K. W. (Producer, Director & Writer; 2004). *2046* [Film]. Culver City, CA: Columbia Pictures Corporation.

Wright, J. (Director; Producers, Bevan, E. & Webster, P.; 2007). *Atonement* [Film]. London, England: Working Title Films.

Wyler, W. (Producer & Director; 1949). *The Heiress* [Film]. Los Angeles, CA: Paramount Pictures.

Wyler, W. (Director; Producer, Goldwyn, S.; 1939). *Wuthering Heights* [Film]. Los Angeles, CA: The Samuel Goldwyn Company.

Yates, D. (Director; Producers, Barron, D., Heyman, D., & Orleans, L.; 2007). *Harry Potter and the Order of the Phoenix* [Film]. Burbank, CA: Warner Bros. Pictures.

Yimou, Z. (Director; Producers, Chiu, F., Kow, F., Tseng, Ch., & Lu, Y.; 1994). *To Live. Huozhe* [Film]. Shanghia, China: Shanghai Film Studio and ERA International.

Zemeckis, R. (Director & Writer; Hale, B.; & Producer, Canton, N., 1985). *Back to the future* [Film]. Burbank, CA: Amblin Entertainment.

Zemeckis, R., & Starkey, S. (Directors; Producers, Bradshaw, J., Starkey, S., & Hanks, T.; 2000). *Cast away.* Los Angeles, CA: DreamWorks SKG.

Zhang, Y. (Producer & Director; Producer, Kong, B.; 2002). *Hero* [Film]. West Hollywood, CA: Beijing New Picture Film Co.

Zhang, Y. (Producer & Director; Producer, Kong, W.; 2004). *House of flying daggers* [Film]. New York, NY: Beijing New Picture Film Company.

Zhang, Y. (Director; Producer, Zhao, Y.; 1999). *Not one less. Yi ge dou bu neng shao* [Film]. Culver City, CA: Columbia Pictures Corporation.

Zhang, Y. (Director & Writer; Producer, Loehr, P.; 2001). *Quitting* [Film]. New York, NY: Iman Film Company.

Zhang, Y. (Director; Zhao, Y.; 1999). *The road home* [Film]. Hong Kong, China: Columbia Pictures Film Production Asia.

Zwick, J. (Director; Producers, Goetzman, G., Hanks, T., & Wilson, R.; 2002). *My big fat Greek wedding* [Film]. Los Angeles, CA: Gold Circle Films.

Zvjagintsev, A. (Director; Producer, Lesnevsky, D.; 2003). *The return* [Film]. New York, NY: Ren Films.

Subject Index

The letters 'f' and 't' following the locators refer to figures and tables respectively

A

The accidental hero, 134, 149
Acupuncture, 167
Adolescence and media
    five tasks (Hill), 62
    sexuality, 63
        films and boys, 65–66
        music, 64–65
    sexuality in other cultures, media images
        of, 66
        age compression, 67
        merchandise reflects film images,
            67–68
        nine themes, *Maxim, Stuff,* and *FHM
            (For Him Magazine)*, 68
        print media reflects film images, 68
        "room tours," 67
        SIECUS, 63
        teens and TV, 69
        television reflects film images, 68–70
    sexualization *vs.* vitality, that is, healthy
        sexuality, 62–63
The adventures of Huckleberry Finn, 246
The adventures of Ozzie and Harriet, 35
Affairs, 100–102, 234
After life, 138
Age compression, 60–61, 64, 67–68
Age gaps (the December/May romance), 108
Aguirre: The Wrath of God, 146
Ain't it cool news, 40
Alchemy for healing and transformation
    behavior modification therapy, 207–209
        See also Behavior modification therapy
            and movie experience
    cinema coaching
        Buddhism, 209
        guidelines for therapists, 209–211
        mindfulness, 209
        sensorimotor sequencing, 209

        somatic experiencing, 209
        watching movies with conscious
            awareness, 209–211
    coaching and movie experience, 219
        cinema alchemy groups, 220
    cognitive and emotional interpretation,
        204–205
        disassociation, 204
        identification through projection, 204
        internalization, 204
    cognitive therapy and movie experience
        business coaches, 220
        corporate coaches, 220
        executive coaches, 220
        identifying cognitive distortions and
            schemas, 216–217
        niche coaches, 220
        personal or life coaches, 220
        sports coaches, 220
        support in understanding cognitive
            model, 215
    couples and family therapy and movie
        experience, 219–220
    doubting voices, 210
    eliciting emotions, 212
    EMDR and movie experience
        narrative therapy and the movie
            experience, 218
        positive psychology EMDR, 218
        resource development and
            installation, 218
    e-motion picture magic, 215t
    film matrix, 213t
    four ways of cinema alchemy, 206–209
        cathartic way, 207
        coaching, 207
        cognitive therapy, 207
        couples and family therapy, 207
        evocative way, 206

Alchemy for healing and transformation (*cont.*)
   laughter, advantages, 208
   methods conducive, 206
   prescriptive way, 206–207
  growth matrix, 214t
  guidelines for questions and instructions
    for clients, 213–215
  hypnotherapy and movie experience
   calming film scene to create a safe
    place, 218
   characters as inner parts like inner
    guide or inner critic, 218
   film re-entry, 217–218
  inner landscape fertile for cinema
    alchemy, 202
   bibliotherapy, 202
  inner strength, 212
   gaining hope and encouragement, 213
   remembering internal resources, 212
   validation, 213
  movie experience in context of
    psychotherapy/coaching, 202–204
   metaphors and symbols,
    usefulness, 203
   multiple "intelligences," 202
   theories of learning and creativity, 202
  movies, integrating
   depth psychotherapy and movie
    experience, 215
   therapeutic reasoning for working with
    unconscious, 215
   viewing films as doorways to
    unconscious, 215
  power of projection, 204
  resistance, overcoming, 211
  risks, to take, 221
   applications of work with certain
    movies, 222
   general guidelines for therapists and
    coaches, 223
   guidelines for cinema alchemy work,
    222–223
   limitations of using movies in
    psychotherapy and coaching,
    223–224
  self-discovery/healing/growth through
    work with matrices, 213
  self matrix, 214t
  supporting process of diagnosis and
    assessment, 211
  transformation
   general guidelines for therapists and
    coaches, 223
   guidelines and limitations, 221
   guidelines for cinema alchemy work,
    222–223
   limitations of using movies in
    psychotherapy and coaching,
    223–224
   possible applications of work with
    certain movies, 222
  ways films aid therapeutic and coaching
    process, 208, 211–212
Alchemy process, ways of cinema alchemy,
    206–211
  cathartic way, 207
  coaching, 207
  cognitive therapy, 207
  couples and family therapy, 207
  evocative way, 206
  laughter, advantages, 208
  methods conducive, 206
  prescriptive way, 206–207
Alcohol and drug abuse, 147
Alice doesn't live here anymore, 24
Ali Zoua: Prince of the streets, 143
Almost famous, 65, 66
Amelie, 124, 129, 138–139, 142
American adolescence and media
  five tasks (Hill), 62
  "holding environment," 52
  infamy, 57–60
  media images of adolescent sexuality in
    other cultures, 66
   age compression, 67
   merchandise reflects film images,
    67–68
   nine themes, *Maxim*, *Stuff*, and *FHM*
    (*For Him Magazine*), 68
   print media reflects film images, 68
   "room tours," 67
   SIECUS, 63
   teens and TV, 69
   television reflects film images, 68–70
  media/sexuality and, 63
   films and boys, 65–66
   music, 64–65
  media *vs.* culture
   "age compression," 60
   commercial symbolism, 61
   cultivation theory, 60
   media images as ideals and stereotypes,
    61–62
   Pussycat Dolls, 61
  responsibility

positive psychology and dawning of
  desire, 71–72
sexualization, 54–57
  Gawker asserts, 56
  "train wreck teens," 54–56
sexualization *vs.* vitality, that is, healthy
  sexuality, 62–63
teen pregnancy, 57–60
vitalization of youth, 52–54
  flexibility, 52
  sexualization, 53
  vitality, 53
American beauty, 45
American graffiti, 53
American pie 2, 100
American Psychological Association (APA),
  9–10, 53–54, 62, 70, 72, 115–116,
  172, 189–190, 248
American Psychological Association Task
  Force on the Sexualization of Girls,
  53, 70
Analyze this, 115–116
*Anatomy of an illness as perceived by the
  patient* (book), 116
And the band played on, 106
Andy Griffith, 25, 35
And your mother, too / Y tu mama
  tambien, 139
An angel at my table, 149, 151
Anger management, 116
Animal house, 53
Annie Hall (1997), 114
Anorexia nervosa, 188
"Anorgasmia," 96
Antonia's line, 118, 131
Antwone Fisher, 115, 116
Anxiety disorders, 145–146
As good as it gets, 176, 222
Art exhibits, 228
Atonement, 52
9/11 attacks, 141, 160, 163, 230
9/11 Press for Truth, 161
Attitude, theories of, 174
Au revoir les enfants, 25
Auteur cinema, 125
  See also International cinema
Awakenings, 120

B
Babe, 7
Babel, 124, 132
Babe: Pig in the city, 7
Babette's feast, 135

Back to the future, 53
Bakara Center for Creative Change, 9
Baraka, 139
The barbarian invasions, 147
Batman begins, 26
A beautiful mind, 190
Behavior modification therapy and movie
  experience
  assertiveness training
    overt/covert modeling, 216
  exposure methods
    preparing aversion therapy and covert
      sensitization, 217
    preparing exposure with response
      prevention, 217
    preparing flooding and
      implosion, 216
    preparing systematic desensitization,
      216
  parts work and the movie experience, 217
Behind the green door, 94
Betrayal from affairs, 101–102
Betty blue, 147–148
The bicycle thief, 133
The Bill Cosby show, 25, 44
Black Rain, 136
Black television, positive images, 44
Blindness and visual impairment, 196
Bliss, 100
The 400 blows, 144
Blue butterfly, 140
Blue lagoon, 53
Body double, 94
Body heat, 94
Bonanza, 35
Born into brothels, 143
Boys don't cry, 104
Boy's town, 25
Boyz'n the hood, 43, 44
Brainstorm, 185
Bratz: The movie, 54
The breakfast club, 53
Breakfast on Pluto, 141
Brideshead revisited, 26
Bridges of Madison County, 22, 100
Brokeback mountain, 26, 105
Bruce almighty, 45
Buffy the vampire slayer, 53
The burning bed, 110–112
The butcher boy, 146
Butterflies are free, 193–194,
  196, 198
Bye, bye, love, 95

C

California Child and Adult Q-sets, 79
  Q-set items most characteristic of *UP* series
    participants at ages 7–49, 80t
California Family Law Act, 36
CanFitPro (Canadian Fitness Professionals), 9
Captains courageous, 26, 45
Casablanca, 21
Catcher in the rye, 40
"Cathartic cinema therapy," 91
Cathartic psychotherapy, 207
Caution, 115–116
  negative image of mental illness, 115
  not good candidates for cinematherapy, 116
  stereotypes, 115
The celebration, 131
Character of Alex Forrest, 103
Character strengths and virtues (Peterson and
    Seligman), 128
Chariots of fire, 7
Charisma, 137
Cheaper by the dozen 2, 7
Children
  and mental health, 143–144
  saving, 236–240
    Hollywood and family, 238–239
Children of a lesser God, 196
Children of men, 141
Chocolat, 135
The chorus, 129t, 130, 137, 144, 149
Cinema alchemy, 206–209
  cathartic way, 207
  coaching, 207
  cognitive therapy, 207
  couples and family therapy, 207
  evocative way, 206
  laughter, advantages, 208
  methods conducive, 206
  prescriptive way, 206–207
Cinema coaching
  Buddhism, 208
  guidelines for therapists, 209–211
  mindfulness, 209
  sensorimotor sequencing, 209
  somatic experiencing, 209
  watching movies with conscious awareness,
    209–211
Cinema education, 10
Cinema paradiso, 129, 143
Cinematherapy, 7, 126–128
  application to real relationship problems
    affairs, 100–101
    betrayal from affairs, 101–102

control and power struggles, 102
divorce, 102
extreme of love addiction, case of fatal
    attraction, 103
fear of commitment, 97–103
sex, love, commitment, and marriage,
    98–100
sustaining a long-term relationship, 100
background, 90–91
  motion pictures, 90
blended families, theme of, 7
case example, 95
case example of cinematherapy, 95
  modeling sexual responses, 96–97
caution, 115–116
  negative image of mental illness, 115
  not good candidates for cinematherapy,
    116
  stereotypes, 115
directions for cinematherapy
  assigning "homework," 95
  commercial films as therapeutic tools,
    94
  film selection, 93–95
  instructions, 93
discussion
  delivery style of therapist, 113
  fitting cinematherapy into therapist's
    orientation style, 113
  formats, 114
  general issues, 112–113
  gestalt therapy, 113
  issues of transference and counter
    transference in films, 114–115
  movie one-liners, 114
  "talkback" technique, 113
further resources, 117–118
  film libraries, developing, 118
  Spiritual Cinema Circle, 118
  traditional practice, 118
identity formation for youths, 7
intelligences, tapped in movie viewing, 117
media's role in perceptions, 126
need for evidence base, 116
  client's own relationship movie, 117
other film guides for clinician, 8–9
practitioners' attitudes, 116
special populations
  gay relationships, 105–106
  new specialized population, 103–104
  positive examples of relationships,
    106–107
  sexual orientation, 104–105

specific issues
  abuse in relationships, 109–112
  age gaps (the December/May
    romance), 108
  female alcoholism, 109
  open marriage, 108–109
  race and class differences, 107–108
  substance abuse and its impact on
    relationships, 109
  into therapist's orientation style, 113
  treatment planning, aids in (Hesley and
    Hesley), 127
uses of
  "cathartic cinema therapy," 91
  continuation of bibliotherapy, 92
  "evocative cinema therapy," 91
  "popcorn cinema therapy," 91
  process and dynamics of cinematherapy,
    92–93
  study directions, 91
  value of cinematherapy, 92
  using international films with international
    clients, 127–128
City of God, 144
The city of lost children, 143
The city of no limits, 137
Client's own relationship movie, 117
A clockwork orange, 123, 147
Clueless, 7, 52, 71
Cognitive and emotional interpretation through
    identification and projection, stages
    of, 204–205
  disassociation, 204
  identification through projection, 204
  internalization, 204
"Cold-hearted and authoritarian", 149
Cold mountain, 104
Coming home, 104, 165
Commercial films as therapeutic tools, 89, 94
Commitment-phobic, 97–98
The constant gardener, 107, 132
Continuation of bibliotherapy, 92
Control, 149
Control and power struggles, 102
The cook, the thief, his wife, and her lover, 146
Corollary syndrome, 96
Cosmopolitan (magazine), 68
Counter dependence, 99
Courtroom, effects and consequences, 177
  "temporary" insanity defense, 177
The courtship of Eddie's father, 7, 35
"Crack" of television networks, 233
The crime of Father Amaro, 142

Crimes and misdemeanors, 21, 95
Crips, South Central (book), 44
Cross-gender identification with film
    characters, 98
Crossing Delancey, 95, 96
CrossRoads, 58
Crouching tiger, hidden dragon, 132
Crush, 108, 113
Cry rape, 160
"Cultivation theory" (Gerbner, George), 172
Culture *vs.* media
  age compression, 60
  commercial symbolism, 61
  cultivation theory, 60
  media images as ideals and stereotypes,
    61–62
  Pussycat Dolls, 61

D
"Daddy-Don Juan" syndrome, 98
The dangerous thread of things, 134
Dan in real life, 45
Danny Deckchair, 140
Deafness and hard of hearing, 196–197
Deconstruction, perspective-making, 228–229
  art exhibits, 228
  critic as dramaturgist, 231
  critic as scientist/engineer
    control of negative outcomes, 229
  critic as television consultant, 231–233
  literally save the children, 236–240
    Hollywood and family, 238–239
  media mythmaking, 245–246
    "Hollywood sophistry," 246
  mindful media, 244–245
    "resident shrink," 245
  morality tales for teens, 240–242
    romanticist values, 240
    teen pregnancy and teen sexuality, 241
  portrayals deconstruct real values, 242–243
    Orders of Mind/Subject to Object
      theories, 243
  real(ity) effects of the media, 233–234
    celebrity worship, 234
  values as mental models, 235–236
    scientific and traditional values, clash
      between, 236
The deer hunter, 104
Delusional disorder, 146, 176
Depersonalization, 158
Derealization, 158
DID, *see* Dissociative Identity Disorder (DID)
Dirty dancing, 64, 66

Dirty, filthy love, 133, 146
Disabilities Act (1990), 195
Disability images, reinterpreting with positive
      psychology
   associate with non-disabled characters, 194
   blindness and visual impairment, 196
   deafness and hard of hearing, 196–197
   media and societal attitudes, 193
   orthopedic disability/mobility impairment,
      197–198
   positive psychology and films
      in clinical settings, 199
      elements of positive psychology
         film, 199
      role of the rehabilitation psychologist,
         199
   Rehabilitation psychology, 194
   stereotypes of disability in films, 194
Dissociative amnesia, 158
Dissociative Identity Disorder (DID), 176
Divorce, 102
   and media, 38–42
The doctor, 118
Don't come knocking, 124, 135
Don't tell, 131
Downfall, 136
Dramaturgist, critic as, 231
Dreams, 129
Dressed to kill, 94
Dr. Strangelove, 197
Duel in the sun, 21
Duets, 45
Dynamics and process of cinematherapy,
      92–93
   viewer's process, steps in, 93
      identification, 93
      identification phase, 93
      introjection phase, 93
      metaphors, use of, 93
      projection, 93

E
Education, using movies for, 125–126
   "cinema education," 125
   Dissociative Identity Disorder, 126
Eldra, 144
Election, 53
Electro-convulsive therapy, 151
Elle (magazine), 68
Elling, 129, 145–146, 148, 150
EMDR and movie experience
   narrative therapy and the movie
      experience, 218

positive psychology EMDR, 218
   resource development and installation, 218
Emmanuelle, 94
Emmanuel's gift, 132
"Emo-man," 100, 107
Emotional abuse, 112
"e-motion picture," 90
e-motion picture magic, 215, 222
The Endurance, 133
Energy work, 155, 167
Equilibrium, 134
Equus, 133, 150–151
Everything is Illuminated, 130
"Evocative cinema therapy," 91
The evocative way, 206, 213
Exorcist, 25
Expedition Robinson, 231
The experiment, 149
The Eye, 148–149
Eyes Wide Shut, 94

F
Failure to launch, 45, 97
Falling down, 39
Family and media
   American movie image of "family," 31
   divorce and the media, 38–42
   healthy family, 45
   healthy relationship holding environment,
      characteristic, 46–47
   Hollywood rules and reflects, 30–32
   homogenization, 31
   International Movie Data Base, 33
   major cycles of family films, 32
   mayhem, reason for, 42–47
   nepotism, 32
   positive images, black television, 44
   rebels without causes, or fathers, 32–36
   teens self-socializing, 30
   twenty most prominent children of
      entertainment industry and their
      family status, 33t
   See also Hollywood and right family
The family of man (photographic exhibit), 88
The family Stone, 7, 45
Fanny and Alexander, 25
Faraway, so close, 130, 138
Fatal attraction, 103
Father knows best, 25, 35, 238
Fathers, importance of, 26–27
Fear of commitment, 97–98, 100, 101
Female alcoholism, 109
Filmist(s)

beyond "happily ever after," 5–6
    father–son/mother–daughter relation-
        ships, 5–6
    happily ever after, or not, 3–5
    movie magic, 2–3
    reach of films, 2
    reciprocal relations, 1–2
Filmist, on being
    "blanking"/setting a blank screen, 12
    dramaturgy, art of storytelling, 11–12
        elements for filmists in social club,
            11–12
    establish what is important, 12–13
    investment, 13
        pre/post-chat, 13–14
Filmist Social Club, 11–12
Film matrix, 213, 214
Film selection, 93–95
Final analysis, 186
The fire within, 147
The first wives club, 45, 101
"Foreign films," 124
Forget Paris, 95
For yourself: The fulfillment of female sexuality
    (book), 97
Four seasons, 95
Four weddings and a funeral, 197, 199
Fresh prince of Bel-Air, 44
Fried green tomatoes, 114, 222
Friendship, 33, 95–96, 98, 135, 143

G
Gandhi, 129t, 136, 141, 221
Gay relationships, 40–41, 105–106, 240
"Gender dysphoria," 105
Genesis, 139
Genital reconstruction surgery, 105
Genocide of Armenians, impact of, 157–158
Gestalt therapy, 113
Girl interrupted, 115–116, 173, 185
God is great and I'm not, 141
Gone with the wind, 18
Good will hunting, 7, 115–116, 165–166
The gospel according to matthew, 142
Grand Canyon, 42–43
Grapes of wrath, 23
Grease, 53
The greatest generation, 24
The great Gatsby, 107
Greece's funniest home videos, 231
Greeks and drama, 202
Growth matrix, 214t
Guess who's coming to dinner, 7, 107

H
The hand, 134
Harry Potter and the goblet of fire, 71
Harry Potter series, 45
Healthy relationship holding environment,
    characteristics, 46–47
Healthy sexuality (vitality) and sexualization,
    62–63
Heavenly creatures, 149
Heaven's bookstore, 134
The heiress, 3, 52
He loves me, he loves me not, 146
Hero, 124, 132
Hero's journey, 220–221
Historical Clinical Risk–20 (HCR-20), 185
Hollywood and right family
    media-holding environment replaces family
        American movie image of "family," 31
        Hollywood rules and reflects, 30–32
        homogenization, 31
        International Movie Data Base, 33
        major cycles of family films, 32
        nepotism, 32
        prominent children of entertainment
            industry and their family status, 33t
        rebels without causes, or fathers,
            32–36
        teens self-socializing, 30
    Southern California, 36
        divorce and the media, 38–42
        healthy family, 45
        healthy relationship holding
            environment, characteristic, 46–47
        mayhem, reason for, 42–47
        positive images, black television, 44
"Hollywood sophistry," 246
Home alone, 45
Homeopathic remedies, 155, 167
Hopalong Cassidy, 18
Hope and glory, 25
Hotel Rwanda, 131, 167
The hours, 146
House of flying daggers, 132
House of fools, 146, 150
How happy can you be?, 142
How the west was won, 237
Huckleberry Finn, 40, 246
Hypnosis, portrayal of, 150
Hypnotherapy and movie experience
    calming film scene to create safe place, 218
    characters as inner parts like inner guide or
        inner critic, 218
    film re-entry, 217–218

I

IDEA (health and fitness professional
    association), 9
Ideology formation, 174
If I never see you again, 118
Implosive therapy, 216
Indiana Jones: Kingdom of the crystal skull,
    26, 46
Indochine, 147
I never sang for my father, 5
Infamy, 57–60
In living color, 44
In my country, 136
Inner guide, 216, 218
Inner landscape fertile for cinema alchemy,
    202
    bibliotherapy, 202
Insanity
    defense, 177, 179–181
        Hinkley case, 181
        media depictions of mentally ill
            defendants, 178–179
    looks of insane people
        "cultivation theory" (Gerbner,
            George), 172
        exposure, 172–174
        ideology formation, 174
        "mere exposure" theory, 173
        theoretical implications, 172
        theories of attitude, 174
    and multicultural issues
        agent of discrimination via myths
            dispersal about mental illness, 187
        *Diagnostic and statistical manual of
            mental disorders*, 184
        effect of media on public perceptions,
            183
        media influence, 185–186
        mental illness, definition (*DSM-IV-TR*),
            184
        National Alliance for the Mentally Ill
            (NAMI), 187
Intelligences, in movie viewing, 117
International cinema
    and accompanying virtues and strengths,
        129t
    auteur film, 124
    cinematherapy, 126–127
        media's role in perceptions, 126
        treatment planning, aids in (Hesley and
            Hesley), 127
        using international films with
            international clients, 127–128

portrayal of treatment
    "cold-hearted and authoritarian," 149
    electro-convulsive therapy, 151
    hypnosis, portrayal of, 150
    international cinema resources, 151
    interventions, 150–151
    role of the psychologist/psychiatrist,
        148–150
    theoretical orientation, 150
portrayals of mental health (in international
    films), 128
    adolescents and mental health, 144–145
    children and mental health, 143–144
    fifteen essential international films and
        accompanying virtues and strengths,
        129t
    friendship, 143
    mental health and recovery, 145
    positive psychology, virtues and
        strengths, 128–143
portrayals of mental illness (in international
    cinema)
    alcohol and drug abuse, 147
    anxiety disorders, 146
    International films portraying
        personality disorders, 147t
    mood disorders, 146
    personality disorders, 147–148
    psychosis, 146
portraying personality disorders, 147t
resources, 151
Third Cinema category, 125
using movies for education, 125–126
    "cinema education," 125
    Dissociative Identity Disorder, 126
Interventions, 150–151, 210
In the company of men, 148
Intimate strangers, 133, 142, 150
Iris, 134
3-Iron, 134
Island on Bird Street, 144
The island on Bird Street, 144
Italian for beginners, 143

J

James' journey to Jerusalem, 141
Japanese story, 135
The Jeffersons, 44
Jesus of Montreal, 142, 149
Journal of Traumatic Stress, 156

K

Kate and Leopold, 106
Keller, Helen, 196

Kiss me again, 108
Kramer vs. Kramer, 5, 102
Kunya Papyrus (Egyptian physicians), 156

L

La cage aux folles: The bird cage, 95,
     147t
La femme Nikita, 147
Lantana, 150
The last emperor, 25, 147
Last king of Scotland, 136, 147t
Last picture show, 53
Last tango in Paris, 94, 146
Laughter, advantages, 207
Leave it to Beaver, 25, 35
Leaving Las Vegas, 109, 222
Less than zero, 34
Liar, liar, 5
Life as a house, 38, 165
Life is beautiful, 124, 129t, 140, 142
"Life test," 105
Like water for chocolate, 66, 134
Lilya 4-ever, 144
Little Buddha, 136, 142
Little daddy, 144
Long life, happiness, and prosperity, 144
Long-term relationship, sustaining, 100
Looking for comedy in the Muslim world, 140
Lord of the rings, 131
Love addiction, case of fatal attraction, 103
Lovers and other strangers, 23
*The Lucifer effect: How good people turn
     evil*, 235

M

"Madonna prostitute" syndrome in men, 98
Major depression, 156
Make an American quilt, 95
Manderlay, 135
A man escaped, 132
The man who cried, 148
March of the penguins, 129t, 137, 138
Maria, full of grace, 144
Marie Antoinette, 140
*The Marilyn syndrome: Breaking your love
     addiction before it breaks you*
     (book), 103
"Marital rape," 111
Marriage, 19–20
     of comfort, 22–23
Marty, 22
Match point, 21
Maxim, Stuff, and *FHM (For Him Magazine)*,
     themes, 68

Mayhem, reason for, 42–47
Mean girls, 53
Media
     mindful, 244–245
          "resident shrink," 245
     mythmaking, 245–246
          "Hollywood sophistry," 246
     real(ity) effects of, 233–234
          celebrity worship, 234
     role in perceptions, 126
     and societal attitudes, 193
Media and loss of American adolescence,
     M I 4 U
     adolescence
          five tasks (Hill), 62
          sexualization *vs.* vitality, that is, healthy
               sexuality, 62–63
     "holding environment," 52
     images of adolescent sexuality in other
          cultures, 66
          age compression, 67
          merchandise reflects film images,
               67–68
          nine themes, *Maxim, Stuff*, and *FHM
               (For Him Magazine)*, 68
          print media reflects film images, 68
          "room tours," 67
          SIECUS, 63
          teens and TV, 69
          television reflects film images, 68–70
     infamy, 57–60
     responsibility
          positive psychology and dawning of
               desire, 71–72
     sexuality and adolescence, 63
          films and boys, 65–66
          music, 64–65
     sexualization, 54–57
          Gawker asserts, 56
          "train wreck teens," 54–56
     teen pregnancy, 57–60
     vitalization of youth, 52–54
          "flexibility," 52
          "sexualization," 53
          vitality, 53
     vs. culture
          "age compression," 60
          commercial symbolism, 61
          cultivation theory, 60
          media images as ideals and stereotypes,
               61–62
          Pussycat Dolls, 61

Media depictions of trauma and impact on
    survivors, 159–163
  9/11 attacks, 160, 163
  Cindy Sheehan, 161
  1999 Columbine school shooting in
    Colorado, 162
  Cry rape, 160
  framing, 159–160
  Jersey girls, 161
  OJ Simpson case, 160
  9/11 press for truth, 161
Media-holding and family
  American movie image of "family," 31
  Hollywood rules and reflects, 30–32
  homogenization, 31
  International Movie Data Base, 33
  major cycles of family films, 32
  nepotism, 32
  rebels without causes, or fathers, 32–36
  teens self-socializing, 30
  twenty most prominent children of
    entertainment industry and their
    family status, 33t
"Media, Myth, and Mental Illness"
  (symposium), 9
Media Psychology Division, 192
Media *vs.* culture
  "age compression," 60
  commercial symbolism, 61
  cultivation theory, 60
  media images as ideals and stereotypes,
    61–62
  Pussycat Dolls, 61
The Media Watch, 9, 115
Me, myself, and Irene, 173
Menace II society, 43
Mental health
  portrayals of (in international films), 128
    adolescents and mental health, 144–146
    children and mental health, 143–144
    fifteen essential international films and
      accompanying virtues and strengths,
      129t
    friendship, 143
    mental health and recovery, 145
    positive psychology, virtues and
      strengths, 128–143
  and recovery, 145
Mental illness
  definition, 186
  myth of, *see* Myth of mental illness in
    movies

  role of psychologist in, *see* Myth of mental
    illness in movies
  validated instruments, 185
"Mere exposure" theory, 173
Mesmer, 151
Microcosmos, 139
*Miller Forensic Assessment of Symptoms Test
  (MFAST)*, 185
*Minnesota Multiphasic Personality Inventory-2
  (MMPI-2)*, 185
*Minnesota Sex Offender Screening Tool
  (MSOST)*, 185
The miracle worker, 193–194, 196
Modeling sexual responses, 96–97
Models of family life, searching for, 27
Mommie dearest, 5
Mongolian ping pong, 130
Monsieur Ibrahim, 143
Monsoon wedding, 67
Monte grande: What is life?, 143
Mood disorders, 146
Mortal transfer, 150
Mostly Martha, 135
Mother Teresa, 141
Motorcycle diaries, 129t, 136, 222
Moulin rouge, 134
Mountain patrol, 132
Movie experience
  behavior modification therapy and
    assertiveness training, 216
    overt/covert modeling, 216
  coaching and, 219
    cinema alchemy groups, 220
  cognitive therapy and
    business coaches, 220
    corporate coaches, 220
    executive coaches, 220
    identifying cognitive distortions and
      schemas, 216–217
    niche coaches, 220
    personal or life coaches, 220
    sports coaches, 220
    support in understanding cognitive
      model, 215
  hypnotherapy and
    calming film scene to create safe place,
      218
  in context of psychotherapy and coaching,
    effect of, 202–203
    metaphors and symbols, usefulness,
      203
    multiple "intelligences," 202
    theories of learning and creativity, 202

See also Alchemy for healing and
    transformation
Movie one-liners, 114
Movies
    as models
        "cinematic elevation," 250
        Positive psychotherapy (PPT), 247–250
        taxonomy for character
            strengths/virtues and films,
            248f
    no film assignment if
        client might infer wrong motives, 224
        client recently had trauma similar to a
            character in movie, 224
        not effective with small children except
            in family therapy, 224
        serious psychiatric disorder seen in
            private practice, 223–224
        violence in client's home, 224
    in psychotherapy and coaching, limitations,
        223–224
Mr. and Mrs. Smith, 102
Mrs. Doubtfire, 38
Multiple Personality Disorder, 176
Music videos and sexualization, 65
My best friend's wedding, 114
My big fat Greek wedding, 7, 107, 222
My first wife, 146
My left foot, 129, 198
My left foot: The story of Christy Brown, 142
My life as a dog, 25
My life at the movies (Pittman, Frank),
    18–19
Myth of mental illness in movies
    courtroom, effects and consequences, 177
        "temporary" insanity defense, 177
    dispelling myths
        courtroom, effect of media portrayal,
            182
        insanity defense, 179–181
        not guilty by reason of insanity,
            181–182
        public perception compared with actual
            use of insanity defense, 181t
    effects and consequences in the
        courtroom, 177
    "faking" insanity and multicultural issues
        agent of discrimination via myths
            dispersal, 187
        *Diagnostic and statistical manual of
            mental disorders*, 184
        effect of media on public perceptions,
            183
    media influence, 185–186
    mental illness, definition (*DSM-IV-TR*),
        186
    National Alliance for the Mentally Ill
        (NAMI), 187
    formulating public perception
        Delusional Disorder, 176
        DID, 178
        media consumption, 175
        media portrayal and public perception,
            175–176
        Multiple Personality Disorder, 176
        Paranoid Delusional Disorder, 176
        violent portrayals, 176–177
        Wahl, Otto (media psychology), 175
    insane people, looks of
        "cultivation theory" (Gerbner, George),
            172
        exposure, 172–174
        ideology formation, 174
        "mere exposure" theory, 173
        theoretical implications, 172
        theories of attitude, 174
    myths and mental illness, role of
        psychologist in, 177, 187
        advocacy, 187–188
        advocacy to the public, 187–188
        endorsing accurate portrayals,
            190–191
        normalizing mental health, 188–189
    role of psychologist in
    successful insanity defense, 177
        media depictions of mentally ill
            defendants, 178–179
My three sons, 25, 35

N
Naked, 147
Naked lunch, 147
Napoleon Dynamite, 53
National Alliance for the Mentally Ill (NAMI),
    187
National Association of Theater Owners, 175
National Lampoon's European vacation, 118
The nativity story, 124, 142
Natural born killers, 116
Nepotism, 32
"Neurotic" (mildly mentally ill), 188
New York University's Medical School., 118
Nobody knows, 132
Noi the albino, 149
No man's land, 129t, 137
Non-disabled characters, associate with, 194

Normalizing mental health
    daily news reporting., 189
    media, 189
    public service announcements (PSAs), 189
North Korea: A Day in the Llife, 135
Not Guilty by Reason of Insanity (NGRI)
    defense, 173, 181–182
Not One Less, 132, 137, 144
Notting Hill, 107, 198–199

O

Obsessive compulsive disorder (OCD), 133,
    146, 176
OCD, *see* Obsessive compulsive disorder
    (OCD)
Omen, 25
One flew over the cuckoo's nest, 116, 185
On golden pond, 7
Open hearts, 148
Open marriage, 108–109
Open marriage (book), 108
Orthopedic disability/mobility impairment,
    197–198
The other side of the mountain, 194, 197
Overture, 129

P

The painted veil, 3
Pan's labyrinth, 143
Paper moon, 24
Paradise now, 142
Paranoid Delusional Disorder, 176
Paris, Texas, 147
Passport to Paris, 66
Pauline and Paulette, 134
Peace one day, 132
Pelle the conqueror, 139, 144
Persona, 122
Personality disorders, 147–148, 147t, 176–177,
    230
Peter Pan, 45
"Peter Pan syndrome," 97
Philadelphia, 106, 222
Phobic disorders, 157
The pianist, 133
Pixote, 144
Pleasantville, 39, 40–42, 47, 246
7 plus seven, 77, 83
"Polyamory," 108
Ponette, 143
"Popcorn cinema therapy," 91
"Popular culture intervention," 90
Populations, special
    gay relationships, 105–107

    new specialized population,
        103–104
    positive examples of relationships,
        106–107
    sexual orientation, 104–105
Portrayals of mental illness (in international
    cinema)
    alcohol and drug abuse, 147
    anxiety disorders, 146
    International films portraying personality
        disorders, 147t
    mood disorders, 146
    personality disorders, 147–148
    psychosis, 146
Positive psychology, 4–5
    disability images, reinterpreting with
        and film
        elements of positive psychology
            film, 195
        films in clinical settings, 199
        Four weddings and a funeral, 197
        role of rehabilitation psychologist, 199
*Positive psychology at the movies: Using
        films to build virtues and character
        strengths* (book), 94, 128, 248
Positive psychology, virtues and strengths,
    128–143
    appreciation of beauty and
        excellence, 138
    citizenship or social responsibility, 135
    courage, 131
    creativity, 129
    curiosity, 132
    essential international films and
        accompanying virtues and
        strengths, 129
    fairness, 136
    forgiveness or mercy, 136–137
    gratitude, 139
    hope and optimism, 139
    humor, 140
    integrity, 133
    kindness, 134–135
    leadership, 136
    love, 133–134
    love of learning, 130–131
    open-mindednes, 130
    persistence, 132
    perspective, 129–130
    prudence, 137
    self-regulation, 137
    social intelligence, 135
    spirituality, 141–142

themes related to Christianity, 142
virtue of humanity, 133
vitality, 133
Positive psychotherapy (PPT), 248
Postcards from the edge, 5, 222
The postman/Il postino, 134
Posttraumatic stress disorder (PSTD), 103,
    156, 158–159
Power and Control Wheel, 111
Power of projection, 204
PPT, *see* Positive psychotherapy (PPT)
Practitioners' attitudes, 116
The prescriptive way, 206–208, 220
Priest, 142
Primal fear, 173, 176, 186
Prince of tides, 111, 116
Princess and the warrior, 149
Prozac nation, 39
PSTD, *see* Posttraumatic stress disorder
    (PSTD)
*PsycCritiques: Contemporary psychology–APA
    review of books*, 248
"Psychic numbing" or "emotional anaesthesia,"
    158–59
Psychologist/psychiatrist, role of,
    148–150
    in myths and mental illness, 177, 187
    advocacy, 189–190
    advocacy to public, 187–188
    endorsing accurate portrayals,
        190–191
    normalizing mental health, 188–189
Psychology and films (book), 8
A psychology of human strengths, 4
*Psychopathy Check List, Revised Edition
    (PCL-R)*, 185
Psychosis, 146
Psychotherapy Networker, 19
PTSD, common symptoms of, 158
Public perception, formulating
    Delusional Disorder, 176
    DID, 176
    media consumption, 175
    media portrayal and public perception,
        175–176
    Multiple Personality Disorder, 176
    Paranoid Delusional Disorder, 176
    violent portrayals, 176–177
    Wahl, Otto (media psychology), 175
Public service announcements (PSAs),
    189, 230
A pure formality, 130
Pursuit of happiness, 7, 44, 195

Q
The queen, 137–138

R
Race and class differences, 107–108
Raisin in the sun, 23
Ratcatcher, 144
Reality television, 233
Reasonable doubts, 197
Rebel without a cause, 24, 34–35, 52
Reconstruction, 134
The Red Foxx show, 44
Rediscovery of childhood, 25–26
"Reel therapy," 92
Rehabilitation Psychology, 194
Reiki, 155, 167
Relationship problems, application to
    affairs, 101–102
    betrayal from affairs, 101–102
    control and power struggles, 102
    divorce, 102
    extreme of love addiction, case of fatal
        attraction, 103
    fear of commitment, 97–98
    sex, love, commitment, and marriage,
        98–100
    sustaining a long-term relationship, 100
*Report of the APA Task Force on the
    Sexualization of Girls*, 62–63
The return, 144
Rey 15-Item Memory Test (MFIT), 185
Ridicule, 140
Riding in cars with boys, 45
The rifleman, 35
Right here, right now, 135
Right now, 129
Risks, taking, 221
    general guidelines for therapists and
        coaches, 223
    guidelines for cinema alchemy work,
        222–223
    limitations of using movies in
        psychotherapy and coaching,
        223–224
    possible applications of work with certain
        movies, 222–223
Risky business, 65, 66
The road home, 134, 137
Rocky, 24, 26
Rolling stone (magazine), 68
Romance and suicide, 20–21
Romeo and Juliet, 21
Rorschach Inkblot test, 230

Rosemary's Baby, 25
The royal Tennenbaums, 45
Rumor has it, 45
Runaway bride, 98
Run Lola run, 129t, 141
Running with scissors, 45
Rushmore, 54

S

Safe place, 216, 218
Salaam Bombay!, 144
Save the last dance, 53
Savior, 144
Say anything, 7
Scenes from a marriage, 116
Science in field of film/psychology, 6
Scientist/engineer, critic as
    use of knowledge in control of negative
        outcomes, 229
The sea inside, 135
Secretary, 94, 102
Secrets of the heart, 130
Self matrix, 214t
Seoul train, 132
September 11, 141
"Sex affirmation surgery," 105
Sex and the cinema (book), 94
Sex in the movies, 94
Sex, love, commitment, and marriage, 98–100
"Sex reassignment surgery," 105
Sexuality Information and Education Council
    of the United States (SIECUS), 63
Sexualization, 54–57
    Gawker asserts, 56
    "train wreck teens," 54–56
Sexual Offender Risk Assessment Guide
    (SORAG), 185
Shenandoah, 25
She's having a baby, 23
Shine, 146, 151
The shining, 39
Shrek (series), 5
SIECUS, *see* Sexuality Information and
    Education Council of the United
    States (SIECUS)
Silence of the lambs, 116, 171, 176
Sky high, 7, 71
Sleepless in Seattle, 25
Snow White, 18
Social learning theory, 95
Something's gotta give, 107, 222
Something to talk about, 94
Son of the bride, 129t, 135, 145

The son's room, 150, 166
The Sopranos, 115
Southern California, 36
    divorce and the media, 38–42
    healthy family, 45
    healthy relationship holding environment,
        characteristic, 46–47
    mayhem, reason for, 42–47
    positive images, black television, 44
Spider, 146, 149
Spiritual Cinema Circle, 118
Splendor in the Grass, 52
Spring, summer, fall, winter. . .and spring, 138
Star wars, 46
Steel magnolias, 5, 166
StepMom, 7, 45
The story of the weeping camel, 137
Strawberry and chocolate, 143
Stress, sources (B. Warheit), 157
Structured Interview of Reported Symptoms
    (SIRS), 185
Substance abuse, 157
    and its impact on relationships, 109
Suicide Club, 146
Summer of '42, 71
Superstar, 64
Survivor, 231
Sweetie, 149
Swimming pool, 130, 148
Swinging, 108
Sylvia, 116, 129
Systems-oriented therapy, 219

T

Take my eyes, 112
"Talkback" technique, 113
Tantric sex practices, 100
Taste of cherry, 131
Taxi driver, 24, 179
Teens
    morality tales for, 240–242
        romanticist values, 240
        teen pregnancy and teen sexuality, 241
    pregnancy, 57–60, 241–242, 244
    and teen sexuality, 67, 240–241
Television consultant, critic as, 231–233
Test of Memory Malingering (TOMM), 185
That obscure object of desire, 123
The man without a past, 145
Theoretical orientation, 150
Therapeutic and coaching, 210
    eliciting emotions, 212
    e-motion picture magic, 215

film matrix, 213t
growth matrix, 214t
guidelines for questions and instructions
    for clients, 213–215
helping to overcome resistance, 211
identifying and reinforcing inner strength,
    212
    gaining hope and encouragement, 213
    remembering internal resources, 212
    validation, 213
integrate movies in therapeutic and
    coaching process
    depth psychotherapy and movie
        experience, 215–216
    therapeutic reasoning for working with
        unconscious, 215
    viewing films as doorways to
        unconscious, 215
self-discovery, healing, and growth through
    work with matrices, 213–214
self matrix, 214t
supporting process of diagnosis and
    assessment, 211
ways films aid therapeutic and coaching
    process, 208, 211–212
Therapist, delivery style of, 113
There's something about Mary, 188
The Story of O, 94
Third Cinema category, 125
Thirteen, 41–42
Three Colors: Red, 143, 166
Three of hearts: A postmodern family, 109
Titanic, 107
To be and to have, 129, 142
To kill a mockingbird, 7, 26, 36, 40, 45
To live, 129t, 132
Tootsie, 94
Touching the void, 133
Tourette's Disorder, 133, 146
Trainspotting, 146
Transamerica, 104
Transference and counter transference in films,
    114–115
Transformation
    general guidelines for therapists and
        coaches, 223
    guidelines and limitations, 221
    guidelines for cinema alchemy work,
        222–223
    limitations of using movies in
        psychotherapy and coaching,
        223–224

possible applications of work with certain
    movies, 222–223
Transformers, 10
Trauma and media
    anecdotal accounts (Trimble), 157
    clinical disorders, 156
    films to consider
        Born on the 4th of July, 146–165
        Coming Home, 165
        Good Will Hunting, 165–166
        Groundhog day, 164
        Hotel Rwanda, 167
        Life as a house, 165
        Ordinary people, 166
        The son's room, 166
        Steel magnolias, 166
        Three colors: Blue, 166
        Truly, madly, deeply, 166
    generalized anxiety disorder, 156
    historic or generational transmission of
        traumas
        genocide of the Armenians, impact of,
            157–158
    integrative approaches, 155
    major depression, 156
    media depictions of trauma and impact on
        survivors, 159–164
        9/11 attacks, 160, 162–163
        Cindy Sheehan, 161
        1999 Columbine school shooting in
            Colorado, 162
        Cry rape, 160
        framing, 159–160
        Jersey girls, 161
        OJ Simpson case, 160
        9/11 press for truth, 161
    people react to/cope with, 158–159
        common symptoms of PTSD, 158
        criterions, 158
        "psychic numbing" or "emotional
            anaesthesia," 158–159
    phobic disorders, 157
    PTSD, 157
    spiritual level, symptoms, 157
    stress, sources (B. Warheit), 157
    substance abuse, 157
    trauma, definition, 157–158
    using film to treat trauma, 164
Travelers and magicians, 141
Treatment, portrayal of (in international films)
    "cold-hearted and authoritarian," 148
    electro-convulsive therapy, 151
    hypnosis, portrayal of, 151

Treatment, portrayal of (*cont.*)
    international cinema resources, 153
    interventions, 150–151
    role of the psychologist/psychiatrist,
        148–150
    theoretical orientation, 150
Tsotsi, 135
"Tweens," 63, 65, 67, 70
Twice adopted, 36
Twin sisters, 134

U
Under the sun, 134
Under the Tuscan sun, 102, 221–222
The unexpected legacy of divorce (book), 37
Unknown white male, 130
7 UP, 77
21 UP, 77
28 UP, 77
35 UP, 77
42 UP, 77
49 UP, 77
49 UP and the UP series as longitudinal study
        of personality and social change
    UP series and psychology, lives in progress,
        78
        Bruce, 84–86
        Jackie, 82–84
        lessons from participants, 86–87
        Neil, 80–82
        quantifying impressions using the
            California Q-Set, 78–80
Uses of cinematherapy
    "cathartic cinema therapy," 91
    continuation of bibliotherapy, 92
    "evocative cinema therapy," 91
    "popcorn cinema therapy," 91
    process and dynamics of cinematherapy,
        92–93
    study directions, 91
    value of cinematherapy, 92
U.S. Senate Commerce Committee, 162

V
Validity Indicator Profile (VIP), 185
Values
    as mental models, 235–236
        scientific and traditional values, clash
            between, 236
    portrayals deconstruct real, 242–243
        Orders of Mind/Subject to Object
            theories, 243

Vanity fair, 55, 57
Vanya on 42nd street, 118
Vera Drake, 134, 149
Veronika Voss, 147
A very long engagement, 140
V for vendetta, 136
Vicky Cristina Barcelona, 21
"Video work," 90
Vincent, 129
Vincent and Theo, 129
Violence Risk Assessment Guide (VRAG), 185
Violent partners (book), 111
Violent portrayals, 176–177
The visual Bible: Gospel of John, 142
Vodka lemon, 140
Voyager, 52

W
Walking on water, 146
Warm water under a red bridge, 138
War of the Roses, 94
The warrior, 138
Water, 130
West side story, 107
Whale rider, 59, 144, 222
When a man loves a woman, 109
Where are you Hilary Duff, 54
Who's afraid of Virginia Woolf?, 109
Why did I get married?, 102
Wilbur wants to kill himself, 146, 149
Wild strawberries, 140
The wind will carry us, 138
Wine and roses, 109
Winged migration, 137
Wings of desire, 129t, 130, 138, 142
"World cinema," 123–124, 127–128, 141, 143,
    151
The world's fastest Indian, 133
Wuthering Heights, 21

Y
16 years of alcohol, 147
"Yellow" journalism, 57
Yesterday, 129t, 133, 142
Yours, mine, and ours, 45
Youth, vitalization of, 52–54
    "flexibility," 52
    "sexualization," 53
    vitality, 53

Z
Zoey 101, 58

CPSIA information can be obtained at www.ICGtesting.com
Printed in the USA
LVOW01s2317311013

359523LV00004B/77/P